The Inquiring Reader

Foundations for College Reading

Richmond Garrigus
Reedley College

Allyn and Bacon
Boston ■ London ■ Toronto ■ Sydney ■ Tokyo ■ Singapore

for Ferne Fetters Garrigus

Vice President, Humanities: Joseph Opiela
Editorial Assistant: Julie Hallett
Marketing Manager: Jennifer Miller
Composition Buyer: Linda Cox
Manufacturing Buyer: Megan Cochran
Cover Administrator: Linda Knowles
Production Administrator: Deborah Brown
Text Design and Electronic Composition: Denise Hoffman
Editorial-Production Service: Anne Cherry and Susan McNally

A Pearson Education Company
160 Gould Street
Needham Heights, MA 02494
Internet: www.abacon.com

Library of Congress Cataloging-in-Publication Data

Garrigus, Richmond, 1941–
The inquiring reader: foundations for college reading / Richmond Garrigus.
p. cm.
ISBN 0-205-30755-8
1. College readers. I. Title.
PE1122.G35 2000
428.6'2—dc21 00-045412

Printed in the United States of America

10 9 8 7 6 5 4 3 2 1 05 04 03 02 01 00

Contents

CHAPTER 2

What Is This About?
Finding Topics and Subtopics 39

CHAPTER 3

What About the Topic?
Recognizing Ideas 75

CHAPTER 10

What's the Difference to Me? Comparing and Grouping 343

To the Instructor

Most high school teachers have quite literally given up on the textbook for the communication of any important content. While understandable, this approach is, of course, ultimately counterproductive. There comes a time in the lives of students—either when they go to college or enter the world of work—when others expect them to read and understand informational text.

—David Pearson

The Inquiring Reader provides the opportunity for students to master the skills essential for success in reading college textbooks. It bases its approach on the belief that there are no easy steps to critical reading. Unpacking text for meaning is demanding on students, and the structuring of that experience for them is not easy for instructors. Yet, ultimately, the effort is very rewarding for both. To help students build a foundation for critical reading, the text uses a metacognitive approach that integrates three components of reading instruction.

1. Active Reading

The Inquiring Reader builds active reading into the machinery of the text. The title of the book and the first chapter stress a questioning attitude as essential to reading as an interactive/metacognitive process. Questioning techniques are used throughout the text: chapter heads include a question; at the beginning of each chapter are listed questions the student will be able to answer; and previewing techniques are integrated and expanded as higher-order thinking skills are introduced.

2. Cognitive Concepts

The text builds a core of concepts and vocabulary about reading that allows for discussion and the practice of analytical reading. Higher-level skills are developed progressively: inference, for example, after being introduced through stories and comics (Chapter 5), is shown to be essential in using context vocabulary clues (Chapter 6) and for determining implied main ideas (Chapter 7). Whereas texts often jump immediately from topics to main ideas, *The Inquiring Reader* devotes a chapter to each of these fundamentals: topic, idea, and main idea.

3. Schema

Many students lack not just specific background information, but any concept of general reference frameworks and the cognitive patterns associated with them (time lines, classifications, etc.) that are presupposed in many college courses. The text demonstrates the process of building schema through exercise that encourage students to begin constructing frameworks and seeing connections among them.

The organization of *The Inquiring Reader* allows a progressive integration of these three concerns.

- Part One, "Reading for Information" (Chapters 1–4) uses a questioning approach to introduce the basics: topics, ideas, main ideas, important details. Materials here are largely factual and require mainly location skills.
- Part Two, "Reading for Understanding" (Chapters 5–8) pushes the student to recognize the need to understand rather than memorize and to explain/summarize in one's own voice, rather than repeat rote facts.
- Part Three, "Reading for Patterns" (Chapters 9–12) engages the student in reading articles and longer textbook passages with graphics. In these chapters, students are introduced to organizational patterns that reflect fundamental cognitive patterns underlying the major fields of study.

AUTHENTIC TEXT EXPERIENCE

Paragraph and short passage exercises have been taken from current text sources, rather than paraphrased or manufactured to support a model. These sources represent the kind of textbooks in general education that college undergraduates must work in. These materials also introduce students to issues and topics that they will need to incorporate as part of their essential background information.

FOUNDATIONS FOR CRITICAL THINKING

The main text contains nearly ninety exercises for improving thinking and reading skills, built around nearly seventy paragraphs for analysis, thirteen textbook graphics, and thirty-five articles and selected textbook passages and excerpts. Chapters progressively build the foundation for skills in

- understanding basic cognitive concepts: general and specific; cause and effect; similarity and contrast; classifying

- recognizing topics and subtopics
- learning what an idea is (distinguishing complete sentences from fragments)
- distinguishing main ideas and major detail (finding "important" ideas)
- inferring implied main ideas and context vocabulary meanings
- recognizing basic organizational patterns and signal words
- using outlines and mind maps to show structure
- developing the ability to say things in one's own words in summaries
- distinguishing between fact and opinion
- understanding purpose and tone

MIND MAP EXERCISES

Mind maps are introduced and distinguished from outlines in Chapter 8. Through examples and exercises students learn that mapping is an aid to understanding organization, and a prerequisite to writing accurate and correctly paraphrased summaries. Mapping is integrated throughout the last four chapters as students experiment with a variety of maps that reflect distinctive idea patterns.

VOCABULARY BUILDING

Students build vocabulary in two ways.

Vocabulary in Context The use of context clues in determining meaning is introduced as an aspect of inference in Chapter 6. Questions on context vocabulary appear in the margins of readings so students can get quick feedback on meaning. At the end of the article, answers to context question give sample explanations of the reasoning process and/or clues that led to correct guesses. Other exercises in Part Three involve students in creating context sentences of their own for new words they meet.

Word Parts The text takes an informal approach to using word parts in building vocabulary. Rather than give exhaustive lists, the text presents a small core of high frequency prefixes and roots. The aim is to make students aware of how word parts form words in the language and how they can be used to learn and retain vocabulary meanings.

STUDY SKILLS

Research has shown that teaching study skills is not effective until students are able to find main ideas and identify major details—i.e., until they can distinguish important material from the less important. This text reflects that view in its approach. Study skills are integrated into the text as concepts are developed. Early chapters focus more on learning behaviors that students are able to control. Working with graphics is introduced in Chapter 8 and each of the last four chapters devotes a section to graphics associated with specific organizational patterns. In Chapter 8, summarizing/paraphrasing is integrated with recognizing and mapping idea patterns. In Part Three, students read and respond to three articles on learning styles and time management.

METACOGNITIVE FEATURES

A Question-Centered Approach

The title of the text—*The Inquiring Reader*—sets the tone for an active reading approach. Chapter 1 introduces the student to the mindset of active reading and foreshadows techniques the student will acquire. Each chapter head includes a question central to the chapter's purpose and each chapter begins with a list of questions that the student will be able to answer. The text reflects an internal metacognitive strategy in looping and building basic skills progressively, sometimes over a number of chapters. Previewing, for example, is introduced in Chapter 5 and expanded in Chapter 8. Outlining is introduced in the second chapter on topics and subtopics (in the form of a table of contents), developed in the chapters on main ideas and important details, and connected to mind maps in Chapter 8. Paragraphs and readings are often reintroduced to be looked at from different angles and to allow the student to see how more advanced skills are built upon fundamentals. The final four chapters of the text provide exercises for analyzing graphics and practicing various forms of mapping techniques.

Active Reading Features

Each chapter contains a section that highlights some aspect of active learning. Beginning in Chapter 8, two features precede longer passages and articles to help students develop previewing techniques and strengthen metacognitive abilities.

"Thinking About Reading" sections give directions and questions to help students identify the topic , activate schema, and make predictions about the main idea and what might be learned.

"Reading with a Purpose" sections strengthen metacognitive abilities by helping students connect information through questions about the importance and organization of details, and whether a main idea hypothesis needs to be modified.

The use of an interactive split text format—with questions, directions, and context vocabulary in the margins—keeps students aware of the need for constant feedback, hypothesis testing, and reevaluation.

READING PORTFOLIO

These assignments at the end of every chapter encourage students to seek out reading materials, reinforce skills that the chapter has introduced, and integrate writing activities that reflect the concerns of the chapter. The assignments help students to build schema, to learn to summarize articles and develop opinions that spring from the reading, and to begin to develop positive lifelong reading habits.

GROUP LEARNING

The text recommends small-group work on the exercises in each chapter. The emphasis is not on getting the right answer so much as understanding the process and the reasons behind choices. Group work is essential for students to share points of view as they work at getting meaning from reading. In addition, group and individual writing assignments can be generated from group discussion questions and from those in the Reading for Understanding sections.

INSTRUCTOR'S MANUAL

The Instructor's Manual contains a variety of instructional materials.

Answer Key The answer key provides answers and completed mind maps for all exercises in the text.

Teaching Strategies and Supplementary Activities Suggestions are provided for overall considerations, as well as for specific chapters. Instructions for additional activities, such as writing story/book reports and keeping a vocabulary notebook, are included, along with examples of student work on such assignments.

Test Bank The test bank supplements the main text by providing four additional full-length articles, two graphics, and forty-six paragraphs. These provide two sets of materials for testing or additional practice for each of six chapter groups: 1–2, 3–4, 5–6, 7–8, 9–10, and 11–12. In addition, two short stories at a more advanced level are included for practice in inference and for use for instructors who choose to require story reports as a class assignment.

ACKNOWLEDGMENTS

I wish to thank editor Joe Opiela for the opportunity to pursue a second reading text project for Allyn & Bacon and to Deborah Brown, Anne Cherry, Denise Hoffman, and Susan McNally for seeing it brought to completion. The text profited greatly from the thoughtful and constructive comments of its reviewers: Patricia Creed, Temple Junior College; Diana Starke, El Paso Community College; Natalie Miller, Joliet Junior College; Joan Hellman, The Community College of Baltimore County, Catonsville Campus; and Patricia Rottmund, Harrisonburg Area Community College. I am especially grateful for the many insights and suggestions that have strengthened the pedagogy of the text.

I am indebted to many colleagues and friends who over the years have been a source of inspiration and ideas. I would like to add a special thanks to Norma Kaser, Marvel Stafford, and Rose Kahn, for their encouragement and their feedback on readings and exercises.

To the Student

Reading is a wonderful activity. Stories and other forms of literature stimulate our imagination and creativity, while at the same time providing us great entertainment. There is, however, another kind of reading that may not be so much fun. That is the kind of reading that you will have to do in many of your college classes. Textbooks in college are often written at a high level of vocabulary and thought, so they can be very difficult and frustrating.

College courses and textbooks ask you not just to find information but to understand it fully, be able to restate it in your own words, and connect it to other information. Often your courses will require high-level thinking skills: recognizing the ways material is organized, reading between the lines for unstated information, and judging evidence used to support ideas. This textbook is aimed at helping you to develop a firm foundation on which you can build higher-level reading skills. A preview of the Table of Contents will show that the parts of this textbook address three basic reading activities:

Part One: Reading for Information
Part Two: Reading for Understanding
Part Three: Reading for Patterns

Most important of all, to improve your reading and study skills, you cannot leave your efforts behind when you leave the reading classroom. Reading is an activity like playing golf or the piano. Only if you practice and apply what you learn will your strategies change. From the beginning of the term, therefore, commit yourself to practicing in your other courses what you learn here about how to find important information and mark a text.

Reading is thinking, and thinking is an active process. Through reading and active learning we not only pick up new information, we change the way we process information. Reading for information and understanding may not be as much fun as reading stories, but you will find that it does indeed provide its own rewards. As you develop reading skills, you will find that you not only have more information, but that reading has changed the way you think and the way you see the world.

Part One

Reading for *Information*

1 Becoming an Active Reader

2 Finding Topics and Subtopics

3 Recognizing Ideas

4 Main Ideas and Supporting Details

CHAPTER 1

How Do I Put My Brain to Work?

Becoming an Active Reader

After reading this chapter, you will know the answers to these questions.

- What is active reading?
- What does "learning to learn" mean?
- Which behaviors lead to college success?
- What information about a word can be found in a dictionary?
- What is the pronunciation key and how is it used?
- What is the purpose of a reading portfolio?

We often think of reading as mainly an activity of the eyes. Yet our vision is just one means of getting messages. The visually handicapped, for example, read by using the sense of touch through the system of braille. But running one's eyes or fingertips over lines of print is not really the full act of reading. Students sometime say that they know all the words in a passage and can read all the sentences but just can't get what it all adds up to. That's because real understanding is not reached just by knowing the words of a language. We can fully understand a message only if our brain goes to work to organize what it has received.

Poor readers are passive readers. That is, they don't get involved with the printed page. They read much like many people watch TV. As you read the following newspaper editorial, think about the answer to this question: "What action is TV viewing most like?"

The Thief of Minds

■ *affliction*: condition showing a bad effect

1 Experts call the affliction "teleconditioning": a change in behavior brought on by watching TV. Parents and teachers know it by its effects: kids whose appetite for external stimulation has reduced their attention spans while leaving their brains lazy and passive. It does not produce an environment that encourages learning.

Why are kids bored? (see ¶1)

2 And that probably greatly increases kids' most common complaint about school: It's boring, they contend. Though that has been around at least as long as there have been classrooms, a 1996 study confirmed what many suspect: It's getting worse.

What results from too much TV and video game playing?

■ *delaying gratification:* giving things up now so one can reach more important goals later

3 Kids raised on an increasing diet of television and video games too often turn out overstimulated but underactive. The condition produces kids who have trouble delaying gratification or developing a thoughtful mind.

■ *kinetic:* full of images, action

4 Despite such warnings, the public appetite for television continues to expand. MTV now reaches an estimated 300 million viewers in 79 countries. (A network TV program offers an average of one new image every nine seconds; on MTV, the average is one every four seconds, and commercials are more kinetic still). Video game sales, likewise, are surging.

■ *engagement:* contact, interaction

What is TV viewing most like?

5 Experts worry most that television stimulus is one-directional; there's no "human engagement" between characters on screen and passive viewers, says David Murray, director of research at Washington's Statistical Assessment Service. A number of studies have found brainwave activity during television viewing closely resembles brain waves during sleep, says sociologist and leisure expert John Robinson at the University of Maryland: "Brainwise, being in front of a TV may be more like being asleep than any other activity."

What should we do and not do?

Should:

Should not:

6 Experts unanimously advise parents to control children's viewing. "We need to shift from trying to improve TV—which is probably a lost cause—to an emphasis to reduce TV," advises social critic Michael Medved.

What percentage of our free time do we spend watching TV weekly?

1. a little under one fourth
2. about one third
3. a little over one half

7 Yet despite the fact that 73 percent of adults surveyed told researchers they'd like to limit kids' viewing, Americans now spend an average of 21 of their 40 free hours in front of a television. The average youth will spend 900 hours a year in school and 1,600 hours watching TV—and 64 percent of American school kids have TVs in their bedrooms. The average U.S. house-

hold has 2.24 television sets; they're on an average 6 hours, 47 minutes daily in those homes.

8 Something has to give. It shouldn't be the minds of an entire generation.

Compared to school hours per week, the time kids watch TV is
1. a little less
2. a little more
3. a whole lot more

EXERCISE 1.1

Questions on *The Thief of Minds*

1. How might the activity of reading be different from that of TV viewing?

____

____

2. Do you agree that TV viewing is bad? Is all TV viewing equally bad?

____

____

3. What advice would you give on solving this problem?

____

____

Active reading is the opposite of passive television viewing. It means your brain is in high gear at all times. But how do you become an active reader? First you must have an attitude suggested by the title of this text. Here are some meanings that dictionaries give for *inquiring:*

"seeking information by asking questions"

"carrying out an examination or investigation"

There is an old saying, "Curiosity killed the cat," but actually curiosity and questions help us survive. We have to want to know about such things as cancer before we can learn why it acts as it does and how we might cure it. There is no better way to become an active reader than to make asking questions a habit.

An important key in active reading is the way good readers become aware of their own learning. They not only think about the material they are reading, but ask themselves questions about how their minds are working. As you read the following short selection, be aware of how your own mind is going about getting meaning from the printed page. The learning skills mentioned here relate to strategies for active reading. This will give you a preview of techniques you will be learning by working in this text.

Learning to Learn

by Lester Lefton

- *cognitive researchers:* those who do studies on how we learn, think, and remember
- *generate:* make, come up with
- *hypotheses:* a statement/ guess that may or may not prove true

What four mental actions are shown by active learners (¶1)?
1.
2.
3.
4.

- *rote learning:* learning facts/ rules but with no understanding

What three strategies do NOT lead to active learning?
1.
2.
3.

- *theoretical:* dealing with broad ideas and concepts in a field.

What definition is given for *metacognition?*

What does SQ3R plus stand for?

S:________ Q:________

3R ________, ________, ________

Plus: ________, ________

- *subsequently:* at a later time

1 Most college seniors believe they are much better students now than they were as first-year students. What makes the difference? How do students learn to learn better? Today, educators and cognitive researchers are focusing on how information is learned, as opposed to what is learned. To learn new information, students generate hypotheses, make interpretations, make predictions, and revise earlier ideas. They are active learners.

2 Human beings learn how to learn; they learn special strategies for special topics, and they devise general rules that depend on their goals. The techniques for learning foreign languages differ from those needed to learn mathematics. Are there general cognitive techniques that students can use to learn better? [Researchers] have argued that lack of effective learning strategies is a major cause of low achievement by university students. They conducted a study to see whether grades would improve overall when rote learning, repetition, and memorization were replaced by more efficient cognitive strategies.

3 To help students become better learners, [researchers] developed a course on learning to learn; it provided practical suggestions for studying and a theoretical basis for understanding learning. It made students aware of the processes used in learning and remembering. This awareness (thinking about thinking, learning about learning) is called metacognition. Learning-skills practice, development of motivation, and development of a positive attitude were also included. Among specific topics were learning from lectures, learning from textbooks, test taking, self-monitoring, reduction of test anxiety, discovering personal learning styles, and learning through such traditional strategies as SQ3R plus (Survey, Question, Read, Recite, Review, plus write and reflect).

4 The learning-to-learn students made gains in a number of areas, including grades and motivation. In later semesters, the students continued to improve. . . . It shows that research into thought processes can lead to more effective thought and, subsequently, to high levels of motivation. Last, this simple study shows that people can be taught to be more efficient learners.

EXERCISE 1.2

Questions on *Learning to Learn*

1. State in your own words what this research shows about learning.

____

____

2. From your own experience and from the reading above, make a list of strategies that might work for better reading comprehension and those that won't.

____

____

There were a number of activities and strategies for learning mentioned in the article:

learning from lectures	development of motivation
learning from textbooks	development of a positive attitude
test taking	reduction of test anxiety
self-monitoring	discovering personal learning styles
study strategies	

All of these interact as very important skills in reading and for success in academic courses. Before the semester is over, you will have learned more about many of these topics.

Active Learning

THE BEHAVIORS OF SUCCESSFUL STUDENTS

Students often think that being "brainy" is the most important ingredient for success in school. Actually, habits of mind and learning behaviors are far better signs for success. One problem is that many times students have learned some very poor study habits and learning behaviors. Developing effective behaviors is more difficult when we must first get rid of old habits, but with hard effort, changes for the better will occur.

EXERCISE 1.3

Successful Behaviors Survey

Below is a list of some of the habits that successful active learners practice. These are the behaviors that you should work to make your own. Rate yourself on the following scale:

4 Always
3 Most of the time
2 Sometimes
1 Seldom
0 Never

Be honest: circle the number that best describes your performance.

1. ***I make every possible effort to attend class.*** 4 3 2 1 0

   Good students just don't miss much class. Kidding yourself that you're coming "most of the time" or deciding to skip "unimportant" class meetings—these behaviors just won't get you where you want to go. Other than real emergencies, there are very few good reasons for missing class. Doctor and dental appointments? Don't schedule them during class. Car problems, car pool problems, child care problems? These can be real, but try to have a backup plan ready. Planning ahead can make all the difference.

2. ***I attend class on time.*** 4 3 2 1 0

   Nothing sends worse messages than coming into class late. Being late says to the instructor "Your class is boring and so are you." It also sends the message that the late student has a "don't care" attitude. Would you get paid on a job for the time you *weren't* there? How long would you last on a job if you were late every day? Constantly coming to class late really deserves the same response: "You're fired!"

3. ***I bring my materials to class.*** 4 3 2 1 0

   Would a carpenter show up at a job site without tools? It's not enough just to be in class on time. Textbooks, notebooks, dictionaries, pencils, pens, calculators, etc.—these are the tools of students. You must have your tools with you to do the job correctly.

4. ***I do my assigned homework.*** 4 3 2 1 0

   Homework is an important part of the tools listed in number 3 above. Many times group work and discussion are built off homework assignments. You can't properly participate or gain from lecture and discussion without completing the needed background work.

5. ***I turn in all other assignments.*** 4 3 2 1 0

Sometimes students fool themselves into thinking that because they do well on the exams, they can slide on other assignments. But many times papers and reports are just as important. Also, doing all the assignments—especially extra credit ones—can sometimes more than make up for a poor test score that can occur in a pressure situation. Don't let any opportunity to gain points or improve a grade slip by you.

6. ***I turn homework and assignments in* on time.** 4 3 2 1 0

Don't lose valuable points or a higher grade by turning things in late. Didn't know the assignment was made? Thought it was due next week? Get a planner. Write down all test dates and assignment due dates. Give yourself a cushion—complete your papers well before the due date.

7. ***I read all handouts carefully and follow instructions.*** 4 3 2 1 0

Instructors often put a lot of effort into making up course outlines and making up instructions on how to complete assignments. Many times students ask questions that show they haven't taken the time to read what has been given out. Be sure you always read carefully and take the time to follow instructions to the letter. If you're not sure, you can always discuss something with your instructor. That will show you're doing your best to do things right.

8. ***If I have the choice, I choose to sit in a power seat.*** 4 3 2 1 0

Don't know where these are? It's easy to find them and take one for your own. In a regular classroom or lecture hall, these are the seats many students *stay away from* like the plague. These are *not* the seats at the back or way off to the side. They're center and front, where active learning is going to take place. In close, it's easy to interact with the instructor and with the other good students who are going to choose these seats when they can.

9. ***I don't sit next to those I am tempted to talk to.*** 4 3 2 1 0

We all want a comfort zone, but sometimes friends can prove to be each other's worst enemy. Avoiding temptation is smart behavior. If you feel you're going to have a hard time not visiting and gossiping with a friend during a class, then don't sit together. Find a place where, in group work, you'll be with people who will help you improve your skills.

10. ***I am always ready to be called on for an answer.*** 4 3 2 1 0

This comes from knowing what's expected and meeting the expectations. Part of preparation is doing reading assignments and written homework. Part of it may be doing optional work, or other readings related in a field or in current events that may help you broaden your background information so you can add something important to discussions.

11. ***I respond willingly if the teacher calls on me.*** 4 3 2 1 0

Sometimes even students who are well prepared may do some strange things when called on: slouch down in their desks, make "why me" faces, or bury their noses in the textbook. Just pretend that responding in class is like visiting the dentist: Be positive, be cheerful, and you'll get through it with much less pain.

12. ***I volunteer to answer questions.*** 4 3 2 1 0

It's good to be prepared to answer and to respond willingly when called on, but it's even better to volunteer. Even if your answer or comment isn't perfect, your instructor will appreciate your effort and you will gain a lot from the practice you get from speaking in class.

13. ***During lessons, I try to know exactly where we are.*** 4 3 2 1 0

Have you ever had the embarrassing experience of being called on to answer a question and finding that you are on the wrong page—or in the wrong chapter? Knowing where you are is a matter of concentration and keeping in contact with the instructor and the class. But sometime or another we all find ourselves lost—whether in a strange city or in a lesson. If it happens, don't be afraid to ask directions. Raise your hand and ask your instructor where you should be.

14. ***I ask questions that show I am interested.*** 4 3 2 1 0

Some questions go beyond simply asking the instructor to make a point or direction clearer. These show that the student is really thinking about a subject. These are the kinds of questions that help to lead a class deeper into a subject, or show that the student sees a way in which a topic has a personal application. Don't be afraid to share your questions and concerns with the class. The instructor will appreciate it.

15. ***I do not talk to others, off task.*** 4 3 2 1 0

Carrying on a private conversation while a speaker is presenting a subject is not just rude; it sends a negative message about your attitude and motivation. The surest way to avoid the temptation to talk is to follow the advice in number 9 above: Take a seat away from those you want to chat with.

16. ***I show attention by keeping eye contact.*** 4 3 2 1 0

Nothing more clearly shows interest and motivation than eye contact. It is also ensures that you follow the advice in number 15 above: there's no way you can talk to others if you're looking directly at your instructor. Keeping eye contact is the one most important behavior for showing that you are a committed and responsible adult.

17. ***I want to know what the right answer is.*** 4 3 2 1 0

After a test, teachers often give students the opportunity to go over the items that they missed. There are good reasons why successful students take advantage of these chances to learn. For one thing, questions on midterm tests have a way of showing up again on final exams. Also, the information that you file away in your memory will eventually connect with something else and—if it is correct—will aid your understanding of it.

18. ***When I miss a question, I want to understand why.*** 4 3 2 1 0

Finding out the right answer is important, but even more important is finding out *why* you missed it. It may simply be a fact that slipped by you or a question you misread. You might, however, have missed an answer because of a broad concept you need to understand or a process of thinking you need to be aware of. Knowing why you missed an answer is the only sure way of making sure that you'll get it right the next time.

19. ***I want to know more about subjects I read about.*** 4 3 2 1 0

One purpose of college is to help you build a broad base of knowledge. Everything you read or hear about will connect to some other piece of information. The more you know, the more you're going to be able to learn. File every new piece of information in the "filing cabinet" of your mind. Don't worry—it has plenty of "memory" for everything you will ever put there.

20. ***I believe that wanting to learn is "cool."*** 4 3 2 1 0

Many times TV shows and movies call students who study hard and get good grades "nerds." "Cool" people are shown as those who party and try to slide through school and life. These media images of students are way off the mark. The very fact that you are in college and have a goal indicates that you don't buy this image and you don't believe learning is "uncool."

21. ***I remember and use new learning strategies.*** 4 3 2 1 0

If you wanted to learn how to play the piano, you would need to take lessons. The purpose of the lesson is really to help you learn how to *practice.* Without applying what you learn to practice sessions, you simply won't improve. Reading is very much the same. Your reading class will give you many new learning strategies. Successful students are the ones who apply the strategies that they learn to other classes and during study time.

22. ***I give up old habits and strategies that don't work.*** 4 3 2 1 0

If you have developed a bad slice in your golf game, it's going to be doubly hard for a golf instructor to teach you the correct swing. Getting rid of old habits must go along with building new, effective ones. This requires us to be honest with ourselves, since we all tend to fall back on behaviors we learned early in life, even when they aren't getting us the results we want.

23. ***I accept responsibility for my actions; I don't give excuses.*** 4 3 2 1 0

Life is choices—and your school record will reflect the choices that you make. Accepting responsibility is the first step to making sure your choices will be positive ones. And forget phony excuses. The dog ate your paper? Your dear, sweet great-aunt passed away unexpectedly, just before your paper was due? Sorry, your instructor has heard them all.

24. ***I know the difference between public and private behavior.*** 4 3 2 1 0

There is a difference between public life and private life, but sometimes students aren't aware of—or ignore—this difference. School and work are part of our public lives, and if we want to succeed, we have to practice certain standards of acceptable speech, dress, and interaction with others. How we talk, dress, and act in our private lives—with our friends and family—is another matter, our own private business. Actually, in today's world, public standards take in a larger range of behaviors than in the past, so meeting public standards in certain areas really shouldn't cramp anyone's lifestyle.

25. ***I seek out the instructor when I have questions or problems.*** 4 3 2 1 0

Don't suffer through a semester where you're never sure of why you did badly on a test or what is expected on a paper. "The doctor is in." Instructors expect and welcome office visits with students. Many times it allows both students and teachers to see each other in a new light.

Now total up your score. _____

Since these are *behaviors,* there's no reason why you can't improve your score to at least 96 or even 100 points. Keep these behaviors in mind for all your classes as the semester progresses. Later on in the semester, you will have a chance to rate yourself again and measure your improvement.

If you really want to improve, you can overcome any problem, no matter how big. For a real-life example of this, read the following article.

Gang Culture Gripped Young Teen, but High School Grad Emerges

1 The Villa family moved to the California coastal town of Eureka five years ago hoping to provide their son Cesar with an escape from the gang culture in Southern California. They found they could not escape for long. Once settled in the small town, Cesar, at that time a middle school student, found himself with few friends and little of the urban excitement he was used to in Santa Barbara. "I began studying I was so bored," Cesar said. "I found out I liked math. I got good grades."

■ *urban:* relating to the city

2 But, by the time he entered high school, Cesar, who once merely imitated gang-identified clothing styles and language favored by older relatives, was fully initiated into Eureka's emerging gang scene. Soon "Schoolboy," as he was known to his friends, found himself expelled from school. Cesar's swift turnaround from this low point, less than two years ago, allowed him to become a valuable member of his community.

■ *initiated:* brought in as a member

3 In his early teens, Cesar befriended other youngsters, including Mexican-Americans who, like himself, hailed from Southern California and Spanish-speaking backgrounds. Eureka had become an emerging center for new Mexican-American and Asian-American immigrants as they looked to escape the distractions Southern California cities often presented their children. In gang activity the two groups often pitted themselves against each other.

■ *distractions:* anything presented that causes loss of attention

4 Cesar found that he had cured himself of boredom, but he had also fallen in with a rough crowd involved with gangs. Soon it became rare for Cesar to come home from the mall without getting in a fight. His father encouraged him to be macho and stand up for himself against rival groups of teenagers. Cesar delivered what could have been a crushing blow to his future, when he assaulted a schoolmate with a crowbar in a personal dispute at the beginning of his junior year. Not only was he

"Gang culture gripped by young teen, but high school grad emerges," in *EDCAL* Volume 28, Number 3, July 17, 1998.

expelled from Eureka High School, he was also barred from attending any other local schools. Cesar, a college-bound student, was devastated, but the intervention of caring Humboldt County educators helped him stick to his plan.

■ *devastated:* stunned; overwhelmed

5 Through his home school teacher, McKaye Lent, Cesar enrolled in classes at the College of the Redwoods and in a work experience program through Eureka High. He also soon became involved in the Humboldt County Office of Education's Gang Risk Intervention Program. Its leaders, through one-to-one counseling and mentoring, helped Cesar direct his energy and emotions in positive ways. "The whole time I spent out of school was a good experience for me," he said. "It helped me think about what I was doing with my life."

■ *intervention:* a coming between in order to change or stop

6 In the fall of 1997, Cesar returned to Eureka High with a remarkable change of attitude. He dropped his gang affiliation, kept up his good grades, and opened himself up to making a diverse group of friends. In fact, he became a leader in the school's Culture Club and organized camping trips and other activities. "A lot of violence comes from not knowing each other's cultures," Cesar said. "Everyone gets along well (in the club). It's really peaceful." Humboldt County Office of Education director Denise Keppel-Jones, who supervises GRIP activities, says Cesar's presence is a valuable asset in her program. "He looks at the unity of all now. At the high school, he enrolls those who are suspicious and distrusting [to become members of the Culture Club]," she said. "He can sell himself and the positive things that can be accomplished."

■ *affiliation:* connection, membership

■ *diverse:* made up of different elements

7 One of Cesar's most remarkable achievements upon returning to school was working with Eureka High School Resource Officer John Turner, once Cesar's arresting officer, to work with gang members on developing conflict resolution skills. "Mainly I try to set an example, especially in the Mexican community, by being a pro-non-violence person," Cesar said.

■ *resolution:* solving, bringing to an end

8 Cesar will enter California State University, Chico, this fall after earning a scholarship for his academic and community service achievements. He is not yet sure of the field he will study, expecting to first concentrate on completing his general education requirements. Cesar is certain, however, that he will continue his outreach to the young people of Eureka. "One of my main interests right now is working with younger kids so they don't have to go through what I did," he said. "I feel like I wasted a lot of time."

■ *concentrate:* give one's attention to

WORKING IN GROUPS

Following are some questions on the preceding article for discussion in small groups. Before answering these questions, here are some guidelines to follow when working in a group:

Role of the Group

- Defines its purpose and sticks to the task
- Budgets the time allowed so the task is finished
- Comes to agreement where possible and states conclusions

Role of a Member

- Shares views but is a good listener
- Keeps an open mind—is willing to change views
- Does an equal share of the work
- Respects the views of others
- Is not afraid to disagree with others' ideas
- Does not get rude or attack others personally

Groups work better if two special roles are assigned

Group Leader

- Helps the group keep to its purpose
- Moves the team along a time line to completion
- Makes sure all have an equal chance to give views

Note Taker

- Keeps track of brainstorming ideas
- Brings together various parts into a final summary
- Gives a short written and/or oral summary of the group's findings

EXERCISE 1.4

Discussing Questions in Groups

Form groups of 4–5 students to discuss the following questions. Select a group leader and note taker before beginning. Compile an answer for each question. If your group does not reach agreement, summarize the different viewpoints.

1. Below are some of the behaviors of successful students listed in the survey you just took. In what ways do Cesar Villa's actions show these behaviors?

   "I believe that wanting to learn is 'cool.'"

   "I give up old habits and strategies that don't work."

   "I accept responsibility for my actions; I don't give excuses."

   "I seek out the instructor when I have questions or problems."

2. According to Cesar Villa, "A lot of violence comes from not knowing each other's cultures." Have you found this true in your own experience? Discuss some ways students could help to solve this problem.

Cesar Villa's turnaround illustrates one other behavior of motivated students that will lead to success, no matter how difficult college may be. The title of the following reading suggests what that behavior is:

When Others Let Go, Hang On and Win

by Harvey Mackay

1 I'm constantly asked what I think the secret of success is. It's a lot of things, but at the top of my list are (a) You need to be a hungry fighter, and (b) a hungry fighter never quits. I've learned over the years that success is largely a matter of hanging on after others let go.

2 When you study the truly successful people, you'll see that they have made plenty of mistakes—but when they were knocked down, they kept getting up . . . and up . . . and up. Like the Energizer Bunny keeps going . . . and going . . . and going.

- Abraham Lincoln failed in business, lost numerous elections and his sweetheart, and had a nervous breakdown. But he never quit. He kept on trying and became, according to many, our greatest president.
- Dr. Seuss' first children's book was rejected by 23 publishers.
- Michael Jordan was cut from his high-school basketball team.
- Henry Ford failed and went broke five times before he finally succeeded.
- Helen Keller, totally deaf and blind, graduated cum laude from Radcliffe College and became a famous author and lecturer.
- The University of Bern rejected Albert Einstein's Ph.D. dissertation, saying it was irrelevant and fanciful.
- Johnny Unitas was cut by the Pittsburgh Steelers, but he kept his dream alive by working in construction and playing amateur foot-

ball while staying in contact with every NFL team. The Baltimore Colts finally responded and he became one of the greatest quarterbacks ever to play the game.

3 I love the story about the high-school basketball coach who was attempting to motivate his players. He stood before the team and said,

"Did Michael Jordan ever quit?"

The team responded, "No!"

He yelled, "What about the Wright brothers? Did they ever give up?"

"No!" hollered back the team.

"Did Muhammad Ali ever quit?"

Again the team yelled, "No!"

"Did Elmer McAllister ever quit?"

There was a long silence. Finally one player was bold enough to ask, "Who's Elmer McAllister? We never heard of him." The coach snapped back, "Of course you never heard of him—he quit!"

4 You see, it's important not to give up. I remember a young jockey who lost his first race, his second, his third, his first 10, his first 20, his first 200, even 260. Finally, Eddie Arcaro won a race—and went on to become one of the all-time great jockeys.

5 Sir Winston Churchill, himself a person who never quit from a lifetime of defeats and setbacks, delivered the shortest and most eloquent commencement address ever given. Despite taking three years to get through eighth grade because of his trouble learning English grammar, Churchill was asked to address the graduates of Oxford University. As he approached the podium with his trademark cigar, cane and top hat, he shouted, "Never give up!" Several seconds passed before he rose to his toes and repeated, "Never, never give up." Then he sat down.

6 The moral of all this: Big shots are little shots who keep shooting.

EXERCISE 1.5

Questions for Discussion

1. Identify the following. What were they famous for?
   a. The Wright brothers
   b. Dr. Seuss
   c. Muhammed Ali
   d. Michael Jordan
   e. Henry Ford
   f. Albert Einstein
   g. Elmer McAllister
2. What famous play (and later movie/TV adaptations) told about the early life of Helen Keller?
3. Who was Winston Churchill? What defeats and setbacks did he have? What is he remembered for?

Active Reading

MAKING THE MOST OF YOUR DICTIONARY

Obviously, knowing the vocabulary is essential to being actively involved in reading material. If you don't know the meanings of a number of words in a passage, you'll have a very difficult time understanding it. In this textbook you will learn some important skills for making intelligent guesses about the meanings of words. But there are many times you will have to look up word meanings in a dictionary. Therefore, it is essential that you know how to use your dictionary to the fullest, not just for looking up meanings but for many uses that promote active learning.

Dictionaries come in many sizes. Your college learning resource center may even have the *Oxford English Dictionary* (*OED*), which has many volumes and may list over one hundred meanings for common words. Other dictionaries may be abridged (shortened) or made easier for school use. A college student should own at least two dictionaries—a paperback or pocket dictionary for carrying, and an up-to-date desk dictionary for home study. There are a number of good dictionaries around—*Webster's New World Dictionary, The American Heritage Dictionary,* and *Random House College Dictionary,* among others.

It is likely that you have looked up words in a dictionary before. If so, what did you want to find out? Check any of the items below for which you have used a dictionary.

1. _____ to spell words
2. _____ to find the meanings (definitions) of words
3. _____ to find one or more synonyms (words that mean about the same) or antonyms (words that mean the opposite)
4. _____ to find where you can use a hyphen to divide a word at the end of a line of print
5. _____ to pronounce words you aren't sure of
6. _____ to find irregular verb forms (*ring/rang/rung*) or noun plural forms (*ox/oxen*)
7. _____ to determine the part or parts of speech of a word (noun, verb, adjective, etc.)
8. _____ to look up the usage label of words (to find, for example, which meanings of *cool* are considered "slang" or "informal")
9. _____ to learn the origin of a word (for example, where *vandalize* came from)
10. _____ to check the meaning of the parts that make up words (prefixes/roots/suffixes)

You probably didn't check all of the above. Students most often use a dictionary for the first three, less often for four through seven, and seldom or never for eight through ten. But dictionaries have a lot more uses than most people are aware of. Study the following section from a dictionary that shows most of the major parts of a word entry.

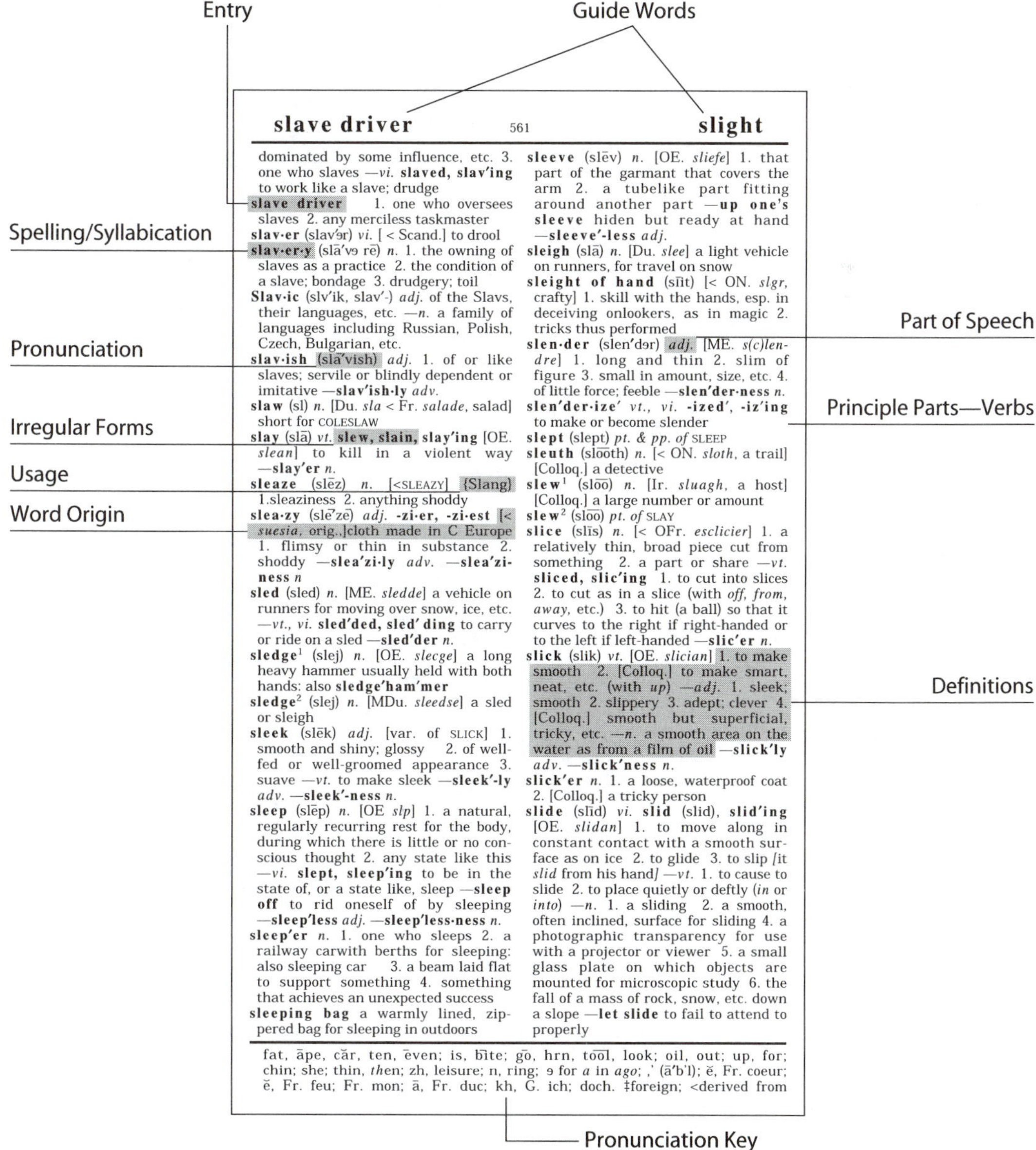

slave driver 561 **slight**

dominated by some influence, etc. 3. one who slaves —*vi.* **slaved, slav'ing** to work like a slave; drudge

slave driver 1. one who oversees slaves 2. any merciless taskmaster

slav·er (slav'ər) *vi.* [< Scand.] to drool

slav·er·y (slā'və rē) *n.* 1. the owning of slaves as a practice 2. the condition of a slave; bondage 3. drudgery; toil

Slav·ic (slv'ik, slav'-) *adj.* of the Slavs, their languages, etc. —*n.* a family of languages including Russian, Polish, Czech, Bulgarian, etc.

slav·ish (slā'vish) *adj.* 1. of or like slaves; servile or blindly dependent or imitative —**slav'ish·ly** *adv.*

slaw (sl) *n.* [Du. *sla* < Fr. *salade*, salad] short for COLESLAW

slay (slā) *vt.* **slew, slain, slay'ing** [OE. *slean*] to kill in a violent way —**slay'er** *n.*

sleaze (slēz) *n.* [<SLEAZY] {Slang} 1.sleaziness 2. anything shoddy

slea·zy (slē'zē) *adj.* **-zi·er, -zi·est** [< *suesia*, orig.,]cloth made in C Europe 1. flimsy or thin in substance 2. shoddy —**slea'zi·ly** *adv.* —**slea'zi·ness** *n*

sled (sled) *n.* [ME. *sledde*] a vehicle on runners for moving over snow, ice, etc. —*vt., vi.* **sled'ded, sled' ding** to carry or ride on a sled —**sled'der** *n.*

sledge[1] (slej) *n.* [OE. *slecge*] a long heavy hammer usually held with both hands: also **sledge'ham'mer**

sledge[2] (slej) *n.* [MDu. *sleedse*] a sled or sleigh

sleek (slēk) *adj.* [var. of SLICK] 1. smooth and shiny; glossy 2. of well-fed or well-groomed appearance 3. suave —*vt.* to make sleek —**sleek'-ly** *adv.* —**sleek'-ness** *n.*

sleep (slēp) *n.* [OE *slp*] 1. a natural, regularly recurring rest for the body, during which there is little or no conscious thought 2. any state like this —*vi.* **slept, sleep'ing** to be in the state of, or a state like, sleep —**sleep off** to rid oneself of by sleeping —**sleep'less** *adj.* —**sleep'less·ness** *n.*

sleep'er *n.* 1. one who sleeps 2. a railway carwith berths for sleeping: also sleeping car 3. a beam laid flat to support something 4. something that achieves an unexpected success

sleeping bag a warmly lined, zippered bag for sleeping in outdoors

sleeve (slēv) *n.* [OE. *sliefe*] 1. that part of the garmant that covers the arm 2. a tubelike part fitting around another part —**up one's sleeve** hiden but ready at hand —**sleeve'-less** *adj.*

sleigh (slā) *n.* [Du. *slee*] a light vehicle on runners, for travel on snow

sleight of hand (slīt) [< ON. *slgr*, crafty] 1. skill with the hands, esp. in deceiving onlookers, as in magic 2. tricks thus performed

slen·der (slen'dər) *adj.* [ME. *s(c)lendre*] 1. long and thin 2. slim of figure 3. small in amount, size, etc. 4. of little force; feeble —**slen'der·ness** *n.*

slen'der·ize' *vt., vi.* **-ized', -iz'ing** to make or become slender

slept (slept) *pt. & pp. of* SLEEP

sleuth (slōōth) *n.* [< ON. *sloth*, a trail] [Colloq.] a detective

slew[1] (slōō) *n.* [Ir. *sluagh*, a host] [Colloq.] a large number or amount

slew[2] (slōō) *pt. of* SLAY

slice (slīs) *n.* [< OFr. *esclicier*] 1. a relatively thin, broad piece cut from something 2. a part or share —*vt.* **sliced, slic'ing** 1. to cut into slices 2. to cut as in a slice (with *off, from, away*, etc.) 3. to hit (a ball) so that it curves to the right if right-handed or to the left if left-handed —**slic'er** *n.*

slick (slik) *vt.* [OE. *slician*] 1. to make smooth 2. [Colloq.] to make smart, neat, etc. (with *up*) —*adj.* 1. sleek; smooth 2. slippery 3. adept; clever 4. [Colloq.] smooth but superficial, tricky, etc. —*n.* a smooth area on the water as from a film of oil —**slick'ly** *adv.* —**slick'ness** *n.*

slick'er *n.* 1. a loose, waterproof coat 2. [Colloq.] a tricky person

slide (slīd) *vi.* **slid** (slid), **slid'ing** [OE. *slidan*] 1. to move along in constant contact with a smooth surface as on ice 2. to glide 3. to slip [it *slid* from his hand] —*vt.* 1. to cause to slide 2. to place quietly or deftly (*in* or *into*) —*n.* 1. a sliding 2. a smooth, often inclined, surface for sliding 4. a photographic transparency for use with a projector or viewer 5. a small glass plate on which objects are mounted for microscopic study 6. the fall of a mass of rock, snow, etc. down a slope —**let slide** to fail to attend to properly

fat, āpe, căr, ten, ēven; is, bīte; gō, hrn, tōōl, look; oil, out; up, for; chin; she; thin, *th*en; zh, leisure; n, ring; ə for *a* in *ago*; ,' (ā'b'l); ë, Fr. coeur; ë, Fr. feu; Fr. mon; ä, Fr. duc; kh, G. ich; doch. ‡foreign; <derived from

Reprinted with the permission of Macmillan General Reference, a wholly owned subsidiary of IDG Books Worldwide, Inc., from *Webster's New World Dictionary,* Third College Edition. Editor in Chief, Victoria Neufeldt; Editor in Chief Emeritus, David B. Guraink. Copyright © 1988 by Simon & Schuster, Inc.

EXERCISE 1.6

Identifying Dictionary Information

Match each number on the dictionary entry with the letter of the information that it gives.

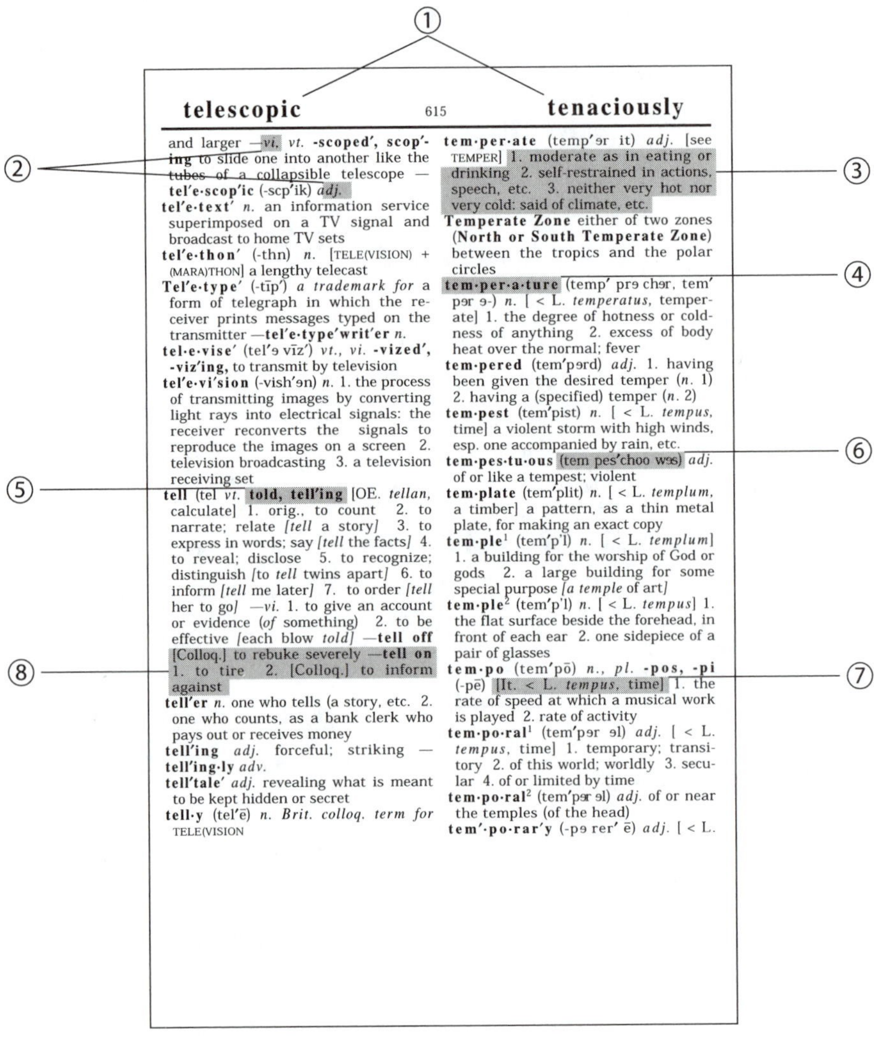

telescopic 615 **tenaciously**

and larger —*vi.* *vt.* **-scoped′, scop′-ing** to slide one into another like the tubes of a collapsible telescope — **tel′e·scop′ic** (-scp′ik) *adj.*
tel′e·text′ *n.* an information service superimposed on a TV signal and broadcast to home TV sets
tel′e·thon′ (-thn) *n.* [TELE(VISION) + (MARA)THON] a lengthy telecast
Tel′e·type′ (-tīp′) *a trademark for* a form of telegraph in which the receiver prints messages typed on the transmitter —**tel′e·type′writ′er** *n.*
tel·e·vise′ (tel′ə vīz′) *vt., vi.* **-vized′, -viz′ing,** to transmit by television
tel′e·vi′sion (-vish′ən) *n.* 1. the process of transmitting images by converting light rays into electrical signals: the receiver reconverts the signals to reproduce the images on a screen 2. television broadcasting 3. a television receiving set
tell (tel *vt.* **told, tell′ing** [OE. *tellan,* calculate] 1. orig., to count 2. to narrate; relate *[tell* a story*]* 3. to express in words; say *[tell* the facts*]* 4. to reveal; disclose 5. to recognize; distinguish *[*to *tell* twins apart*]* 6. to inform *[tell* me later*]* 7. to order *[tell* her to go*]* —*vi.* 1. to give an account or evidence (*of* something) 2. to be effective *[*each blow *told]* —**tell off** [Colloq.] to rebuke severely —**tell on** 1. to tire 2. [Colloq.] to inform against
tell′er *n.* one who tells (a story, etc. 2. one who counts, as a bank clerk who pays out or receives money
tell′ing *adj.* forceful; striking — **tell′ing·ly** *adv.*
tell′tale′ *adj.* revealing what is meant to be kept hidden or secret
tell·y (tel′ē) *n. Brit. colloq. term for* TELE(VISION

tem·per·ate (temp′ər it) *adj.* [see TEMPER] 1. moderate as in eating or drinking 2. self-restrained in actions, speech, etc. 3. neither very hot nor very cold: said of climate, etc.
Temperate Zone either of two zones (**North or South Temperate Zone**) between the tropics and the polar circles
tem·per·a·ture (temp′ prə chər, tem′ pər ə-) *n.* [< L. *temperatus,* temperate] 1. the degree of hotness or coldness of anything 2. excess of body heat over the normal; fever
tem·pered (tem′pərd) *adj.* 1. having been given the desired temper (*n.* 1) 2. having a (specified) temper (*n.* 2)
tem·pest (tem′pist) *n.* [< L. *tempus,* time] a violent storm with high winds, esp. one accompanied by rain, etc.
tem·pes·tu·ous (tem pes′choo wəs) *adj.* of or like a tempest; violent
tem·plate (tem′plit) *n.* [< L. *templum,* a timber] a pattern, as a thin metal plate, for making an exact copy
tem·ple[1] (tem′p′l) *n.* [< L. *templum*] 1. a building for the worship of God or gods 2. a large building for some special purpose *[a temple* of art*]*
tem·ple[2] (tem′p′l) *n.* [< L. *tempus*] 1. the flat surface beside the forehead, in front of each ear 2. one sidepiece of a pair of glasses
tem·po (tem′pō) *n., pl.* **-pos, -pi** (-pē) [It. < L. *tempus,* time] 1. the rate of speed at which a musical work is played 2. rate of activity
tem·po·ral[1] (tem′pər əl) *adj.* [< L. *tempus,* time] 1. temporary; transitory 2. of this world; worldly 3. secular 4. of or limited by time
tem·po·ral[2] (tem′pər əl) *adj.* of or near the temples (of the head)
tem′·po·rar′y (-pə rer′ ē) *adj.* [< L.

1. _____
2. _____
3. _____
4. _____
5. _____
6. _____
7. _____
8. _____

a. usage
b. guide words
c. pronunciation
d. irregular forms
e. word origin
f. entry/spelling
g. parts of speech
h. definitions

LOCATING AN ENTRY QUICKLY

Before using a dictionary for any purposes, you must find the word that you want to learn about. That isn't always as simple as it might seem. Fortunately, the dictionary has features to help you find words and find them fast. Large dictionaries have fingertip slots at the edge of the pages that allow you to go quickly to a section. These sections are arranged alphabetically and the entries within each section are also in alphabetical order, just as items are in a phone book or a filing cabinet. To work in a dictionary quickly and correctly, you first must be confident about using alphabetical order:

a b c d e f g h i j k l m n o p q r s t u v w x y z

Alphabetizing can be very simple. For example, arrange these words in alphabetical order:

warrant harbor permit noisy acorn zebra debate

____

____

____

____

____

____

____

Since each word begins with a different letter, these can easily be put in order:

*a*corn
*d*ebate
*h*arbor
*n*oisy
*p*ermit
*w*arrant
*z*ebra

It's is more difficult when words begin with two or more letters that are alike:

gorge goofy gorgeous gorilla gorgon gopher

____

____

____

____

____

____

In this example all the words begin with two letters alike (*go*), four share three (*gor*), three words have four (*gorg*), and two have five letters in common (*gorge*):

*go*ofy
*go*pher
gorge
*gorge*ous
*gorg*on
*gor*illa

Note that *gorge* is listed before *gorgeous.* If a second word contains all the letters of the first, the shorter word will be listed first.

Words that are long and unfamiliar to you can make alphabetizing quite a challenge. For example, here is a list of difficult words from a single page of a dictionary:

synchronize syncarpous syncopate symphysis symposium syncline

____

____

____

____

____

____

Because these words and their letter combinations are not so common, you had to take more time to put this list in order:

symphysis
symposium
syncarpous
synchronize
syncline
syncopate

Using Guide Words

At the top left and right of each page are *guide words.* The word on the left indicates the *first* entry for that page; the word on the right indicates the *last* entry on the page. All words that fall between these guide words will be on that page. Thus for a word to be on a page, it must come alphabetically after the first entry word but before the second entry word. For example, suppose you turned to a dictionary page with these guide words:

kink **kith**

Circle the two that would be on this page.

kilt kitchen kindly kitten kite

Remember that an entry word must come after the first guide word but before the second. In this list, all the words begin with *ki* so we must start with the third letter. You should have circled the words *kitchen* and *kite* in the list above. An easy way to see this is by listing all seven words in alphabetical order:

kilt
kindly
kink
kitchen
kite
kith
kitten

The *t* in *kitchen* and in *kite* comes after the *n* in **kink,** and their fourth letters, *c* and *e,* come before the *h* in *kith.* In contrast, the *l* in *kilt* comes before the *n* in *kink* and the *d* in *kindly* comes before the second *k* in *kink,* so these would be on a previous page. The second *t* in *kitten* comes after the *h* in *kith;* so it would be on a page following this one.

EXERCISE 1.7

Using Guide Words

Two of the entry words in the right column belong on a page headed by the guide words in the left column. Match the two correct letters to each number.

		Guide Words	
_____	_____	1. **breastpin**	**brig**
_____	_____	2. **brigade**	**broadminded**
_____	_____	3. **broadside**	**Brown**
_____	_____	4. **brownie**	**buckram**
_____	_____	5. **bucksaw**	**bulldog**

Entry Words	
a. broadside	f. brighten
b. bridge	g. browse
c. buffer	h. brevity
d. buckeye	i. browbeat
e. brindled	j. bucktooth

FINDING CORRECT SPELLINGS

Suppose you heard a word, mentioned in connection with a poisoning, that sounded something like "TOE MAIN." Now look it up in your dictionary.

Did you find it under TOE?
Did you find it under TO?
Did you ever find it?

The answer is NO to the first two questions and probably NO to the last. The reason is that the first letter in the word is not *t* but a silent *p.* This points to a big problem with the English spelling system: Sounds are not always represented by the same letters. There are a number of interesting reasons for this situation. For instance, many English spellings became fixed in print before a number of changes occurred in how words were pronounced and, also, English has borrowed thousands of words from other languages. This has made English a richer language, but has led also to some real problems for modern-day spellers—and for students trying to find words in the dictionary.

Checking on correct spellings is one of the most common uses of the dictionary. Yet, as you can see, if we aren't sure of the spelling, particularly the beginning letter, we won't find the word. If you wanted to write about a friend who has "NEW MON YA" or if you were writing a report about the "NITES" of the Round Table, would you be able find these in order to check the spelling? Chances are you would have a better chance of finding *pneumonia* and especially *knight* than you would have *ptomaine* because you probably have seen these before and would have a picture in your mind of the silent letter at the beginning.

It is true that English spelling can be very confusing and frustrating, and yet English spelling is more regular than many people think. The first thing to keep in mind always is this truth about written language:

Letters aren't sounds. They are used to represent sounds.

In some written languages the relation of letters and sounds is very regular. In others, like English, there is a lot of variation. As you have already seen, letters may be silent, representing no sound at all. Pairs of letters may represent only one sound, for example, the letters *sh* as in *share.* The same sound can be represented by different letters (the *g* in *general* and the *j* in *jam*) or different sounds can be represented by the same letter (the *g* in *general* and the *g* in *game*). A letter may have no one sound all its own. Look, for example, at the letter *c* in these pairs:

cell	sell
cello	chair
call	kite

When not combined with other letters, *c* can have the same sounds as those represented by *s, ch,* and *k.* It represents no special sound of its own.

Matching sounds and letters can be confusing and can make it hard to locate entries for words. There are, however, some things you can try if you can't find a word in the letter section in which you think it belongs.

1. If you can't find a word that sounds like it starts with *s* or *k,* then look under *c* (*cell, call*).
2. The letter combination *ch* represents the sound in *chart* but it also can represent other sounds. If you can't find a word that sounds like it should start with *sh* or *k,* then look under *ch* (*chevron, chorus*).
3. Many words begin with silent letters. If you can't find a word that sounds like it begins with
   - *n,* look under *kn, gn,* or *pn* (examples: *know, gnat, pneumatic*).
   - *s,* look under *p* (*psychology, pseudonym*).
   - *r,* look under *w* (*wrap, wrench*).
4. The sound we think of when we see the letter *j* can also be represented by *g* (*general, ginger*).
5. Many words begin with *ph,* which represents the same sound the letter *f* usually does (*phrase, physical*).
6. The letters *qu* usually represent the sound blend [kw] (*quick, quack*).
7. The letter *x* can represent the two separate sound pairs [k] [s] as in (*exit*) or [g] [z] as in (*exempt*). At the beginning of a word, *x* often represents the sound of [z] (*xylophone*).

8. The letter combination *sc* may represent the sound blend [sk] (*scold*) or the *c* may be silent (*science*). The combination *sch* may be the spelling for the sound blend [sk] as in (*school*) or the sound [sh] as in (*schnauzer*).

These guidelines can also apply to spellings in the middle or at the end of words. In addition, in these positions the letter *s* sometimes represents the [z] sound (*please, business*) and the letter combination *gh* may be pronounced like [f] as in *tough*. The common word ending *-tion* is usually pronounced like the word *shun* (*action, petition*).

All of the preceding examples are of *consonant* sounds. These are sounds produced when the breath stream is blocked—for example, [t, d, k] when the tongue touches the teeth or roof of the mouth, or [p, b, m] when the lips are brought together. The spellings for consonants are fairly regular, but the same is not true of the *vowel* sounds. These are sounds made when there is no blocking of the breath by the speech organs. The vowels sounds are represented by the letters *a, e, i, o, u,* and sometimes *y.* There are, however, more vowel sounds than there are letters. Different letters or letter combinations can represent the same sound (examples: *beat/beet/be* and *bed, said, head*) and different sounds can have the same letters (*bead/dead*). This makes the spelling of vowels very tricky. You will learn more about this problem in the section on the pronunciation of words.

EXERCISE 1.8

Finding Correct Spellings

The words below are spelled incorrectly. In some of these, the beginning sound of the word is spelled with the letter most often associated with it; in others, the misspelling occurs with sounds in the middle or at the end of the word. Apply the rules above to find the word and write its correct spelling.

1. akshun __________
2. skeme __________
3. narled __________
4. frenology __________
5. trof __________
6. rangler __________
7. teeze __________
8. salm __________
9. zenofobia __________
10. kwestion __________
11. egzistence __________
12. jeranium __________
13. karakter __________
14. sharades __________
15. soriasis __________
16. senario __________
17. akselerate __________
18. gofer __________
19. ekstend __________
20. selery __________

PRONOUNCING WORDS CORRECTLY

Suppose while studying you run across the word *lymphocytosis* in a science text. You've never heard the word before, and there's no one around to help you. But, by yourself, you could still figure out how to say it correctly. The dictionary gives you the way to pronounce just about any word in the language.

If you look at the dictionary entry for a word, you will see dots between some of letters. These dots serve two purposes. They can tell you where to break a word at the end of a line of print. But they also help you solve the first problem you face in pronouncing a word: trying to figure out how many sections there are. You know when you hear a word or a name that it often sounds like it has more than one part. These "sound parts" are known as *syllables* and the dots between the letters tell you how many of these sound parts are in the word. For example, the entry for *lymphocytosis* looks like this, indicating it has five syllables:

lym • pho • cy • to • sis

A syllable is a unit made with just *one vowel sound,* though it may be blended with a number of consonants. Look at these examples:

to
top
pots
stops
strips
sprints
freeze

The first six words in the list have from one to six consonant sounds, but in each word they are part of only one syllable. The last word, *freeze,* has three vowel letters, but only one vowel sound. Therefore, it has only one syllable. Now look at these pairs:

print printed
dump dumped

Print and *dump* both have one syllable. When the *-ed* ending is added to *print,* it has two syllables, *print • ed,* but how many syllables does *dumped* have? The answer is only one; the letter *e* is not pronounced, so there is still only one vowel sound.

EXERCISE 1.9

Making Syllable Divisions

Look up these words in your dictionary and write the boldface entry the way it appears, with dots between syllables. Then write the number of syllables on the line to the right. The first has been done for you:

1. syllable	syl • la • ble	three
2. aspirin	__________	_____
3. paleontology	__________	_____
4. hypothetical	__________	_____
5. splurge	__________	_____
6. chiaroscuro	__________	_____
7. complexion	__________	_____
8. dowry	__________	_____
9. breadth	__________	_____
10. unknowing	__________	_____

You have already seen a number of instances of how sounds can be spelled in many ways. For another example, match the words in the list below with the words they rhyme with:

_____	1. rough	a. too
_____	2. cough	b. no
_____	3. through	c. cuff
_____	4. though	d. off

This should remind you of what you learned before: In our spelling system, letters aren't sounds; they only represent sounds. Of course, a language in which every sound was represented by its own special letter would be easy to pronounce and easy to spell. In fact, a number of systems, such as the International Phonetic Alphabet, have been developed to help people pronounce various languages accurately. Your dictionary provides a system for pronouncing words through a *pronunciation key* that helps you say each syllable of a word correctly. Look at the first part of the dictionary entry for the word we previously divided into syllables:

lym • pho • cy • to • sis (lim fō sī tō sis)

Notice that the word has been repeated in parentheses, but with some changes and with some different-looking symbols. Each letter represents one and only one sound. [o] has a special sound and so does [i]. But how do you know what that special sound is?

To discover this, you must turn to the pronunciation key. This is located and explained at the beginning of the dictionary. It may be reproduced in other sections, most often on the inside of the dictionary's front and back covers. Also, part of the guide (usually showing less common vowel sounds) may be printed at the bottom of every right-hand-side page. But a word of caution: not all dictionaries use the same pronunciation key, so you should always check to be sure. The pronunciation key here is from *Webster's New World Dictionary,* Third Edition:

Pronunciation Key

Symbol	*Key Words*	*Symbol*	*Key Words*
a	asp, fat, parrot	b	bed, fable, dub, ebb
ā	ape, date, play, break, fail	d	dip, beadle, had, dodder
ä	ah, car, father, cot	f	fall, after, off, phone
		g	get, haggle, dog
e	elf, ten, berry	h	he, ahead, hotel
ē	even, meet, money, flea, grieve	j	joy, agile, badge
i	is, hit, mirror	k	kill, tackle, bake, coat, quick
ī	ice, bite, high, sky	l	let, yellow, ball
		m	met, camel, trim, summer
ō	open, tone, go, boat	n	not, flannel, ton
ô	all, horn, law, oar	p	put, apple, tap
oo	look, pull, moor, wolf	r	red, port, dear, purr
o͞o	ooze, tool, crew, rule	s	sell, castle, pass, nice
yo͞o	use, cute, few	t	top, cattle, hat
yoo	cure, globule	v	vat, hovel, have
oi	oil, point, toy	w	will, always, swear, quick
ou	out, crowd, plow	y	yet, onion, yard
ʉ	up, cut, color, flood	z	zebra, dazzle, haze, rise
ur	urn, fur, deter, irk	ch	chin, catcher, arch, nature
ə	a in ago	sh	she, cushion, dash, machine
	e in agent	th	thin, nothing, truth
	i in sanity	*th*	then, father, lathe
	o in comply	zh	azure, leisure, beige
	u in focus	ŋ	ring, anger, drink
ər	perhaps, murder	ʼ	[indicates that a following l or n is a syllabic consonant, as in *cattle* (kat''l), *Latin* (lat''n); see full explanation on p. xiii]

Notice what the key will tell us about how to pronounce our sample word:

lym • pho • cy • to • sis (lim fō sī tō sis)

The symbol [o] has the sound of the *o* in *open,* the symbol [i] has the sound of the *i* in *ice,* the symbol [f] indicates that *ph* has the sound of the *f* in *fall.* As you can see, the dictionary makers assume that you have some familiarity with basic words and sounds in the language. Using the key, see if you can now pronounce the sounds of the sample words correctly.

Note that there are some rather strange-looking symbols in the key for sounds we don't always recognize as special. The symbol [ŋ] stands for the single sound we hear at the end of *ring* and the [zh] symbol represents the sound we hear in *azure,* which is similar to but not the same as the sound represented by the [z] symbol, as in *zebra.*

Because there are more vowel sounds than vowel letters, a lot of different symbols are needed to show those sounds (the entire left column). Also, look at the upside-down *e* symbol [ə], which stands for the "schwa" sound. This is the vowel sound in syllables that get little or no emphasis. It's the sound we get when we casually say "uh." It's important to note that the schwa sound can be represented by any of the vowel letters, as shown in the key. Read the following aloud, pronouncing the key word as you normally would in a sentence, and listen for the sound "uh" as it is represented by various letters:

a as in *a*go
e as in ag*e*nt
i as in san*i*ty
o as in c*o*mply
u as in foc*u*s

When you listen to words being pronounced, you hear that not all syllables receive the same emphasis or *stress.* As you saw above, syllables with the schwa sound have very little or no stress at all. For example, the word *ago* sounds like "a GO" whereas the word *sanity* sounds like "SAN i ty." Your dictionary uses *accent marks* following a syllable to show where the emphasis falls. If you look again at the entry for our sample word, you'll notice that it contains accent marks as well as sound symbols:

lym • pho • cy • to • sis (lim′ fō sī tō**′** sis)

There are two accents here, but the second one is wider and bolder than the first. That means the first syllable [lim′] gets some stress but the fourth syllable [tō′] receives the heaviest stress, i.e., "lim pho cy TO sis." Different forms of a base word may have different syllable breaks and the accent may switch to a different syllable. For example, *pronounce* is accented on the second syllable: "pro NOUNCE." The noun form of the word, however, has a syllable break between *n* and *c* and puts the accent on the fourth syllable: "pro nun ci A tion." Also, sometimes a word may be pronounced differently depending on its function. For instance, *produce* is pronounced differently as a verb than it is as a noun:

produce (verb): [prō do͞os′]

"People at airports are often asked to produce some identification."

produce (noun): [präd′ o͞os]

"The produce in a supermarket is not as fresh as that at a fruit stand."

As a verb, the first syllable has an unaccented schwa sound; as a noun, the *d* is part of the accented first syllable.

EXERCISE 1.10

Using the Pronunciation Key

Use the pronunciation key on page 29 to pronounce these words. In some cases a word may have two different pronunciations. Write what you think the correct spelling is and use your dictionary to look up the entry to see if you are correct. If you can't find the word, use the rules you learned above for different ways a sound can be spelled. In the column at the right, write the syllable that has the main accent. The first has been completed for you as an example.

	Correct Spelling	*Accented Syllable*
1. [jen′ ər əs]	generous	gen
2. [prez′ ənt]	______	______
3. [pri zent′]	______	______
4. [lē′ zhʉr]	______	______
5. [di spīt′]	______	______
6. [äm′ ni bəs]	______	______
7. [äm nip′ ə tənt]	______	______

8. [fär′ mə sē] ____________ ____________
9. [ī′ brou] ____________ ____________
10. [riŋ′ k‘l] ____________ ____________
11. [skol′ ʉr] ____________ ____________
12. [sel′ yo͞o lʉr] ____________ ____________
13. [so͞o′ də nim] ____________ ____________
14. [kas kād′] ____________ ____________
15. [gär′ dē ən] ____________ ____________
16. [jel′ əs ē] ____________ ____________
17. [zō äl′ ə jē] ____________ ____________
18. [jip′ sē] ____________ ____________
19. [kwäl′ ə tē] ____________ ____________
20. [nē′ kap] ____________ ____________

■ Group Activity

1. Use the pronunciation guide to write your complete name so that a classmate should be able to pronounce it correctly. Be sure to include an accent mark on the syllable that receives the greatest stress. Use the schwa symbol for unaccented syllables.

   Printed Name ____________________________

   Pronunciation ____________________________

2. Work in a group of three to four with dictionaries. Practice pronouncing unfamiliar words that look difficult. Select five difficult-looking words from different sections of the dictionary. After your group agrees on a pronunciation for each of these words, have your instructor listen to you.

Reading Portfolio

A READING SURVEY

One project that will help you to build good reading skills and lifelong reading habits is to keep a reading portfolio. At the end of each chapter you will have an activity to complete. Your reading portfolio should be a separate ring binder, or a section of your class binder, whichever your instructor prefers. You need filler paper for some of the activities and you should get or make some dividers so that you can organize assignments as you go.

The first part of your portfolio will contain your responses to a variety of assignments that ask you to work with material in magazines and newspapers. You will collect and comment on articles and, as the term progresses, you will file in your portfolio articles that you find, summarize, and respond to.

Your first activity is to complete the reading survey below. It will give your instructor some helpful ideas about your background and your interests. When your instructor returns it to you, file it at the beginning of your portfolio.

Reading Survey

Reading Background

1. What other English classes are you taking this semester?

____

____

____

2. What other English courses have you completed?

____

____

____

3. What is your first language? ______________________________

4. What was the last school you attended? ______________________________

   When? ______________________________

5. Do you like to read? Yes ____ No ____

6. Is vocabulary a problem for you in reading? Yes ____ No ____

7. Do you often reread to understand better? Yes ____ No ____

8. What kind of reading material do you find easiest?

____

____

____

____

9. What kind of reading material do you find hardest?

____

____

____

10. How many hours a week do you watch TV or movies or surf the Web?

____

Give some examples of your favorite programs, movies, or Web sites:

____

____

11. Do you read magazines or newspapers regularly? Yes ____ No ____

12. What job or career are you preparing yourself for?

____

13. What has been your favorite subject(s) in school?

____

____

14. What subject(s) have you most disliked in school?

____

____

Reading Interests

You may be a regular reader or read only once in a while. In either case, some things interest you more than others. Complete the following questionnaire to determine your interests.

Newspapers and Magazines

1. How often do you read a newspaper? ______________________

2. List newspapers you are familiar with, listing them in order of those you read most often to those you read the least:

____

____

____

3. Which part of the newspaper do you turn to first?

____

4. Which parts of the newspaper do you read? Write A for always, O for often, S for seldom, and N for never:

____ local news
____ regional news
____ state news
____ national news
____ international news
____ comic pages
____ sports pages
____ crossword puzzles
____ obituaries
____ other:
____ editorials
____ featured columns
____ classified ads
____ movie/TV previews and reviews
____ business, stock market
____ real estate
____ horoscopes and advice columns and features

5. Do you read any magazines regularly? ____________________

If so, name them:

____

____

____

____

6. Check any of these subjects in newspapers/magazines you would like to read about:

____ sports
____ TV and movie celebrities
____ politics and political leaders
____ nutrition and physical fitness
____ fashion/beauty
____ computers/other new technologies
____ home and child care
____ love and romance
____ motor vehicles
____ home building projects
____ gardening and lawn care
____ saving and investing money

7. What magazines would someone find around your house?

____

____

____

Books

1. Check any of the following types of reading that appeal to you.

   Fiction (made-up)

   ____ mystery novels
   ____ romance novels
   ____ historical novels
   ____ western novels
   ____ science fiction novels
   ____ short stories

   Nonfiction (factual/informational)

   ____ biographies
   ____ books of essays
   ____ self-help advice books

2. Do you enjoy reading comic books? _____

   Which are your favorites?

   ____

   ____

   ____

   ____

3. What are some books you have read in the last year or so?

   ____

   ____

   ____

   ____

   ____

   ____

Write a paragraph on each of the following. Be as honest and as specific as you can.

1. What scares you most about being in college or in a reading class?

   ____

   ____

   ____

   ____

   ____

2. What improvements do you hope to make in your reading skills?

3. What is your plan for bringing about these improvements?

CHAPTER 2

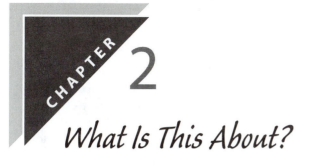

What Is This About?

Finding Topics and Subtopics

After reading this chapter, you will know the answers to these questions.

- What is the difference between general and specific?
- What are topics and subtopics?
- How do outlines relate to topics and subtopics?
- How will previewing help in finding topics and subtopics?
- What is context and how do we use it to find meanings?
- Why are parts of speech important for finding meanings?
- What effects can reading problems have on our lives?

A feature on the educational show *Sesame Street* began "One of these things is not like the other," and then the young viewer was asked to decide which of four items did not fit in a group. For example, children might see this list:

BANANA   MILK   SHOE   SANDWICH

The answer SHOE would be correct, but why? The exercise may look simple, but to get the right answer, the child must use some important thinking skills that are basic to reading comprehension.

GENERAL AND SPECIFIC

To get the correct answer SHOE, the viewer must look for connections and come up with something new. In this example, three of the items share a connection—they are all things that we eat. They belong to a category in our minds—food—that is larger than any one item. A shoe is not a food; therefore it doesn't belong in that group. But suppose the list had read like this:

BANANA SHOE HAT COAT

Now BANANA would not belong. The other three belong to the group "things we wear," and we normally don't wear bananas.

We apply the word *general* to items that are broad—that is, they name a large category like "things we wear," which includes other items. Through our experiences we have built up many such categories. In each list below, one item is a larger category to which the other three belong. Look for connections and circle what you think the correct answers are:

A	B	C
planting the seeds	dancers	seat
preparing the soil	singers	legs
creating a garden	actors	back
watering/weeding regularly	entertainers	chair

The answers above represent different kinds of general categories:

- an action requiring several steps (creating a garden)
- members that make up a group (entertainers)
- a whole thing made up of its parts (chair)

The individual items that make up a category are *specific*—they give you a more definite picture. What comes to your mind when you think of "entertainer"? Now compare that to what you picture when you think of "dancer." Which delivers a sharper image? For some further examples, circle the item in the pairs below that is the most *specific:*

transportation	ship
iced tea	beverage
activity	running
blue	color
headwear	baseball cap

Notice how the specific items—*ship, iced tea, running, blue, baseball cap*—appeal more directly to your senses and create a sharper mental image than do the general terms. The exercise below will give you some more practice in telling the difference between general and specific terms.

EXERCISE 2.1

General and Specific Terms

■ PART A

Each group contains four specific items and one general term. Circle the general category.

1. poem	short story	literature	novel	play
2. mother	family	brother	father	sister
3. exercise	running	lifting weights	hiking	swimming
4. modem	keyboard	monitor	printer	computer
5. cake	birthday party	candles	presents	games
6. coffee	hot chocolate	drink	cola	lemonade
7. French fries	burger	hot dog	fast food	pizza
8. brass	French horn	trumpet	tuba	trombone
9. oak	maple	pine	cedar	wood
10. index	table of contents	chapter	textbook	glossary

■ PART B

Each group contains five specific items. Cross out the one that doesn't fit. Then write the name of the general category that the other four belong to. (Watch out: 8, 9, and especially 10 are more difficult!)

					General Category
1. knife	plate	rifle	bow and arrow	sword	____________
2. toilet	vanity	refrigerator	bathtub	shower	____________
3. paint	mow lawn	rake leaves	prune bushes	trim hedge	____________
4. low pay	dirty work	good benefits	no job security	mean bosses	____________
5. book	newspaper	magazine	journal	movie	____________
6. rainy	windy	snowy	cloudy	sandy	____________
7. happy	angry	asleep	afraid	joyful	____________

8. pen	pencil	paper clip	highlighter	chalk	__________
9. lake	river	pond	ocean	stream	__________
10. pop	mom	did	wow	kid	__________

■ PART C

Suppose you decide to buy an automobile but you're not exactly sure what you want. When you arrive at the car lot, the salesman asks some questions to pin down what it is you want. Note as you answer at each level how your description grows more and more specific and how the image of the automobile you want takes a clearer shape.

What make of car would you most be interested in? ________________

What model? ________________

Two-door or four-door? ________________

New or used? ________________

Color? ________________

Standard or automatic shift? ________________

Number of cylinders? ________________

Special features? ________________

RECOGNIZING TOPICS

It is necessary to understand the meaning of *general* in order to master the very important ability to identify *topics* in reading materials. The term *topic* means about the same as *subject.* Every sentence, paragraph, article, chapter, or book deals with a subject—its topic—and gives information about it. As we noted earlier, active reading means the reader must keep asking questions and looking for answers. The first question you will always ask is

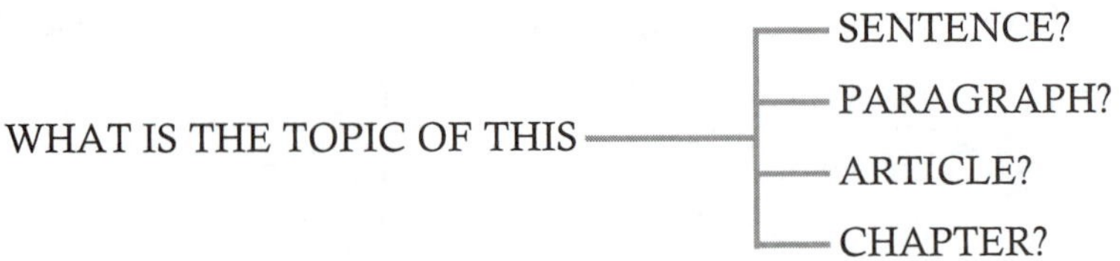
WHAT IS THE TOPIC OF THIS
SENTENCE?
PARAGRAPH?
ARTICLE?
CHAPTER?

EXERCISE 2.2

Identifying Topics in Sentences and Paragraphs

■ PART A Determining the Topics of Sentences

For each of the following sentences, ask yourself "What is the topic of this sentence?" Then make the best selection from the three choices given.

1. A fossil is recognizable, physical evidence of an organism that lived long ago.
   a. fossils
   b. physical evidence
   c. organisms
2. After they are processed, "cacao beans" end up in chocolate products.
   a. processing
   b. cacao beans
   c. chocolate products
3. Most of the life of a bottom-dwelling fish is spent hiding from predators.
   a. ocean life
   b. bottom-dwelling fish
   c. predators
4. Millions of years ago, vast forests in Africa gave way to grasslands.
   a. the past
   b. forests in ancient Africa
   c. grasslands
5. Supervisors control those who actually produce goods or deliver services.
   a. supervisors
   b. production of goods
   c. delivery of services
6. Most Americans are satisfied with their jobs but are not too excited about them.
   a. most Americans
   b. job satisfaction
   c. exciting events

7. Work is one of life's unpleasant necessities.
   a. work
   b. life
   c. necessities
8. The labor force excludes anyone who is not paid for work and is not seeking a paying job.
   a. the labor force
   b. unpaid work
   c. paying jobs
9. People who are satisfied with their jobs have better physical health and live longer.
   a. people
   b. job satisfaction effects
   c. physical health
10. Though diet and exercise are related to heart disease, job dissatisfaction is more closely linked to the cause of death.
    a. diet and exercise
    b. disease
    c. job dissatisfaction

■ PART B Determining the Topics of Paragraphs

Here are five paragraphs on different topics taken from a science textbook. For each, ask yourself, "What is the topic of this paragraph?" Look for repeated words or phrases that may help you determine it.

■ *isolated:* separated

■ *intermittent:* starting and stopping at various times

1. Populations of most species are not stretched out continuously, with one merging into the others. Most often they are isolated geographically to some extent, with gene flow being more of an intermittent trickle than a steady stream. But sometimes barriers form and shut off even the trickles. This can happen rapidly, as when a major earthquake changed the course of the Mississippi River in the 1800s and isolated some populations of insects that could not swim or fly. Geographic isolation also

From *Biology: Concepts and Applications,* hardcover version, 2nd edition, by C. Starr. © 1994. Reprinted with permission of Brooks/Cole Publishing, a division of Thomson Learning.

happens slowly. Millions of years ago, owing to long-term shifts in rainfall, vast forests in Africa gave way to grasslands, and subpopulations of forest-dwelling apes became isolated from one another. One of the subpopulations of African apes may have started the divergence that led to modern humans. (p. 204)

■ *divergence:* moving apart from a common starting point

A key word that points to the topic occurs four times (once in a different form) in this paragraph. Circle that word. It combines twice with another word to name the topic of the paragraph. Write it here:

___

2. *T. cacao* evolved in Central America, where wild animals ate its fruits and dispersed its seeds. Today its trees flourish on vast plantations in Central America, the West Indies, and West Africa. Growers harvest its seeds, or "cacao beans." These are processed into cocoa butter and essences, which end up in chocolate products. Unknown interactions among the 1,000 or so compounds in chocolate exert compelling (some say addictive) effects on the human brain. Each year, for instance, the average American feels compelled to buy 8 to 10 pounds of the stuff. With that kind of demand, growers do their very best to keep cacao trees growing and reproducing. (p. 353)

■ *dispersed:* spread out

■ *compelling:* forceful

The topic of this paragraph is repeated in different phrases in the paragraph. Write it here:

___

___

3. "Fossil" comes from a Latin word for something that has been "dug up." As generally used, a fossil is recognizable, physical evidence of an organism that lived long ago. Most fossils are body parts, such as bones, teeth, shells, leaves, and seeds. Some are tracks, burrows, and other telltale impressions of past life. All were preserved because they were gently buried before they could decompose or fall apart. (p. 211)

■ *impressions:* imprints made by pressure

■ *decompose:* rot

The repetition of what word indicates that it is the topic of the paragraph?

___

■ *vertebrates:* creatures with a backbone

■ *predatory:* killing and eating other animals

■ *propulsive:* providing thrust

4. Collectively, living fishes are the most numerous and diverse vertebrates. Their body form tells us about their watery world. Being about 800 times denser than air, water resists rapid movements. Predatory fishes of the oceans are streamlined for pursuit, with a long trim body that reduces friction. Their tail muscles are organized for propulsive force and forward motion. Bottom-dwelling fishes spend most of their lives hiding from predators or prey. Their flattened body is easy to conceal, but the shape tells us these fishes are sluggish, not Corvettes of the deep. (p. 314)

What topic best covers the material in this paragraph?

a. body form of living fishes

b. development of vertebrates

c. how predatory fishes get food

d. the habits of bottom-dwelling fishes

■ *allele:* different form of a gene that allows variations in a trait

■ *recessive:* controlled by; overpowered by a dominant allele

5. We all have genes for thousands of traits, such as earlobes, cheeks, lashes, and eyeballs. Most of the traits vary in their details from one person to the next. Remember, humans inherit pairs of genes, on pairs of chromosomes. In some pairings, one allele has powerful effects and overwhelms the other's contribution to a trait. The outgunned allele is said to be recessive to the dominant one. If you have detached earlobes, dimpled cheeks, long lashes, or large eyeballs, you carry at least one and possibly two dominant alleles that influence the trait in a particular way. (p. 122)

No one word will cover the topic of this paragraph. Which phrase best states what the paragraph is about?

a. genes, alleles, and chromosomes

b. how different traits are inherited

c. a thousand traits

d. earlobes, cheeks, lashes, and eyeballs

IDENTIFYING SUBTOPICS

Topics are broad categories that can be broken into smaller groups—called subtopics—which, in turn, might be broken into even smaller subtopics containing individual items. This wide range from the very general to the very specific allows us to speak of some topics and subtopics as more or less general or specific than others:

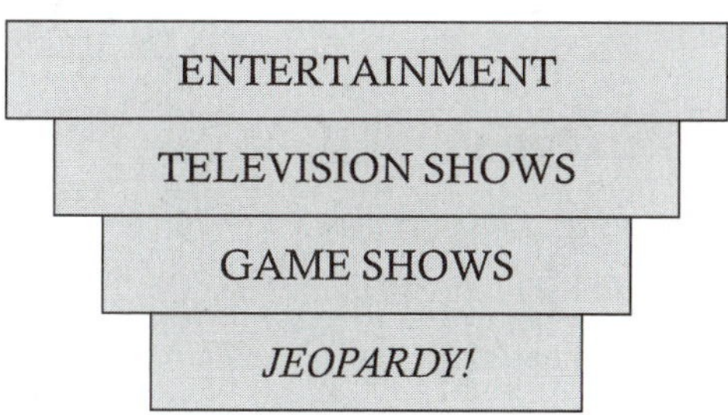

Entertainment is a very general topic that covers many categories. One main subtopic, *TV Shows,* is less general than *Entertainment* but more general than *Game Shows,* which is a more specific subtopic than *TV Shows* but more general than a specific game show, *Jeopardy!*

An example of the importance of understanding topics and subtopics occurs in the process of narrowing down writing assignments. Suppose you were asked to write a composition on a famous person. Famous People is very general *topic,* which would include subtopics such as famous actors, politicians, religious leaders, and so on. To narrow your writing topic, you might select the subtopic Athletes, which is more specific than Famous People. But there are many different sports in which athletes compete, so you would need a smaller subtopic, such as Golfers. Finally, you choose the person you want to write on, for instance, Tiger Woods, a specific individual.

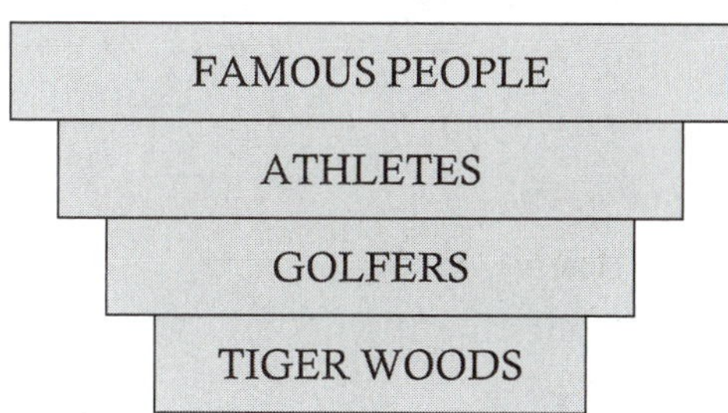

These terms depend on how broad a subject is being dealt with. In a short essay, Tiger Woods would be the topic. In a book covering a wide topic like entertainment, Tiger Woods might be a subtopic in a section on golf.

To help students see the structure of the book and the organization of its chapters, most textbooks contain a *table of contents.* A table of contents uses an outline form that helps you visually to grasp how topics and subtopics fit. The text itself often uses boldface print and various sized headings that reflect the outline. For example, here are the contents of part of a chapter as listed in the table of contents of a college psychology textbook.

Sensation and Perception

Lester Lefton, *Psychology,* 5th ed., Table of Contents.

Note how the size of the print, the use of boldface, and indented lines help you to see the movement from general to specific. *Sensation and Perception* is a very broad topic. *The Visual System* is one subtopic under that grouping. That, in turn, is broken into even smaller subtopics or aspects: *The Structure of the Eye, The Electrical Connection,* etc.

EXERCISE 2.3

Determining Topics and Subtopics from an Outline

The table of contents of a college biology textbook contains this listing for a chapter.

C. Starr, *Biology,* 2nd ed.

From the outline form, the size of the print, and the use of boldface, you should be able to determine the following:

1. The overall topic of the chapter: ______________________________

2. The three main subtopics of the chapter:

____

____

____

3. The five subdivisions of the subtopic *The World's Biomes:*

____

____

____

____

____

The topic of a paragraph or passage is usually, but not always, stated near the beginning. It is often restated, sometimes more than once, in the rest of the text. A statement of the topic should be as specific as possible while still covering all the material that relates to it.

EXERCISE 2.4

Determining Subtopics in Paragraphs

The next five paragraphs relate to the general topic Work in America. To determine the subtopics developed in these paragraphs, look for the word or phrase that is most specific while still broad enough to cover all the material.

- *specialization:* doing only one narrow job
- *initiative:* the drive to begin and carry through with something
- *profound:* deeply important or very insightful
- *dehumanizing:* degrading, making less than human

1 Specialization of work, if carried too far, leaves little room for responsibility or initiative by the worker. It can mean that some people are assigned the job of controlling those who actually produce goods or deliver services. When Studs Terkel (1974) interviewed workers, he found "the most profound complaint is 'being spied on.' There's the foreman at the plant, the supervisor listening in at Ma Bell's, the checker who gives the bus driver a hard time." Moreover, by tying the worker to an isolated task, to a small part of some large task, specialization can empty jobs of their meaning. The result can be dehumanizing for some workers, as Terkel found when he interviewed people across the country: "'I'm a machine,' says the spotwelder. 'I'm caged,' says the bank teller. 'I'm a mule,' says the steelworker. 'A monkey can do what I do,' says the receptionist."

Which of the following phrases best covers the material in this paragraph?

a. worker initiative

b. dehumanizing activities

c. specialization of work

d. mules, machines, and monkeys

2 Although it is unpleasant to be a temporary worker, does permanent full-time employment bring happiness? Are Americans really happy with their jobs? In many studies during the last two decades representative samples of workers have been asked whether they would continue to work if they inherited enough money to live comfortably without working. More than 70 percent replied that they would. When asked how satisfied they were with their jobs, even more—from 80 to 90 percent—replied that they were very or moderately satisfied. But when asked whether they would choose the same line of work if they could begin all over again, most said no. In short, most Americans seem to like their jobs but are not too excited about them.

■ *decades:* periods of ten years

■ *moderately:* somewhat, partly

The paragraph begins with two questions. What topic is suggested by these paragraphs?

____

3 In a survey, only 26 percent of American workers still held the traditional view of work. Some of these workers said that "the more I get paid, the more I do." Others agreed that "work is one of life's unpleasant necessities. I wouldn't work if I didn't have to." A bumper sticker says it all: "Work sucks, but I need the bucks." In contrast, a large majority (73 percent) of the respondents expressed more positive attitudes toward work. Many agreed with the statement: "I have an inner need to do the very best I can, regardless of pay." They most frequently rated as "very important" certain nonmonetary, inherent qualities of work, such as interesting jobs, developing their own skills, and seeing how good the results of their work are. The American work ethic has taken on a new quality.

■ *nonmonetary:* not having to do with pay

■ *inherent:* within the thing itself, not outside of it

Which of the following best covers the material in this paragraph?

a. traditional attitudes toward work

b. negatives attitudes toward work

c. positive attitudes toward work

d. attitudes toward work

■ *gainfully:* with wages

■ *dramatic:* very noticeable, big

4 The labor force includes all those over 16 years of age who are gainfully employed as well as those who are jobless but are actively seeking paid employment. It excludes full-time homemakers, students, and retired people—anyone who is not paid for his or her work and is not seeking a paying job. In 1988 about 66 percent of Americans over the age of 16 were in the work force—this figure is expected to grow to 69 percent in 2000—compared with about 55 percent in 1940. This increase has been accompanied by dramatic shifts in what American workers do and who makes up the work force.

The topic is stated in a two-word phrase in two places in the paragraph. One word is different in the two phrases. Write the two phrases below:

____

____

■ *white-collar:* nonmanual labor; professional, salaried

■ *blue collars:* those doing skilled and unskilled manual labor

■ *psychosomatic:* showing a link between mind and body

■ *impaired:* damaged, made worse

■ *genetics:* the inherited traits of an individual

5 People with satisfying jobs have better mental health than those with less satisfying work. Thus, white-collar workers are less likely than blue collars to suffer from psychosomatic illnesses, low self-esteem, worry, anxiety, and impaired interpersonal relationships. People who are happy with their jobs also tend to have better physical health and to live longer. Although diet, exercise, medical care, and genetics are all related to the incidence of heart disease, job dissatisfaction is more closely linked to the cause of death. (pp. 298–301)

The topic of this paragraph covers the connection between

a. white-collar workers and blue-collar workers
b. mental health and job satisfaction
c. physical health and job satisfaction
d. mental and physical health and job satisfaction

The preceding five paragraphs occur in a section with the heading "Work in America." Write the number of the paragraph or paragraphs you think belong under the subtopic headings. (There are two paragraphs in the second section.)

Work in America
- The Labor Force _____
- Job Satisfaction _____ _____
- Attitudes Toward Work _____
- The Changing Workplace _____

TOPICS AND SUBTOPICS IN TEXTBOOK PASSAGES

Recognizing topics and subtopics in textbooks is the foundation for deciding what information is most important to remember. While many textbooks will help you by giving outlines or headings of different sizes, in others you may have to decide on topics and subtopics on your own. Two selections in the next exercise will give you practice in surveying longer textbook passages for topics and subtopics.

EXERCISE 2.5

Determining Topics and Subtopics in Textbook Passages

■ PART A

The following passage contains some of the text outlined earlier in this chapter on "The World's Biomes." The text defines a *biome* as "A broad, vegetational subdivision of a biogeographical realm shaped by climate, topography, and composition of soils." As you read, the concept of a biome should become clearer to you. But first, look up the meanings of these words to help you understand this definition.

biogeographical: ____

realm: ____

topography: ____

Before you read the selection, look back at the five subtopics under "The World's Biomes." Think about what you know about these. Are some more familiar? Do you know more about deserts than, for example, tundras? Write down any information you have about these areas.

____

____

____

____

____

____

____

____

Look at the beginning of the article. What do you think the subtopic of ¶s 1–3 will be?

___

What gave you the hint?

___

___

The World's Biomes

by Cecie Starr

Deserts

■ *potential:* possibility

■ *extensive:* far reaching

1 Deserts exist where the potential for evaporation greatly exceeds rainfall. Such conditions prevail at latitudes of about 30° north and south. There we find the deserts of the American Southwest, northern Chile, Australia, northern and southern Africa, and Arabia. Farther north are the vast Gobi of Asia, the Kyzyl-Kum east of the Caspian Sea, and the high deserts of eastern Oregon. These northern deserts result largely from the rain shadow effect of extensive mountain ranges.

Which *two* subtopics does this paragraph mainly give information about?

a. how to survive on a desert

b. what causes desert conditions

c. where deserts are located

d. what plants grow in the desert

■ *erode:* wear away

2 Vegetation cover is limited in deserts. The infrequent rains often fall in heavy, brief pulses that erode the unprotected soil. Humidity is so low, solar rays easily penetrate the air and quickly heat the ground surface. The surface radiates heat and cools quickly at night.

What smaller subtopic of "deserts" do you get information about in this paragraph?

a. types of vegetation in a desert

b. physical conditions of a desert

c. the unbearable hotness of a desert

3 Although arid or semiarid conditions do not favor large, leafy plants, deserts show plenty of diversity. A patch of Arizona desert may have deep-rooted evergreen shrubs, including creosote, and fleshy-stemmed, shallow-rooted cacti. It may have tall saguaro, short prickly pear, and ocotillo—which drops leaves more than once a year, then grows new ones after a rain. Its annuals and perennials flower spectacularly but briefly after spring rains. Mesquite, cottonwood, and other deep-rooted species may grow near streambeds with a permanent underground water supply.

- *arid:* very dry
- *semiarid:* somewhat dry
- *annuals:* plants that die after one season
- *perennials:* plants that live more than two years

All the details in this paragraph deal with what subtopic of "deserts"?

____

Dry Shrublands and Woodlands

4 Western or southern coastal regions of continents between latitudes 30° and 40° have a semiarid climate, like that around the Mediterranean Sea. They get more rain than deserts, but not much more. Rain falls mostly during mild winter months, and the summers are long, hot, and dry. Dry shrublands and woodlands prevail in these regions and other areas with related climates. Their dominant plants often have hard, tough, evergreen leaves.

- *prevail:* dominate, have the greatest number

Judging from the section heading, what two subtopics will paragraphs 4–6 be about?

____

____

¶4 introduces the subtopic of

a. dry shrublands

b. dry woodlands

c. both of the above

5 Dry shrublands dominate when annual rainfall is less than 25 to 60 centimeters. These biomes have exotic local names, such as fynbos and chaparral. California alone has 2.4 million hectares (6 million acres) of chaparral-covered hills, where dominant plants may form a nearly impenetrable vegetation cover. These plants are woody, multibranched, and a few meters tall

- *impenetrable:* not capable of being entered

at most. Every so often, lightning-sparked firestorms sweep through these biomes. Many of the shrubs have highly flammable leaves, and their above ground parts burn rapidly. Yet they are exquisitely adapted to episodes of fire and quickly resprout from their root crowns. Trees (and suburban housing developments) do not fare as well in firestorms. The shrubs—which feed the fires—have the competitive edge.

■ *exquisitely:* intricately, perfectly

What is the subtopic of ¶5?

a. California chaparral

b. woody plants

c. the dangers of fire in the shrublands

d. dry shrublands

6 Dry woodlands dominate when annual rainfall is about 40 to 100 centimeters. The dominant trees can be tall, but they do not form a dense, continuous canopy. Eucalyptus woodlands of southwestern Australia and oak woodlands of the Pacific states are like this.

■ *canopy:* overhead covering

What is the subtopic of ¶6?

____

Grasslands and Savannas

7 Grasslands sweep across parts of southern Africa, Australia, South America, and midcontinental regions of North America and the Soviet Union. The main types are shortgrass prairie, tallgrass prairie, and tropical savannas. Usually the land is flat or rolling. Warm temperatures prevail in summer in temperate zones and throughout the year in the tropics. The 25 to 100 centimeters of annual rainfall prevents deserts from forming but is not enough to support forests. The dominant animals are grazing and burrowing types. Grazing and periodic fires keep shrublands and forests from encroaching on the fringes of many grasslands.

■ *temperate:* moderate, mild

■ *encroaching:* moving into an area that belongs to another

■ *fringes:* edges, outskirts

The heading for this section is "Grasslands and Savannas." What part of this subtopic does ¶7 introduce?

a. grasslands

b. savannas

c. both parts

8 Tallgrass prairie once extended west from the temperate deciduous forests of North America. Daisies, sunflowers, and other composites as well as legumes also were abundant. Most tallgrass prairie has been converted to farmland. Large areas are now being restored in several locations. Shortgrass prairie prevails when winds are strong, rainfall light and infrequent, and evaporation rapid. Plant roots above the permanently dry subsoil soak up the brief, seasonal rain. In the 1930s, the shortgrass prairie of the American Great Plains was largely overgrazed and plowed under for wheat, which requires more moisture than the region sometimes provides. Strong prevailing winds, drought, and poor farming practices turned much of the prairie into a Dust Bowl. Steinbeck's *The Grapes of Wrath* and Michener's *Centennial,* two historical novels, speak eloquently of the disruption of this biome and its consequences.

■ *deciduous:* losing leaves each year

■ *eloquently:* movingly, gracefully

■ *disruption:* interference, breaking up of

What subtopics are covered in ¶8?

a. savannas and grasslands

b. savannas and prairies

c. two types of prairie

9 Tropical savannas cover broad belts of Africa, South America, and Australia. Where rainfall is low, rapidly growing grasses dominate. Scattered patches of acacia and other shrubs exist where there is slightly more moisture. Where more rain falls, savannas grade into tropical woodlands with tall, coarse grasses.

What is the subtopic of ¶9?

____

10 Monsoon grasslands thrive in parts of southern Asia. "Monsoon" refers to a season of heavy rain that corresponds to a shift in prevailing winds over the Indian Ocean. It alternates with a pronounced dry season. The climate favors dense stands of tall, coarse grasses. These die back and often burn during the dry season.

■ *pronounced:* very definite

■ *dense:* thick

What is the subtopic of ¶10?

____

Forests

11 In the world's major forests, tall trees grow together closely enough to form a fairly continuous canopy over a broad region. The trees fall into three general categories. Which category prevails in a region depends partly on distance from the equator. "Evergreen broadleafs" dominate between latitudes 20° north and south. "Deciduous broadleafs" are most common at moist, temperate latitudes where winters are not severe. "Evergreen conifers" are most common at higher, colder latitudes and in the mountains of temperate zones. (Starr, pp. 393–96)

¶11 introduces a section on the subtopic "forests." What three smaller subtopics will this section cover?

____

____

____

■ PART B

Look at the title of the following selection. What do you think the topic of the selection will be?

____

What definition of famine is given in the first paragraph?

____

____

Have you heard or read about famines in areas other than Africa? Write down any information you have on the general topic of famines:

____

____

____

____

____

____

____

____

Famine in Africa

by Michael Bradshaw

1 Famine is a severe shortage of food occurring over a wide area and causing deaths by starvation and by diseases that take advantage of a reduced ability to fight them following malnutrition. Famines occurred in various parts of the world throughout human history, but in the last twenty years most have occurred in Africa south of the Sahara. Despite huge injections of aid from other parts of the world, many countries remain in danger of famine from year to year. It is likely that Africa will continue to be the hungry continent into the next century as its population growth outstrips economic growth.

■ *malnutrition:* condition due to not getting proper foods

■ *outstrips:* goes beyond

What is the topic of ¶1?

a. food shortages

b. South Africa

c. famines

d. aid from countries

2 Famine results from shocks to natural and human systems that upset them and disrupt food production or distribution. Natural shocks include drought, river flooding, insect plagues, and plant diseases. Human shocks include wars, civil conflict, widespread poverty, inefficient food distribution, and population growth that exceeds the ability of a country or region to feed the extra mouths.

■ *disrupt:* break up, stop

■ *inefficient:* not effective

The topic of ¶2 is

____

____

3 It is often not so much the immediate result of such shocks but the failure of human systems to cope with them, that causes famines. For example, recent African famines have occurred on the semi-arid margins of deserts where droughts that are part of climate changes have had greater famine impacts than before.

The reasons for these greater impacts include pressures from increasing populations, civil wars that disrupt transportation systems, and the abandonment of long-established systems of cultivation and livestock keeping that made allowances for coping with drought.

- *abandonment:* giving up, leaving
- *allowances:* adjustments

The topic of ¶3 is famines that are caused by

a. droughts in Africa
b. failure of human systems
c. civil wars
d. pressure from increasing populations

4 The much publicized famines in Ethiopia and Somalia occurred when stresses resulting from drought were made worse by the difficulties of getting food to populations cut off from supplies by civil war. By mid-1992 it was estimated that up to 4.5 million people in Somalia were faced with starvation. Baidos and Bordera, two small towns west of the capital, Mogadishu, lie in some of the country's best farmland. After refugees from other areas moved in, famine struck both. At Baidos, where the population was swollen to 60,000, over 100 died each day; in Bordera, 30 to 40 died each day. Neither town had community kitchens and the timing of the issue of dry food was irregular.

¶4 is mainly about famines in which country?

a. Ethiopia
b. Somalia
c. Baidos
d. Mogadishu

5 Famines in Zimbabwe and southern Sudan occurred when the drought impacts were increased by the arrival of hundreds of thousands of refugees from war in Mozambique or famine in Ethiopia respectively. Famine in Mali and Niger occurred when livestock herds had to be slaughtered because the grass had dried up rapidly when overgrazing was followed by drought.

The topic of ¶5 is causes of famines in

a. Zimbabwe and Sudan
b. Mozambique and Ethiopia
c. Mali and Niger
d. both a and b

6 Famines get emergency attention from governments and from international aid agencies. Governments can usually cope with the onset of famine if they have distribution systems that deal equally with urban and rural areas. Famines are more prevalent in rural areas where provision is uneven, where transportation is poor, and where it is difficult for the people to immigrate rapidly into the better provisioned urban areas. Rural areas are also at a disadvantage since many people there are undernourished compared to those in towns. Poor nourishment gives famine conditions a start as the young and old succumb rapidly to starvation and killing diseases.

provisioned: provided with supplies

succumb: give in to, die

¶6 mainly deals with famine in

a. government
b. urban areas
c. rural areas
d. areas of poverty

7 International agencies bring food and medical aid to emergency situations. They are limited in what they can do by response time and local access to affected areas. It takes time to assemble staff and purchase, ship, and deliver emergency food to the needy country. Once there, internal transportation is often so poor that only limited quantities can be shipped rapidly. Such emergency food often brings wheat flour and milk powder not normally consumed by local people, who may need a cultural shift to continue consuming such food. (p. 100)

The topic of ¶7 is problems in

a. giving food and medicine
b. providing shelter
c. transporting victims
d. all of the above

Write the numbers of the paragraphs that deal with the following subtopics:

the definition of famine __________

the causes of famine __________

trying to solve famines __________

DICTIONARY SKILLS: WORDS WITH MULTIPLE MEANINGS

Just as general categories may have many specific members, and just as topics can have many subtopics, so too can a word be viewed as a kind of general category with several different specific meanings (for example, the word *place* has more than twenty-five different meanings in one desk-size dictionary). Because words have more—sometimes many more—than just one meaning, there are times when finding the right meaning requires some real effort and thought. For example, suppose while reading that you run across the word *discharge* in this sentence:

> Antony's father was able to *discharge* his son's gambling bills by writing a check for the full amount.

Not sure of its meaning, you look up the word and find this entry:

> **dis•charge** (dis charj′) v.t. 1. to release or dismiss: as *discharged* from the army. 2. to unload (a cargo) 3. to shoot (a gun or projectile) 4. to emit, as the sore *discharges* pus 5. to pay (a debt) or perform (a duty) 6. in *electricity,* to remove stored energy from a battery.

What does the word mean in your sentence? As you can see, *discharge* can have many different meanings. We can't really say what the word means until we look at the *context,* what goes on around the word, to help us decide which of these meanings fits. From the situation—the context—you would be able to figure out that here the meaning in definition 5, "to pay (a debt)" would best fit. A sentence with a different context would give a very different meaning:

> The cannon *discharged* as the enemy troops mounted the hill.

Here the context—a battle—tells us the correct meaning is definition 3: "to shoot (a gun or projectile)."

That words can have more than one meaning is only one problem in finding the right definition of a word. A word can belong to two or more parts of speech (groups of words with similar functions), each with several meanings. This is especially true for parts of speech like *nouns, verbs,* and *adjectives.* When you are puzzled by a word that can be more than one part of speech, you may be unable to figure out the meaning unless you can first identify how the word is being used—its part of speech—in a particular sentence.

You may have been asked in school to identify the parts of speech in a sentence; if so, you may have been given some rules like the following for these parts of speech:

nouns (n.) are the names of persons, places, things, or ideas

adjectives (adj.) describe nouns by telling which or what kind of

verbs (v.) show action

adverbs (adv.) tell how an action is performed

But suppose you ran across a word like *agminate,* whose meaning you did not know. Would you be able to decide on its part of speech using these rules? Does it show or describe an action? Does it name or describe a person, place, thing, or idea? The truth is, trying to identify parts of speech only by their meaning or general function doesn't always work. But there are other things that can help you. Examine the sentence below. Despite the fact that you would probably say that you don't know what the words mean, make a guess on the parts of speech of the words in the sentence:

The borful floogs garfly sporfed some corfable tarkons by the horkle.

You will be surprised by how much agreement there is with your classmates. Odds are that most of the class will have arrived at the following:

	adj.	**n.**	**adv.**	**v.**		**adj.**	**n.**			**n.**
The	borful	floogs	garfly	sporfed	some	corfable	tarkons	by	the	horkle.

But if you know none of the words in this sentence, how can you decide on their parts of speech?

First of all, it's not true that you don't know any of the words. Look again: *the, some,* and *by* are words you are familiar with. You also know that the name of something (a noun) must sooner or later follow a *the.* Second, parts of the made-up words do have a kind of meaning. You know that *-s* added to a word like "floog" can mean "more than one," that many describing words (adjectives) have *-ful* endings as in "borful" (help*ful,* care*ful*), or *-able* endings as in "corfable" (laugh*able,* work*able*) and that adverbs often end in *-ly* as in "garfly" (slow*ly,* sad*ly*). You might know that verbs have various endings to show past, present, and future. The *-ed* on "sporfed" tells us that the "sporfing" (whatever it might mean) happened in the past. You also get some clues from position. Nouns often fill the subject positions—what the sentence is about (floogs)—and adjectives come between words like *the* or *some* and a noun ("some *corfable* tarkons").

You probably know more than you thought you did about figuring out parts of speech. Reviewing the guidelines below and doing the practices will help you find the part of speech and meaning for words you will meet.

Nouns

The word *noun* comes from a Latin word that means "name." We most commonly think of nouns as words that name persons, places, and things: *Roberto, Las Vegas, car, city, table,* etc. Nouns also are names given to events (*a wedding, the Super Bowl*), to feelings (*love, dislike, fear*), or to ideas or concepts (*truth, honor, beauty, fate*). Nouns also have special features and locations in a sentence that help us identify them.

1. A word used as a noun usually can be made to show *more than one* of something (its plural form). Most nouns can be made plural by adding *-s* or *-es,* but there are other forms as well:

   dog/dog*s* box/box*es* child/child*ren*

   Look at the two sentences with the word *present* below:

   A. The mayor will present him with a medal.

   B. Maria was very happy with the present she received.

   In which sentence is *present* being used as a noun? _____

   How do you know? ____

2. Most nouns can appear alone with *the* or *a/an* or with **pronouns** like *my, his, their,* etc.: *the* house, *a* party, *an* orange, *her* sister. Any word that would make sense in the blanks would be a noun:

   A ____________________ came down the road.

   She gave away **her** ____________________.

3. Nouns are very often the subjects of sentences. The subject is **who** or **what** a sentence is about, and usually occurs near the beginning. **Who** or **what** is the subject of these sentences? Circle one word in each.

   A large dog ran into the road.

   The final exam will be the hardest.

   Justice must apply equally to everyone.

Circle the words below (nouns) that will fit into the subject blank in this sentence:

The ____________________ is very old.

long	story
house	difficult
stupid	radio
unfair	carefully

4. Nouns can stand alone with words that show relationships like time, direction, position, such as *of, after, through, upon:*

   After *lunch,* we went for a *walk* by the *river.*

   During the *holidays,* rooms in *hotels* are expensive.

   In which of the sentences below is *chocolate* being used as a noun? _____

   A. After dinner I ate a chocolate cookie.

   B. Every evening I drink a cup of chocolate.

   How do you know? ____

Adjectives

This part of speech includes words that tell us about what things are like. They answer **which** or **what kind** of questions about nouns, giving us information like the following:

size: tall, small, tiny, huge

shape: round, oval, square, triangular, lopsided

color: brown, red, yellow

condition: old, new, dirty, used, clean, firm, rotten

value: good, bad, excellent, worthless, superior

Here are some special features of adjectives that help us to identify them.

1. Many adjectives can make comparisons. Some take the endings *-er* and *-est* to do this, while others use *more* and *most.* Examples:

big	bigg*er*	bigg*est*
beautiful	*more* beautiful	*most* beautiful

2. Adjectives most often are placed after *the, an/a,* or pronouns like *my, his, their,* etc., in order to describe a noun:

the *yellow* fence	a *delicious* pizza	an *open* window
a *big, dirty, yellow* dog	my *old, shabby* coat	

Look again at the sentences using the word *chocolate.*

A. After dinner I ate a *chocolate* cookie.

B. Every evening I drink a cup of *chocolate.*

In which of the sentences is *chocolate* being used as an adjective? _____

How do you know? ____

Adjectives often follow the word *very.* Circle the words (adjectives) that will fit into the blank at the end of this sentence:

The test was very ____________________.

long	story
house	difficult
stupid	radio
unfair	carefully

Verbs

Words used as verbs often can be used as other parts of speech. There are some simple rules for testing whether a word is being used as a verb.

1. Verbs answer **what is it doing** or **what did it do** about the subject.

   Good students are eager to *ask* questions.
   (**What do** good students **do**? They *ask* questions.)

   Look at the two sentences with the word *produce* below:

   A. The *produce* from these farms rotted before it could be taken to market.

   B. These farms *produce* only enough for one family to make a living.

   In which sentence is *produce* telling us about **what the farms do?** _____

2. Verbs have forms that show time: He walk*s*/is walk*ing* to school (present time); He walk*ed* to school (past); He *will* walk to school (future). We can decide if a word in a sentence is a verb if we can change its form to show time. In the example with *produce,* we could also decide that the word is

being used as a verb in sentence B because we could make changes in time:

These farms *are* produc*ing*/produc*ed*/*will* produce only enough for one.

In sentence A, *produce* is used as a noun and cannot make these changes. Sentences beginning with these changes would not make sense:

The *will produce* from these farms rotted.

The *are producing* from these farms rotted.

Adverbs

This traditional part of speech contains a number of groups with different features. The most common adverbs end in *-ly* and tell how an action is done:

The professor spoke *slowly* to the class.
(How did the professor speak?)

You will not have to make any decisions about the part of speech of these words, because adverbs ending in *-ly* cannot be used as any other part of speech. However, don't assume that all words with this ending are adverbs. Here is a quick way to test. Most of these adverbs come in pairs with adjectives (*sad/sadly*). Therefore if you drop the *-ly* from an adverb, you will usually be left with an adjective with a similar meaning (*timidly/timid*). However, if you drop the *-ly* from a word that is not an adjective, you would end up with something that is not a word (*silly/sil*). Circle any of the following that are *not* adverbs.

fabulously	holly
rely	weakly
strong	starry
carefully	bully

How did you know? ____________________________

EXERCISE 2.6

Parts of Speech and Definitions in Context

Using the preceding guide, determine the part of speech of the italicized word in each of the three sentences in the following groups (parts of speech for the first group is given). Use the context and the dictionary entries that are given to determine the correct meaning of each word. Then explain what helped you to make your decision on the part of speech and how a particular meaning for a part of speech would fit the context. Use the sample below as a guide.

Sample Dictionary Entry

present *noun* 1. a moment of time between past and future; now. 2. a gift *adj.* 1. current, at this time 2. being in attendance, at hand *verb* 1. to introduce 2. to exhibit or display 3. to put forward, as a petition 4. to make a gift or formal presentation of

1. I like my *present* job better than my last one.

   Part of speech: adjective

   Reason: placed between "my" and the noun "job"

   Meaning: (1) current, at this time

   Context clue: "present" means the opposite of "last"

2. The little boy got the *present* that he wanted for his birthday.

   Part of speech: noun

   Reason: stands alone with "the"; can be made plural ("presents")

   Meaning: (2) a gift

   Context clue: people get gifts on their birthdays

3. The governor will *present* the mayor with a check for the new pool.

   Part of speech: verb

   Reason: could show past time: "the governor presented"

   Meaning: (4) to make a gift or formal presentation of

   Context clue: money is being given for a city project

Dictionary Entry

> **second** *noun* 1. A unit of time equal to 1/60 of a second. 2. A brief period of time; a moment. 3. The official attendant in a contest such as a duel or a boxing match. *adj.* 1. Coming after the first. 2. Another: *a second chance.* 3. Inferior to another: *second to none.* *verb* 1. To attend (a boxer, for example) as an aide. 2. To promote or encourage. 3. To support (a motion or a nomination) as a requirement for a discussion or vote.

1. The *second* game was much better than the first.

   Part of speech: adjective

   Reason: ______________________________

   Meaning: ______________________________

   Context clue: ______________________________

2. Only one *second* remained in the game.

   Part of speech: noun

   Reason: ______________________________

   Meaning: ______________________________

   Context clue: ______________________________

3. Most committee members will *second* only a motion that they intend to support.

   Part of speech: verb

   Reason: ______________________________

   Meaning: ______________________________

   Context clue: ______________________________

Dictionary Entry

burst *noun* 1. A sudden, intense event: *raining in bursts.* 2. A quick, intense increase; a rush: *a burst of speed.* 3. The explosion of a bomb on impact. *adj.* 1. Overwhelmed or broken by emotion: *a burst heart* 2. Blown apart; exploded. *verb* 1. To come open or fly apart suddenly; to explode. 2. To come forth, emerge, or arrive suddenly. 3. To give sudden expression to: *burst into tears.*

1. With a *burst* of energy, the fullback charged into the end zone.

Part of speech: ______________________

Reason: ______________________

Meaning: ______________________

Context clue: ______________________

2. The tire *burst* when the attendant kept adding air.

Part of speech: ______________________

Reason: ______________________

Meaning: ______________________

Context clue: ______________________

3. A *burst* pipe was the cause of the flooding.

Part of speech: ______________________

Reason: ______________________

Meaning: ______________________

Context clue: ______________________

Dictionary Entry

pilot *noun* 1. One who operates an aircraft. 2. The helmsman on a ship. 3. A part that steadies or guides the action of a tool. *adj.* 1. Acting as a model for future action or development 2. Serving as a guide or control. *verb* 1. To act as the pilot of. 2. To guide or lead, as through a difficult situation.

1. They introduced a *pilot* program for teaching phonics to children.

   Part of speech: ________________

   Reason: ________________

   Meaning: ________________

   Context clue: ________________

2. The *pilot* was badly injured in the crash of the jetliner.

   Part of speech: ________________

   Reason: ________________

   Meaning: ________________

   Context clue: ________________

3. Many business people *pilot* their own planes to work.

   Part of speech: ________________

   Reason: ________________

   Meaning: ________________

   Context clue: ________________

Active Learning

THE TOPIC IS READING

In *Speaking of Reading,* author Nadine Rosenthal examines the topic of reading and its importance in people's lives. The book includes oral responses from many people from all walks of life—rich and poor, educated and uneducated—who, in their own words, answered this question: "What is your reading history and how does reading affect the rest of your life?"

Here and in later chapters, you will read some short selections from the chapter "Learning to Read as Adults." These include the author's observations and oral histories of people who have had trouble with reading but are on the road to success. Their experiences should give you a better understanding of the importance of active reading and learning in general to success and happiness. You may also find that some of their experiences are similar to your own.

EXERCISE 2.7

Overcoming Reading Difficulties

In this selection, the author shows how problems in reading can have harmful effects on people's lives. As you read, note the examples the author gives from her teaching experience of the ways nonreaders must adjust on the job and in their personal lives.

from *Learning to Read as an Adult*

by Nadine Rosenthal

1 Adults who can't read develop complex coping mechanisms to save face in countless situations. My students described how they ask directions without letting on they are unable to read street signs, or call up manufacturers to "doublecheck" instructions; they are forever "forgetting" their glasses, and claim they don't use a checkbook because it "might get stolen." They seldom carry paper or pen to write messages on.

2 Many nonreaders cope by carefully controlling their interactions with others. One of my students admitted she was naturally an outgoing person, but that as an adult she learned to be cautious around other people. She avoided church activities because she dreaded having to read something in a meeting, and she didn't join her friends at restaurants because she would be confronted with reading a menu. Another had the "gotta go" syndrome—retreating quickly to save embarrassment in front of peers. "Every time I enter a political discussion at work," he confessed, "I risk others noticing my knowledge on the subject is thin. They accuse me of making broad generalizations, but that's all I know."

3 Many nonreaders control their interactions at work so successfully they become model workers. They work without complaint to cover up their reading disabilities. They have learned to think ahead to avoid potential disasters, and use this skill for both themselves and their company's welfare. Some decline promotions to supervisory positions because of potential paperwork, while others work hard in fear of losing their jobs. They know they may have to fill in employment papers for a future job without having the opportunity to get their spouses' help.

Reprinted with permission of Nadine Rosenthal: *Speaking of Reading* (Heinemann, a division of Reed Elsevier, Inc., Portsmouth, N.H., 1995), pp. 121–30.

In groups of 3–4, complete the following:

1. The author states that "Adults who can't read develop complex coping mechanisms to save face in countless situations." List three examples she gives of how students hide reading problems:

   (1) ____________________

   (2) ____________________

   (3) ____________________

2. "Many nonreaders cope by carefully controlling their interactions with others." Give two examples from the text of these behaviors.

   (1) ____________________

   (2) ____________________

3. "Many nonreaders control their interactions at work so successfully they become model workers." Give two examples from the text of successful ways in which nonreaders cope on the job. List two negative effects that the inability to read has on a worker's career:

   Successful:

   (1) ____________________

   (2) ____________________

   Negative:

   (1) ____________________

   (2) ____________________

4. Have you ever experienced or witnessed situations similar to the examples the author gives? If so, list and briefly discuss what they were and how you felt.

   ____

   ____

5. "What is your reading history and how does reading affect the rest of your life?" Give your own answer to the book's question:

   ____

   ____

   ____

Reading Portfolio

SEARCHING THE RESOURCE LEARNING CENTER

Visit the areas in your library/learning resource center that have the periodicals (magazines, newspapers, journals) and/or computer access to the Internet or other resource materials.

1. Browse through the magazine section or go on-line to find and write the names of five magazines. Then search the table of contents of one of them and write down the names of two articles you might want to read. Include the names of the authors.
2. Do the same for newspapers. Write down the names of three newspapers. Select one and write the full headlines for two articles that look interesting to read. Include the names of the authors, if given.

CHAPTER 3

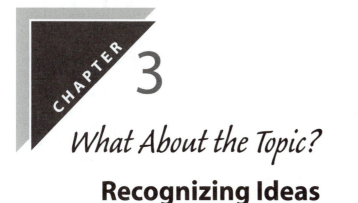

What About the Topic?

Recognizing Ideas

After reading this chapter, you will know the answers to these questions:

- What is the difference between a topic and an idea?
- How do questions lead from topics to ideas?
- What kinds of questions lead to identifying ideas?
- What effects does illiteracy have upon society in general?

You have discovered that the first step in understanding reading material is to find the topic: the subject (who or what) the material deals with. The topic of a paragraph or article might be surfing, or taxes, or computers—anything at all that people are interested in. But simply naming a topic does not result in communication or understanding. A good reader must go beyond knowing what the topic is to finding out what the author wants to communicate *about* that subject.

FROM TOPIC TO IDEA

The topic tells us the subject area but it doesn't tell us exactly what a writer will talk about in what may be a very big area of information. For example, two writers may be worried about water pollution, but the information in one article may be very different from that in another. We use the term *idea* to refer to any statement that a writer makes *about* a topic. A topic is stated as a fragment, a part of a sentence; an idea must be a complete statement, a whole sentence. For example, here is a paragraph you read in the last chapter:

> **Evergreen Broadleaf Forests.** These biomes sweep across tropical zones of Africa, the East Indies, southeastern Asia, the Malay Archipelago, South America, and Central America. Annual rainfall can exceed 200 centimeters and is never less than 130 centimeters. (Starr, pp. 593–96)

The broad topic, **Evergreen Broadleaf Forests,** is shown by the use of boldface. Notice that it is only a *topic,* not a complete sentence.

Taken by itself, "Evergreen Broadleaf Forests" doesn't communicate anything clearly to us. If a biology teacher walked into a classroom and announced "evergreen broadleaf forests," all the students would be left thinking, What *about* evergreen broadleaf forests? The rest of the above paragraph does tell us *about* this topic—that is, it communicates ideas about evergreen broadleaf forests. These ideas are stated in *complete sentences:*

> These biomes sweep across tropical zones. . . .
>
> Annual rainfall can exceed 200 centimeters. . . .

Unlike topics, ideas are statements that we can prove or disprove, agree or disagree with. "Action movies" is a topic. We can't prove or disprove it, agree or disagree with it. Compare that to ideas *about* "action movies."

> Eddie Murphy has appeared in many action movies.
>
> Eddie Murphy's action movies are terrific fun.

These sentences provide us with ideas we can react to. We can prove the first (true, Eddie Murphy has appeared in many action movies) and we can agree or disagree with the second, depending on our tastes.

EXERCISE 3.1

Distinguishing Topics from Idea Sentences

For both Parts A and B, ask yourself the following questions about each item:

> Is it a complete sentence?
>
> Does it tell *about* the topic?
>
> Could I prove/disprove it or agree/disagree with it?

■ PART A

In each of the following pairs, write I for Idea sentence and T for Topic fragment.

1. _____ During heavy snowfalls, skiing advanced slopes can be dangerous.
   _____ The dangers of skiing advanced slopes, especially during heavy snowfalls.
2. _____ Returning to college, completing an education, then many students being successful.
   _____ Many students have become successful after returning to complete their education.
3. _____ Health and energy increase on a diet of fresh fruit, vegetables, and whole grain breads.
   _____ Fresh fruit, vegetables, along with whole grain breads, leading to health and energy.
4. _____ Christmas is a special time of year, with holly, songs, and presents around the tree.
   _____ A special time of year, with Christmas trees, holly, songs, and presents.
5. _____ The differences between ideas and topics, proving/disproving, agreeing/disagreeing.
   _____ Unlike topics, ideas are statements we can prove or disprove, agree or disagree with.

■ PART B

Decide which of the following items are complete ideas and which are fragments. Write I for Idea sentence and T for Topic fragment.

1. _____ Computers changing the way we live, improvement for all of us in our lives.
2. _____ If mall parking is inadequate, many customers will opt to shop elsewhere.
3. _____ The widespread use of home fireplaces has clearly increased air pollution.
4. _____ With many potential voters too turned off to vote, democracy is threatened.
5. _____ New advancements in Internet shopping, the risks, benefits, and future of it.
6. _____ Good study habits, motivation, organizational skills, the likelihood of high grades.

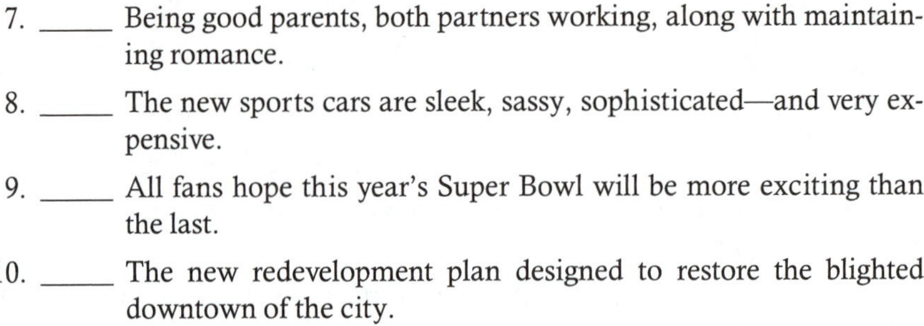
7. _____ Being good parents, both partners working, along with maintaining romance.
8. _____ The new sports cars are sleek, sassy, sophisticated—and very expensive.
9. _____ All fans hope this year's Super Bowl will be more exciting than the last.
10. _____ The new redevelopment plan designed to restore the blighted downtown of the city.

Every complete sentence expresses an idea, and, even in a single paragraph, many different ideas can be stated about a topic. Authors report on what they have experienced and wondered about. Writing, therefore, is a result of authors creating ideas by answering their own questions. Fortunately, our language contains words that allow us to ask different *kinds* of questions about the things around us:

Who, Which, What questions help us to identify and describe.

Where questions show our concern with locations and how things fit together.

What kind(s)/type(s)/group(s) of questions let us put things in categories.

When questions reflect how important time is to us in arranging our lives.

How questions help us understand the way things work and to see the steps in a process.

Why questions lead to identifying causes and effects and to solving problems.

Asking questions is the key to active reading and writing. It is the most important means we use to create many different ideas about a topic:

Topic	*Question*	*Idea*
Pets	*How* can you keep your dog in good health?	Provide a good diet and plenty of exercise to keep your dog healthy.
Heart disease	*Why* are some people more likely than others to have heart disease?	Both heredity and lifestyles contribute to the risk of heart disease.
Economic classes	*What groups* are identified as the main economic and social classes in the U.S.?	Upper, middle, and lower are the three major class groupings for U.S. families.

EXERCISE 3.2

Relating Questions to Topics and Ideas

Following are ten statements. Some are topics (stated in fragments) and some are ideas (stated in complete sentences). Two examples are given below to show you how to complete the exercise. Study them carefully before you go on.

EXAMPLE

Research shows that TV viewing brings down the reading skills of young children.

What is the topic? TV viewing and reading skills

Is there a complete idea? yes

If no, ask a question about the topic; your answer (a complete sentence) will be an idea.

Question: [no answer needed]

Answer/Idea: [no answer needed]

EXAMPLE

Work requirements for people on welfare.

What is the topic? work requirements for people on welfare

Is there a complete idea? no

If no, ask a question about the topic; your answer (a complete sentence) will be an idea.

Question: "What effect will work requirements have for people on welfare?"

Answer/Idea: "Work requirements for people on welfare will result in a need for more educational programs."

1. The American diet today has too much fat and too many calories.

What is the topic? ______

Is there a complete idea? ______

If no, ask a question about the topic; your answer (a complete sentence) will be an idea.

Question: ______________________

____

Answer/Idea: ______________________

____

2. Pressure by parents on kids in junior sports.

What is the topic? ______________________

Is there a complete idea? ______________________

If no, ask a question about the topic; your answer (a complete sentence) will be an idea.

Question: ______________________

____

Answer/Idea: ______________________

____

3. Many people don't vote because they feel candidates are owned by special interests.

What is the topic? ______________________

Is there a complete idea? ______________________

If no, ask a question about the topic; your answer (a complete sentence) will be an idea.

Question: ______________________

____

Answer/Idea: ______________________

____

4. The very alarming high school dropout rates in this country.

What is the topic? ______________________

Is there a complete idea? ______________________

If no, ask a question about the topic; your answer (a complete sentence) will be an idea.

Question: ______________________________

____

Answer/Idea: ______________________________

____

5. The all too often tragic consequences of drinking and driving.

What is the topic? ______________________________

Is there a complete idea? ______________________________

If no, ask a question about the topic; your answer (a complete sentence) will be an idea.

Question: ______________________________

____

Answer/Idea: ______________________________

____

6. Many young people are showing a spirit of volunteerism.

What is the topic? ______________________________

Is there a complete idea? ______________________________

If no, ask a question about the topic; your answer (a complete sentence) will be an idea.

Question: ______________________________

____

Answer/Idea: ______________________________

____

7. There are many benefits but also some dangers in shopping on the Internet.

What is the topic? ______________________________

Is there a complete idea? ______________________________

If no, ask a question about the topic; your answer (a complete sentence) will be an idea.

Question: ______________________________

____

Answer/Idea: ______________________________

____

8. The connection between good study skills and behaviors and success in college.

What is the topic? ______________________________

Is there a complete idea? ______________________________

If no, ask a question about the topic; your answer (a complete sentence) will be an idea.

Question: ______________________________

____

Answer/Idea: ______________________________

____

9. The dangers of secondhand smoke in public areas.

What is the topic? ______________________________

Is there a complete idea? ______________________________

If no, ask a question about the topic; your answer (a complete sentence) will be an idea.

Question: ______________________________

____

Answer/Idea: ______________________________

____

10. Some afternoon talk shows are giving young people poor adult role models.

What is the topic? ______________________________

Is there a complete idea? ______________________________

If no, ask a question about the topic; your answer (a complete sentence) will be an idea.

Question: ______________________________

____

Answer/Idea: ______________________________

____

Below are some of the paragraphs from the last chapter for which you identified topics. Following these are questions which are answered by the paragraph. These answers are the ideas of the paragraph.

EXERCISE 3.3

Answering Questions to Find Ideas

Work together in small groups of 4–5 in doing this assignment and discuss your answers fully. Sometimes you will need to complete a question before answering. The meanings of highlighted vocabulary items were given in the original exercise. Look back if you cannot recall these (p. 45). Be careful to write answers in *complete sentences.*

■ PART A

1. "Fossil" comes from a Latin word for something that has been "dug up." As generally used, a fossil is recognizable, physical evidence of an organism that lived long ago. Most fossils are body parts, such as bones, teeth, shells, leaves, and seeds. Some are tracks, burrows, and other telltale impressions of past life. All were preserved because they were gently buried before they could decompose or fall apart.

   Topic: *fossils*

   Questions:

   Where did the word "fossil" come from? ______________________________

   ____

   What is a fossil? ______________________________

   ____

   What are they mainly? ______________________________

   ____

What else might fossils be? ______________________________

____

Why were they not destroyed? ______________________________

____

2. *T. cacao* evolved in Central America, where wild animals ate its fruits and dispersed its seeds. Today its trees flourish on vast plantations in Central America, the West Indies, and West Africa. Growers harvest its seeds, or "cacao beans." These are processed into cocoa butter and essences, which end up in chocolate products. Unknown interactions among the 1,000 or so compounds in chocolate exert compelling (some say addictive) effects on the human brain. Each year, for instance, the average American feels compelled to buy 8 to 10 pounds of the stuff. With that kind of demand, growers do their very best to keep cacao trees growing and reproducing.

Topic: *cacao (cocoa)*

Questions:

Where did cacao come from? ______________________________

____

Where is cacao mainly found today? ______________________________

____

What happens to the cacao seeds? ______________________________

____

Why do Americans feel compelled to buy chocolate products? __________

____

Why will growers keep up production of cacao trees? ______________

____

3. Collectively, living fishes are the most numerous and diverse vertebrates. Their body form tells us about their watery world. Being about 800 times denser than air, water resists rapid movements. Predatory fishes of the oceans are streamlined for pursuit, with a long trim body that reduces friction. Their tail muscles are organized for propulsive force and forward motion. Bottom-dwelling fishes spend most of their lives hiding from predators or prey. Their flattened body is easy to conceal, but the shape tells us these fishes are sluggish, not Corvettes of the deep.

Topic: *living fishes*

Questions:

What group composes the most numerous and diverse vertebrates? ______

______

What does their body form tell us about them? ______

______

Why do predatory fishes have a long, streamlined body? ______

______

For **what** are the tail muscles of predatory fish designed? ______

______

Why do bottom-dwelling fishes have a flattened body? ______

______

What does their shape indicate to us? ______

______

4. Populations of most species are not stretched out continuously, with one merging into the others. Most often they are isolated geographically to some extent, with gene flow being more of an intermittent trickle than a steady stream. But sometimes barriers form and shut off even the trickles. This can happen rapidly, as when a major earthquake changed the course of the Mississippi River in the 1800s and isolated some populations of insects that could not swim or fly. Geographic isolation also happens slowly. Millions of years ago, owing to long-term shifts in rainfall, vast forests in Africa gave way to grasslands, and subpopulations of forest-dwelling apes became isolated from one another. One of the subpopulations of African apes may have started the divergence that led to modern humans.

Topic: *geographic isolation of species*

Questions:

How are the populations of most species arranged? ______

______

What is the movement of the gene flow compared to? ______

______

What can shut off the gene flow? ______________________

____

When did forests in Africa change to grasslands? ______________________

____

Where might the divergence that led to modern humans have occurred?

____

With **what kind** of group might have started the divergence that led to humans? ______________________

____

■ PART B

Following are paragraphs you worked with in Chapter 2 on the topic "Work in America" (p. 50). Each paragraph deals with an aspect or subtopic of that main topic. Select the correct subtopic for each paragraph from the list below:

Subtopics

- specialization of work
- job satisfaction
- attitudes toward work
- the American work force
- health and job satisfaction

Some questions about the paragraph have been stated for you. Write the answers to these (the ideas of the paragraph) in complete sentences. Other questions require you to complete the question before answering it. In places you are directed to answer questions directly stated in the text or to make up questions and answer them in complete sentences.

1. Specialization of work, if carried too far, leaves little room for responsibility or initiative by the worker. It can mean that some people are assigned the job of controlling those who actually produce goods or deliver services. When Studs Terkel (1974) interviewed workers, he found "the most profound complaint is 'being spied on.' There's the foreman at the plant, the supervisor listening in at Ma Bell's, the checker who gives the bus driver a hard time." Moreover, by tying the worker to an isolated task, to a small part of some large task, specialization can empty jobs of their meaning. The result can be dehumanizing for some workers, as Terkel found when he interviewed people across the country: "'I'm a ma-

chine,' says the spotwelder. 'I'm caged,' says the bank teller. 'I'm a mule,' says the steelworker. 'A monkey can do what I do,' says the receptionist."

Subtopic (from the list provided): ______________________________

Questions:

What effect can specialization of work have on worker initiative? _____

____

What effect can specialization of work have on job assignments? _____

____

What is the biggest ____________________ of workers?

Answer: ____

Why might some workers end up feeling ____________________?

Answer: ____

2. Although it is unpleasant to be a temporary worker, does permanent full-time employment bring happiness? Are Americans really happy with their jobs? In many studies during the last two decades, representative samples of workers have been asked whether they would continue to work if they inherited enough money to live comfortably without working. More than 70 percent replied that they would. When asked how satisfied they were with their jobs, even more—from 80 to 90 percent—replied that they were very or moderately satisfied. But when asked whether they would choose the same line of work if they could begin all over again, most said no. In short, most Americans seem to like their jobs but are not too excited about them.

Subtopic (from the list provided): ______________________________

Questions:

What did studies show about workers' opinions on working even if they didn't need the money? ______________________________________

____

What did studies show about workers' jobs ____________________?

Answer: ____

How did workers respond to a question on whether they would _______

____?

Answer: ____

Write the answer that the paragraph gives to the two questions at the beginning:

____

____

3. In a survey, only 26 percent of American workers still held the traditional view of work. Some of these workers said that "the more I get paid, the more I do." Others agreed that "work is one of life's unpleasant necessities. I wouldn't work if I didn't have to." A bumper sticker says it all: "Work sucks, but I need the bucks." In contrast, a large majority (73 percent) of the respondents expressed more positive attitudes toward work. Many agreed with the statement: "I have an inner need to do the very best I can, regardless of pay." They most frequently rated as "very important" certain nonmonetary, inherent qualities of work, such as interesting jobs, developing their own skills, and seeing how good the results of their work are. The American work ethic has taken on a new quality.

Subtopic (from the list provided): ______________________

Questions:

What view of work was held by 26 percent of workers? ______________

____

What attitudes about work did this view show? ______________

____

Write and answer two questions, like the above, about the rest of the workers:

____

Answer: ______________________________________

____

Answer: ______________________________________

4. The labor force includes all those over 16 years of age who are gainfully employed as well as those who are jobless but are actively seeking paid employment. It excludes full-time homemakers, students, and retired people—anyone who is not paid for his or her work and is not seeking a paying job. In 1988 about 66 percent of Americans over the age of 16 were in the work force—this figure is expected to grow to 69 percent in 2000—compared with about 55 percent in 1940. This increase has been accompanied by dramatic shifts in what American workers do and who makes up the work force.

Subtopic (from the list provided): ______________________________

Questions: Ask and answer two questions about **who is** and **who isn't** in the work force:

(Is/Are) ____?

Answer: ____

(Isn't/Aren't) ____?

Answer: ____

How does the number of workers over 16 in 1988 compare to other years?

Answer: ____

Write and answer a question for the last sentence of the paragraph:

____

Answer: ____

5. People with satisfying jobs have better mental health than those with less satisfying work. Thus, white-collar workers are less likely than blue collars to suffer from psychosomatic illnesses, low self-esteem, worry, anxiety, and impaired interpersonal relationships. People who are happy with their jobs also tend to have better physical health and to live longer. Although diet, exercise, medical care, and genetics are all related to the incidence of heart disease, job dissatisfaction is more closely linked to the cause of death.

Subtopic (from the list provided): ______________________________

Questions: Write, and answer in a complete sentence, four questions about the paragraph:

____

Answer: ____

____

Answer: ____

____

Answer: ____

____

Answer: ____

The short selection below appeared in a health handbook. Its main topic, indicated by the title, is divided into two sections, which are then further subdivided into smaller paragraph subtopics. Read the article and complete the exercise that follows.

Tension Headaches

1 More than 90% of headaches are caused by tension. Tension headaches are often caused by tight muscles in the neck, back, and shoulders. Both emotional stress and physical stress, such as sitting at a computer too long, can cause muscle tension. A previous neck injury or arthritis in the neck can also cause tension headaches.

2 A tension headache may cause pain all over the head, pressure, or a feeling of having a band around the head. The head may feel like it is in a vise. Some people feel a dull, pressing, burning sensation above the eyes.

3 The pain may also affect the jaw, neck, and shoulder muscles. You can rarely pinpoint the center or source of pain.

Prevention

4 ■ Reduce emotional stress. The next time you do something that causes a headache, take time to relax before and afterwards.

5 ■ Reduce physical stress. Change positions often during desk work and stretch for 30 seconds each hour. Make a conscious effort to relax your jaw, neck, and shoulder muscles.

6 ■ Evaluate your neck and shoulder posture at work and make adjustments if needed.

7 ■ Daily exercise helps relieve tension.

8 ■ Cut down on caffeine. People who drink a lot of caffeinated beverages often develop a headache several hours after they have their last beverage, or may wake with a headache that is relieved by drinking caffeine.

Kaiser Permanente Healthwise Handbook, 11th ed., copyright © 1994, 129.

EXERCISE 3.4

Topics, Subtopics, and Ideas in *Tension Headaches*

1. What is the overall topic of the selection? ______________________

2. The section including ¶s 1–3 deals with
   a. frequency of tension headaches
   b. causes and effects of tension headaches
   c. treatment of tension headaches

3. Write the correct subtopics on the lines below (¶s 1–3) from the following list:

   - other areas affected by the pain of tension headaches
   - cause of tension headaches
   - feelings in the head caused by a tension headache

   Then turn the subtopic into a question and answer it in a complete sentence using the information in the paragraph. The first has been done for you.

   ¶1 Subtopic: ______________________

   Question: What are the causes of most tension headaches?

   Idea: Tight muscles, emotional stress and physical stress, or a previous neck injury or arthritis in the neck can cause tension headaches.

   ¶2 Subtopic: ______________________

   Question: ______________________

   Idea: ______________________

   ¶3 Subtopic: ______________________

   Question: ______________________

   Idea: ______________________

4. The heading tells us that ¶s 4–8 are concerned with ________________ of tension headaches.

5. Write the correct subtopics in the spaces for ¶s 4–8 from the following list:

   - neck and shoulder posture
   - daily exercise
   - reducing physical stress
   - cutting down on caffeine
   - reducing emotional stress

   Then turn the topic into a question and answer it in a complete sentence using the information in the paragraph.

   ¶4 Subtopic: ________________________________

   Question: ________________________________

   Idea: ________________________________

   ____

   ¶5 Subtopic: ________________________________

   Question: ________________________________

   Idea: ________________________________

   ____

   ¶6 Subtopic: ________________________________

   Question: ________________________________

   Idea: ________________________________

   ____

   ¶7 Subtopic: ________________________________

   Question: ________________________________

   Idea: ________________________________

   ____

¶8 Subtopic: ______________________________

Question: ______________________________

Idea: ______________________________

____

The following selection from a college textbook will give you practice in identifying topics, asking questions, and stating ideas in paragraphs. Before you begin reading, look at the title and the first sentence of paragraph 1. "Deprivation" is defined as a state or condition in which something necessary is lacking or has been taken away. The first sentence mentions children. From this a good guess would be that the topic of this selection has to do with what happens (results) to children who have been denied something. But what? Based on your own experience and background information, write down a few important things that you think children might be deprived of:

____

____

____

____

EXERCISE 3.5

Determining Topics, Subtopics, and Ideas in a Textbook Selection

Answer the questions after reading each paragraph. In places you must make up or complete a question before you answer it. *Be sure that all your answers are stated in complete sentences.*

The Results of Deprivation

by Alex Thio

1 Since the fourteenth century there have been more than 50 recorded cases of "feral children"—children supposedly raised by animals. One of the most famous is "the wild boy of Aveyron." In 1797 he was captured in the woods by hunters in southern France. He was about 11 years old and completely naked. The "wild boy" ran on all fours, had no speech, preferred

What definition of "feral children" is given?

uncooked food, and could not do most of the simple things done by younger children. A group of experts pronounced him hopelessly retarded. But Jean Itard, a physician, disagreed. He set out to train the boy, whom he later called Victor. After three months Victor seemed a little more human. He wore clothing. He got up at night to urinate in the toilet. He learned to sit at a table and eat with utensils. He started to show human emotions such as joy, gratitude, and remorse. But, although he lived to be more than 40 years old, he neither learned to speak nor ever became a normal person.

- *pronounced:* declared, labeled
- *remorse:* feeling of regret, shame over one's actions

What is the topic of ¶1?

a. deprived children of France

b. Victor, a "feral" child

c. the viewpoint of experts

d. Dr. Itard's techniques

When and **where** was Victor captured?

___

___

How is Victor described?

___

___

What did the experts think of him?

___

___

What did Dr. Itard do?

___

___

How did Victor respond?

___

___

In what way was his development still limited?

___

___

2 There is some doubt that Victor was raised by animals. He was probably old enough to scavenge for food himself when he was abandoned. Nevertheless, he was certainly deprived of normal socialization, and he bore the marks of this loss throughout his life. Less extreme cases also illustrate the significance of socialization. In the United States, there have been three well-known instances of such deprivation. They involved three children—Anna, Isabella, and Genie—who were kept secluded in their homes with their mothers.

- *scavenge:* to collect by searching
- *socialization:* development of proper relationships in society

What is the topic of ¶2?

a. Victor's socialization

b. child abuse in the United States

c. Victor and other deprived children

d. Anna, Isabella, and Genie

How did Victor survive if he was not raised by animals?

____

What result did lack of socialization have on Victor?

____

How many other famous cases of deprivation are known and **where** did they occur?

____

What did Anna, Isabella, and Genie have in common?

____

3 Anna was born in Pennsylvania in 1932 as an illegitimate child, a fact that outraged her mother's father. After trying unsuccessfully to give Anna away, the mother hid her in the attic. Anna was fed just enough to keep her alive, was neither touched nor talked to, neither washed nor bathed. She simply lay still in her own filth. When she was found in 1938 at the age of 6, Anna looked like a skeleton. She could not talk or walk. She did nothing but lie quietly on the floor, her eyes vacant and her face expressionless. Efforts to socialize her were not very successful. Eventually she could do simple things such as walk, feed herself, brush her teeth, and follow simple directions. But she never learned to speak and was far from normal. She died at the age of 11.

- *illegitimate:* born out of wedlock
- *outraged:* shocked and angered greatly

What is the topic of ¶3?

____

____

Why was the father of Anna's mother so angry?

____

Where did her mother put her?

____

How was Anna treated?

____

How did she react?

____

What things did she learn to do?

____

In what ways was her development still limited?

____

- *secluded:* kept apart, hidden
- *hostility:* intense anger
- *systematic:* orderly, planned

4 Isabella's story is a far happier one. Like Anna, she was an illegitimate child who was 6 years old when she was found in Ohio in 1938. Her grandfather had kept her and her deaf-mute mother secluded in a dark room. Isabella was more fortunate than Anna because she could interact with her mother. When she was discovered, Isabella showed great fear and hostility toward people and made a strange croaking sound. Specialists who examined her thought she was feebleminded and uneducable. Nevertheless, she was put on a systematic and skillful program of training. After a slow start, she began to talk. In only nine months she could read and write, and within two years she was attending school. She had become a very bright, cheerful, and energetic girl. Apparently, the intensive training by the specialists, coupled with the earlier interaction with her mother, made it possible for Isabella to develop into a normal person.

What is the topic of ¶4?

____

____

Why was Isabella more fortunate than Anna?

How did she act when first discovered?

What did specialists think of Isabella?

What results did her program of training have?

Why was Isabella able to develop normally?

5 Intensive training, however, did not work out for Genie, who was found in California in 1970, primarily because she had been deprived of normal socialization for 12 years—twice as long as Isabella. From about 1 to 13 years of age, Genie had been isolated in a small, quiet room. During the day she was tied to her potty seat, able only to flutter her hands and feet. At night, if she was not forgotten, her father would straitjacket and cage her in a crib with an overhead cover. He would beat her if she made any noise. He never spoke to her except to occasionally bark or growl like a dog at her. Her terrified mother, forbidden to speak to Genie, fed her in silence and haste. When she was discovered, at age 13, Genie could not stand straight, was unable to speak (except whimper), and had the intelligence and social maturity of a 1-year-old. For the next eight years, psycholinguists, speech therapists, and special education teachers worked with her, but at the end, when she was 21, her language abilities could go no further than the 4 year-old level. She was finally placed in an institution.

■ *psycholinguists:* those who study the relationship of the mind and language

What is the topic of ¶5?

Why did a program of training not work for Genie?

Write and answer three more questions for this paragraph:

____

Answer: ______________________________

____

____

Answer: ______________________________

____

____

Answer: ______________________________

____

■ *cubicles:* tiny compartments for sleeping, work, or study

6 These four cases are, to say the least, unusual. But even less severe forms of deprivation can be harmful. In 1945 psychologist Rene Spitz reported that children who received little attention in institutions suffered very noticeable effects. In one orphanage, Spitz found that infants who were about 18 months old were left lying on their backs in small cubicles most of the day without any human contact. Within a year, all had become physically, mentally, emotionally, and socially retarded. Two years later, more than a third of the children had died. Those who survived could not speak, walk, dress themselves, or use a spoon.

What is the topic of ¶6?

a. four unusual cases of deprivation
b. more feral children
c. children in orphanages
d. social retardation

What did Spitz conclude in his report?

____

How were the children in one orphanage treated?

____

How did they react in the first year?

____

What happened to more than a third of the children?

____

How did the rest act?

____

7 Since Spitz's pioneering work, many other psychologists have documented the damage done to children who are placed in institutions in which they receive little human contact, attention, or stimulation. Normal human development seems to require, at the least, that infants have some continuing interaction, some bond of attachment, with another person. (Thio, pp. 93–95)

What is the topic of ¶7?

a. Spitz's pioneering work
b. further findings about institutional children
c. human development

What have other psychologists documented?

____

What is the most important thing a child needs for normal development?

____

In the newspaper article that follows, identify the topic of the article and subtopics of each paragraph and make notes where indicated. In the margins, write questions that you think the paragraph answers.

Kicking Asphalt

by Jodi Garber

1 If you see a grown man or woman riding around town on an overgrown scooter with a large front wheel, your eyes are not deceiving you. It might be world-class marathoner Matt Carpenter cross-training on his Kickbike, a state-of-the-art scooter with hand brakes. Or it could be someone he sold one to, for Carpenter also is a distributor of the Kickbike, which is relatively new to the United States but popular in Europe.

Main Topic:

Subtopic ¶1:

- *marathoner:* one who runs a marathon (26 plus miles)
- *state-of-the-art:* best, most up-to-date
- *distributor:* one who deals out or sells goods directly

Reprinted by permission of *The Gazette,* July 30, 1998. Colorado Springs, CO.

Subtopic ¶2:

- *integrated:* brought together
- *regimen:* systemized plan

2 After owning his Kickbike for about a month, Carpenter had integrated it into his training regimen. He finds it especially useful after races because the workout achieved on a Kickbike is close to running but without the shock. "I just finished this really long race in Italy, and I was really sore. I could use the Kickbike and still work out," says Carpenter, who lives in Colorado Springs, Colo.

Subtopic ¶3:

- *sole:* only, single
- *impact:* force, shock

3 The Kickbike is a good cross-training tool for runners, says Harald Fricker, president of Kickbike USA, whose Eagle distributorship is the sole distributor for North America. "It uses the same muscles, yet is lower impact, and it really re-creates running for them," says Fricker, a long-distance runner himself. In fact, a Kickbike workout uses even more muscles than running, Fricker says. The Kickbike is propelled by pushing off with alternate legs in a motion very similar to running.

Subtopic ¶4:

4 Carpenter views his Kickbike as another toy to add to his collection. "That's the neatest part for me, keeping it fun," he says. "This is fun for me because you get such a crazy workout. Going uphill on that thing is almost harder than biking or running. It's kind of like, you go up like you're running, and you come down like you're on a road bike."

Subtopic ¶5:

- *physiologist:* one who studies the functions of organisms and their parts

5 The Kickbike was developed in the last 10 years in Finland by physiologist Hannu Vierikko. In Europe, organized competitions include a Kickbike division nearly every weekend, according to Fricker. America is just catching on, but Fricker expects the process to be rapid. Kickbikes have been distributed in the United States and Canada since early July. After a little more than two weeks, 250 Kickbikes had been shipped out, at least one to every state, he says.

Subtopic ¶6:

- *components:* parts
- *alloy:* a mixture of metals

6 The adult-sized scooters sell for $349 plus $90 shipping. How can they charge so much for a scooter? It is most likely that scooters from your childhood were not made of high-tech bicycle components like aluminum alloy handlebars and a full-sized bicycle wheel in the front. Fricker says Kickbikes use Trans X components, which are found in many high-end mountain bikes.

Subtopic ¶7:

7 In addition to being a great workout, the Kickbike also is a good way to get around. "I use mine to go to the grocery store," Carpenter says. He also says if he were in college, he would use a Kickbike to get from class to class. Apparently, Kickbike manufacturers have thought of that as well: They make book baskets that attach on the front. Unlike bicycles, Kickbikes do not have chains or gears and so are clean and lack the dreaded bicycle

grease. They are also compact, weighing 19 pounds. Fricker says two can fit in the trunk of any car.

8 When Carpenter says the Kickbike delivers a good workout, he isn't kidding. Over hilly terrain, 20 minutes on a Kickbike is equal to about 115 minutes on a road bike, Fricker says. But for those not concerned with calories, the Kickbike is lots of fun, kind of like a high-tech skateboard/scooter. It's the perfect thing for all those garages where there are kayaks and baseball bats and bicycles," Carpenter says. "It's just one more tool to stay fit."

Subtopic ¶8:

terrain: surface features of an area of land

EXERCISE 3.6

Subtopics and Ideas in Articles

Write the topic of the article here: ______________________

Below are listed the subtopics for the eight paragraphs of the topic. Compare the list to the subtopics you wrote in the margin. Match the letter of the subtopic to the correct paragraph.

¶1 _____
¶2 _____
¶3 _____
¶4 _____
¶5 _____
¶6 _____
¶7 _____
¶8 _____

a. materials and parts
b. increasing popularity
c. fitness and fun
d. who's riding them
e. Matt Carpenter's training program
f. use as transportation
g. Carpenter's workouts for fun
h. cross-training for runners

Following are questions that are answered in the preceding paragraphs. Compare any questions you came up with to those that follow. Then answer the questions in short but complete idea sentences.

¶1 **Who** is riding Kickbikes? ______________________

____

¶2 **How** did Carpenter use his Kickbike? ______________________

____

Why does he find the Kickbike especially useful? ________________________

____

¶3 **How** does the Kickbike benefit runners? ________________________

____

Who is Harald Fricker? ________________________

____

How is the Kickbike operated? ________________________

____

¶4 **Why** does Carpenter value his Kickbike? ________________________

____

¶5 By **whom** and **where** was the Kickbike developed? ________________________

____

Where is the Kickbike becoming popular? ________________________

____

¶6 **How much** does the adult-sized Kickbike cost? ________________________

____

What are they made of and **what** parts do they have? ________________________

____

¶7 **What** practical use does the Kickbike have? ________________________

____

How do Kickbikes differ from bicycles? ________________________

____

¶8 **How** does the workout on a Kickbike compare to that of a bicycle? ________

____

For **what** other purpose than burning calories can the Kickbike be used?

____

____

Active Learning

"NEVER GIVE UP!"

Nowhere is the importance of reading more clearly illustrated than in the workplace. An inability to read on the job can lead not just to wasted money and lost jobs but to personal injury or even death. In the first passage below, Nadine Rosenthal discusses and illustrates these consequences for society. Following the selection is the oral history of an adult reader who continues to struggle to overcome problems with reading that have affected her in her personal relationships and in the workplace. These selections are followed by questions regarding the ideas developed in the passages and your thoughts about them. Write all your answers in complete idea sentences.

EXERCISE 3.7

The Effects of Illiteracy in the Workplace

■ **PART A**

1 Management is finding that many of its workers' skills are not up to the demands of even non-technical or semi-technical jobs. One of my adult literacy students confessed that he incorrectly rebuilt a car engine because he was unable to read an updated section in the manual. His error caused the rebuilt engine to malfunction, which resulted in a serious accident. This accident was the crisis that brought him to my class. Poor workmanship and lowered production attributable to illiteracy result in losses of hundreds of billions of dollars each year. A few more enlightened companies are now developing their own literacy programs in response to their need for a more skilled work force.

2 What happens to people when they lose their jobs and are unable to find or maintain new jobs because of their poor literacy skills? They remain chronically unemployed or underemployed. Seventy-five percent require additional reading and writing skills to enable them to successfully compete for entry-level job openings. The government has put into place a number of programs to address this need. Yet learning to read as an adult can be an enormous undertaking. Rather than endure the years it takes to make up for their educational deficit, nonreaders can become disillusioned and opt for a short-cut. A small percentage turn to crime to make up the deficit in their pocketbook. (Rosenthal, p. 124.)

1. What solution (¶1) is being offered by companies to create a more skilled work force?

____

____

____

2. List the long-range unwanted consequences (¶2) that the author feels eventually result from poor literacy skills. Give any examples you can add from your personal observation and/or experience.

____

____

____

■ PART B

Here is the oral history of Helen Garrett. As you read, note any ways in which her reading problems affected her ability to function actively in the world of work.

Helen Garrett

1 When you can't read, you're always a little bit on guard. I'm a very private person, almost standoffish. Even if I could read better, I think I would still be a private person, but because I have this reading disability, maybe that made me the way I am, too. Which came first, I don't know, but I think my reading played a big part in it all. I have people who I'm close to, but I don't get so close to anyone that I have to tell them about my reading. I don't trust what they'll do when they find out.

2 I dated men who never knew I couldn't read. I was afraid that if I told them they might have kept on dating me, but maybe would start joking about me with their friends later on. That would have hurt me. I once dated a man who wanted me to put my voice on his answering machine, and he wrote out what he wanted me to say. I said, "Fine, but let's do it later, I don't want to do it now." He got upset with me and did it himself. Maybe he would have continued dating me if I told him, but I'm sure he would have thrown things up in my face later on. I married the right man; my husband would never do such a thing, never. . . .

3 I've been married for seven years, but my husband only found out about my reading two years ago. We have a business, and even before we got married he wanted me to help him with it. I would make excuses, but finally I started helping him. When I would have to spell something like

a person's name or the name of a company, I would call my mother to spell it out for me over the telephone. Finally, one day I told him about my reading. He said, "Helen, I did notice your spelling, sometimes you would spell something wrong, but I really didn't know you couldn't read." He was really sympathetic, and thank God for him because a lot of men wouldn't even want to date me if they knew I couldn't read. He helps me a lot now.

4 Sometimes I ask him if people know I can't read. He says, "No, nobody would ever guess it." He says that God lets things happen to people for certain reasons. Once he said to me, "Maybe if you could read you would be uppity. As you are, you're really down to earth." Maybe he's right that not being able to read humbles me. I know God is not going to put so much on me that I can't bear it, but it's rough.

5 I have to worm myself out of so many things. One time a friend mailed me something and then asked me, "Helen, did you read it?" I had to make up an excuse. I said, "I haven't had time to read it." Another time I was at a friend's baby shower and she wanted me to read the cards. I said I didn't have my glasses. In church, I would go to classes and I get so nervous because the pastor might call on me to read something. My husband told me to be truthful with him, so I pulled him aside one day and told him I had a reading problem. He said he understood, and that there were other people out there who couldn't read also.

6 About four years ago, I went on an interview where these people wanted to hear my voice, so they asked me to read something off a card. I asked them, "Can I do it later?" They said, "Can we ask you a question? Can you read?" I said, "I can read but not very well." You can imagine how I felt when I got out of there. I felt backed against a wall. I cried all the way home. Later they told me they still wanted me, but I never went back. I never told anyone about it, either. I only told my husband a couple of months ago. Every time I think about that incident, I almost cry.

7 I've been back in school a few years now. I've learned my vowels that I wasn't sure about as a child: a-e-i-o-u and sometimes y. I've learned about using periods, commas, and question marks. I've learned to not skip something I don't know, but to go back and sound it out. Now I'll use my dictionary, and I'll write a letter. At one time I couldn't even look up a word, and I wouldn't dare write a letter to no one.

8 I expected that in six months to a year it would all come together for me, but it doesn't happen like that. Learning to read is a long process. Sometimes, sure, I might get frustrated, but that's not going to help. I used to break down and ask my teacher, "How am I doing? It seems like I'm not doing very well." But she said I was doing fine. I've come up maybe two or three levels in a few years, and that's pretty good.

9 I don't want what happened to me to happen to my daughter. She's eighteen months. I've wondered if I should tell her about my reading problem, but she's my child and I think I should be truthful to her. I buy little children's books for her and I read them over and over until I know the words thoroughly, and then I read them to her.

10 I'll keep on fighting until I can read. I'm never going to give up. (Rosenthal, 125–28.)

In groups of 3–4, complete the following:

1. List examples from Helen Garrett's history that show how her reading disability affected
   a. her personality (¶s1, 4):
   b. her feelings about dating and marriage (¶s 2–3):
   c. work (¶s 3, 6):
2. "Adults who can't read develop complex coping mechanisms to save face in countless situations." Find two examples in ¶5 of how Helen Garrett hid her reading problem.
   a.
   b.
3. Based on your reading of ¶s7–10, how much progress has Helen Garrett made?
4. Do you think she will continue to improve and succeed? Why?
5. What steps is Helen Garrett taking to make sure that her daughter will become a good reader?

6. Recall Winston's Churchill's advice (Chapter 1): "Never give up!" How does that apply to the speaker in this passage?

____

7. Have you ever experienced or witnessed similar situations? If so, briefly discuss what they were and how you felt.

____

____

Reading Portfolio

FINDING IDEAS IN ARTICLES

For your last assignment, you went to your learning resource center and looked at the titles and table of contents of several magazines and newspapers. Now do the following:

1. Survey again the table of contents of one of the magazines that interested you and decide on an article to read. Which article did you first select?

   ____

   Did you stay with it? _______ If not, why not?

   ____

2. For the article you ended up with, answer the following:

   Author: _______________

   Title: _______________

   Name of magazine: _______________

   Topic: _______________

3. Why did you select it?

   ____

4. What did you know about the topic before you read the article?

   ____

5. What did you think you would learn about it?

   ____

6. Write ten questions that are answered in the article. Space the questions so that the entire article is covered. Then answer the questions. Be careful to write your answers in complete sentences.

Question: ______________________________

Answer: ______________________________

Question: ______________________________

Answer: ______________________________

Question: ______________________________

Answer: ______________________________

Question: ______________________________

Answer: ______________________________

Question: ______________________________

Answer: ______________________________

Question: ______________________________

Answer: ______________________________

Question: ______________________________

Answer: ______________________________

Question: ______________________________

Answer: ______________________________

Question: ______________________________

Answer: ______________________________

Question: ______________________________

Answer: ______________________________

CHAPTER

4

What's the Big Idea?

Main Ideas and Supporting Details

After reading this chapter, you will know the answers to these questions:

- What are main ideas?
- What are supporting details?
- What signals point to main ideas?
- How do topical and main idea organization differ?
- How do we decide what information is important?
- What is the difference between major and minor detail?

Below is an exercise that you completed in the last chapter. Reread the paragraph, and read the questions and answers that follow it.

> Collectively, living fishes are the most numerous and diverse vertebrates. Their body form tells us about their watery world. Being about 800 times denser than air, water resists rapid movements. Predatory fishes of the oceans are streamlined for pursuit, with a long trim body that reduces friction. Their tail muscles are organized for propulsive force and forward motion. Bottom-dwelling fishes spend most of their

lives hiding from predators or prey. Their flattened body is easy to conceal, but the shape tells us these fishes are sluggish, not Corvettes of the deep.

Topic: *living fishes*

Questions:

a. **What** are the most numerous and diverse vertebrates?
   Living fishes are the most numerous and diverse vertebrates.

b. **What** does their body form tell us about them?
   Their body form tells us about their watery world.

c. **Why** do predatory fishes have a long, streamlined body?
   Predatory fishes are streamlined for frictionless pursuit.

d. **For what** are the tail muscles of predatory fish designed?
   Their tail muscles are organized for propulsive force and forward motion.

e. **Why** do bottom-dwelling fishes have a flattened body?
   Their flattened body is easy to conceal from predators or prey.

f. **What** does their shape indicate to us?
   The shape tells us these fishes are sluggish.

Five of the above questions are answered completely in the sentence that follows. One of these ideas, however, requires a lot more information to be answered fully. Write the letter of that answer: _____

FINDING MAIN IDEAS AND SUPPORTING DETAILS

If you answered "b" above, you're correct, and on your way to learning the most important skill in reading: finding the *main idea.* You have learned about the difference between general and specific and how a topic (a general subject or category) can have subtopics (more specific subcategories.) The same applies to ideas: Some are more general than others. A main idea is a general idea that covers a broad area. It gives unity to a section by providing a focus for all the other specific ideas. In the example above, question b is a general question with a general answer: "Their body form tells us about their watery world." Then note how the answers to c, d, e, and f all contribute to an understanding of what the body form of fishes tells about where they live and what they do. Because it is a general idea that determines what information belongs in the paragraph, this sentence is the main idea.

Sometimes the main idea of a paragraph is called the *topic sentence.* The main idea of an article or a report may also be referred to as a *controlling idea* or *thesis.* The rest of the ideas in a unit of writing are the *supporting details* (sometimes called *specific details* or *concrete details*) because they help to develop the main idea. In an outline or map form, we can show the relationship of the ideas in the paragraph by putting the supporting details under the main idea:

1. The body form of fishes tells us about their watery world.
   a. Predatory fishes are streamlined for frictionless pursuit.
   b. Their tail muscles are organized for propulsive force and forward motion.
   c. The flattened body of bottom-dwellers is easy to conceal from predators or prey.
   d. Their shape tells us these fishes are sluggish.

Usually all the specific details in a paragraph will relate directly to the main idea. Sometimes, however, a sentence may not directly develop the topic sentence. Instead, it's there to give some needed factual background information or to introduce the topic area. In the example above, the first sentence of the paragraph—"Collectively, living fishes are the most numerous and diverse vertebrates"—doesn't give any details about what the body form of fishes reveals about them. The author includes it as an introduction to the general topic area.

EXERCISE 4.1

Identifying Main Ideas and Supporting Details

In each group of four sentences, one idea is the main idea and the others are supporting details. Circle the letter of the main idea.

1. a. Yolanda enjoys playing hockey.
   b. Tennis is Yolanda's favorite sport.
   c. Yolanda is very active in sports.
   d. Every Saturday night Yolanda bowls with her family.

2. a. Pickups have some advantages over cars.
   b. Pickups can be driven over rough terrain.
   c. You can use a pickup to haul large items.
   d. Pickups have the power to carry heavy loads.

3. a. Multiscreen theaters throughout the country are enjoying success.
   b. Movies can make money for a lot of people.
   c. Movie stars get fantastic sums of money for their performances.
   d. Companies that make movies can make huge profits.
4. a. Exercise helps to control weight gain.
   b. Exercise benefits you in many ways.
   c. Stress and tension can be relieved by exercise.
   d. Exercise can help prevent heart attacks.
5. a. We should include healthy foods in our diets.
   b. Foods with fiber are essential to good health.
   c. Green and yellow vegetables are important elements in a healthy diet.
   d. Carbohydrates and unsaturated fats must be included in our diets.
6. a. Before a test, Rocha carefully reviews the notes she has taken.
   b. Rocha has some excellent study habits.
   c. Rocha frequently meets with a study group.
   d. Rocha owns a good desk dictionary and a thesaurus.
7. a. Fights erupt in baseball when batters are intentionally beaned by pitchers.
   b. Brawls seem to be a regular part of hockey games.
   c. Basketball players frequently get into fights that are set off by fouls.
   d. Many sports are marred by violence.
8. a. The unemployment rate is currently very low.
   b. Interest rates are low so more people are able to buy homes.
   c. The U.S. economy is doing very well.
   d. The rate of inflation is almost zero.
9. a. Yang delivers papers in the mornings.
   b. Yang makes money at a number of jobs.
   c. After school, Yang works as a bag boy at the local market.
   d. On weekends, Yang does yard work for several neighbors.
10. a. A flat-head screwdriver has several uses.
    b. Paint can lids can be pried off with a flat-head screwdriver.
    c. Grout can be cleaned with a flat-head screwdriver.
    d. A flat-head screwdriver is used to drive in a screw with a single slot on the head.

A topic sentence is most often the first sentence of a paragraph, but it may be placed at the end and, indeed, can occur anywhere in the paragraph. That means that finding the main idea is not always easy. In the last two chapters you practiced the first two steps in finding main ideas: identifying the topic and thinking of questions that the paragraph answers. The next step, as you learned above, is to check whether the paragraph focuses on one general question. There are also a number of features that can help you locate the main idea sentence. For example, what is the main idea of the following paragraph?

> Why is it that so many borful floogs are sporfing tarkons? There are a number of dorphans for this prawlsey. First, floogs have a nern for corfable tarkons. Also, they mortate in the horkles where tarkons are frebitting. Finally, floogs have fewer other cronders to sporf on nowadays.

Since this is a "nonsense" paragraph we could say that it can't have any ideas at all. Yet most of us would probably pick the second sentence as the main idea.

SIGNALS TO HELP LOCATE MAIN IDEAS

We would pick the second sentence as the main idea because the paragraph contains some clues that help us to locate main ideas. Below is a list of the most common signals that help us to identify main idea sentences:

Questions A question is never a main idea, but the answer to it, especially if the question is at or near the beginning of a paragraph, often is. In the example above, the fact that the second sentence appears to answer a question would make it likely that it is the main idea of the paragraph.

Listing Phrases These usually put a number word (e.g., *three, several, a few, a number of, some*) with a plural word naming a group of things (e.g., *steps, types, reasons, traits, factors*):

- As student body president, Alva showed *some important leadership qualities.*
- The achievements of the two schools are similar *in several respects.*
- To start your lawnmower, follow *these steps.*
- The shopping mall went through *several key stages* as it grew.
- The restaurant has a *number of different types of* salads.

- For a great barbecue sauce, you need to include *some special ingredients.*
- The police are aiming to solve *a few major problems.*
- High school graduates should think of going to college *for several good reasons.*

In the nonsense paragraph, the second sentence contains a listing phrase: "There are a number of . . ." Because a listing phrase is general and signals that a list of specific items will follow, the sentence it occurs in, especially if it is at or near the beginning of the paragraph, is usually the topic sentence.

Details in a List Listing phrases are often followed by words—e.g., *next, also, second, finally, then*—that indicate the specific items in a list or steps in a process. Signal words and phrases that go with the first item in such a list—e. g., *first, step 1, one reason, the initial stage* (and, occasionally, *for example*)—often directly follow the main idea. In the nonsense paragraph above, the signal words *first, also,* and *finally* make up a list of items; the position of *first,* along with the other clues, would tell us that "There are a number of dorphans for this prawlsey" is the main idea.

Examples A sentence that is supported by one or more examples has a good chance of being the main idea. It is easier to see this connection when authors use signal words to indicate examples, e.g., *to illustrate, for instance, for example, including.* If you see one of these signal phrases near the beginning of a paragraph, the sentence that it follows is likely to be the main idea.

Change of Direction Signals Sometimes a writer starts with an idea but changes directions and develops a different one. This is usually to get the reader's attention. An author might start with something we know and switch to something that we aren't aware of. Sometimes a paragraph begins with something we all think is true, but develops a main idea that shows we may be wrong. Words and phrases that show contrast or difference—e.g., *yet, but, however, although, in contrast, in truth, actually*—are often used to change directions; the sentence they appear in is the main idea.

Summary/Conclusion Signals For a description of a process or report on a scientific study, the sentence that gives a summary or draws a conclusion from the evidence is a good choice for the main idea sentence. It's an easier job to identify a topic sentence of this type when it includes a signal word—e.g., *therefore, thus, in summary, in conclusion, indeed, clearly*—pointing to a general summary or conclusion. Occasionally, the main idea of a paragraph may be introduced and then later repeated in another sentence, usually the last one in the paragraph. Signal words (e.g., *thus, therefore, clearly*) often introduce this *restatement* of the main idea.

EXERCISE 4.2

Using Signals to Find Main Ideas in Paragraphs

Work together in small groups in doing this assignment and discuss your answers fully.

■ PART A

Read each paragraph and identify the topic or subtopic. Then answer the questions regarding main ideas and identifying signals.

1. Delayed reproduction slows the tendency toward growth and lowers the average number of children in each family. In China, for example, the government has established the most extensive family planning program in the world. Couples who pledge not to have more than one child are given extra food, better housing, free medical care, and salary bonuses. Their child will be granted free tuition and preferential treatment when he or she enters the job market. Those who break the pledge forego benefits and sometimes pay penalties. (Starr, p. 548.)

■ *extensive:* wide-ranging

■ *tuition:* fee for schooling

■ *preferential:* favorable, special

Topic:

a. the government of China

b. delayed reproduction

c. lucky couples

The main idea is supported by an example.

What signal phrase indicates this? ______________________

What is the example about? ______________________

Write the main idea: ______________________

____

2. When contact between initially hostile groups occurs under certain conditions, prejudice between them does seem to decrease. For example, increased contact between Jews of Middle Eastern origin and Jews of European or American origin has been found to reduce in-group bias among Israeli soldiers. Similarly, increased contact between African Americans and whites has been found to reduce prejudice between them in the United States. Thus, increased social contact, under appropriate conditions, offers another useful means for reducing prejudice. (Robert Baron, *Essentials of Psychology.* p. 537. © 1996 by Allyn and Bacon. Reprinted by permission.)

■ *prejudice:* opinion formed beforehand, without knowing or looking at the facts

■ *bias:* a preference that keeps one from being fair in judging

Topic:

a. how prejudice begins

b. bias among Israeli soldiers

c. decreasing prejudice

This paragraph is developed by two examples.

What signal word or phrase introduces the first?

____

What two groups are the first example about?

______________ ______________

What signal word or phrase introduces the second example?

____

What two groups are the second example about?

______________ ______________

In this paragraph, the main idea is stated twice.

Write the sentence that first states the main idea:

____

____

What signal word of conclusion indicates the main idea is being restated?

____

Write the sentence that restates the main idea:

____

____

■ *erodes:* wears away slowly

3. Water plays several key roles on our planet. First, the oceans cover more than two-thirds of the planet's surface. They act as a huge heat storage reservoir and redistribute heat from low to high altitudes by ocean currents. Second, water falls on land in the form of rain or snow. As it runs off to the sea, water erodes rocks and soils and creates landscapes and landforms. This flow moves nutrients from one location to another, which also influences the distribution of plant and animal life. Third, water in the air moves huge quantities of heat from one place to

another by absorbing surface heat in evaporation over warm oceans and releasing that latent heat in condensation over cooler regions. (Allen Strahler and Arthur Strahler, *Physical Geography,* 4e, p. 88. Copyright © 1997. Reprinted by permission of John Wiley & Sons, Inc.)

- *absorbing:* taking in
- *latent:* hidden, present but not active

Topic:

a. the formation of planet Earth

b. the importance of the earth's oceans

c. water on our planet

Write the sentence that contains the main idea:

____

____

What listing phrase appears in the main idea sentence?

____

What signal word introduces the first item in a list?

____

4. Research indicates that exercise can have a significant impact on our mental health. For example, exercise has been found to improve self-concept, alleviate feelings of depression, and reduce anxiety. These effects are particularly apparent just after a workout, but there may also be some benefits from long-term participation in exercise. Changes in mood following exercise may result from socializing and being involved with others; running with a friend may improve mood because of the companionship the exercise provides. (Baron, p. 437.)

- *alleviate:* relieve, lessen

Topic:

a. mental health and physical exercise

b. the benefits and dangers of exercise

c. the importance of socializing

The main idea is supported by an example. What signal phrase shows this?

____

Write the main idea:

____

____

■ *precipitation:* forms of water that fall on the earth

5. Upon reaching the land surface, precipitation has three fates. First, it can evaporate and return to the atmosphere as water vapor. Second, it can sink into soil and then into the surface rock layers below. This subsurface water emerges from below to feed rivers, lakes, and even ocean margins. Third, precipitation can run off the land, concentrating in streams and rivers that eventually carry it to the ocean or to a lake in a closed inland basin. This flow of water is known as *runoff.* (Strahler and Strahler, p. 91.)

Topic:

a. land surfaces

b. precipitation

c. evaporation of water

Write the sentence that contains the main idea:

____

____

What listing phrase appears in the main idea sentence?

____

What signal word introduces the first item in the list that follows the main idea?

____

■ *criteria:* standards or tests on which judgments can be made

■ *essentially:* basically

■ *infinite:* without end

6. Language uses symbols for communicating information. In order for a set of symbols to be viewed as a language, however, several additional criteria must be met. First, information must actually be transmitted by the symbols—the words and sentences must carry meaning. Second, although the number of separate sounds or words in a language may be limited, it must be possible to combine these elements into an essentially infinite number of sentences. Third, the meanings of these combinations must be independent of the settings in which they are used. In other words, sentences must be able to convey information about other places and other times. Only if all three of these criteria are met can the term *language* be applied to a system of communication. (Baron, p. 536.)

Topic:

a. communication between people

b. criteria for language

c. the meaning of words

In this paragraph, the main idea is stated twice. The first statement of the main idea is indicated by three signals.

What change of direction signal does the sentence contain?

____

What listing phrase does it contain?

____

What "first item in a list" follows it?

____

Write the sentence that first states the main idea:

____

____

The main idea is restated later in the paragraph.

What listing phrase occurs in the restatement of the main idea?

____

Write the sentence that restates the main idea:

____

____

7. Next to water, proteins are the most abundant substances in the human body. Proteins are major components of nearly every cell and have been called the "body builders" because of their role in the development and repair of bone, muscle, skin, and blood cells. Proteins are also the key elements of the antibodies that protect us from disease, of enzymes that control chemical activities in the body, and of hormones that regulate bodily functions. Moreover, proteins aid in the transport of iron, oxygen, and nutrients to all of the body's cells and supply another source of energy to body cells when fats and carbohydrates

are not readily available. In short, adequate amounts of protein in the diet are vital to many body functions and to your ultimate survival. (R. Donatelle and L. Davis, *Health, The Basics,* p. 155. Copyright © 1999 by Allyn and Bacon. Reprinted by permission.)

Topic:

a. substances in the body

b. proteins and disease

c. importance of proteins

What signal phrase of conclusion does the main idea contain?

___

Write the sentence that states the main idea:

___

___

■ *prospered:* succeeded; grew wealthy

■ *proportion:* a share in relation to the whole

8. Much has been said about the frontier as a "safety valve." The theory is that when hard times came, the unemployed who cluttered the city pavements merely moved west, took up farming, and prospered. In truth, relatively few city dwellers, at least in the populous eastern centers, migrated to the frontier during depressions. Most of them did not know how to farm; few of them could raise enough money to transport themselves west and then pay for livestock and expensive machinery. The initial outlay for equipment had become so heavy by the 1880s and 1890s that the West was decreasingly a land of opportunity for farmers, though it might be for ranchers, miners, and day laborers. A large proportion of the settlers who moved west came from farms on the older frontier, which was within striking distance of the new frontier. (Thomas A. Bailey and David M. Kennedy, *The American Pageant,* 11e, p. 614. Copyright © 1998 by Houghton Mifflin Company. Reprinted with permission.)

Topic:

a. the frontier as a "safety valve"

b. farming on the frontier

c. the disadvantages of city life

The main idea sentence contains what change of direction signal?

___

Write the sentence with the main idea:

____

____

The next two paragraphs deal with different aspects of stereotypes. Select a subtopic for ¶s 9–10 from the choices below:

- stereotypes and prejudice
- the effects of stereotypes

9. Stereotypes are cognitive frameworks consisting of knowledge and beliefs about specific social groups—frameworks suggesting that, by and large, all members of these groups possess certain traits. Like other cognitive frameworks, or schemas, stereotypes exert strong effects on the ways in which we process social information. For example, information relevant to a particular stereotype is processed more quickly than information unrelated to it. Similarly, stereotypes lead us to pay attention to specific types of information—usually information consistent with the stereotypes. And they may actually block our ability to pay attention to stereotype-inconsistent information. Finally, stereotypes also determine what we remember—usually, again, information that is consistent with these frameworks.

- *cognitive:* relating to processes involved in thinking
- *relevant:* having a bearing on the matter at hand
- *inconsistent:* not regular; not fitting with

Subtopic (from the two choices above): ______________

Write the sentence that contains the main idea:

____

____

What listing phrase appears in the main idea sentence?

____

What signal word introduces the first item in a list?

____

10. What is the relevance of such effects to prejudice? Together, they tend to make stereotypes somewhat self-confirming. Once an individual has acquired a stereotype about some social group, she or he tends to notice information that fits readily into this cognitive framework and to remember "facts" that are consistent with it more readily than "facts" inconsistent with

■ *induce:* lead, cause

it. As a result, the stereotype strengthens with time. Indeed, even exceptions to it tend to make it stronger, for they simply induce the persons holding the stereotype to bring more supporting information to mind. In short, our tendency to create cognitive frameworks to hold and organize social information may contribute to the development and persistence of many forms of prejudice. (Baron, p. 536.)

Subtopic (from the two choices above): ____________________

In this paragraph, the main idea is stated twice.

In what way does the first sentence signal that a main idea is coming?

____

Write the sentence that first states the main idea:

____

____

What signal word of conclusion indicates the main idea is being restated?

____

Write the sentence that restates the main idea:

____

____

■ PART B

For each paragraph, identify the topic and select the number of the sentence that is the main idea. Then decide what signals led you to your answer.

1. [1]Studies have shown that gender bias often gets in the way of correct diagnosis of psychosocial disorders. [2]In one study, for instance, 175 mental health professionals, of both genders, were asked to diagnose a patient based upon a summarized case history. [3]Some of the professionals were told that the patient was male, others that the patient was female. [4]The gender of the patient made a substantial difference in the diagnosis given (though the gender of the clinician did not). [5]When sub-

jects thought the patient was female, they were more likely to diagnose hysterical personality, a "women's disorder." [6]When they believed the patient to be male, the more likely diagnosis was antisocial personality, a "male disorder." (Donatelle and Davis, p. 40.)

Topic: ____

____

Main Idea: ______

This is the main idea because it

a. is followed by an example with a signal word

b. has a change of direction signal

c. has no signal but states a general idea that all details support

d. both a and b

e. none of the above

2. [1]How many times have you heard of a woman who is repeatedly beaten by her partner or spouse and asked, "Why doesn't she just leave him?" [2]There are many reasons why some women find it difficult, if not impossible, to break their ties with their abusers. [3]Many women, particularly those having small children, are financially dependent on their partners. [4]Others fear retaliation against themselves or their children. [5]There are women who hope that the situation will change with time (it rarely does), and others who stay because their cultural or religious beliefs forbid divorce. [6]Finally, there are women who still love the abusive partner and are concerned about what will happen to him if they leave. (Donatelle and Davis, p. 74.)

Topic: ____

____

Main Idea: ______

This is the main idea because it

a. answers a question stated in the paragraph

b. has a listing phrase

c. is followed by an example with a signal word

d. both a and b

e. all of the above

3. [1]Some women do abuse and even kill their partners. [2]Approximately 12 percent of men reported that their wives engaged in physically aggressive behaviors against them in the past year—nearly the same percentage as women. [3]The difference between male and female batterers is twofold. [4]First, although the frequency of physical aggression may be the same, the impact of physical aggression by men against women is drastically different: women are typically injured in such incidents two to three times more often than are men. [5]These injuries tend to be more severe and have resulted in significantly more deaths. [6]Women do engage in moderate aggression, such as pushing and shoving, at rates almost equal to men. [7]But the severe form of aggression that is likely to land the victim in the hospital is almost always a male-against-female form of aggression. [8]Second, a woman who is physically abused by a man is generally intimidated by him: she fears that he will use his power and control over her in some fashion. [9]Men, however, generally report that they do not live in fear of their wives. (Donatelle and Davis, p. 75.)

Topic: ____

____

Main Idea: ______

This is the main idea because it

a. has a listing phrase
b. is followed by a "first item in a list" signal word or phrase
c. has a change of direction signal
d. has a summary/conclusion signal
e. both a and b
f. both b and c

4. [1]Although most of us have a fairly clear idea of the distinction between a friend and a lover, this difference is not always easy to verbalize. [2]Some people believe that the major difference is that there is no intimate physical involvement between friends. [3]Others have suggested that intimacy levels are much lower between friends than between lovers. [4]But people can be intimate with each other without being sexually involved. [5]Confused? [6]You are probably not alone. [7]Surprisingly, there has not been a great deal of research to clarify these terms. (Donatelle and Davis, p. 89.)

Topic: ____

____

Main Idea: ______

This is the main idea because it

a. answers a question stated in the paragraph
b. is followed by an example with a signal word
c. has no signal but states a general idea that all details support
d. both a and b

5. [1]Once you begin to recognize the causes of your behaviors and have an understanding of the potential risks, the choices are yours. [2]Choices, however, are seldom clear-cut, and choosing among alternatives is difficult, particularly when society, your family and friends, and your own values system come into play. [3]For example, "just saying no" is, of course, one choice when you are handed a glass of beer at a party. [4]However, if you want to fit in and the people with whom you identify are all drinking, or if you like the taste of beer and are thirsty, the decision becomes harder. [5]By practicing decision making skills prior to having that drink put into your hands, your chances of making the choice you really want to make will increase. (Donatelle and Davis, p. 21.)

Topic: ______________________________

____

Main Idea: ______

This is the main idea because it

a. answers a question stated in the paragraph
b. has a change of direction signal
c. has a summary/conclusion signal
d. has no signal but states a general idea that all details support
e. both a and c

6. [1]Several techniques are used to diagnose heart disease. [2]An electrocardiogram (ECG) is a record of the electrical activity of the heart measured during a stress test. [3]Patients walk or run on treadmills while their hearts are monitored. [4]A more accurate method of testing for heart disease is angiography (often referred to as cardiac catheterization), in which a needle-thin tube called a catheter is threaded through blocked heart arteries, a dye is injected, and an X-ray is taken to discover which areas are blocked. [5]A more recent and even more effective method of measuring heart activity is positron emission tomography, also called a PET scan, which produces three-dimensional images of the heart. (Donatelle and Davis, p. 296.)

Topic: ____

____

Main Idea: ______

This is the main idea because it

a. answers a question stated in the paragraph
b. has a listing phrase
c. is followed by a "first item in a list" signal word or phrase
d. has no signal but states a general idea that all details support
e. both b and c

7. [1]Everyone copes with stress in different ways. [2]For some people, drinking and taking drugs help them to cope. [3]Others choose to get help from counselors. [4]Still others try to keep their minds off stress or to engage in positive activities such as exercise or relaxation techniques. [5]Stress inoculation is one of the newer techniques for helping people prepare for stressful events. [6]Through stress inoculation, people are able to prepare for potential stressful events ahead of time. [7]For example, if you were petrified over speaking in front of a class, practicing in front of friends, in front of a video camera, or other strategies may inoculate or prevent the chances of your freezing up on the day of the presentation. (Donatelle and Davis, p. 60.)

Topic: ____

____

Main Idea: ______

This is the main idea because it

a. has a listing phrase
b. is followed by an example with a signal word
c. has a change of direction signal
d. has a summary/conclusion signal
e. has no signal but states a general idea that all details support

8. [1]Stress management calls for mental action in two areas. [2]First, positive self-esteem, which can help you cope with stressful situations comes from learned habits. [3]Successful stress management involves mentally developing and practicing self-esteem skills. [4]Second, because you can't always anticipate what the next stressor will be, you need to

develop the mental skills necessary to manage your reactions to stresses after they have occurred. [5]Most of all, you must strive to become more aware of potential threats to your stress levels and act quickly to avoid or to deal with potential stressors. [6]Rather than seeing stressors as adversaries, learn to view them as exercises in life. (Donatelle and Davis, p. 61.)

Topic: ____

____

Main Idea: ______

This is the main idea because it

a. has a listing phrase
b. is followed by an example with a signal word
c. has a change of direction signal
d. has a summary/conclusion signal
e. has no signal but states a general idea that all details support

9. [1]Passionate love will not occur unless three conditions are met. [2]First, the person must live in a culture in which the concept of "falling in love" is idealized. [3]Second, a "suitable" love object must be present. [4]If the person has been taught by parents, movies, books, and peers to seek partners having certain levels of attractiveness or belonging to certain racial groups or having certain socioeconomic status and none is available, the person may find it difficult to allow him- or herself to become involved. [5]Finally, for passionate love to occur, there must be some type of physiological arousal that occurs when a person is in the presence of the object of desire. [6]Sexual excitement is often the way in which such arousal is expressed. (Donatelle and Davis, p. 90.)

Topic: ____

____

Main Idea: ______

This is the main idea because it

a. answers a question stated in the paragraph
b. has a listing phrase
c. is followed by a "first item in a list" signal word or phrase
d. all of the above
e. b and c

10. [1]The United Nations defines seven basic types of families, including single-parent families, communal families (unrelated people living together for ideological, economic, or other reasons), extended families, and others. [2]But most Americans think of family in terms of the "family of origin" or the "nuclear family." [3]The family of origin includes the people present in the household during a child's first years of life—usually parents and siblings. [4]However, the family of origin may also include a stepparent, parents' lovers, or significant others such as grandparents, aunts, or uncles. [5]The family of origin has a tremendous impact on the child's psychological and social development. [6]The nuclear family consists of parents (usually married, but not necessarily) and their offspring. (Donatelle and Davis, p. 89.)

Topic: ____

____

Main Idea: ______

This is the main idea because it

a. answers a question stated in the paragraph
b. is followed by a "first item in a list" signal word or phrase
c. is followed by an example with a signal word
d. has a change of direction signal
e. has a summary/conclusion signal

EXERCISE 4.3

Finding Subtopics and Main Ideas in Textbook Passages

Work together in small groups. Read and discuss the passages and identify the topic or subtopic, the main idea, and any signals that led you to your choice.

■ PART A Work in America

You identified topics and ideas for some of the paragraphs in this passage in earlier chapters. Match one of these subtopics with each of these paragraphs:

Subtopics: ¶1–6

- other important changes in the work force
- satisfaction with work: groups
- satisfaction with work: individuals
- work and our self-concept

- work specialization
- changes in gender in the work force

Write down anything you can remember from your earlier reading about the topic of work in America:

____

____

____

____

____

____

1. When Americans meet strangers, one of their first questions is likely to be, "What do you do?" We answer, "I am a salesperson" or "I am a cabdriver" or a doctor or lawyer, or whatever. Work is not just a way to make enough money to pay the bills. For many of us, work helps define our identity and our sense of self-worth.

Subtopic (from the list provided): ______________________

Main Idea: ______________________________

____

Check and complete all of the following that helped you make your choice.

This is the main idea because it

_____ answers a question stated in the paragraph

_____ has a listing phrase: ______________________

_____ is followed by a "first item in a list" signal word or phrase:

____

_____ is followed by an example with a signal word or phrase:

____

_____ has a change of direction signal: ______________________

_____ has a summary/conclusion signal: ______________________

_____ has no signal but states a general conclusion that all details lead to

■ *projected:* extended forward

2. The composition of the American labor force has changed, with the most publicized change occurring in its gender. In 1984 the U.S. Department of Labor announced that since 1960 the number of women in the labor force had nearly doubled. Today, about 53 percent of women are in the labor force, compared with just 33 percent in 1960. The number of women workers will continue to rise, which is projected to account for about two-thirds of the entire labor force growth between 1982 and 1995.

Subtopic (from the list provided): ____________________

Main Idea: ______________________________

____

Check and complete all of the following that helped you make your choice.

This is the main idea because it

_____ answers a question stated in the paragraph

_____ has a listing phrase: ____________________

_____ is followed by a "first item in a list" signal word or phrase:

____

_____ is followed by an example with a signal word or phrase:

____

_____ has a change of direction signal: ____________________

_____ has a summary/conclusion signal: ____________________

_____ has no signal but states a general conclusion that all details lead to

■ *declined:* gone down

■ *fueled:* caused, stimulated

3. Important changes have also occurred in the age and racial composition of the work force. In the last two decades, the employment rate for men older than 65 declined significantly. But in recent years, a growing industrial demand for cheaper labor has fueled a dramatic increase in labor-force participation among Americans of African, Hispanic, or Asian descent, as well as among immigrants. These minorities will account for 88 percent of work-force growth between 1989 and 1999.

Meanwhile, there will be proportionately fewer white men in the labor force.

■ *proportionately:* in its ratio to the whole

Subtopic (from the list provided): ______________________

Main Idea: ______________________________

____

Check and complete all of the following that helped you make your choice.

This is the main idea because it

_____ answers a question stated in the paragraph

_____ has a listing phrase: ______________________

_____ is followed by a "first item in a list" signal word or phrase:

____

_____ is followed by an example with a signal word or phrase:

____

_____ has a change of direction signal: ______________________

_____ has a summary/conclusion signal: ______________________

_____ has no signal but states a general conclusion that all details lead to

4. Studies have also shown that job satisfaction varies from one group to another. Generally, older workers are more satisfied than younger ones. One reason is that older workers, being more advanced in their careers, have better jobs. Another reason is that younger workers are more likely to expect their jobs to be highly interesting and stimulating, hence are more likely to be disillusioned because of the difficulty in realizing their high aspirations. White-collar workers, especially professionals and business people, are also more likely than blue collars to feel genuinely satisfied with their jobs.

■ *aspirations:* desires, goals

Subtopic (from the list provided): ______________________

Main Idea: ______________________________

____

Check and complete all of the following that helped you make your choice.

This is the main idea because it

_____ answers a question stated in the paragraph

_____ has a listing phrase: ______________________________

_____ is followed by a "first item in a list" signal word or phrase:

____

_____ is followed by an example with a signal word or phrase:

____

_____ has a change of direction signal: ____________________

_____ has a summary/conclusion signal: ____________________

_____ has no signal but states a general conclusion that all details lead to

5. Although it is unpleasant to be a temporary worker, does permanent full-time employment bring happiness? Are Americans really happy with their jobs? In many studies during the last two decades, representative samples of workers have been asked whether they would continue to work if they inherited enough money to live comfortably without working. More than 70 percent replied that they would. When asked how satisfied they were with their jobs, even more—from 80 to 90 percent—replied that they were very or moderately satisfied. But when asked whether they would choose the same line of work if they could begin all over again, most said no. In short, most Americans seem to like their jobs but are not too excited about them.

Subtopic (from the list provided): ____________________

Main Idea: ______________________________

____

Check and complete all of the following that helped you make your choice.

This is the main idea because it

_____ answers a question stated in the paragraph

_____ has a listing phrase: ______________________________

_____ is followed by a "first item in a list" signal word or phrase:

____

_____ is followed by an example with a signal word or phrase:

____

_____ has a change of direction signal: ________________

_____ has a summary/conclusion signal: ________________

_____ has no signal but states a general conclusion that all details lead to

6. For doctors and lawyers and other professionals, specialization of work may stimulate the mind while it fattens the checkbook. But for less-educated manual workers, specialization can be numbing and can produce mindless, repetitive tasks. A person working in the slaughter industry, for example, can be a stock scraper, belly shaver, crotch buster, gut snatcher, gut sorter, snout puller, ear cutter, eyelid remover, stomach washer, hindleg-toenail puller, frontleg toenail puller, or oxtail washer. Sorting the guts of hogs eight hours a day is far from an interesting job. Neither is identification of oneself as a gut sorter likely to boost one's ego. (Thio, pp. 298–301.)

Subtopic (from the list provided): ________________

Main Idea: ________________________________

____

Check and complete all of the following that helped you make your choice.

This is the main idea because it

_____ answers a question stated in the paragraph

_____ has a listing phrase: ________________

_____ is followed by a "first item in a list" signal word or phrase:

____

_____ is followed by an example with a signal word or phrase:

____

_____ has a change of direction signal: ________________

_____ has a summary/conclusion signal: ________________

_____ has no signal but states a general conclusion that all details lead to

■ PART B Health, Diet, Exercise

For each paragraph, first select the number of the sentence that is the main idea. Then decide what signals led you to your answer.

1. [1]In recent years, diagnosticians have revised their definition of obesity. [2]Although body weight is certainly an important factor, they believe that the real indicator of obesity is how much fat your body contains. [3]A male weight lifter may be 30 to 40 percent overweight according to the charts and yet still not be obese because of the heaviness and relative density of his muscle tissue. [4]Similarly, a 40-year old woman who prides herself on weighing the same 130 pounds that she did in high school may be shocked to learn that her body now contains over 40 percent fat compared to 15 percent fat in her high school days. [5]Weight by itself, though a useful guide, is not an indicator of obesity. (Donatelle and Davis, p. 180.)

   Main Idea: ______

   Check and complete all of the following that helped you make your choice.

   This is the main idea because it

   _____ has a listing phrase: ______________________________

   _____ is followed by a "first item in a list" signal word or phrase:

   ____

   _____ is followed by an example with a signal word: ____________

   _____ has a change of direction signal: ______________________

   _____ has a summary/conclusion signal: ______________________

2. [1]With all of the techniques available for calculating how fat you really are, how do you decide which is the best for you? [2]Perhaps the best way is to ask yourself how much an exact measure of your body fat means to you. [3]If you are interested in obtaining the most accurate measure before and after a program of diet and exercise, you may find the expense of some of the more sophisticated measures worth the investment. [4]If you simply want a general idea of how much body fat you are carrying around, an inexpensive pinch test or skinfold measure may be all that you need. [5]On the other hand, if you know, based on the bulges around your middle or the size and fit of your jeans, that you are obese,

perhaps the exact amount of fat that you have does not matter as much as the fact that you need to take action. (Donatelle and Davis, p. 181.)

Main Idea: ______

This is the main idea because it

_____ answers a question stated in the paragraph

_____ has a listing phrase: ______________________________

_____ has a summary/conclusion signal: ______________________

_____ all of the above

_____ none of the above

3. [1]You probably know someone who seems to be able to eat you under the table and does not appear to exercise more than you do, yet never seems to gain weight. [2]Although the person's schedule may not include running or strenuous exercise, it probably includes a high level of activity. [3]Walking up a flight of stairs rather than taking the elevator, speeding up the pace while mowing the lawn, getting up to change the TV channel rather than using the remote, and doing housework vigorously all burn extra calories. [4]Or, perhaps in some subtle ways, these people just manage to burn more calories through extra motions. [5]Clearly, any form of activity that helps your body burn additional calories helps you maintain your weight. (Donatelle and Davis, p. 89.)

Main Idea: ______

This is the main idea because it

_____ answers a question stated in the paragraph

_____ has a listing phrase: ______________________________

_____ is followed by a "first item in a list" signal word or phrase:

____

_____ has a summary/conclusion signal: ______________________

4. [1]College students often face a challenge when trying to eat healthy foods. [2]Some students live in dorms and do not have their own cooking or refrigeration facilities. [3]Others live in crowded apartments where everyone forages in the refrigerator for everyone else's food. [4]Still others eat at university food services where food choices may be limited. (Donatelle and Davis, p. 171.)

Main Idea: ______

This is the main idea because it

_____ is followed by an example with a signal word: _______________

_____ has a change of direction signal: ___________________________

_____ has a summary/conclusion signal: ___________________________

_____ has no signal but states a general idea that all details support

TOPICAL VERSUS MAIN IDEA ORGANIZATION

Not all paragraphs, articles, chapters, or books have a main idea. This is particularly true for writing that is mainly giving factual information or instructions. Often writers use a *topical* paragraph to give some necessary background information. In topical organization, no single general idea holds all of the other ideas together. Instead, all the ideas in the paragraph are more or less of equal importance; they connect together in that they all relate to a topic.

Learning to recognize the difference between topical and main idea organization is very important in determining your strategy in reading textbooks. As you mark texts and take notes, it is important to know what kind of information you are looking for. Though texts in all fields can show a mixture of the two, those in the sciences—biology and geology, for example—tend more toward factual information organized around topics and subtopics. Courses in the humanities and social sciences, such as philosophy, history, or political science, tend to stress concepts that provide main ideas for paragraphs and sections.

The difference between topical and idea organization can be shown by two different maps. For topical organization we can use a *pinwheel* map to show relationships. For example, this paragraph, which you worked with earlier, is a good example of a topical paragraph:

> "Fossil" comes from a Latin word for something that has been "dug up." As generally used, a fossil is recognizable, physical evidence of an organism that lived long ago. Most fossils are body parts, such as bones, teeth, shells, leaves, and seeds. Some are tracks, burrows, and other telltale impressions of past life. All were preserved because they were gently buried before they could decompose or fall apart. (Starr, p. 211.)

The topic of this paragraph is "fossils" and its individual sentences answer a number of questions of equal importance about that topic:

> **Where** did the word "fossil" come from?
> **What** is the definition of a fossil?
> **What** are they mainly made from?
> **What** other things can leave impressions?
> **Why** were they not destroyed?

None of these questions, however, is broad enough to include all the others. Their answers give us information on various aspects of the topic of fossils. A pinwheel map will show this topical relationship:

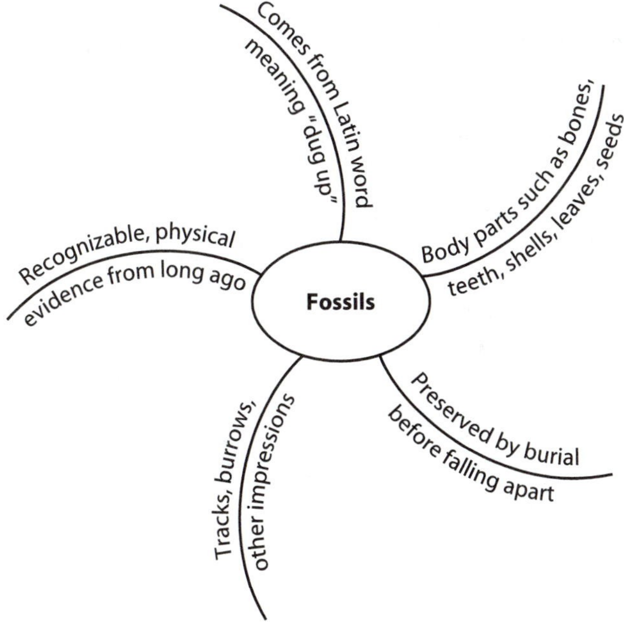

To show relationships in main idea organization, we can use a *cartwheel* map. For example, below is a paragraph that appeared on the same page as the topical paragraph:

> The fossil record is uneven for some organisms and environments are better represented than others. For example, fossils of hard-shelled mollusks and bony fishes are abundant. Fossils of jellyfishes and other soft-bodied animals are not. Floodplains, seafloors, swamps, and natural traps such as caves and tar pits favor fossilization. Rapidly eroding hills do not. (Starr, p. 211.)

The general topic is still "fossils" but the focus of the paragraph is on a subtopic, *the fossil record.* The paragraph answers a number of questions about this topic:

> **Why** is the fossil record uneven?
> **Which** fossils are abundant?
> **Which** are not?
> **Which** environments favor fossilization?
> **Which** do not?

Is the answer to any of these a main idea that is broad enough to cover all the rest? The presence of the signal phrase "for example" would suggest that the first sentence may be a main idea sentence:

> The fossil record is uneven for some organisms and environments are better represented than others.

Do all the other questions in the paragraph contribute to answering the first? Since they are all examples of how the fossil record is uneven, we would determine that they are supporting detail for the main idea. A cartwheel map shows how all the ideas in the paragraph are held together.

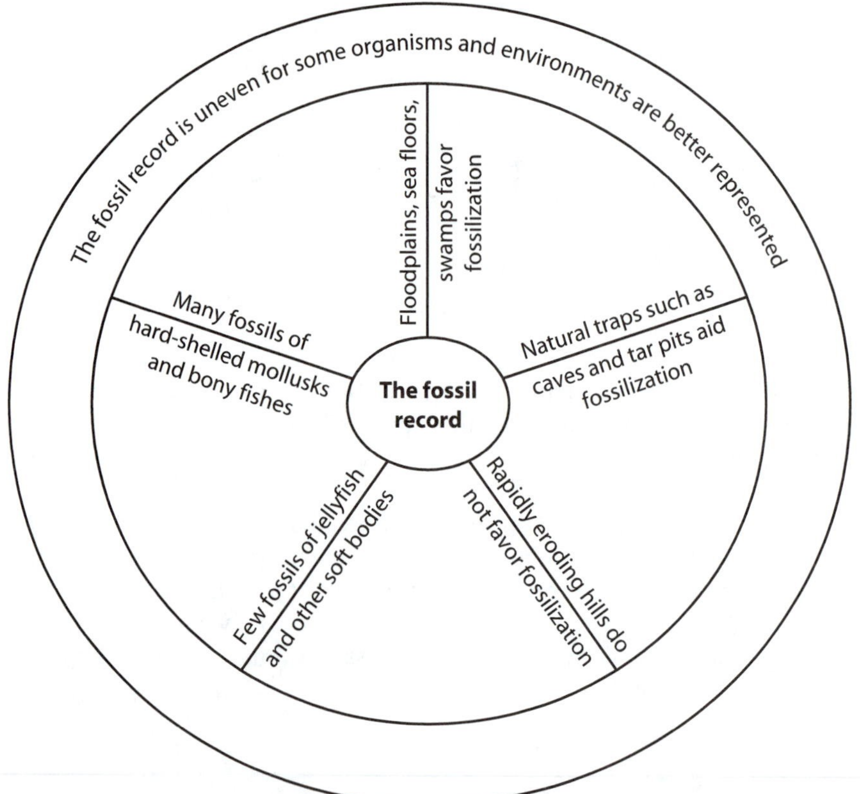

The spokes of the wheel (the supporting details) have unity beyond just the topic (the hub) because they all support and develop a more general main idea (the rim).

When paragraphs contain definitions, recognizing the difference between topical and main idea patterns can be difficult. Definitions, especially when they appear near the beginning of a paragraph, can help us identify the topic. For example, in the first paragraph on fossils, the author indicates the topic and helps the reader understand what it is by including two sentences of definition:

> "Fossil" comes from a Latin word for something that has been "dug up." As generally used, a fossil is recognizable, physical evidence of an organism that lived long ago."

It is tempting to pick a definition, especially one at the beginning of a paragraph, as a main idea, but the truth is, a definition very seldom is. The paragraph may be topical, as with the preceding example. Or, in a paragraph with a main idea, the definition may introduce the topic but not be the main idea sentence:

> **Stereotypes are cognitive frameworks consisting of knowledge and beliefs about specific social groups—frameworks suggesting that by and large, all members of these groups possess certain traits.** Like other cognitive frameworks, or schemas, stereotypes exert strong effects on the ways in which we process social information. For example, information relevant to a particular stereotype is processed more quickly than information unrelated to it. Similarly, stereotypes lead us to pay attention to specific types of information—usually information consistent with the stereotypes. And they may actually block our ability to pay attention to stereotype-inconsistent information. Finally, stereotypes also determine what we remember—usually, again, information that is consistent with these frameworks. (Baron, p. 536.)

The first sentence defines stereotypes, but the main idea (signaled by the phrase "for example") relates to the effect they have:

> Like other cognitive frameworks, or schemas, stereotypes exert strong effects on the ways in which we process social information. For example, . . .

There are, of course, times when a definition is the main idea. This occurs usually when there is confusion or a lack of agreement about a word's meaning. An author may want to distinguish between two terms—for example, "love" versus "infatuation"—or sharpen the definition of a term that others may be misusing:

> If you were to examine even the most pristine family under a microscope, you would likely find some type of dysfunction. No group of people who live together day in and day out can interact perfectly all the time. However, many people have begun to overuse the term dysfunctional to refer to even the smallest problems in the family unit. As such, the term becomes relatively meaningless. True dysfunctionality refers to settings where negative interactions are the norm rather than the exception. Children raised in these settings tend to face tremendous obstacles to growing up healthy. Coming to terms with past hurts may take years. (Donatelle and Davis, p. 94.)

In this example, the author notes how a term has been misused before giving the main idea:

> True dysfunctionality refers to settings where negative interactions are the norm rather than the exception.

EXERCISE 4.4

Identifying Topical and Idea Paragraphs

■ PART A

In the following pairs, one paragraph is topical and one is controlled by a main idea. Ask questions and look for main idea signals to see if a paragraph is organized around a main idea or by a topic only. Following the two paragraphs are a pinwheel map for topical organization and a cartwheel map for main idea organization. Match the letter of each paragraph to the right map and complete the map using the list below each paragraph.

1 Anabolic steroids are artificial forms of the male hormone testosterone that promotes muscle growth and strength. Most steroids are obtained through black market sources. It is estimated that approximately 17 to 20 percent of college athletes use steroids. Overall, it is estimated that there are 1 million steroid abusers in the United States, many of whom take steroids for noncompetitive bodybuilding. Steroids are available in two forms: injectable solution and pills. Anabolic steroids produce a state of euphoria, diminished fatigue, and increased bulk and

power in both sexes. These qualities give steroids an addictive quality. When users stop, they appear to undergo psychological withdrawal, mainly caused by the disappearance of the physique they have become accustomed to.

Items for the Map

- Anabolic steroids.
- Steroids are artificial forms of testosterone for muscle growth/strength.
- Most steroids are obtained through black market sources.
- 17 to 20 percent of college athletes use steroids.
- 1 million steroid abusers in the United States.
- Steroids are available in two forms: injectable solution and pills.
- Effects of steroids give them an addictive quality.

2 Several adverse effects occur in both men and women who use steroids. These drugs cause mood swings (aggression and violence), sometimes known as "roid rage"; acne; liver tumors; elevated cholesterol levels; hypertension; kidney disease; and immune system disturbances. There is also a danger of AIDS transmission through shared needles. In women, large doses of anabolic steroids trigger masculine changes, including lowered voice, increased facial and body hair, male pattern baldness, enlarged clitoris, decreased breast size, and changes in or absence of menstruation. When taken by healthy males, anabolic steroids shut down the body's production of testosterone, causing men's breasts to grow and testicles to atrophy. (Donatelle and Davis, pp. 248–49.)

Items for the Map

- Steroid use may cause mood swings ("roid rage").
- Effects of steroids.
- Abuse of steroids can stop production of testosterone in men.
- Several adverse effects occur in both men and women who use steroids.
- There is a danger of AIDS transmission through shared needles.
- Use can result in acne or ailments like liver tumors and kidney disease.
- Large doses cause masculine changes in women, such as increased facial and body hair.

Idea Organization

¶ ______

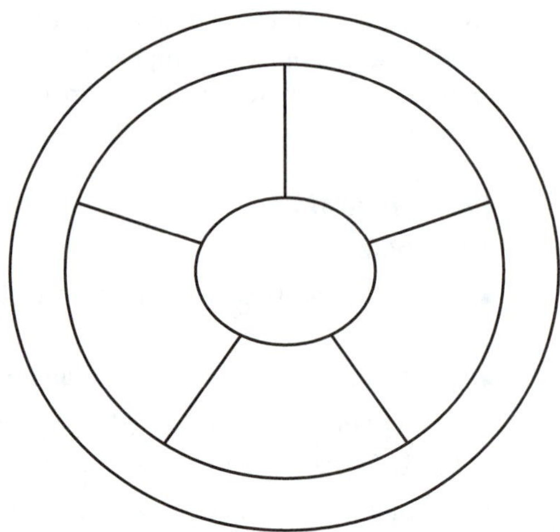

Topical Organization

¶ ______

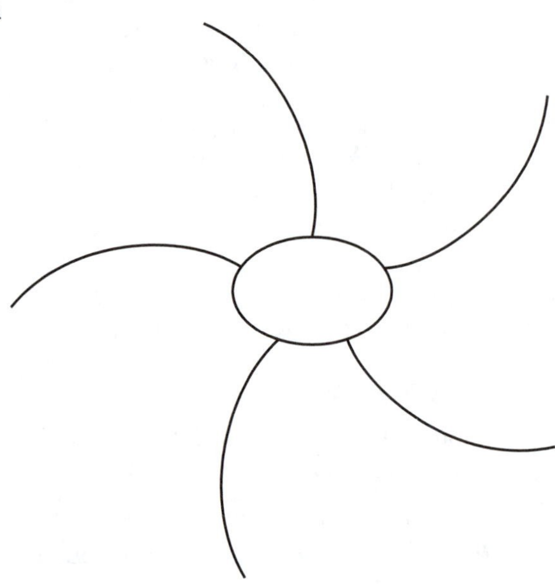

1 The labor force includes all those over 16 years of age who are gainfully employed as well as those who are jobless but are actively seeking paid employment. It excludes full-time homemakers, students, and retired people—anyone who is not paid for his or her work and is not seeking a paying job. In 1988 about 66 percent of Americans over the age of

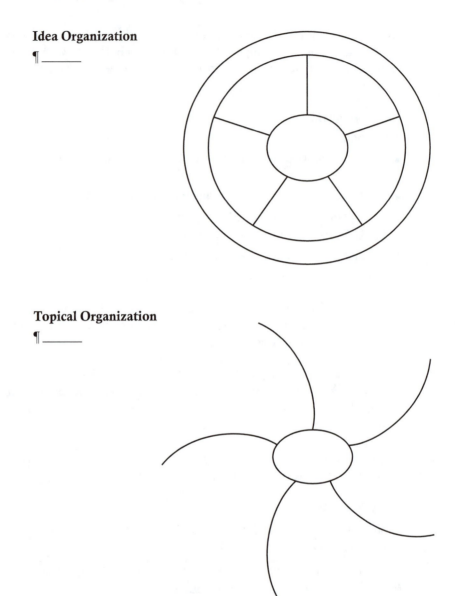

16 were in the work force—this figure is expected to grow to 69 percent in 2000—compared with about 55 percent in 1940. This increase has been accompanied by dramatic shifts in what American workers do and who makes up the work force.

Items for the Map

- The labor force.
- The labor force includes all over 16 wage earners plus active job seekers.
- The labor force excludes unpaid non-job-seekers.
- In 1988, 66 percent of Americans over 16 were in the work force.
- By 2000, 69 percent of Americans over 16 will be in the work force.
- In 1940, 55 percent of those over 16 were in the labor force.
- Big changes have occurred in types of jobs and who is in the work force.

2 In a survey, only 26 percent of American workers still held the traditional view of work. Some of these workers said that "the more I get paid, the more I do." Others agreed that "work is one of life's unpleasant necessities. I wouldn't work if I didn't have to." A bumper sticker says it all: "Work sucks, but I need the bucks." In contrast, a large majority (73 percent) of the respondents expressed more positive attitudes toward work. Many agreed with the statement: "I have an inner need to do the very best I can, regardless of pay." They most frequently rated as "very important" certain nonmonetary qualities of work, such as interesting jobs, developing their own skills, and seeing how good the results of their work are. The American work ethic has taken on a new quality. (Thio, pp. 298–99.)

Items for the Map

- American work ethic.
- Only 26 percent workers held the traditional view "Work sucks, but I need the bucks."
- A large majority (73 percent) had more positive attitudes toward work.
- Many feel an inner need to do the very best regardless of pay.
- They most frequently rated as "very important" certain nonmonetary qualities of work.
- The American work ethic has taken on a new quality.

Idea Organization

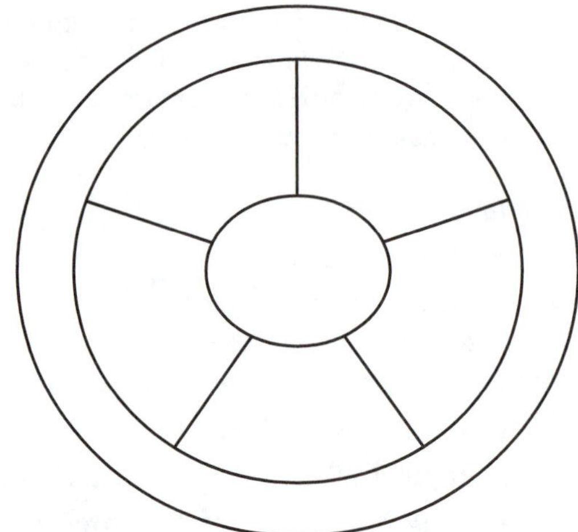

Topical Organization

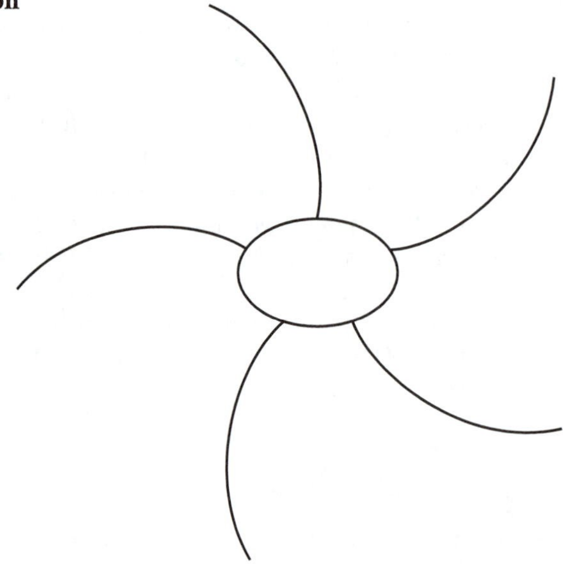

■ PART B

The following sets of paragraphs concern a common topic. In each pair, one paragraph is topical and one has a main idea. For each paragraph, select the letter of the correct response.

Topic: *calorie consumption*

1 Americans consume more calories per person than does any other group of people in the world. A calorie is a unit of measure that indicates the amount of energy we obtain from a particular food. Calories are eaten in the form of proteins, fats, and carbohydrates, three of the basic nutrients necessary for life. Three other nutrients, vitamins, minerals, and water, are necessary for bodily function but do not contribute any calories to our diets.

a. Americans consume more calories per person than does any other group in the world.
b. A calorie is a unit of measure that indicates the amount of energy we obtain from a particular food.
c. Calories are eaten in the form of proteins, fats, and carbohydrates.
d. Three other nutrients, vitamins, minerals, and water, are necessary for bodily function.
e. None of the above. This paragraph has a topical organization.

2 Excess calorie consumption is a major factor in the tendency to be overweight. However, it is not so much the quantity of food we eat that is likely to cause weight problems and resultant diseases as it is the relative proportion of nutrients in our diets and our lack of physical activity. Americans typically get approximately 38 percent of their calories from fat, 15 percent from proteins, 22 percent from complex carbohydrates, and 24 percent from simple sugars. Nutritionists recommend that complex carbohydrates be increased to make up 48 percent of our total calories and that proteins be reduced to 12 percent, simple sugars to 10 percent, and fats to no more than 30 percent of our total diets. (Thio, pp. 149–150.)

a. Excess calorie consumption is a major factor in the tendency to be overweight.
b. Weight problems and resultant diseases are caused less by quantity of food than by the relative proportion of our nutrients and our lack of physical activity.
c. Americans get their calories from fat, proteins, complex carbohydrates, and simple sugars.
d. Nutritionists recommend that complex carbohydrates be increased and that proteins, simple sugars, and fats be reduced.
e. None of the above. This paragraph has a topical organization.

Topic: *chronic fatigue*

3 Fatigue is a subjective condition in which people feel tired before they begin activities, lack the energy to accomplish tasks that require sustained effort and attention, or become abnormally exhausted after normal activities. To many Americans, such symptoms are all too common. In the late 1980s, however, a characteristic set of symptoms including chronic fatigue, headaches, fever, sore throat, enlarged lymph nodes, depression, poor memory, general weakness, nausea, and symptoms remarkably similar to mononucleosis were noted in several U.S. clinics. Despite extensive testing, no viral cause has been found to date.

a. Fatigue is a condition in which people feel tired before they begin activities.
b. To many Americans, such symptoms are all too common.
c. In the late 1980s a characteristic set of symptoms were noted.
d. Despite extensive testing, no viral cause has been found to date.
e. None of the above. This paragraph has a topical organization.

4 Today, in the absence of a known pathogen, many researchers believe that the illness, now commonly referred to as chronic fatigue syndrome (CFS), may have strong psychosocial roots. According to Harvard psychiatrist Arthur Barsky, our heightened awareness of health makes some of us scrutinize our bodies so carefully that the slightest deviation becomes amplified. The more we focus on our body and on our perception of our health, the worse we feel. (Donatelle and Davis, pp. 345–46.)

a. There is no known pathogen for chronic fatigue syndrome.
b. Many researchers believe that CFS may have strong psychosocial roots.
c. Our awareness of health makes some of us scrutinize our bodies very carefully.
d. The more we focus on our body and our perception of our health, the worse we feel.
e. None of the above. This paragraph has a topical organization.

Topic: *eating disorders*

5 Bulimics are binge eaters who take inappropriate measures, such as secret vomiting, to lose the calories/weight that they have just acquired. Up to 3 percent of adolescents and young female adults are bulimic, with male rates being about 10 percent of the female rate. Bulimics also have an obsession with their bodies, weight gain, and how they appear to others. Unlike anorectics, bulimics are often "hidden" from the public eye,

as their weight may only vary slightly or be within a normal range. Also, effective treatment appears to be more likely with bulimia than with anorexia.

a. Bulimics are binge eaters who take inappropriate measures to lose the calories/weight that they have just acquired.
b. Bulimics are obsessed with their bodies, weight gain, and how they appear to others.
c. Unlike anorectics, bulimics are often "hidden" from the public eye.
d. Effective treatment appears to be more likely with bulimia than with anorexia.
e. None of the above. This paragraph has a topical organization.

6 Disordered eating patterns are the result of many factors other than an addiction to food or low self-esteem. Often, they are partially the result of poor self-concept, but other factors, such as a perceived lack of control in their lives, may trigger these problems. To win social approval by maintaining a thin body and to gain control of some aspects of their lives, anorectics or bulimics take rigid control over eating. (Donatelle and Davis, p. 89.)

a. Disordered eating patterns are the result of many factors.
b. Disordered eating patterns are the result of addiction to food or low self-esteem.
c. Most eating problems result from a perception of lack of control over one's life.
d. The causes of disordered eating, plus rigid control by anorexics and bulimics.
e. None of the above. This paragraph has a topical organization.

READING FOR IMPORTANT INFORMATION

Students are told that they should highlight or mark important items in their textbooks, but how do we decide what is important? Clearly, the first place to start is identifying topics and marking main ideas, skills you worked on in the last few chapters. Seeing main ideas for paragraphs and larger units of reading material will help you summarize and remember the main points you need to recall. Being able to tell the difference between topical and idea organization is also important, especially as it relates to study skills. Topical organization requires you to identify various aspects of a subject. It also may involve more memorization of factual material.

But after you have identified main topics and main ideas, a lot of idea statements remain. For your study purposes, some ideas in the material are going to be more necessary to remember than others. To decide on what to mark and what to remember for a test or what to include in a report, you must make decisions about the supporting ideas. You need to identify what is *major* and what is *minor* detail.

Major details are more general than minor details. They are often needed for the main idea to be clear; if they were left out of a summary, for example, we would probably not clearly understand what the author is saying. Just as major supporting details develop main ideas; so too do minor details support and develop major details. Minor details help in backing up statements and in making reading material vivid and interesting. However, if minor details were left out, we would still have the most important ideas in the material. As an example, here is a paragraph you saw earlier:

Main Point **Specialization of work, if carried too far, leaves little room for**
responsibility or initiative by the worker. *It can mean that some people are*
Major Details *assigned the job of controlling those who actually produce goods or deliver services.*
When Studs Terkel interviewed workers, he found "the most profound complaint
is 'being spied on.' There's the foreman at the plant, the supervisor listen-
Minor Detail ing in at Ma Bell's, the checker who gives the bus driver a hard time."
Main Point **Moreover, by tying the worker to an isolated task, to a small part of**
some large task, specialization can empty jobs of their meaning. *The re-*
Major Details *sult can be dehumanizing for some workers, as Terkel found when he interviewed*
people across the country: "'I'm a machine,' says the spotwelder. 'I'm
Minor Detail caged,' says the bank teller. 'I'm a mule,' says the steelworker. 'A monkey can do what I do,' says the receptionist."

In this paragraph, a main point about the effects of specialization is made in the first sentence. But to understand how specialization leads to loss of responsibility and initiative, we need more details. Therefore the second sentence and third sentences give us important major details about why there is a loss of responsibility: Workers feel controlled by bosses. The fifth and sixth sentences give us additional major points about the result of all this: Workers who become small cogs feel less than human.

The rest of the paragraph is minor detail. The quotations from workers add greatly to our interest in the writing but if these were left out we would still have the basic information:

> Specialization of work, if carried too far, leaves little room for responsibility or initiative by the worker. It can mean that some people are assigned the job of controlling those who actually produce goods or de-

liver services. When Studs Terkel interviewed workers, he found "the most profound complaint is 'being spied on.'" Moreover, by tying the worker to an isolated task, to a small part of some large task, specialization can empty jobs of their meaning. The result can be dehumanizing for some workers, as Terkel found when he interviewed people across the country.

Outlining is a good way of separating major and minor detail and seeing what is important to remember and what we can leave out. Outlines thus serve as a good basis for making a summary or for studying for a test. An outline of the above would look like this:

I. Overspecialization of work erodes responsibility/initiative of the worker.
   A. Bosses make workers feel controlled.
   B. Workers complain of "being spied on."
      1. plant foreman
      2. Ma Bell supervisor
      3. bus driver checker
II. Overspecialization dehumanizes workers.
   A. Worker tied to isolated task.
   B. Jobs lose meaning
      1. spotwelder as a machine
      2. caged bank teller
      3. steelworker like a mule
      4. receptionist like a monkey

Making useful notes and underlying or highlighting important information in textbooks requires this ability to tell major from minor detail. In reading a textbook, a student needs to ask questions about the material, mark main ideas and other important details that answer those questions, and look up any vocabulary words or terms that are not clear. The passage above, for example, might be marked like this:

Specialization of work, if carried too far, leaves little room for responsibility or initiative by the worker. It can mean that some people are assigned the job of controlling those who actually produce goods or deliver services. When Studs Terkel interviewed workers, he found "the most profound complaint is 'being spied on.' There's the foreman at the plant, the supervisor listening in at Ma Bell's, the checker who gives the bus driver a

key point!! bosses control workers

profound: far-reaching, beyond the obvious.

What are workers upset about?

spied on by bosses

key point!! causes isolation

What effect does doing the same small job have?

workers feel like machines!

good examples

hard time." Moreover, by tying the worker to an isolated task, to a small part of some large task, specialization can empty jobs of their meaning. The result can be dehumanizing for some workers, as Terkel found when he interviewed people across the country: "'I'm a machine,' says the spotwelder. 'I'm caged,' says the bank teller. 'I'm a mule,' says the steelworker. 'A monkey can do what I do,' says the receptionist."

EXERCISE 4.5

Reading for Important Information

Following is a paragraph that will give you practice in finding and marking main ideas and major details.

1. First, determine the main idea by reading the paragraph and completing the main idea checklist that follows. Mark and look up the meanings of any words you are unsure of.
2. Next, reread and mark your text to show important information. Do the following:
   a. Highlight or underline the main idea and the question that it answers; write "main point" in the margin next to it.
   b. Major details are frequently introduced by signal words of addition:

also	first	finally	moreover
in addition	second	last	furthermore
and	next		

   Find and double-underline the four signal words that indicate major detail. Underline or highlight the phrasing that states the major detail. The first has been done for you.
   c. In the margin write a short question that the major detail answers, and write the answer to it using key words. The first has been done for you.
   d. Do not mark minor detail other than to write "EX." for "example."
   e. Circle any words in the text that you need to look up definitions for. In the margin write only the definition that fits the way the word is being used in the sentence.
3. Finally, complete the outline that follows the paragraph.

So how can we get the couch potatoes off the couch? Some research suggests that starting and then maintaining an exercise program requires that people arrange their environment so that it supports the desired exercise behavior and weakens competing behaviors. First, it is important to arrange effective cues that become a signal to exercise. Working out in the same location, doing a similar warm-up routine, and recording and posting the results of one's physical activity can be effective in cueing future exercise behavior. It is also important to arrange when exercise occurs, to minimize the effects of the cues for competing behaviors. For example, individuals who have a tendency to work late should establish a morning training routine to minimize competition with a busy work schedule. Also, it is also important to arrange for consequences that maintain exercise behavior. Initially, it is critical for new exercisers to seek out sources of rewards for their exercise behavior and avoid potential sources of punishment, including muscle soreness, fatigue, and injury. Finally, the presence of a strong social support network can greatly increase adherence to a lifelong exercise habit. (Baron, p. 438.)

How do we develop exercise behaviors?

set up cues for exercise

Topic: ______________________________

Main Idea: ______________________________

____

This is the main idea because it

a. answers a question stated in the paragraph
b. is followed by a "first item in a list" signal word or phrase
c. is followed by an example with a signal word or phrase
d. has a change of direction signal
e. both a and b
f. both b and d

Use notes in your text above to complete the outline with these items:

- muscle soreness, fatigue, injury
- a strong social support network increases adherence to lifelong exercise
- do similar warm-up routine
- arrange cues to signal exercise
- individuals who work late need morning training routine
- arrange for consequences that maintain exercise behavior
- find sources of rewards for exercise behavior
- arrange when exercise occurs

Outline

I. Main Idea: To start and maintain an exercise program, arrange the environment to support the desired behavior and weaken competing behaviors.

A. First, ______________________________

1. work out in same location
2. ______________________________
3. record/post the results

B. Also ______________________________

1. minimize effects of competing cues
2. example: ______________________________

C. Third, ______________________________

1. new exercisers: ______________________________
2. avoid potential sources of punishment: ______________________________

D. Finally, ______________________________

Active Learning

STRATEGIES OF ACTIVE READERS

Below is a list of strategies that good readers use when reading and studying textbooks. Rate yourself on your own habits. Use the following scale:

4 Always **3** Most of the time **2** Sometimes **1** Seldom **0** Never

Circle the number that best describes your performance.

1. I look at the title to try to discover the topic.

   4 **3** **2** **1** **0**

2. I think about what I already know about this topic.

   4 **3** **2** **1** **0**

3. I ask questions about the title.

   4 **3** **2** **1** **0**

4. I read the first paragraph or introduction and the last paragraph or conclusion.

   4 3 2 1 0

5. I survey major headings.

   4 3 2 1 0

6. From the above I make a good guess (hypothesis) as to the main idea of the reading.

   4 3 2 1 0

7. If I can't understand something on the first reading, I go back and reread it.

   4 3 2 1 0

8. As I read, I relate details to my main idea guess.

   4 3 2 1 0

9. If what I read doesn't fit with my guess, I reread paragraphs and revise my main idea guess.

   4 3 2 1 0

10. I look for signals that indicate main ideas.

    4 3 2 1 0

11. I mark the topic sentences of paragraphs that have one.

    4 3 2 1 0

12. I mark the text and write in the margin to show important information (major details).

    4 3 2 1 0

13. I look up words I don't know and find meanings that fit the sentence.

    4 3 2 1 0

14. I make outlines to help me write summaries and study for tests.

    4 3 2 1 0

15. I ask for help from my instructor when I can't figure things out.

    4 3 2 1 0

Reading Portfolio

READING FOR MAIN IDEAS AND MAJOR DETAILS

For this assignment you need to find an article that interests you in a magazine or newspaper or from the Internet.

Author: ______________________________

Title: ______________________________

Publication/Source: ______________________________

Topic: ______________________________

Check the reading strategies you followed before you read:

_____ I looked at the title.

_____ Did it suggest or state the topic?

_____ Did it suggest or state an idea?

_____ I asked a question about the title.

_____ I read the first paragraph or (introduction) and the last paragraph (conclusion).

_____ Did the introduction contain a statement that might be the main idea?

_____ Did the conclusion state (or restate) a possible main idea?

_____ From the above I made a good guess (hypothesis) as to the main idea:

____

____

Check the reading strategies you followed as you read.

_____ I related details to my main idea guess.

_____ I marked and wrote comments in the margin for major sections and details (or, if not your own copy, took notes on a separate piece of paper).

_____ I did not mark a lot of minor details.

_____ My reading and checking back showed my main idea guess was right.
If not, how did it change? ______________________________

_____ I made an outline of the article.

Save the article and the outline you did for this assignment. You will use it again in the next portfolio assignment.

Part Two

Reading for *Understanding*

CHAPTER 5

Do I Really Know What This Means?

Making Inferences and Explaining Ideas

After reading this chapter, you will know the answers to these questions:

- What is reading for understanding?
- What is inference?
- Why is inference important in reading stories?
- What's the difference between fact and opinion?
- How do the terms *purpose* and *tone* relate to reading?

In the last few chapters you have asked questions about the subject the writer is presenting. The answers to these questions are the ideas about the topic. Answering these questions has been mainly a matter of looking back, locating facts, and organizing them. In this chapter you will learn about a purpose in reading that goes beyond reading just for information.

READING FOR INFORMATION IN LONGER PASSAGES

To prepare yourself for this next level, you will need to practice the techniques of reading for information in a more demanding and longer textbook selection. Below is a five-paragraph passage, "The Spanish Conquistadores," that will give you practice in reading for important information.

EXERCISE 5.1

Finding Important Information in Longer Passages

1. Before you read the passage, write down any information that comes to mind about this topic:

   What do you think *conquistador* means? ______________________

   What names do you think of when you hear this word? What were they known for?

   ____

   What time period/dates do you associate these with names?

   ____

2. Read for important information.
   - Decide on the main idea of each paragraph and complete the main idea checklist that follows. Highlight or underline the main idea; write "main point" in the margin.
   - Circle any signal words that indicate major detail. Underline or highlight the phrasing that states the major detail.
   - In the margin write a short question that the major detail answers, and write the answer to it using key words.
   - Do not mark minor detail other than to write EX. for "example."
   - Circle any words in the text that you need to look up definitions for. In the margin write *only* the definition that fits the way the word is being used in the sentence.
3. Complete the outline of the most important information for the entire passage.
4. After you finish reading, think about what you have learned. Look again at the questions at the start of this exercise; correct any information you wrote down that you discovered was not accurate.

The Spanish Conquistadores

1 In 1492, the same year that Columbus sighted America, the great Moorish city of Granada, in Spain, fell after a ten-year siege. For five centuries the Christian kingdoms of Spain had been trying to drive the North African Muslim Moors ("the Dark Ones," in Spanish) off the Iberian peninsula, and with the fall of Granada they succeeded. But the lengthy "Reconquista" had left its mark on Spanish society. Centuries of military and religious confrontation nurtured an obsession with status

and honor, bred religious zealotry and intolerance, and created a large class of men who regarded manual labor and commerce contemptuously. With the Reconquista ended, some of these men turned their restless gaze to Spain's New World frontier.

Topic: ______________________________

Main Idea: ______________________________

____

This is the main idea because it:

a. has a change of direction signal
b. has a listing phrase
c. has a signal word of summary or conclusion
d. has no signal but states a general conclusion that all details lead to

2 At first, Spanish hopes for America focused on the Caribbean and on finding a sea route to Asia. Gradually, however, word filtered back of rich kingdoms on the mainland. Between 1519 and 1540, Spanish conquistadores swept across the Americas in two wide arcs of conquest—one driving from Cuba through Mexico into what is now the southwestern United States, the other starting from Panama and pushing south into Peru. Within half a century of Columbus's arrival in the Americas, the conquistadores had extinguished the great Aztec and Incan empires and claimed for church and crown a territory that extended from Colorado to Argentina, including much of what is now the continental United States.

Topic: ______________________________

Main Idea: ______________________________

____

This is the main idea because it:

a. has a change of direction signal
b. has a listing phrase
c. is followed by a "first item in a list" signal word
d. has no signal but states a general conclusion that all details lead to

3 The military conquest of this vast region was achieved by just ten thousand men, organized in a series of private expeditions. Hernan Cortes, Francisco Pizarro, and other aspiring conquerors signed contracts with the Spanish monarch, raised money from investors, and then went about recruiting an army. Only a small minority of the conquistadores—leaders or followers—were nobles. About half were professional

soldiers and sailors; the rest comprised peasants, artisans, and members of the middling classes. Most were in their twenties and early thirties, and all knew how to wield a sword.

Topic: ______________________________

Main Idea: ______________________________

____

This is the main idea because it:

a. answers a question asked in the paragraph

b. has a listing phrase

c. is followed by a "first item in a list" signal word

d. has no signal but states a general conclusion that all details lead to

4 Diverse motives spurred these motley adventurers. Some hoped to win royal titles and favors by bringing new peoples under the Spanish flag. Others sought to assure God's favor by spreading Christianity to the pagans. Some men hoped to escape dubious pasts, and others sought the kind of historical adventure experienced by heroes of classical antiquity. Nearly all shared a lust for gold. As one of Cortes's foot soldiers put it, "We came here to serve God and the king, and also to get rich."

Topic: ______________________________

Main Idea: ______________________________

____

This is the main idea because it:

a. answers a question asked in the paragraph

b. has a listing phrase

c. is followed by an example with a signal word or phrase

d. has a change of direction signal

5 Armed with horses and gunpowder and preceded by disease, the conquistadores quickly overpowered the Indians. But most never achieved their dreams of glory. Few received titles of nobility, and many of the rank and file remained permanently indebted to the absentee investors who paid for their equipment. Even when an expedition captured exceptionally rich booty, the spoils were unevenly divided: men from the commander's home region often received more, and men on horseback generally got two shares to the infantryman's one. The conquistadores lost still more power as the crown gradually tightened its control in the New World. By the 1530s in Mexico and the 1550s in Peru, colorless colonial administrators had replaced the freebooting conquistadores.

Topic: ______________________________

Main Idea: ______________________________

____

This is the main idea because it:

a. has a change of direction signal
b. has a listing phrase
c. is followed by a "first item in a list" signal word
d. has a signal word of summary or conclusion

6 Nevertheless, the conquistadores achieved a kind of immortality. Because of a scarcity of Spanish women in the early days of the conquest, many conquistadores married Indian women. The soldiers who conquered Paraguay received three native women each, and Cortes's soldiers in Mexico—who were forbidden to consort with pagan women—quickly had their lovers baptized into the Catholic faith. Their offspring, the "new race" of mestizos, formed a cultural and biological bridge between Latin America's European and Indian races. (Bailey and Kennedy, pp. 16–17.)

Topic: ______________________________

Main Idea: ______________________________

____

This is the main idea because it:

a. has a change of direction signal
b. has a listing phrase
c. is followed by a "first item in a list" signal word
d. has a signal word of summary or conclusion

Use these items to complete the outline that follows:

- All wanted gold, riches
- Colonial administrators brought in, replaced them
- Focus on mainland and wealth, not route to Asia through Caribbean
- Did receive "immortality" in a different way
- Cortes, Pizarro, others making contracts, raising money, signing up army
- Offspring—mestizos—helped unify Latin America's races
- After the Reconquista, great attraction to Spain's New World
- Mainly soldiers/sailors, peasants, artisans—not nobles
- Ended up in debt forever to investors in Spain

- Did not get equal share of the booty
- Many different reasons for going on the venture

1. With fall of Granada (1492), Moors driven off by Spanish Christians
   A. ______________________________
   B. Result a class of intolerant men after honor/status
2. Within fifty years, Aztec and Incan empires destroyed, territory taken by Spain
   A. ______________________________
   B. 1519–1540, conquistadores in two groups spread through the Americas
3. Got victory with only about ten thousand men
   A. ______________________________
   B. ______________________________
4. ______________________________
   A. Hoped conquering people and land for Spain would get them titles/favors
   B. Bring Christianity to those considered pagans
   C. Wanted excitement and adventure, get away from past mistakes
   D. ______________________________
5. Desires of most not achieved
   A. Very few titles of nobility
   B. ______________________________
   C. ______________________________
   D. ______________________________
6. ______________________________
   A. Spanish women scarce; married Indian women
   B. ______________________________

VOCABULARY IN TEXTBOOK PASSAGES

Textbooks often give definitions of key terms but there will still be terms that you will need to look up. The instructions for the preceding exercises asked you to do the following: "Circle any words in the text that you need to look up definitions for. In the margin write only the definition that fits the way the word is being used in the sentence." Following is an exercise that will probably include many of the words you circled in the text. You should now have a good idea of what those words mean.

EXERCISE 5.2

Deciding on Vocabulary Meanings in a Textbook Passage

The list below contains words taken from the six-paragraph passage on the conquistadores. The column at the right contains the meanings of these words as used in that passage. Match the letters of the meanings at the right to the words at the left.

_____ 1. siege
_____ 2. manual
_____ 3. conquistadores
_____ 4. Iberian
_____ 5. peninsula
_____ 6. Granada
_____ 7. nurtured
_____ 8. obsession
_____ 9. zealotry
_____ 10. intolerance
_____ 11. contemptuously
_____ 12. extinguished
_____ 13. aspiring
_____ 14. middling
_____ 15. wield
_____ 16. diverse
_____ 17. lust
_____ 18. pagans
_____ 19. dubious
_____ 20. antiquity
_____ 21. preceded
_____ 22. rank and file
_____ 23. absentee
_____ 24. freebooting
_____ 25. immortality

a. of questionable character; shabby, shameful
b. helped to grow or develop
c. non-Christians, heathens
d. hopeful, ambitious
e. came before
f. Spanish conquerors of Mexico and Peru
g. not present
h. province and city in Spain, former Moorish capital
i. physical, by hand
j. ancient times, especially before the Middle Ages
k. prejudice, discrimination
l. the surrounding of something in order to capture it
m. excessive enthusiasm; fanaticism
n. intense desire
o. plundering, looting
p. utterly destroyed
q. ordinary soldiers
r. average, ordinary
s. designating area containing Spain and Portugal
t. varied, different
u. endless existence; enduring fame
v. a strong fixed idea that directs one's behavior
w. scornfully
x. manipulate, use
y. long projection of land into water, connected by mainland to an isthmus

READING FOR UNDERSTANDING

Here is a part of paragraph 1 from "The Conquistadores":

> The lengthy "Reconquista" had created a large class of men who regarded manual labor and commerce contemptuously. With the Reconquista ended, some of these men turned their restless gaze to Spain's New World frontier.

Here are some questions that might be asked:

Did the Reconquista last a long time? ___________

Was the class of men created big or small? ___________

What two things did these men dislike? ___________ ___________

The answers to these questions give us a certain amount of information—facts about this era. They are also either right or wrong: we can look back at the text to check if we have the right answer. But does being able to answer simple questions mean that we really understand the passage? Suppose in a study group some different questions were brought up. How would you answer these?

Why is the term *Reconquista* used for this period?

What were these men probably doing during the Reconquista?

What sorts of activities would "commerce" cover and why would they dislike it?

What part of the New World is being referred to here?

Why is the New World called a frontier? What were conditions like there?

Why would these men be attracted to this new area?

Asking questions is a part of active reading, but some questions require more brainpower from the reader. We would not truly be ready to *explain* the passage unless we can answer this second group of questions. To answer these, we have to do some "reading between the lines" and our answers would not all be the same. Some questions above require thinking deeply about connections the author does not directly state—for instance, why these men would dislike manual labor and business. Some require having background information—for example, knowing something about the history of Spain and about the geography of the time.

The first group of questions involves *reading for information.* The second group requires *reading for understanding.* Reading for understanding rather than just for facts requires a much deeper level of active questioning and thinking. Professor Mortimer Adler has given this explanation of this important difference:

> Both information and understanding are knowledge in some sense. Getting more information is learning, and so is coming to understand what you did not understand before. What is the difference? To be informed is to know simply that something is the case. To be enlightened is to know, in addition, what it is all about: why it is the case, what its connections are with other facts, in what respects it is the same and different, and so forth. Most of us are acquainted with this distinction in terms of the difference between being able to remember something and being able to explain it. If you remember what an author says, you have learned something from reading him. If what he says is true, you have even learned something about the world. But whether it is a fact about the book or the world, you have gained nothing but information if you have exercised only your memory. You have not been enlightened. That happens only when, in addition to knowing what an author says, you know what he means and why he says it. (From Mortimer Adler, *How to Read a Book,* pp. 35–36. Copyright © 1940, 1967.)

EXERCISE 5.3

Reading for Understanding

Work together in small discussion groups to complete these exercises.

■ PART A

For the questions that follow, put answers in your own words and add any examples that might make a point more clear.

1. Explain in what ways information and understanding are alike.

____

____

____

____

____

2. ". . . you have gained nothing but information if you have exercised only your memory. You have not been enlightened. That happens only when, in addition to knowing what an author says, you know what he means and why he says it." (¶2) Can you give an example from your own educational experience that would show the difference between being "informed" and being "enlightened"?

3. "Most of us are acquainted with this distinction [between information and understanding] in terms of the difference between being able to remember something and being able to explain it." (¶2) How do remembering and explaining differ? Can you come up with an example from your own experience, perhaps from school, where you remembered something (such as a formula or definition) but didn't understand it?

■ PART B

You read the selection "The Conquistadores" and completed an outline that included major detail. This involved you in reading for information and gave you knowledge of the basic facts on the topic. Here are some short passages from that selection, with questions that will involve you in reading more actively for understanding. Some may require you to seek some background information.

1. "For five centuries the Christian kingdoms of Spain had been trying to drive the North African Muslim Moors ("the Dark Ones," in Spanish) off the Iberian peninsula, and with the fall of Granada they succeeded." (¶1)

   a. Who were the Moors and where did they come from?

   b. Why would these two groups want to fight each other for so long?

2. "At first, Spanish hopes for America focused on the Caribbean and on finding a sea route to Asia. Gradually, however, word filtered back of rich kingdoms on the mainland." (¶2)

   a. Where would you find the Caribbean on a map?

   ____

   b. What was Columbus looking for originally? How does a map help explain why he didn't find it?

   ____
   ____
   ____

   c. Why did he name the people he found Indians?

   ____
   ____

   d. Was there already a sea route to India? What was so desirable about finding a new one?

   ____
   ____

   e. Whose kingdoms are being referred to here? What present-day areas are being referred to as "the mainland"?

   ____
   ____

   f. What kind of wealth did the "rich kingdoms" supposedly have? How accurate were the reports?

   ____
   ____
   ____

3. "Armed with horses and gunpowder and preceded by disease, the conquistadores quickly overpowered the Indians." (¶5)

   a. What does the author mean by "preceded by disease"? What had happened to the Indians?

   ____
   ____

b. What were the Indians armed with? Why was this a disadvantage?

____

____

4. "Nevertheless, the conquistadores achieved a kind of immortality." Which sentence from ¶6 most fully explains what this means?

   a. Because of a scarcity of Spanish women in the early days of the conquest, many conquistadores married Indian women.
   b. The soldiers who conquered Paraguay received three native women each.
   c. Cortes's soldiers in Mexico—who were forbidden to consort with pagan women—quickly had their lovers baptized into the Catholic faith.
   d. Their offspring, the "new race" of mestizos, formed a cultural and biological bridge between Latin America's European and Indian races.

■ PART C

The following statement appeared in a newspaper column about computers:

> The Compaq Presario 2254 has a 233 megahertz Advanced Micro Devices K6 processor; 32 megabytes of memory; a four-gigabyte hard drive; a 56K fax-modem; and a 64-bit 3-D graphics card.

Make up two groups of questions for this passage. The second group will be much harder to do.

1. Questions for information (answer these):

   a. ____
   b. ____
   c. ____

2. Questions for understanding (Can you think of any? Could you answer them?):

   a. ____
   b. ____
   c. ____

READING FOR INFORMATION AND UNDERSTANDING IN NEWSPAPERS

Newspapers aim to deliver information clearly and accurately. Reporters are trained to ask and answer the key questions that are part of active learning: Who? What? When? Where? Why? and How? However, even though articles stress factual information, stories will often suggest issues and ideas that require reading for understanding.

The subject in the next article is compared to one of the deprived children you read about earlier in Chapter 3. Write down anything you can remember about Genie and the other children:

____

____

____

____

____

____

____

As you answer the questions that relate to the facts of the case, think about what this story tells us of the conditions and effort that are needed to help children learn and use language successfully.

Girl's Pleas Are Wordless

by Raymond Smith

1 They are two girls whose stories gripped the nation. One was discovered chained to a bed in a Norco, California house; the other was found imprisoned in a small bedroom in Temple City nearly 30 years ago. The child rescued in Norco remains in Loma Linda University Medical Center as doctors evaluate her condition and try to decide how best to help her. The child was malnourished and unable to speak, communicating only with moans and small sounds. A linguist says doctors may have better luck dealing with her inability to speak than did the doctors who tried to help the girl rescued in 1970.

How long ago was the first child found?

Where is the child?

How did she communicate?

Reprinted by permission of the *Press-Enterprise,* Riverside, California. This article appeared in the September 12, 1999 edition.

Who is Genie?

When was she rescued?

Why was Genie studied?

2 "Genie," the girl from Temple City, had been imprisoned by her father, strapped into a harness and forced to sleep in an infant crib covered with wire mesh. During the day she was strapped to a potty seat, unable to move anything but her fingers and her toes. For years she was separated from a normal life, until a social worker discovered her plight. She was rescued from her captivity when she was 13. She could understand few words and could say only "Stopit" and "Nomore." She could barely walk, according to an account of her life. Researchers studied Genie, as they dubbed her, to see how she would learn to talk.

What must be done to help the child develop normally?

What will result from delays in learning?

■ *robustness:* strength; ability to keep on going

3 Learning to speak also is an important issue in the case of the six-year-old Norco girl discovered Tuesday. Police and a neighbor say the Norco child could communicate only with moans and other small sounds. Breaking that language barrier will be crucial as doctors and therapists work to build a more normal life for the youngster, a speech expert said. Language skills are a critical part of interaction with others and overall human development, said Mabel Rice, a professor of speech, language and hearing at the University of Kansas. Delays in learning those skills can permanently stunt a person's grasp and use of language, she said. Still, even extreme obstacles can be overcome in some cases. "There's just a huge amount of robustness in human language capabilities," Rice said.

Found by Accident

How was Genie's situation discovered?

How was the Norco child's situation found out?

How much did the child weigh?

4 There are similarities between the two cases, though they are separated by almost 30 years. Genie's plight was discovered almost by accident when her mother, who was nearly blind, walked into a Los Angeles County Social Services office. Genie's mother was looking for the offices for services for the blind to get help for herself. The Norco child was discovered when Riverside County sheriff's deputies went to a home to check out a report of a missing child. Deputies found the malnourished girl wearing only a diaper. She weighed 30 pounds.

Emotional Problems

■ *linguistic:* relating to language

What type of problems will the child need treatment for?

5 The doctor treating the girl, Clare Sheridan, said that linguistic abilities are one aspect of treatment that would be needed for a child brought up in isolation. Sheridan said she could not comment directly on the treatment of the girl, but she did say that any child subjected to this type of neglect would need treatment for physical problems, intellectual problems—such as linguistic skills—and emotional problems.

6 The most serious of the three would be the emotional problems, she said. "Without anyone to emotionally bond with at the earliest ages, a child would be forced to repress all their emotions," she said. "What happens is they pretty much stop feeling them at all." Until the amount of isolation and neglect the child endured has been ascertained, it would be impossible to say how much treatment would be required, Sheridan said. One of the first steps for people trying to help the girl is to gain her trust, Rice said. "She's been ripped out of the only familiarity she's used to, as bad as that was," Rice said.

What will result from a lack of an emotional bond?

■ *ascertained:* determined

What first step needs to be taken?

Retardation Feared

7 According to a 1997 Nova program on PBS, Genie wound up in an adult foster care home in Southern California. Genie was wearing a diaper when she was rescued and weighed 59 pounds. Genie's mother was acquitted of child abuse. Her father, blamed for Genie's treatment, killed himself the morning he was to appear in court to face abuse charges. He reportedly had imprisoned his daughter because he thought she was retarded and feared that people would exploit her, according to the 1993 book "Genie: An Abused Child's Flight From Silence," by Russ Rymer.

What did Genie's father do?

Why did her father treat Genie the way he did?

8 Doctors at Loma Linda University Medical Center said the Norco child is responding to a positive environment and attention. Determining the best approach for treatment could take weeks or even months. Rice, who has heard of the Norco case but is not involved in the girl's treatment, said the years from age 8 to 12 are critical for language development. There is no way yet to know whether the child can make up for missed time, Rice said. Vocabulary can be learned, even in some cases involving severe neglect. But understanding sentence structure, tenses and the need for nouns and verbs might be lost forever if language skills are not developed soon enough, Rice said.

How is the Norco child progressing?

Which years are the key to language development?

What will be lost if language skills don't develop early?

9 In Genie's case, she eventually learned to use words but could never form full sentences. "The outlook for the Norco girl is probably better because this child is younger, but it won't be an easy thing," Rice said. Developing language skills can be difficult, even for otherwise bright people, Rice said. Children without proper skills have a harder time making friends and expressing themselves. The resulting frustration can make children withdraw, leading to perceptions that they are immature or not particularly intelligent, she said.

How much progress was Genie able to make?

What happens to children who lack proper language skills?

EXERCISE 5.4

Reading for Information and Understanding

■ PART A Reading for Information

The article has a mixture of paragraphs organized around topics and paragraphs with a main idea. For the five paragraphs below, identify two that have a topical organization by selecting answer *e.* For the three main idea paragraphs, select the main idea sentence from choices *a* through *d.* Reread the paragraphs carefully before answering.

1. (¶2) a. Genie had been imprisoned by her father, strapped into a harness and forced to sleep in an infant crib covered with wire mesh.
   b. She was rescued from her captivity when she was 13.
   c. She could understand few words and could say only "Stopit" and "Nomore."
   d. Researchers studied Genie, as they dubbed her, to see how she would learn to talk.
   e. None of the above. This paragraph has a topical organization.
2. (¶4) a. There are similarities between the two cases, though separated by almost 30 years.
   b. Genie's plight was discovered by accident.
   c. Genie's mother was seeking services for the blind to get help for herself.
   d. Deputies found the malnourished girl who weighed only 30 pounds.
   e. None of the above. This paragraph has a topical organization.
3. (¶6) a. The most serious of the three would be the emotional problems.
   b. It would be impossible to say how much treatment would be required.
   c. One of the first steps for people trying to help the girl is to gain her trust.
   d. "She's been ripped out of the only familiarity she's used to, as bad as that was."
   e. None of the above. This paragraph has a topical organization.
4. (¶7) a. Genie wound up in an adult foster care home in southern California.
   b. Genie was wearing a diaper when she was rescued and weighed 59 pounds.

c. Her father killed himself the morning he was to appear in court to face abuse charges.

d. He imprisoned his daughter because he thought she was retarded and feared that people would exploit her.

e. None of the above. This paragraph has a topical organization.

5. (¶9) a. In Genie's case, she learned to use words but could never form full sentences.

b. The outlook for the Norco girl is probably better because this child is younger, but it won't be an easy thing.

c. Developing language skills can be difficult, even for otherwise bright people.

d. Frustration can make children withdraw, leading to perceptions that they are immature or not particularly intelligent.

e. None of the above. This paragraph has a topical organization.

■ PART B Reading for Understanding

Discuss the following in small groups. Then write your own responses to the questions.

> Developing language skills can be difficult, even for otherwise bright people. Children without proper skills have a harder time making friends and expressing themselves. The resulting frustration can make children withdraw, leading to perceptions that they are immature or not particularly intelligent.

1. According to this passage from ¶9, what is the relationship between language skills and intelligence?

____

2. What connection exists between language skills and social skills?

____

3. Why, according to ¶6, would the child's most serious problem be emotional?

____

4. What do you think causes people to treat children in such a manner and what might be done to prevent such tragedies?

____

____

MAKING INFERENCES IN READING

Imagine the following situations:

A. You return home from a vacation. A large box has been pulled up to the kitchen window. Inside, a stool has been moved in front of the kitchen cabinets. You discover that all the cookies and candy bars in the cabinets are gone, as are the ice cream bars in the refrigerator. A jar filled with loose change is missing.

B. You're gone for the weekend. When you return Sunday night, you find the back door has been pried open. All the beverages and TV dinners in the refrigerator are gone. The living room TV is on; empty beer and soda cans, cigarette butts, and the remains of TV dinners litter the floor.

C. You go to the market Saturday morning, at the same time you always do. You return home an hour later to find that your front door has been kicked in. Every drawer in the bedroom dresser is open. Jewelry and cash have been taken along with your TV, stereo components, computer, and telephone.

Now match these conclusions with the above and think of some reasons for your choices.

_____ Professional thieves have robbed you.
_____ Some young neighborhood kids got into your home.
_____ Teenagers partied in your house.

Situation A indicates the presence of young kids. We would decide this on the basis of what was taken (candy, cookies, small change) and from the size of the thieves (needing a box to reach things). It's also likely they are neighborhood kids who would have a chance to observe you getting ready for the vacation. Situation B points toward teenagers. Nothing of real value was taken—the motive for the break-in is to eat, drink, and have fun. Situation C looks like the work of professionals. They have been watching your routine. Extreme force has been used to enter. Items of value are taken swiftly. The fact that all the dresser drawers are open indicates a professional thief at work. They pull out drawers starting at the bottom to save the time it takes to push each drawer back in to look at the next.

In situations like the above, we are making *inferences:* reasonable guesses and conclusions drawn from the available evidence. Inferences are what is probable or most likely, the conclusion that best fits with and explains the evidence. In situation A above, we could have concluded that it was not children but a bunch of hungry dwarfs who had gotten into the house, but that would be a lot less likely to happen.

All of us make inferences every day throughout our lives. From our experiences as children, we draw conclusions about dangers—fire, for example, or busy highways—and learn to avoid them if we are to survive. In later life we decide about careers we want to follow, places we want to live, or relationships (marriage, friendships, etc.) we want to continue or end. These decisions require making judgments and drawing conclusions, often on a limited amount of evidence.

We must be able to make sound inferences in reading for understanding. This can be hard work, especially since authors sometimes take for granted that we are making connections between ideas and don't directly state them. When we must "read between the lines," make reasonable guesses, or draw conclusions, we are making inferences. For example, the previous exercise had this passage:

> At first, Spanish hopes for America focused on the Caribbean and on finding a sea route to Asia. Gradually, however, word filtered back of rich kingdoms on the mainland.

The author doesn't directly state that the Spanish gave up the search for a sea route, but we would make that inference on the basis of the information in the rest of the paragraph that relates to the conquest of the mainland.

You will do a lot of work in later chapters in this text with reading skills that require using inference. The exercise below will give you some practice on using inference before you move on to other materials.

EXERCISE 5.5

Making Inferences from Cartoons

Cartoons, jokes, and other kinds of humor often require us to make inferences. We may have to make reasonable guesses about what has happened or why, or we may have to make connections between characters. Working together in small groups, read the following cartoons, examine the drawings carefully, and then answer the questions on inference that follow.

1. What is the relationship between the young people in the cartoon? How do you know?

____

____

2. To whom is the man related? How do you know?

____

____

3. What is the next line that the girl will say? What is she in the process of doing?

____

____

4. What is the girl going to wish for?

____

____

5. Why would she make that particular wish?

____

____

1. What time is this taking place? How do you know?

____

____

2. Is the general happy or sad? How do you know?

____

____

3. Where has the general been? How do you know?

____

____

4. What is the relationship between the general and the woman?

____

____

5. Does the woman seem supportive or unsupportive of the general? How do you know?

____

____

6. What's the real answer to the woman's question?

____

____

7. What happened? Why does the general not want to talk about it?

____

____

Reading stories and novels can be hard because they make us do a lot of reading between the lines. We decide what characters are like from what they say and do, and from what others say about them. The following story deals with an incident involving a young girl in school. As you read, think of what words you would use to describe the people involved. Look up the meanings of any words you aren't sure of.

The Scholarship Jacket

by Marta Salinas

1 The small Texas school that I attended carried out a tradition every year during the eighth grade graduation; a beautiful gold and green jacket, the school colors, was awarded to the class valedictorian, the student who had maintained the highest grades for eight years. The scholar-

ship jacket had a big gold S on the left front side and the winner's name was written in gold letters on the pocket.

2 My oldest sister Rosie had won the jacket a few years back and I fully expected to win also. I was fourteen and in the eighth grade. I had been a straight A student since the first grade, and the last year I had looked forward to owning that jacket. My father was a farm laborer who couldn't earn enough money feed eight children, so when I was six I was given to my grandparents to raise. We couldn't participate in sports at school because there were registration fees, uniform costs, and trips out of town; so even though we were quite agile and athletic, there would never be a sports school jacket for us. This one, the scholarship jacket, was our only chance.

3 In May, close to graduation, spring fever struck, and no one paid any attention in class; instead we stared out the windows and at each other, wanting to speed up the last few weeks of school. I despaired every time I looked in the mirror. Pencil thin, not a curve anywhere, I was called "Beanpole" and "String Bean" and I knew that's what I looked like. A flat chest, no hips, and a brain, that's what I had. That really isn't much for a fourteen-year-old to work with, I thought, as I absentmindedly wandered from my history class to the gym. Another hour of sweating in basketball and displaying my toothpick legs was coming up. Then I remembered my P.E. shorts were still in a bag under my desk where I'd forgotten them. I had to walk all the way back and get them. Coach Thompson was a real bear if anyone wasn't dressed for P.E. She had said I was a good forward and once she even tried to talk Grandma into letting me join the team. Grandma, of course, said no.

4 I was almost back at my classroom's door when I heard angry voices and arguing. I stopped. I didn't mean to eavesdrop; I just hesitated, not knowing what to do. I needed those shorts and I was going to be late, but I didn't want to interrupt an argument between my teachers. I recognized the voices: Mr. Schmidt, my history teacher, and Mr. Boone, my math teacher. They seemed to be arguing about me. I couldn't believe it. I still remember the shock that rooted me flat against the wall as if I were trying to blend in with the graffiti written there.

5 "I refuse to do it! I don't care who her father is, her grades don't even begin to compare to Marta's. I won't lie or falsify records. Marta has a straight A plus average and you know it." That was Mr. Schmidt and he sounded very angry. Mr. Boone's voice sounded calm and quiet.

6 "Look, Joann's father is not only on the Board, he owns the only store in town; we could say it was a close tie and—"

7 The pounding in my ears drowned out the rest of the words, only a word here and there filtered through. ". . . Marta is Mexican. . . .

resign. . . . won't do it. . . ." Mr. Schmidt came rushing out, and luckily for me went down the opposite way toward the auditorium, so he didn't see me. Shaking, I waited a few minutes and then went in and grabbed my bag and fled from the room. Mr. Boone looked up when I came in but didn't say anything. To this day I don't remember if I got in trouble in P.E. for being late or how I made it through the rest of the afternoon. I went home very sad and cried into my pillow that night so Grandmother wouldn't hear me. It seemed a cruel coincidence that I had overheard that conversation.

8 The next day when the principal called me into his office, I knew what it would be about. He looked uncomfortable and unhappy. I decided I wasn't going to make it any easier for him so I looked him straight in the eye. He looked away and fidgeted with the papers on his desk. "Marta," he said, "there's been a change in policy this year regarding the scholarship jacket. As you know, it has always been free." He cleared his throat and continued. "This year the Board decided to charge fifteen dollars—which still won't cover the complete cost of the jacket."

9 I stared at him in shock and a small sound of dismay escaped my throat. I hadn't expected this. He still avoided looking in my eyes.

10 "So if you are unable to pay the fifteen dollars for the jacket, it will be given to the next one in line."

11 Standing with all the dignity I could muster, I said, "I'll speak to my grandfather about it, sir, and let you know tomorrow." I cried on the walk home from the bus stop. The dirt road was a quarter of a mile from the highway, so by the time I got home, my eyes were red and puffy.

12 "Where's Grandpa?" I asked Grandma, looking down at the floor so she wouldn't ask me why I'd been crying. She was sewing on a quilt and didn't look up.

13 "I think he's out back working in the bean field."

14 I went outside and looked out at the fields. There he was. I could see him walking between the rows, his body bent over the little plants, hoe in hand. I walked slowly out to him, trying to think how I could best ask him for the money. There was a cool breeze blowing and a sweet smell of mesquite in the air, but I didn't appreciate it. I kicked at a dirt clod. I wanted that jacket so much. It was more than just being a valedictorian and giving a little thank you speech for the jacket on graduation night. It represented eight years of hard work and expectation. I knew I had to be honest with Grandpa; it was my only chance. He saw me and looked up.

15 He waited for me to speak. I cleared my throat nervously and clasped my hands behind my back so he wouldn't see them shaking. "Grandpa, I have a big favor to ask you," I said in Spanish, the only lan-

guage he knew. He still waited silently. I tried again. "Grandpa, this year the principal said the scholarship jacket is not going to be free. It's going to cost fifteen dollars and I have to take the money in tomorrow, otherwise it'll be given to someone else." The last words came out in an eager rush. Grandpa straightened up tiredly and leaned his chin on the hoe handle. He looked out over the field that was filled with the tiny green bean plants. I waited, desperately hoping he'd say I could have the money.

16 He turned to me and asked quietly, "What does a scholarship jacket mean?"

17 I answered quickly; maybe there was a chance. "It means you've earned it by having the highest grades for eight years and that's why they're giving it to you." Too late I realized the significance of my words. Grandpa knew that I understood it was not a matter of money. It wasn't that. He went back to hoeing the weeds that sprang up between the delicate little bean plants. It was a time consuming job; sometimes the small shoots were right next to each other. Finally he spoke again.

18 "Then if you pay for it, Marta, it's not a scholarship jacket, is it? Tell your principal I will not pay the fifteen dollars."

19 I walked back to the house and locked myself in the bathroom for a long time. I was angry with Grandfather even though I knew he was right, and I was angry with the Board, whoever they were. Why did they have to change the rules just when it was my turn to win the jacket?

20 It was a very sad and withdrawn girl who dragged into the principal's office the next day. This time he did look me in the eyes.

21 "What did your grandfather say?"

22 I sat very straight in my chair.

23 "He said to tell you he won't pay the fifteen dollars."

24 The principal muttered something I couldn't understand under his breath, and walked over to the window. He stood looking out at something outside. He looked bigger than usual when he stood up; he was a tall gaunt man with gray hair, and I watched the back of his head while I waited for him to speak.

25 "Why?" he finally asked. "Your grandfather has the money. Doesn't he own a small bean farm?"

26 I looked at him, forcing my eyes to stay dry. "He said if I had to pay for it, then it wouldn't be a scholarship jacket," I said and stood up to leave. "I guess you'll just have to give it to Joann." I hadn't meant to say that; it had just slipped out. I was almost to the door when he stopped me.

27 "Marta—wait."

28 I turned and looked at him, waiting. What did he want now? I could feel my heart pounding. Something bitter and vile tasting was

coming up in my mouth; I was afraid I was going to be sick. I didn't need any sympathy speeches. He sighed loudly and went back to his big desk. He looked at me, biting his lip, as if thinking.

29 "Okay, damn it. We'll make an exception in your case. I'll tell the Board, you'll get your jacket."

30 I could hardly believe it. I spoke in a trembling rush. "Oh, thank you, sir!" Suddenly I felt great. I didn't know about adrenaline in those days, but I knew something was pumping through me, making me feel as tall as the sky. I wanted to yell, jump, run the mile, do something. I ran out so I could cry in the hall where there was no one to see me. At the end of the day, Mr. Schmidt winked at me and said, "I hear you're getting a scholarship jacket this year."

31 His face looked as happy and innocent as a baby's, but I knew better. Without answering I gave him a quick hug and ran to the bus. I cried on the walk home again, but this time because I was so happy. I couldn't wait to tell Grandpa and ran straight to the field. I joined him in the row where he was working and without saying anything I crouched down and started pulling up the weeds with my hands. Grandpa worked alongside me for a few minutes, but he didn't ask what had happened. After I had a little pile of weeds between the rows, I stood up and faced him.

32 "The principal said he's making an exception for me, Grandpa, and I'm getting the jacket after all. That's after I told him what you said."

33 Grandpa didn't say anything, he just gave me a pat on the shoulder and a smile. He pulled out the crumpled red handkerchief that he always carried in his back pocket and wiped the sweat off his forehead.

34 "Better go see if your grandmother needs any help with supper."

35 I gave him a big grin. He didn't fool me. I skipped and ran back to the house whistling some silly tune.

EXERCISE 5.6

Making Inferences in Story Reading

For each sentence, write *Yes* if it is an inference strongly suggested by the reading and *No* if is not. Then explain your choice by telling your reasoning and giving evidence for it.

1. _____ Marta's school is located in a large city.

   Reasoning/evidence: ______________________________

   ____

2. _____ The principal believes the jacket fee policy is right and just.

Reasoning/evidence: ______________________________

____

3. _____ Grandfather has strong beliefs about what is right and just.

Reasoning/evidence: ______________________________

____

4. _____ Marta is a better student than Rosie was.

Reasoning/evidence: ______________________________

____

5. _____ Mr. Boone shows some prejudices.

Reasoning/evidence: ______________________________

____

6. _____ Marta has more than one sister.

Reasoning/evidence: ______________________________

____

7. _____ Joann is really not a very good student.

Reasoning/evidence: ______________________________

____

8. _____ Grandfather would respect Mr. Boone, described as "calm and quiet," more than Mr. Schmidt, who is "very angry."

Reasoning/evidence: ______________________________

____

9. _____ Mr. Boone knows Marta overheard the conversation.

Reasoning/evidence: ______________________________

____

10. _____ Grandfather is very proud and happy that Marta will be given the jacket.

Reasoning/evidence: ______________________________

____

FACTS AND OPINIONS

In reading for information, you are reading mainly for *facts*—statements that we agree on because they can be proved by our senses, by data from scientific studies, or from the records of history. The following are all examples of factual statements:

The sun is 93 million miles from the earth.

Ronald Reagan was elected president in 1980.

Plants give off carbon dioxide into the air.

When we read for understanding, we may find that we disagree about statements. The evidence may be mixed or there may not be enough evidence to be sure. Statements that can't be proved completely we call *opinions* or *judgments.* Even if most people agree on it, a statement is still an opinion as long as an opposite viewpoint can be supported. Inferences are examples of opinion. They are only probable or highly likely; they are not "sure things." They are not facts, though they are based on facts, and some inferences can be better supported than others. Some opinions involve the truth of what really happened. For example, the facts surrounding the murders of John F. Kennedy and Martin Luther King, Jr. continue to be debated. Some opinions show judgments of value—we think a movie or book is good whereas someone else might think it poor entertainment. Many of our opinions are about what actions we should take—for example, to vote for one candidate over another. These are indicated by words like *should, must, ought to* and supported by reasons that we give.

EXERCISE 5.7

Telling Facts from Opinions

The following pairs have one sentence that is factual and one that is opinion. Underline the factual statement in each pair.

1. Belinda got an A on her last biology exam.
   Belinda is an excellent student.
2. *Rocky* is a heartwarming and inspiring story.
   Rocky tells the story of a washed-up fighter who becomes the champ.
3. We should allow no more commercial development of agriculture land.
   Some farmland is being turned into housing developments.

4. The Democrats won the majority of seats in the last state election.
   Next year, you should vote Republican.
5. Pauline painted her bedroom light blue.
   Light blue is a more restful color than light green.
6. William Shakespeare wrote Hamlet and Macbeth.
   Shakespeare is the greatest writer of all time.
7. You should have a physical every year.
   Many people have a routine checkup each year.
8. Shauna thinks Brett acts like a big jerk.
   The truth is that Brett acts like a big jerk.
9. The *Titanic* sank after it collided with an iceberg.
   It was the captain's fault alone that the *Titanic* sank.
10. More vanilla is sold than any other flavor of ice cream.
    Vanilla is the best flavor of ice cream.

Our constitution ensures that we all have a right to our own opinions, but does that mean that all opinions are equally good? Some opinions are strictly a matter of personal taste: "Vanilla is the best flavor of ice cream." In education and in public discussions, however, opinions are rated as weak or strong depending on how reasonable they are and how strong the supporting evidence is. If, for example, we want to express an opinion on a candidate or a political issue—that someone can't be trusted or gun control laws should be passed—we must give evidence or reasons for our views.

EXERCISE 5.8

Supporting Opinions with Evidence

When we read stories or see movies, we often use inference to make opinions about characters. Here are some opinions about Marta in "The Scholarship Jacket." Decide if the opinion is well supported by asking these questions: Does the evidence really relate to the opinion? Is there evidence that points to a different conclusion? Then circle either *Agree* or *Disagree* for each of the following and explain your decision. If you disagree, include any evidence that supports the opposite of the stated opinion.

1. Marta dislikes physical activities.
   Evidence: She doesn't go out for sports.
   Agree Disagree

Explanation: ____

____

2. Marta is smart.

Evidence: She has been a straight A student for eight years and has the highest average.

Agree Disagree

Explanation: ____

____

3. Marta has very low self-esteem.

Evidence: Her family gave her away. She doesn't get a chance to succeed at sports. She's not beautiful.

Agree Disagree

Explanation: ____

____

4. Marta will give in somewhat on her beliefs on what is right.

Evidence: She tells the principal she will talk to her grandfather. She tries to convince her grandfather to pay for the jacket "even though I knew he was right."

Agree Disagree

Explanation: ____

____

5 Marta wants to be recognized for her work.

Evidence: She "looked forward to owning that jacket"; "the scholarship jacket was our only chance"; "I wanted that jacket so much; It represented eight years of hard work."

Agree Disagree

Explanation: ____

____

6. Marta is snoopy.

Evidence: She sneaks near the classroom and listens to the conversation between her teachers.

Agree Disagree

Explanation: ____

____

7. Marta is usually lazy and inattentive.

   Evidence: She is just like her classmates: "spring fever struck, and no one paid any attention in class; instead we stared out the windows and at each other."

   Agree Disagree

   Explanation: ______________________________

   ____

8. Marta is not vain about her looks.

   Evidence: Marta "despaired every time I looked in the mirror." She is called "Beanpole" and "String Bean" and says "I knew that's what I looked like."

   Agree Disagree

   Explanation: ______________________________

   ____

9. Marta is jealous of others.

   Evidence: She doesn't think it's fair that Joann should get the jacket. She wants to outdo her sister Rosie's accomplishments.

   Agree Disagree

   Explanation: ______________________________

   ____

10. Marta is respectful of her elders.

    Evidence: She doesn't talk back to her teachers or her principal. She accepts the decisions of her grandparents.

    Agree Disagree

    Explanation: ______________________________

    ____

PURPOSE AND TONE

Two important terms allow us to talk about how writers and readers connect through written materials. *Purpose* refers to why the author is writing: to give you information, to prove the truth about something, or to try to persuade you to do something. *Tone* is a term we are familiar with in daily life. We apply it, for example, to the way people speak to us; a tone of voice can be described, for example, as rude, comforting, hostile, or friendly. We also apply the term to a writer's attitude about the subject and the reader—for example, lighthearted or serious, humorous or angry, matter-of-fact or emotional.

These terms have a close connection with inference. Usually an author does not directly state the purpose; it may be obvious or, in some cases, we have to infer what an author is up to. Tone is something we always must infer. We must pay careful attention to the author's choice of words to decide what tone is being conveyed. Often a writer has a choice of words that may reveal positive or negative feelings. For example, a writer could choose to describe a woman in high society as "sophisticated" or "snobbish." The first carries a tone of approval; the second conveys disapproval.

Purpose and tone are also closely connected with fact and opinion. If the purpose is simply to give information, the material will be mainly factual; if opinions are included, they will be reported rather than expressed. Writing that expresses opinions is largely aimed at more than just giving information; it aims to convince the reader of the truth about something or persuade the reader to act. An author's purpose also often determines the tone that writing conveys. For example, factual, informational writing would usually be described as "objective," "matter-of-fact," or "neutral." Purposes that involve opinions and emotions would have much more emotional tones.

EXERCISE 5.9

Determining Purpose and Tone in Writing

■ PART A

In the paragraphs and passages you have read from textbooks, the author's purpose has been mainly to give information, and thus we would describe the tone as generally neutral and matter-of-fact. In some of the articles, however, opinion and feeling have played a role and a more emotional tone has been conveyed. For each of these readings, three purposes have been listed, some of which are more important than others. Rate each group as follows:

1 the author's primary purpose
2 a purpose, but secondary to the first
3 the least important purpose or not a purpose

1. "When Others Let Go, Hang On and Win" by Harvey Mackay (Chapter 1)
   _____ entertain with information about successful people
   _____ show the reader that success is possible
   _____ persuade the reader to adopt a never-give-up attitude

2. "Gang Culture Gripped Young Teen, But High School Grad Emerges" (Chapter 1)
    _____ tell the facts about a student who changed directions
    _____ emphasize how students' lives can be turned around
    _____ persuade gang members to give up the gang life
3. "Famine in Africa" by Michael Bradshaw (Chapter 2)
    _____ give information about famines, especially those in Africa
    _____ convince the reader that famines are bad
    _____ persuade the reader to contribute to organizations fighting famine
4. "Kicking Asphalt" by Jodi Garber (Chapter 3)
    _____ convince the reader that Kickbikes give the best workouts
    _____ get the reader to buy a Kickbike
    _____ give information about a new and useful exercise/training device
5. "The Effects of Illiteracy in the Workplace" by Nadine Rosenthal (Chapter 3)
    _____ describe the skills needed in the workplace
    _____ show through examples that illiteracy leads to workplace problems
    _____ persuade readers that literacy programs along with other solutions are needed

■ PART B

Match the description of tone on the right that you think best describes the reading on the left:

_____ 1. "The Effects of Illiteracy"

_____ 2. "Kicking Asphalt"

_____ 3. "Famine in Africa"

_____ 4. "Gang Culture Gripped Young Teen"

_____ 5. "When Others Let Go"

a. lighthearted in an informative way
b. optimistic and enthusiastic
c. serious and concerned
d. objective and scientific
e. pleased and approving

■ PART C

Determine the tone of each sentence by looking carefully at the word choices. Write *Positive* for the sentence in each group that shows a tone of approval, *Negative* for the one that reveals disapproval, and *Neutral* for the one that conveys no feelings.

EXAMPLE

Neutral ______ Bryan is 5 feet 8 inches and weighs 215 pounds.

Positive ______ Bryan is compact and stocky.

Negative ______ Bryan is short and fat.

1. ______ Manny is a grade grubber.

______ Manny has a straight-A average.

______ Manny is a brilliant student.

2. ______ The Miami Dolphins choked up and blew the play-off game.

______ The Miami Dolphins played valiantly in their one-point loss.

______ The Miami Dolphins lost the play-off game by a point.

3. ______ Bruce Willis's new action-jammed movie opened this month.

______ Bruce Willis is appearing in a new adventure movie this month.

______ Bruce Willis is mugging his way through a boring film this month.

4. ______ Cecelia bought a new Porsche for $90,000.

______ Cecelia tossed away $90,000 on a new Porsche.

______ Cecelia invested $90,000 in buying a new Porsche.

5. ______ The new shopping mall has added an exciting four acres to the city.

______ The new strip mall has eaten up some more valuable land.

______ The new shopping center has stores covering four acres.

Active Learning

THE MOTIVATION TO SUCCEED

The history of America continues to be one of a country of great diversity in language, ethnic backgrounds, and economic circumstances. The college population reflects this diversity, containing students who belong to minority groups, come from other language backgrounds, are returning to school after a long time, or have physical or learning handicaps. As a result, many students face a variety of obstacles on their road to success.

EXERCISE 5.10

Becoming an Active Learner

This is the oral history of an adult reader who was able to overcome problems caused by reading difficulties, both in his personal life and on the job. Before you read the article, write down some observations about your own educational experiences and background.

James Rich

1 I've always had a problem with reading. I lived with my grandparents in South Carolina and went up to third grade there, then I went to New York to live with my mother. I was terrified going to school in New York because it was a big school with kids of all ethnic groups. I was shy and quiet so my teacher, who had thirty-five kids in the classroom, was happy to have a kid who didn't give her any trouble. Unfortunately, she never helped me with my reading. We moved a lot and I changed from one school to another, so I never got to feel comfortable. I just didn't open up in school.

2 My mother only had a fourth-grade education, but she could read. She worked long hours doing domestic work, so I didn't see her much. Actually, no one I knew read much, no teachers ever encouraged me, and no one ever picked me out to talk to about reading. In 1955, when I was in the sixth grade, I moved back to South Carolina and began school there once again. The kids were pretty sharp and I couldn't keep up. It was an all-black school with all-black teachers who were strict and very traditional. They made the kids go up to the board and do their math, for example, and there weren't too many kids in the classroom. I was so far behind I quit school to go to work. At that point I probably read at second- or third-grade level.

3 Soon I moved back to New York to live with my father. He had a third grade education, but he was a hardworking man, very determined, very ambitious. He read the Bible and taught Bible school. I stayed away from the school because they made us read out loud to each other, and I didn't want to be embarrassed.

4 By the time I was eighteen, I got a girl pregnant, got married, and went to work. Eventually we had ten children together. During that time I would try to read occasionally by getting the newspaper and trying to pick out as many words as I could and guess the rest. I became good at picking up the drift of an article. My wife had finished high school and read very well. When she read a book or newspaper article to me, I'd listen carefully and remember what I heard because I have a very good memory.

5 I worked two jobs most of the time I was married, and I memorized as many words as I could on my jobs. For a while I worked as a chemical operator in a plant mixing chemicals and sending samples to the lab. They would send back written instructions detailing how much acid, let's say, to put into the chemical and at what temperature. It could explode if the temperature was too high. No one knew I couldn't read. I got a helper to read things to me sometimes, and other times I would call the lab up and say, "The instructions got wet, what do they say?" It took a tremendous amount of my energy just to maintain.

6 Finally, at age forty, I went back to school, to adult education. The most difficult thing for me was sitting and reading one word at a time like I was a kid. It just didn't feel good, especially since I moved pretty well in the world; it was hard on my ego, on my self-esteem. But I struggled long and hard with my reading for a number of years and finally got good enough to work towards my high school equivalency diploma, my G.E.D.

7 I work better when I set a goal, so six months before my forty-fifth birthday I decided I wanted to get my G.E.D by that date. I got up really early every morning and studied, and had three tutors who each studied with me one night a week. Fortunately, I was able to connect up with the local adult literacy program so the tutors were free. With the tutors helping me figure out how to read the paragraphs and answer the questions, I slowly moved through the G.E.D study books. I put in an incredible amount of work and actually got my G.E.D a month ahead of time!

8 Now I'm attending a community college and I'm beginning to understand how a person learns and knows how to read. My first class was a public speaking class because speaking is one of my strong interests—I had already been through the Toastmasters program. Next, I learned how to read articles and write papers on them. I had decided to be honest with the teachers about my background, so I went up and told my

first writing teacher what a bad speller I was. She really tried hard with me. She thought my content was pretty good, and just corrected my spelling. Now my spelling is getting better, and I've gone from writing three, four, five words at a time to writing whole essays. I use a dictionary, but spelling is still the most difficult thing. Now I can ask someone how to spell a word and I don't feel bad because I know I've already given it my best.

9 The most important thing I've learned is that if I want to learn how to read, I have to read a lot. I have to face where I'm at to start moving from here. I have a lot of endurance because I'm a long-distance runner; running helps me focus and clear my head. In turn, reading has helped my running—I now have more information available to me about running. If you can read, you can do almost anything.

10 Reading has made me a lot more aware of the world around me. For instance, with issues and events, I don't have to just listen to the news and only hear what others say, I can also read and form my own opinions. I started voting in '84 after I went back to school by educating myself on the issues with my tutors. For the last few years I've been an inspector at the polls.

11 The overall result of reading is that it has enriched my life and changed my relationships with people. I can be a lot more open and comfortable with people because I'm not trying to hide anything. I have new and different kinds of friends now who I've met at school or through my various activities. People used to wonder what was wrong with me because I was so closed. Reading has a hell of a lot to do with your personality. (Rosenthal, pp. 128–30.)

1. List some of the factors and experiences (¶s 1–3) that had negative effects on James Rich's education in his early life.

____

____

____

____

2. List the strategies (¶4–5) that James Rich used to make up for his lack of vocabulary and comprehension skills. How effective were these?

____

____

____

____

3. What inferences would you draw about the possible success of the plan James Rich developed (¶7) to reach his goal of getting the G.E.D?

____

____

4. What example (¶5) is given of a dangerous consequence that might happen as a result of a lack of reading skills on the job?

____

____

5. Discuss the ways James Rich's experiences with reading affected his
   a. running (¶9)

   ____

   ____

   b. civic participation (¶10)

   ____

   ____

   c. personality and relationships (¶11)

   ____

   ____

   d. What evidence in ¶10 would indicate that James Rich has developed some active learning strategies?

   ____

   ____

6. Which of the following best describes the author's purpose in writing this account?
   a. get the reader to sympathize with him over the obstacles in his life
   b. share his experiences regarding reading with others
   c. express his complaints about the way life has treated him
7. Which of the following best describes the author's tone in writing this account?
   a. humorous and lighthearted
   b. thoughtful and serious
   c. angry and sarcastic

Reading Portfolio

READING FOR UNDERSTANDING

In your last portfolio assignment, you were told to keep the article you used for further use. You followed reading strategies that helped you find the topic, the main idea, and the major details. Now do the following:

1. Review your outline and read the article again. As you read, ask yourself if you really understand the information well enough to explain it to a friend.
2. Locate up to five passages in the article that require reading for understanding. For each passage, write an explanation in your own words. If you can't, indicate what information or concepts you think you would need to know in order to understand the ideas fully.

CHAPTER 6

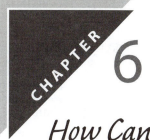

How Can I Build Vocabulary?

Using Context and Word Parts

After reading this chapter, you will know the answers to these questions:

- What signals indicate a definition in the text?
- What is a glossary and where is it located?
- What are context clues and how are they used?
- How does writing context sentences increase vocabulary?
- What are word parts and how do they help build vocabulary?
- What are the costs of illiteracy in the workplace?

Vocabulary is a very important part of comprehension. If you don't know a lot of the words on the page, it's hard to read for facts and information. It's even more difficult to read with deep understanding. There are a number of techniques you can use that will help you to learn and remember new words.

DEFINITIONS IN THE TEXT

Sometimes an author will help you out by giving the definition of the word right in the text. The definition can be indicated by quotation marks, dashes, colons, boldface type, underlining, or italics. Definitions are often given in textbooks. A number of the passages that you studied in the last few chapters used this technique. Sometimes a definition is given in a single sentence:

> Experts call the affliction "teleconditioning": a change in behavior brought on by watching TV.

Here the definition after the colon tells us what teleconditioning means. Sometimes the definition is in a separate sentence or may need more than one sentence:

> While several processes play an important role in the formation of prejudices, perhaps the most important of these involves the formation and impact of **stereotypes.** Stereotypes are cognitive frameworks consisting of knowledge about specific groups—frameworks suggesting that by and large, all members of these groups possess certain traits.

Even when a definition is given, there may be a problem in truly understanding it. For instance, a student could memorize the definition of stereotype without really understanding what was meant by "a cognitive framework consisting of knowledge about specific groups." Sometimes the text will give more explanations or helpful examples to make the meaning clear. In any case, always try to get to the point where you can explain the term so that you're sure you really understand it.

Some definitions may be hard to spot, especially if the definition comes before the term or is spread out before and after. Look carefully at this example:

> Stone Age skulls containing neatly drilled holes have been uncovered by archaeologists in Europe and South America. One colorful explanation for such operations, known as "trephining," is that they were performed in order to permit the escape of evil spirits. (Baron, p. 447.)

To decide what trephining means, you have to find the reference for "such operations" back in the first sentence and put together a definition with information that follows the term: "an operation by which holes are drilled in skulls; in Stone Age times, possibly performed to permit evil spirits to escape."

EXERCISE 6.1

Recognizing Dictionary Definitions

■ PART A

The following are examples of terms defined in a text. Decide what term is being defined and what its definition is. This may require putting together information from before and after the term.

1. "Attitudes are lasting patterns of feelings, beliefs, and behavior tendencies toward other people, ideas or objects. Our attitudes are shaped by how other people perceive us and by how we think other people see us." (Lefton, p. 574.)

   Term being defined: ______________________________

   Definition: ______________________________

2. "Have you ever experienced panic—very high levels of physical arousal coupled with the intense fear of losing control? If you have, don't worry: Almost everyone has had this experience at some time or other. But persons who suffer a psychological condition known as panic attack disorder experience such reactions often, and sometimes without any specific triggering event. Such attacks can involve all or several of the following symptoms: pounding heart, chest pains, nausea, dizziness, trembling or shaking, fear of losing control or going crazy, chills, hot flashes, and numbness." (Baron, p. 459.)

   Term being defined: ______________________________

   Definition: ______________________________

   Term being defined: ______________________________

   Definition: ______________________________

3. "Because of a scarcity of Spanish women in the early days of the conquest, many conquistadores married Indian women. Their offspring, the 'new race' of mestizos, formed a cultural and biological bridge between Latin America's European and Indian races." (Bailey and Kennedy, p. 17)

   Term being defined: ______________________________

   Definition: ______________________________

4. "Both children and adults use two processes to deal with new ideas: assimilation and accommodation. Assimilation is the process by which a person absorbs new ideas and experiences, and uses them later in similar situations. Accommodation is the process of modifying previously developed cognitive structures and behaviors to adapt them to a new concept." (Lefton, pp. 291-92.)

   Term being defined: ______________________________

   Definition: ______________________________

   Term being defined: ______________________________

   Definition: ______________________________

5. "Labels are an essential ingredient of prejudice. Labels cause selective perception; that is, they lead people to see certain things and blind them to others." (From James M. Henslin, *Sociology: A Down-to-Earth Approach,* third edition, p. 320. Copyright © 1997 by Allyn and Bacon. Reprinted by permission.)

   Term being defined: ______

   Definition: ______

6. Review the definitions above. Which do you fully understand and could explain clearly?

   ______

   ______

7. For which would you need more information or specific examples to understand fully?

   ______

   ______

■ PART B

For each paragraph, identify its organization by circling either *Topical* or *Main Idea.* If the paragraph has a main idea, write the number of the sentence that best states that idea and identify any signals that helped you to find it. Then give the meaning of terms that the paragraph defines.

1. [1]Public awareness of anabolic steroids has recently been heightened by media stories about their use by amateur and professional athletes, including Arnold Schwarzenegger during his competitive bodybuilding days. [2]Anabolic steroids are artificial forms of the male hormone testosterone that promote muscle growth and strength. [3]These ergogenic drugs are used primarily by young men to increase their strength, power, bulk (weight), and speed. [4]These attributes are sought either to enhance athletic performance or to develop the physique that users perceive will make them more attractive and increase their sex appeal. (Donatelle and Davis, p. 248.)

   Organization: Topical or Main Idea: ______

   This is the main idea because it:

   a. answers a question stated in the paragraph
   b. has a listing phrase
   c. has a change of direction signal
   d. has a summary/conclusion signal

Term being defined: ______________________________

Definition: ______________________________

2. [1]Anger is a spontaneous, usually temporary, biological feeling or an emotional state of displeasure that occurs most frequently during times of personal frustration. [2]Since life is stressful, anger becomes a part of daily life experiences. [3]Anger can range in intensity from irritation to rage, a violent and extreme form of anger. [4]Aggression is a spontaneous, impulsive act of anger. [5]It is an observable behavior that can depreciate, threaten, or hurt a person or destroy an object. [6]It is unplanned and usually occurs during times of acute stress. [7]Verbal aggression and actual physical aggression are its most common forms. (Donatelle and Davis, p. 69.)

Organization: Topical or Main Idea: ________

This is the main idea because it:

a. answers a question stated in the paragraph
b. has a listing phrase
c. has a change of direction signal
d. has a summary/conclusion signal

Term being defined: ______________________________

Definition: ______________________________

Term being defined: ______________________________

Definition: ______________________________

Term being defined: ______________________________

Definition: ______________________________

3. [1]The term vegetarian means different things to different people. [2]Strict vegetarians, or vegans, avoid all foods of animal origin, including dairy products and eggs. [3]The few people who fall into this category must work hard to ensure that they get all of the necessary nutrients. Far more common are lacto-vegetarians, who eat dairy products but avoid flesh foods. [4]Their diet can be low in fat and cholesterol, but only if they consume skim milk and other low or nonfat products. [5]Ovo-vegetarians add eggs to their diet, while lacto-ovo-vegetarians eat both dairy products and eggs. [6]Pesco-vegetarians eat fish, dairy products, and eggs, while semivegetarians eat chicken, fish, dairy products, and eggs. [7]Some people in the semivegetarian category prefer to call themselves "non-red-meat eaters." (Donatelle and Davis, pp. 167–68.)

Organization: Topical or Main Idea: ________

This is the main idea because it:

a. answers a question stated in the paragraph
b. has a listing phrase
c. has a change of direction signal
d. is followed by a "first item in a list" signal word or phrase

Term being defined: ______________________________

Definition: ______________________________

Term being defined: ______________________________

Definition: ______________________________

Term being defined: ______________________________

Definition: ______________________________

Term being defined: ______________________________

Definition: ______________________________

Term being defined: ______________________________

Definition: ______________________________

Term being defined: ______________________________

Definition: ______________________________

4. [1]Many social scientists maintain that love may be of two kinds: companionate and passionate. [2]Companionate love is a secure, trusting attachment, similar to what we may feel for family members or close friends. [3]In companionate love, two people are attracted, have much in common, care about each other's well-being, and express reciprocal liking and respect. [4]Passionate love is, in contrast, a state of high arousal, filled with the ecstasy of being loved by the partner and the agony of being rejected. [5]The person experiencing passionate love tends to be preoccupied with his or her partner and to perceive the love object as being perfect. (Donatelle and Davis, p. 90.)

Organization: Topical or Main Idea: ________

This is the main idea because it:

a. answers a question stated in the paragraph
b. has a listing phrase
c. has a change of direction signal
d. has a summary/conclusion signal

Term being defined: ______________________________

Definition: ______________________________

Term being defined: ______________________________

Definition: ______________________________

5. [1]Behaviors, thoughts, and feelings always occur in a context—the situation. [2]Situations can be divided into two components: the events that come before and those that come after a behavior. [3]Antecedents are the setting events for a behavior; they cue or stimulate a person to act in certain ways. [4]Antecedents can be physical events, thoughts, emotions, or the actions of other people. [5]Consequences—the results of behavior—affect whether a person will repeat a behavior. [6]Consequences can also be physical events, thoughts, emotions, or the actions of other people. (Donatelle and Davis, p. 21.)

Organization: Topical or Main Idea: ________

This is the main idea because it:

a. answers a question stated in the paragraph
b. has a listing phrase
c. has a change of direction signal
d. has a summary/conclusion signal

Term being defined: ______________________________

Definition: ______________________________

Term being defined: ______________________________

Definition: ______________________________

Term being defined: ______________________________

Definition: ______________________________

When no definition is given for a word you don't know, you will need to look it up. The fastest place to find a definition is in a *glossary*—a list of definitions of key terms, in alphabetical order, located at the end of a textbook usually just before the index. A glossary can save you a lot of valuable study time and effort in looking up words and trying to find exact meanings. You should always preview every textbook you use carefully to find any special features, including a glossary, that it might have.

If a text does not contain a glossary, then you must go to your dictionary. As you learned in Chapter 2, finding the right meaning for a word in a dictionary can get complicated because words can have more than just one meaning. Sometimes you must decide on the correct part of speech, and you must always pay attention to the context (the environment in which a word occurs) if you have to decide among several possible meanings. As you discovered, you must look at the *context,* what goes on around the word, before you can decide which of the possible meanings fits.

USING CONTEXT CLUES TO BUILD VOCABULARY

You might hear a teacher say, "Learn the following list of words and their definitions."

garrulous = very talkative

mendacious = untruthful

indolent = lazy

antipathy = intense dislike

intractable = hard to control

Students are often given lists of 20–25 words and told to look up their meanings. If you studied these words and memorized them, you should do well on a matching or fill-in-the-blank test. But you would probably find, a week or so later, that the meanings of most of them had slipped from your memory.

Building vocabulary takes time and there is no simple key. However, rather than spend a lot of time memorizing lists of words and definitions, you can develop some approaches to vocabulary building that active readers have found more effective. One of these is using inference—the art of making reasonable guesses—to discover the meanings of words without going to the dictionary. A sentence or group of sentences may contain enough clues in the context for you to make a good guess about the meaning of a word. The more often you recognize the meaning of a word in context, the better chance you will have of building a meaning for it and remembering it. Eventually, the word will become a part of your writing and speaking vocabulary as well; at this point, the word will be yours for a lifetime.

Using the context requires some hard effort in thinking, but you will increase your vocabulary and also develop a skill that will help you in reading textbooks and other materials. There are several kinds of context clues that help you guess the meaning of a word.

Examples

If we don't know a word, sometimes a specific example will indicate its meaning.

> In China, couples who pledge not to have more than one child are given extra food, better housing, free medical care, and salary bonuses. Their child will be granted free tuition and *preferential* treatment when he or she enters the job market.

The list of things couples may be given—extra food, better housing, medical care, bonuses, free tuition for child—are all examples of special treatment. This would lead us to guess correctly that preferential would mean "especially favorable." Example clues may be introduced by signals like *for example, for instance, such as, to illustrate,* or *including:*

> Workers most frequently rated as 'very important' certain *nonmonetary,* qualities of work, such as interesting jobs, developing their own skills, and seeing how good the results of their work are.

The signal phrase "such as" tells us that examples of nonmonetary qualities are being given. Since these examples relate to values and personal interests rather than making money, we would decide that nonmonetary means "without relation to money or material gain."

Similar Words

Sometimes in a sentence you find two words or phrases that seem to have about the same meaning. If you know one of the words, you can figure out the other:

> Exercise has been found to improve self-concept, *alleviate* feelings of depression, and reduce anxiety.

This sentence tells us of the benefits of exercise: it makes a good thing (self-concept) better and it makes a bad thing (anxiety) decrease. Since depression is also something bad, we can figure that alleviate means something like *reduce.* Therefore we would arrive at a good guess for alleviate: "to lessen, make less severe."

Words that mean about the same thing (*synonyms*) may be signaled by various words or phrases (*and, or, just as, like, similarly*) and they may also be indicated by punctuation marks such as commas, dashes, or parentheses:

> *Egocentrism*, **or** self-centeredness, shapes all behavior; it is the inability to understand that the world does not exist solely to satisfy one's interests and needs.

Note in this example how the last part actually gives us a definition: "the inability to understand. . . ." But we don't really need it to get the meaning of the word. The signal word **or** and the use of commas tells us that egocentrism and self-centeredness mean the same thing.

Contrast

Sometimes the meaning of an unknown word can be guessed because of an **antonym**—a word with a meaning opposite of another. If we know that two words or phrases mean about the opposite, and we already know one of them, we can figure out the meaning of the other:

> Populations of most species are not stretched out continuously, with one merging into the others. Most often they are *isolated* geographically to some extent.

The first sentence tells how species populations are *not* arranged; the second sentence tells us the true facts. Therefore, isolated is the opposite of "stretched out continuously" and has to mean "separated from."

Contrast may be signaled by a number of words such as *but, however, in contrast, although, yet, rather than*:

> Tobacco could be planted easily. Sugar cane, *in contrast,* required arduous land clearing.

The signal phrase *in contrast* here shows that tobacco and sugar cane require different degrees of effort in planting. Therefore, arduous has to mean the opposite of easy: "requiring great difficulty or effort."

Drawing Conclusions

Probably most meanings we guess depend on clues we get from background information we have or through thinking processes that lead us to draw conclusions about how a word is being used—what some might call "logic" or "common sense":

> When asked how satisfied they were with their jobs, from 80 to 90 percent of workers replied that they were very or *moderately* satisfied.

If you are familiar with situations involving polls, you would know that they usually ask for a range of responses. From the information here, we would think that "very satisfied" represents the most favorable end. Since two groups have been lumped together here, we would guess that they represent the range of favorable responses. Moderately would therefore have to fall somewhere between "very" and "unsatisfied" and we would conclude that it means "somewhat, partially."

Another thinking process we use is recognizing how details, such as statistics, support a general statement:

> In 1912, on the night when the *Titanic* sank, social class was a major *determinant* of who survived and who died. Among the females on board, 3 percent of the first-class passengers drowned, compared with 16 percent of the second class and 45 percent of the third-class passengers.

Here the statistics support the conclusion that social class was the key to who survived. Therefore determinant would have to mean "factor, cause."

Situations involving causes and results often let us make good guesses about what words might mean:

> In recent years, a growing industrial demand for cheaper labor has *fueled* a dramatic increase in labor-force participation among minorities and immigrants.

The facts tell us cheap labor is needed and that the labor force has grown. These two are clearly connected: the first has led to the second. Therefore fueled here means "caused, stimulated."

Of course, you need to keep in mind that often there are no clues or only limited clues to the meaning of a word. In these cases, use your dictionary to find the exact meaning.

> When she was discovered, Isabella showed great fear and *hostility* toward people and made a strange croaking sound.

We could guess from the context that hostility is some kind of antisocial reaction, but quite a few meanings would fit the context: "shyness, dread, submissiveness." Without further clues, we would need to go to the dictionary to find that hostility means "aggressive behavior."

Context questions involve a good deal of honest mental effort. In all the vocabulary in context exercises that you do in this text, take the time to really think about how you are getting your answer. Think out the meaning of a word without going to the dictionary. (If you already know the word, pretend that you don't.) You will be repaid for your efforts through an increase in vocabulary and with improvement in your ability to read with real understanding.

EXERCISE 6.2

Using Context to Find Meaning

■ PART A

In the following exercise are sentences with context clues that should help you decide on the meaning of the italic words. Many of these have been taken from earlier passages in this text. Decide on the meaning of each word and indicate which type of clue you used to make your guess. Write down any words or punctuation signals that gave you a clue. Be ready to explain how you used clues to figure out the meaning. In some cases you will need to check and comment on more than one clue. Here is an example:

> Unknown interactions among the 1,000 or so compounds in chocolate exert *compelling* (some say addictive) effects on the human brain. Each year, for instance, the average American feels compelled to buy 8 to 10 pounds of the stuff. With that kind of demand, growers do their very best to keep cacao trees growing and reproducing.

The example clue shows that use of chocolate is heavy and that Americans show a real need for it. At the same time, in parentheses a near synonym, *addictive,* is given for compelling. From these two clues we would conclude that compelling must mean something like "forceful."

In some of the sentences there are not enough clues present to make a reasonably certain guess. In these cases make a guess if you wish, but check the "not enough clues" line.

1. The result of specialization of work can be *dehumanizing* for some workers: "I'm a machine," says the spotwelder. "I'm caged," says the bank teller.

   Meaning: a. useful
   b. uncertain
   c. degrading
   d. advantageous

   Clues: _____ example clue Signal word(s)? ______________
   _____ similar word clue ______________
   _____ contrast clue ______________
   _____ information led to drawing a conclusion ______________
   _____ not enough clues to decide

Explain your reasoning: ____

____

2. Vegetation cover is limited in deserts. The infrequent rains often fall in heavy, brief pulses that *erode* the unprotected soil.

Meaning: a. wear away
b. replace
c. build up
d. avoid

Clues: _____ example clue Signal word(s)? _______________
_____ similar word clue _______________
_____ contrast clue _______________
_____ information led to drawing a conclusion _______________
_____ not enough clues to decide

Explain your reasoning: ____

____

3. Fossils were preserved because they were gently buried before they could *decompose* or fall apart.

Meaning: a. reproduce
b. break down
c. be found
d. flee

Clues: _____ example clue Signal word(s)? _______________
_____ similar word clue _______________
_____ contrast clue _______________
_____ information led to drawing a conclusion _______________
_____ not enough clues to decide

Explain your reasoning: ____

____

4. Important changes have also occurred in the age and racial composition of the work force. In the last two decades, the employment rate for men older than 65 *declined* significantly.

Meaning: a. remained the same
b. went up
c. went down
d. was changed

Clues: _____ example clue Signal word(s)? _____________
_____ similar word clue _____________
_____ contrast clue _____________
_____ information led to drawing a conclusion _____________
_____ not enough clues to decide

Explain your reasoning: ______________________________

____

5. The Spanish fused with the Native Americans through marriage, *incorporating* their culture into their own rather than shunning and eventually isolating the Indians as the English would do.

Meaning: a. destroying
b. considering
c. evading
d. bringing together

Clues: _____ example clue Signal word(s)? _____________
_____ similar word clue _____________
_____ contrast clue _____________
_____ information led to drawing a conclusion _____________
_____ not enough clues to decide

Explain your reasoning: ______________________________

____

6. Educational *inequality* exists everywhere. In the former Soviet Union, for example, most children of high status families attended schools that would lead to a profession. They avoided vocational schools that lead to farm or factory work. (Thio, p. 313.)

   Meaning: a. not having the same privileges or status
   b. access to opportunity
   c. facilities and supplies
   d. leadership by professionals

   Clues: _____ example clue Signal word(s)? ______________
   _____ similar word clue ______________
   _____ contrast clue ______________
   _____ information led to drawing a conclusion ______________
   _____ not enough clues to decide

   Explain your reasoning: ____

   ____

7. There is some doubt that Victor was raised by animals. He was probably old enough to *scavenge* for food himself when he was abandoned.

   Meaning: a. work
   b. beg
   c. search
   d. pay

   Clues: _____ example clue Signal word(s)? ______________
   _____ similar word clue ______________
   _____ contrast clue ______________
   _____ information led to drawing a conclusion ______________
   _____ not enough clues to decide

   Explain your reasoning: ____

   ____

8. Although *arid* conditions do not favor large, leafy plants, deserts show much variety.

Meaning: a. warm
b. economic
c. very dry
d. humid

Clues: _____ example clue Signal word(s)? ______________
_____ similar word clue ______________
_____ contrast clue ______________
_____ information led to drawing a conclusion ______________
_____ not enough clues to decide

Explain your reasoning: ____________________________________

____

9. Younger workers are more likely to expect their jobs to be highly interesting and stimulating, hence are more likely to be disappointed because of the difficulty in realizing their high *aspirations.*

Meaning: a. expenses
b. hopes, goals
c. budgets
d. limitations

Clues: _____ example clue Signal word(s)? ______________
_____ similar word clue ______________
_____ contrast clue ______________
_____ information led to drawing a conclusion ______________
_____ not enough clues to decide

Explain your reasoning: ____________________________________

____

10. About 2,000 years ago, the poet Horace expressed feelings familiar to many Americans: "In Rome, you long for the country; in the country you praise the city to the skies." Many Americans have tried to solve this *dilemma* by moving to the suburbs. (Thio, pp. 352, 360.)

Meaning: a. situation requiring a choice between opposites
b. unsolvable riddle
c. opportunity for economic advancement
d. unnecessary choice

Clues: _____ example clue Signal word(s)? _____________
_____ similar word clue _____________
_____ contrast clue _____________
_____ information led to drawing a conclusion _____________
_____ not enough clues to decide

Explain your reasoning: ____

____

11. Smokeless tobacco also *impairs* the sense of taste and smell, causing the user to add salt and sugar to food.

Meaning: a. depends on
b. decreases
c. accompanies
d. repairs

Clues: _____ example clue Signal word(s)? _____________
_____ similar word clue _____________
_____ contrast clue _____________
_____ information led to drawing a conclusion _____________
_____ not enough clues to decide

Explain your reasoning: ____

____

12. A stereotype strengthens with time. Indeed, even exceptions to it tend to make it stronger, for they simply *induce* the persons holding the stereotype to bring more supporting information to mind.

Meaning: a. prohibit
b. discourage
c. lead, cause
d. dare

Clues: _____ example clue Signal word(s)? ____________
_____ similar word clue ____________
_____ contrast clue ____________
_____ information led to drawing a conclusion ____________
_____ not enough clues to decide

Explain your reasoning: ____

____

13. He started to show human emotions such as joy, gratitude, and *remorse.*

Meaning: a. hopefulness
b. regret for actions
c. appreciation of others
d. reverence

Clues: _____ example clue Signal word(s)? ____________
_____ similar word clue ____________
_____ contrast clue ____________
_____ information led to drawing a conclusion ____________
_____ not enough clues to decide

Explain your reasoning: ____

____

14. In the late 1800s and early 1900s, logging destroyed most of the coniferous forests that once *flourished* around the northern Great Lakes.

Meaning: a. grew in great numbers
b. burned
c. disappeared
d. were discovered

Clues: _____ example clue Signal word(s)? _____________
_____ similar word clue _____________
_____ contrast clue _____________
_____ information led to drawing a conclusion _____________
_____ not enough clues to decide

Explain your reasoning: ____

____

15. Higher income students in *elite* universities learn independent thinking skills useful in leadership positions. Meanwhile, in average universities and colleges, middle class youth are taught responsibility, and dependability—qualities needed for middle-level professions and occupations.

Meaning: a. old
b. very large
c. state-controlled
d. of highest status

Clues: _____ example clue Signal word(s)? _____________
_____ similar word clue _____________
_____ contrast clue _____________
_____ information led to drawing a conclusion _____________
_____ not enough clues to decide

Explain your reasoning: ____

____

16. The automobile greatly *facilitated* the movement to the suburbs. It encouraged people to leave the crowded inner city for the comfortable life of the suburbs.

Meaning: a. helped bring about
b. disrupted
c. increased the expenses of
d. slowed

Clues: _____ example clue Signal word(s)? ____________
_____ similar word clue ____________
_____ contrast clue ____________
_____ information led to drawing a conclusion ____________
_____ not enough clues to decide

Explain your reasoning: ______________________________

____

17. Within half a century of Columbus's arrival in the Americas, the conquistadores had *extinguished* the great Aztec and Incan empires and claimed for church and crown a territory that extended from Colorado to Argentina.

Meaning: a. respected the rights of
b. praised
c. destroyed completely
d. failed to conquer

Clues: _____ example clue Signal word(s)? ____________
_____ similar word clue ____________
_____ contrast clue ____________
_____ information led to drawing a conclusion ____________
_____ not enough clues to decide

Explain your reasoning: ______________________________

____

18. Armed with horses and gunpowder and *preceded* by disease, the conquistadores quickly overpowered the Indians.

Meaning: a. free of
b. immune to
c. coming before in time
d. greatly weakened

Clues: _____ example clue Signal word(s)? _____________
_____ similar word clue _____________
_____ contrast clue _____________
_____ information led to drawing a conclusion _____________
_____ not enough clues to decide

Explain your reasoning: ___________________________________

____

19. By about 5,000 years ago, humans had developed more powerful technologies. Thanks to *innovations* like the ox-drawn plow, irrigation, and metallurgy, farmers could produce more food.

Meaning: a. new machines
b. inventions in transportation
c. reliable tools of the past
d. new discoveries and techniques

Clues: _____ example clue Signal word(s)? _____________
_____ similar word clue _____________
_____ contrast clue _____________
_____ information led to drawing a conclusion _____________
_____ not enough clues to decide

Explain your reasoning: ___________________________________

____

20. In rural communities people feel bound to each other in a personal way. In industrial societies people are *alienated* from one another and relationships are impersonal. In the country people help their neighbor build a barn. In the city they stand by while a neighbor is mugged or even murdered.

Meaning: a. protected, shielded
b. disconnected, isolated
c. different, varied
d. responsive, sociable

Clues: _____ example clue Signal word(s)? ____________
_____ similar word clue ____________
_____ contrast clue ____________
_____ information led to drawing a conclusion ____________
_____ not enough clues to decide

Explain your reasoning: ______________________________

____

■ PART B

The following short passages contain more than one word for which there are sufficient context clues to make a good guess. Read the entire passage carefully when deciding on the meaning; clues may occur both before and after the word. Explain your reasoning in arriving at your choices and note any types of signals that gave you clues.

1. Excessive TV viewing reduced children's attention spans while leaving their brains *lethargic* and passive. It does not produce an environment *conducive* to learning.

lethargic

a. diseased
b. not active
c. strong
d. interested

Explain your reasoning and identify the clues you used: __________

____

conducive

a. helpful, encouraging
b. difficult
c. expensive
d. disappointing

Explain your reasoning and identify the clues you used: ___________

____

2. Robert Swanson was already relatively rich 10 years ago, but since then he has gotten richer. A decade ago, when he founded a semiconductor firm, he paid himself $125 in salary. Today the California *entrepreneur* earns $360,000 a year and his net worth has soared to $15 million. He *revels* in being rich, often riding around in a 1992 Porsche. (Thio, p. 138.)

   entrepreneur

   a. a crook, swindler
   b. a person who creates a business and assumes the risks for it
   c. an elected public official
   d. real estate salesman

   Explain your reasoning and identify the clues you used: ___________

   ____

   revels

   a. enjoys greatly
   b. feels guilty
   c. shows
   d. rebels

   Explain your reasoning and identify the clues you used: ___________

   ____

3. The safety-valve theory is that when hard times came, the unemployed who *cluttered* the city pavements merely moved west, took up farming, and prospered. In truth, relatively few city dwellers, at least in the populous eastern centers, migrated to the frontier during *depressions.* But the safety-valve theory does have some *validity.* Free acreage did *lure* to the West a host of immigrant farmers, who otherwise might have remained in the eastern cities to clog the job markets.

cluttered

a. died on
b. built
c. overcrowded
d. avoided

Explain your reasoning and identify the clues you used: ___________

____

Which of the following meanings of *depression* best fits the context?

a. an area sunk below its surroundings; a hollow.
b. the condition of feeling sad or low in spirit.
c. a period of major economic slowdown and unemployment
d. a psychotic or neurotic condition characterized by lack of concentration, sadness

Explain your reasoning and identify the clues you used: ___________

____

validity

a. danger
b. truthfulness
c. importance
d. real doubt

Explain your reasoning and identify the clues you used: ___________

____

lure

a. cheat
b. bankrupt
c. employ
d. attract with promise of reward

Explain your reasoning and identify the clues you used: ___________

____

4. In their bodies Europeans carried the germs that caused smallpox, yellow fever, and malaria. Indeed, Old World diseases would quickly *devastate* the Native Americans. During the Indians' long period of isolation

in the Americas, most of the Old World's killer *maladies* had disappeared from among them. But generations of freedom from those illnesses had also wiped out protective *antibodies. Devoid* of natural resistance to Old World sicknesses, Indians died in *droves.* (Bailey and Kennedy p. 14.)

devastate

a. destroy completely

b. be resisted by

c. be a nuisance to

d. strengthen

Explain your reasoning and identify the clues you used: ___________

____

maladies

a. illnesses, afflictions

b. rival Indian tribes

c. economic hardships

d. criminals

Explain your reasoning and identify the clues you used: ___________

____

antibodies

a. poisons, viruses

b. doctors and nurses

c. coverings

d. substances that give immunity to disease

Explain your reasoning and identify the clues you used: ___________

____

devoid of

a. supplied with

b. upset by

c. lacking completely

d. interested in

Explain your reasoning and identify the clues you used: ___________

____

droves

a. hospitals
b. pairs
c. wagons
d. very large numbers

Explain your reasoning and identify the clues you used: ____________

____

WRITING GOOD CONTEXT SENTENCES

You can help to make a word part of your vocabulary by using it in a sentence of your own so that the meaning is clear. You'll be surprised how often you will remember a word, not from any dictionary definition, but because your own sentence will pop into your mind. There are a number of exercises in this text that will ask you to write context sentences for vocabulary words. Sometimes the choice of these words will be up to you. Here are some guidelines for doing the next exercise.

1. When you select the words, pick those that you really don't know. Words selected should be nouns, verbs, adjectives, or adverbs. These are the parts of speech for which clear clues can be given.
2. Decide on the meaning of the word by going to the dictionary. You learned earlier that many words function as more than one part of speech and their meanings change accordingly. If you pick the wrong part of speech, the definition won't fit the context. For example, look at the word *grave* in this sentence:

   Sources report that the terrorist situation in Ireland is very grave.

   Here grave is an adjective meaning "serious/dangerous"; you would be in error if you identify it as a noun meaning "a place of burial."
3. Write down only the definition or a synonym for the word in *the context where you found it.* Copying out all the meanings for a word—some of which are very different—won't help you to decide the meaning that makes sense in the context of the sentence. For example, in this sentence—"Back pain is often the result of a *sedentary* job"—sedentary means "requiring much sitting." If you used the meaning "remaining in one area; not migratory," your definition would be correct if you were talking about birds, but it does not fit this situation.

4. Watch out for "circular" definitions. To save space, dictionaries often give the root meaning for only the most basic form of a word. For example, a definition for *chaotic* such as "characterized by chaos" doesn't help us learn what the word means. A definition that never defines a word's root just takes us in a circle, back to our starting point. Here you need to look up the basic form (chaos means "wild disorder") to make a useful definition of the adjective form chaotic: "wildly confused, disordered."

5. Sometimes words have wordy definitions. For example, *psychokinesis* is defined in the dictionary as "the production of motion, esp. in inanimate and remote objects, by the exercise of psychic powers." A student may find and copy the right definition for this word but without really understanding what it means. The best method is to put definitions in words of your own that make sense to you. For example, you could define psychokinesis as "moving things with the power of your mind." And remember: You can always ask your instructor if you aren't sure what a definition means.

6. A similar problem can exist with using synonyms. For example, the word *indifferent* has many synonyms, including *apathetic*. Saying that indifferent means apathetic won't help you at all if you don't know what either one means. Try to come up with a meaning that makes sense to you such as "having no strong feeling one way or the other" or "having no preference," if you're sure of what preference means.

7. Before writing your context sentence, think up a situation that could contain clues to help you use the word in a way to make its meaning clear. It's best *not* to write sentences on the same topic as the sentence in which you found the word. Write instead about things you know. Your sentences don't have to be connected to a single topic. You may write each sentence on any topic you wish.

8. When you write your context sentence, be sure there are enough specific clues so that someone who doesn't know the meaning of the word could guess it. If you need to write more than one sentence, feel free to do so. But just making a sentence that includes a word is not the same thing as writing a good context sentence. Don't settle for a "one size fits all" sentence into which many words of a certain part of speech can fit. For example:

   It was very ________. (any adjective)

   I ________ yesterday. (many verbs)

   Completing these will make sentences, but they are poor context sentences because they have no clue to the meaning to help the reader narrow down the possible meanings of the word. For example, in the sentence "It was very chaotic," the word *chaotic* could have the meaning of just about any adjective in the language. "The party was chaotic" is a little better, but chaotic still could mean anything that a party might be: "crowded," "free," "fun," "exciting," "boring," "out of control." Revising the sentence again to read "We left the party because it was too chaotic" is much better. We wouldn't leave a party because it was "too fun" or "too exciting" or "too free." However, more than one choice still fits the context: "We left the party because it was too boring/crowded/disordered."

A really good context sentence leaves only one possible meaning: "We left the party because it was so chaotic that we were afraid the place would be wrecked and the police might come." Now only "disordered" fits all the details in the sentence. Therefore this would be considered a good context sentence.

EXERCISE 6.3

Recognizing Good Context Clues

This exercise will help you to recognize when there are enough clues to guess a word's meaning. Study the sample and explanation carefully before doing the exercise.

SAMPLE

None A. Everyone who was there was in agreement that it was very *enthralling.*

Some B. Everyone agreed that the ballerina's performance was very *enthralling.*

Good C. The performance of the ballerina was so *enthralling* that the audience sat spellbound, thrilled by her every move.

Sentence A gives us no clue at all. "It" can refer to anything. *Enthralling* here could have any adjective meaning: "old, tall, expensive, rough, boring," etc.

Sentence B is better but we still need to narrow the meaning. Here any word that makes a judgment would fit: "clumsy, boring, spellbinding, mediocre," etc. A good context sentence leaves only one meaning possible.

Sentence C gives a clear and complete context clue. From the very positive reaction of the audience we know that enthralling here can only mean "spellbinding" or "captivating."

In each set of sentences, label one *None* (gives no clue at all), label one *Some* (needs more clues), and label one *Good* (gives clues that allow only one meaning). Then decide, without using a dictionary, what the word seems to mean. Be ready to explain your choices.

1. ________ A. Jerry has many good qualities, but unfortunately he is also very *indolent.*

   ________ B. Although his brother is hardworking, Jerry is quite *indolent.*

   ________ C. They all agreed that it was true that he is very *indolent.*

   Meaning: ____

2. ________ A. When home prices in Mario's neighborhood fell, his home also *depreciated* in value.

   ________ B. In their opinion the latest reports showed that it had definitely *depreciated.*

   ________ C. During this past year, the value of Mario's home has *depreciated* greatly.

   Meaning: ____

3. ________ A. They knew that it was clearly something that they should definitely soon *reciprocate.*

   ________ B. We decided to *reciprocate* when they invited us to their home for dinner.

   ________ C. The Taylors invited us to a barbecue last week, so to *reciprocate* we are taking them to the movies.

   Meaning: ____

4. ________ A. Among Alvin's clever inventions is an *ingenious* washing machine that runs efficiently on a lawn mower engine.

   ________ B. There was no doubt that it was indeed definitely *ingenious.*

   ________ C. Over the years, Alvin has built many *ingenious* machines.

   Meaning: ____

5. ________ A. It seemed to all of those who were present that they were acting *petulantly.*

   ________ B. When his mother refused to buy him a toy ship, the little boy reacted *petulantly* by screaming and stamping his feet.

   ________ C. The little boy responded *petulantly* to his mother's decision at the store.

   Meaning: ____

6. _______ A. All Tina could find was a leftover *remnant* of cloth, much too small to make a doll dress.

_______ B. After looking everywhere for material, Tina finally found a *remnant* in a drawer.

_______ C. Tina looked everywhere throughout the house, but never found the *remnant* she was looking for.

Meaning: ____

7. _______ A. Our team has the reputation of being very *ferocious.*

_______ B. When neighborhood dogs wander over onto our property, our cat Patches becomes very *ferocious.*

_______ C. On the football field, Jamarr is a *ferocious* blocker and tackler, but at home he is as gentle and playful as a kitten.

Meaning: ____

8. _______ A. Fidel's yard sale got rid of all the junk he has *accumulated* over the years.

_______ B. The neighbors stated that they were the ones who *accumulated* it.

_______ C. Over the years, Myrna and her family have *accumulated* a lot of money.

Meaning: ____

9. _______ A. Mary advised her husband that the most important thing at the meeting was to speak *tactfully.*

_______ B. When he had to do them, the president would always do things *tactfully.*

_______ C. Mike's boss delivered his evaluation *tactfully,* speaking gently and choosing words very carefully.

Meaning: ____

10. _______ A. The campaign manager agreed with the agency that the ad campaign could use some *alterations.*

_______ B. Due to high blood pressure, Ralph made major *alterations* in his lifestyle, including more exercise and fewer fatty foods.

_______ C. It was generally agreed that there would be some *alterations.*

Meaning: ____

EXERCISE 6.4

Writing Context Sentences from Situation Clues

In this exercise, a meaning for the word has been given. You will be given "situation clues" that might help you think of a way to use the word. The first one is done for you as a sample. These clues are general—you will need to think of specific examples. Make sure your sentence clearly answers such questions as **who, what, when, where, why, how.** To test to see if your sentence is a good context sentence, ask yourself this: Would someone who doesn't know the word be able to guess the meaning from the clues in the sentence?

SAMPLE

destitute: lacking resources or the means to subsist; impoverished

Situation clue: head of family loses job

Sentence: After my great-grandfather lost his job, he and his family were evicted and ended up wandering the streets, completely destitute.

1. **apathetic:** lacking interest or spirit

   Situation clue: reaction to a bad report/grade

   Sentence: ______________________________

2. **defective:** not in working order; flawed

   Situation clue: bought a new appliance

   Sentence: ______________________________

3. **genial:** friendly, kind

   Situation clue: visiting an older relative

   Sentence: ______________________________

4. **hilarious:** very funny

   Situation clue: being entertained

   Sentence: ______________________________

5. **incredible:** astonishing, not believable

   Situation clue: giving an excuse

   Sentence: ____

   ____

Examine the sample entry below before doing the exercise that follows. It shows you what to do for words you select on your own.

SAMPLE

Sentence from an article:

> The best professors always *illuminate* difficult concepts through clear explanations and many concrete examples.

1. Look up the word in the dictionary.

il lu mi nate *v.* **-nat ed, -nat ing, -nates.** —*tr.* 1. To provide or brighten with light. 2. To decorate or hang with lights. 3. To make understandable; clarify. 4. To enlighten intellectually or spiritually. 5. To endow with fame or splendor; celebrate. 6. To adorn (the pages of a book, for example) with ornamental designs, miniatures, or letters in brilliant colors,or precious metals. 7. To expose to or reveal by radiation. —*intr.* 1. To become lighted; glow. 2. To become exposed to or reveal by radiation. —*n.* (-nit). One who has or professes to have an unusual degree of enlightenment.

2. Decide on the part of speech of the word as used in the article. A total of nine meanings as a verb are given, and one as a noun. One test for a verb is that it can show past tense. The entry shows the past tense for *illuminate* as regular—in this case you add only a **-d.** You can make the substitution—"The best professors always illuminated difficult concepts." "Illuminated" also tells us what the subject (professors) did. With these clues, you would identify the word as a verb.
3. Decide on the correct meaning, and write down only what you can understand. After looking at the nine verb meanings, you would decide that only 3 and 4 could fit, and after further thought you would determine that 3 is closest to the meaning. If you don't know what "clarify" means, you would probably be better off just using the phrase "To make understandable," or, picking up the words "clear" and "explanation" from the context, you might add your own phrase, "explain clearly."

4. Write a context sentence of your own, on a different topic. You want a sentence with enough specific clues so that someone who didn't know the word could guess its meaning: Your completed entry would look like this:

illuminate

1. Part of speech, definition: Verb: "to make understandable, explain clearly"

2. Sentence: "My friend Roberto tries to illuminate the rules of soccer by showing me different situations and plays, but I still don't understand how the game is played."

EXERCISE 6.5

Completing a Vocabulary Entry

Use the preceding sample as a guide to do a vocabulary in context entry for the word in the sentence below:

Apple Corporation announced a price cut today in the hopes that the move will *spur* new sales.

> **spur** *n.* 1. One of a pair of spikes or spiked wheels attached to a rider's heels and used to urge a horse forward. 2. An incentive; stimulus. 3. A spurlike attachment or projection 4. A lateral ridge projecting from a mountain or mountain range. 5. An oblique reinforcing prop or stay of timber or masonry. 6. *Bot.* A tubular extension of the corolla or calyx of a flower, as in a columbine or larkspur. 7. A spur track. **—spurred, spur ring, spurs.** *—tr.* 1. To urge (a horse) on by the use of spurs. 2. To incite, stir to action. *—intr.* To ride quickly by horseback by making use of spurs.

1. Determine the correct part of speech. *Spur* here is being used as a(n)

____

2. Determine the meaning. *Spur* in this sentence means:

____

3. Write a context sentence of your own; think of a situation on a different topic.

   Situation: ______________________________

   Sentence: ______________________________

   ____

spur

1. Part of speech, definition: ______________________________

   ____

2. Sentence: ______________________________

   ____

USING WORD PARTS TO BUILD VOCABULARY

Look at the following groups of words. What similarities do you see within each group?

A.	**B.**	**C.**	**D.**
compel	regain	actor	psychology
expel	reelect	director	geology
repel	reborn	mediator	biology

You probably noticed that all the words in A contain the letter group *pel,* the words in B begin with *re,* those in C end in *or,* and the words in D end in *ology.* But are these similar in meaning as well as spelling? To compel is to force or push something; to expel (from school or a country, for example) means to force or thrust out; things that repel us we would want pushed or thrust away from us. We would conclude that the letter group *pel* has the meaning "to push, thrust, or force." In group B, *re* in front of each word adds the meaning "again": "to gain again, to elect again, to be born again." The *or* ending in C adds the meaning "one who" to act, direct, and mediate.

Many of the vocabulary words of English are made up of these smaller word parts. You are familiar with many word parts, though you may not be aware of it. You know, for example, that *un* and often *in* and *im* mean "not" and make opposites when added to words:

clear	unclear
happy	unhappy
sane	insane
possible	impossible

Word parts are divided into three main types:

Roots These are the foundations of words. A word may be made of more than one root ("blackboard") or can be a single root by itself ("track"). Many roots can't stand by themselves. For example, there is no word **pel* in the language that stands alone to mean "push or force." Many roots must always be combined with other word parts.

Prefixes These attach in front of roots and can make a big change in the meaning. For instance, the prefix *in* added to *visible* makes a word that means the opposite: *invisible. Re* in group B is a very common prefix that attaches to many words.

Suffixes These parts follow roots: their main function is to change a word's part of speech. For example, if we add the suffix *ation* to a verb like "condemn" we create a noun form: *condemnation*—the act of condemning. The words in group D above all name fields of study. The suffix *logy* means "the study of" and combines with roots that appear in many words in the language: *psych* (mind), *geo* (earth), *bio* (life). Thus psychology is the study of the mind, geology the study of the earth, and biology the study of life-forms.

Combining what you know of word parts with using context clues can give you a powerful one-two punch for vocabulary. For example, here is a sentence from a previous chapter:

> The result of specialization can be *dehumanizing* for some workers, as Terkel found when he interviewed people across the country: "I'm a machine," says the spotwelder. "I'm caged," says the bank teller.

The examples are context clues that give you a general idea of the meaning of the word, but knowing that the prefix *de* means "down" or "away from" provides more support for deciding that "dehumanizing" means "taking away human qualities, degrading."

When context clues are weak or absent, you may use your knowledge of word parts to guess meanings. Below are some examples of sentences you worked with earlier that lack enough context clues but contain word parts that will help unlock the meaning of the word:

> People with satisfying jobs have better mental health than those with less satisfying work. Thus, white-collar workers are less likely than blue collars to suffer from *psychosomatic* illnesses, low self-esteem, worry, and anxiety.

If you know that *psycho* means "mind" and *soma* means "body," you can understand what a psychosomatic illness is: one that shows symptoms of an ailment in the body but was actually created only by the mind.

> Important changes have also occurred in the age and racial composition of the work force. In the last two decades, the employment rate for men older than 65 *declined.*

We know the rate changed, but there's no definite clue here if the change is a rise in the rate or a fall. Knowing, however, that the prefix *de* means "down" gives us the information we need to decide that decline means "go down."

> During the Indians' *millennia* of isolation in the Americas, most of the Old World's killer maladies had disappeared from among them.

We can tell from the clues that "millennia" refers to a period of time, but how long is it? Many years? Many centuries? If we know that *mille* refers to "thousand," we can decide that the time span refers to a period of two thousand years or more.

English is from the Germanic group of languages and its most basic words are of Germanic origin. But throughout its history English has borrowed a lot of vocabulary from other languages. Many words came from Greek and Latin and also from the Romance languages (those that descended from Latin, the language of Rome). If your primary language is one of the Romance languages like French, Italian, Spanish, or Portuguese, you have a real advantage in recognizing word parts. English words often show similarities to words in these languages. For example, the root *aqua* means "water" in such words as *aquarium* and *aqueduct.* The Spanish word is *agua*. The word manuscript combines *manu* (hand) with *script* (written) to mean "written by hand." The Spanish words are *mano* and *escriben.*

You should keep some things in mind when you are working with word parts. Sometimes what looks like a word part may be a part of another unit. For example, *unanimous* does not mean "not animous." In this case, *un* is a form of a different word part, *uni,* meaning "one." Also, the meaning of a word part may not be very clear in a word's general usage. The word parts of *prevent* mean "to come before"; the meaning of *pre* as "before" is not very clear in our current use: "to keep or stop from doing." Finally, your dictionary might not list all the words that can combine with some common prefixes. For example, if you try to look up a word beginning with the prefix *anti* in a pocket-size dictionary, you may not find it listed. If you don't, look up the base word and add the meaning of the prefix to it.

EXERCISE 6.6

Using Common Prefixes

Here are some prefixes that combine to form many words.

Prefix	*Meaning*	*Examples*
pre	before	preflight, predict, prejudice
super	above	supervise, supernatural, superintendent
re	again	repeat, restate, reclaim
mis	wrong	misplace, misspell, misbehave
over	too much	overweight, overconfident, overeager
counter	opposite	counterweight, counterpart, counterbalance
out	go beyond	outdo, outrage, outshine

Below are some common words that combine with these prefixes. For each word, make a list of other words that can be formed by using the prefixes above.

EXAMPLES: write *miswrite, rewrite, overwrite*
charge *recharge, supercharge, overcharge, countercharge*

1. date ____________ ____________ ____________ ____________
2. plan ____________ ____________ ____________ ____________
3. take ____________ ____________ ____________ ____________
4. cook ____________ ____________ ____________ ____________
5. draw ____________ ____________ ____________ ____________
6. write ____________ ____________ ____________ ____________
7. view ____________ ____________ ____________ ____________
8. play ____________ ____________ ____________ ____________
9. think ____________ ____________ ____________ ____________
10. pay ____________ ____________ ____________ ____________
11. heat ____________ ____________ ____________ ____________
12. act ____________ ____________ ____________ ____________
13. use ____________ ____________ ____________ ____________
14. turn ____________ ____________ ____________ ____________
15. spend ____________ ____________ ____________ ____________

Active Learning

THE ALTERNATIVE IS EXPENSIVE

When active learning is not nurtured or encouraged, the long-lasting effects upon the child are devastating. Poor reading and writing skills, coupled with limited vocabulary, have a damaging effect not just upon personal lives but upon society at large as well. In the following passage, Nadine Rosenthal discusses the wide-ranging consequences that threaten a surprisingly large number of Americans. Some vocabulary words in the passage have been listed at the beginning. Other words, listed in the margin, can be figured out by using context clues. Help in finding context clues is offered at the end of the reading.

EXERCISE 6.7

The Costs of Illiteracy

Preview Vocabulary

tentatively: (¶1) uncertainly, hesitantly

strenuous: (¶2) very difficult, demanding

profoundly: (¶4) absolutely, to a great degree

humiliation: (¶5) condition of having one's self-esteem lowered

The Costs of Illiteracy

by Nadine Rosenthal

1 Throughout the many years I taught adult reading classes, I observed my students as they walked tentatively over the threshold into my classroom for the first time. One student expressed his discomfort clearly: "As I was walking into your class that first day I thought about my third-grade teacher, who embarrassed me in front of my friends by having me read out loud when she knew full well I couldn't read to save my life. That was when I decided I'd never read again. Unfortunately I didn't." He came to my class because he was tired of guarding his reading secret. But, as he embarked on his reading studies, he had little idea of the new difficulties he would encounter.

■ *embarked:*
a. set out on
b. became afraid of

2 Learning to read as an adult is generally more difficult than learning to read as a child. When adults return to their education after a long hiatus, they seldom learn as quickly as they could have when they were children. When adults who read at the third-grade level begin adult reading classes, they may find it takes several years of night classes to bring their reading up to even the fourth-grade level. The differences between an adult learning to read and a child learning to read are significant. Eight-year-old third graders spend perhaps five hours a day on reading-related activities at the time in their lives when their minds are primed for learning, and when learning is their main occupation. In addition, they don't have the self concept as a failure that comes from the years of covering up the fact that they can't read. By contrast, adults learning to read generally attend classes and tutoring sessions only two to six hours a week, yet also raise children, work in jobs that are often strenuous, pay bills, shop for food and clothing, and cope with a myriad of family issues. . . .

■ *hiatus:*
a. trip
b. an interruption in time

3 National literacy statistics depict a dire educational situation. A functionally literate person is defined as having the reading and writing skills necessary for everyday living. It is estimated that there are 27 million American adults (15 percent of the total population) who are functionally illiterate—whose reading skills are too low to read medicine bottle labels, consumer product directions and warnings, TV schedules, bus schedules, traffic signs, or job advertisements. An additional 45 million (25 percent of the total population) are barely able to meet the more demanding reading requirements of the workplace, bringing the total to 72 million American adults (40 percent of the total population) with marginal or nonfunctional reading skills. A truly literate populace, one capable of analyzing complex material, forming critical opinions, or making informed decisions necessary for full participation in democracy, requires far more than these marginal skills. . . .

■ *dire:*
a. familiar
b. alarming

■ *marginal;*
a. barely meeting a low standard
b. improving

4 For every $1 spent on preschool education, perhaps $4 are saved in future welfare and prison costs. If you consider the fact that preschool is where the children with parents who don't or can't read to them first encounter the prereading skills that will prepare them to learn to read later, and that without such preschool experiences children enter kindergarten already behind, this statistic makes the importance of funding education, especially early childhood education, profoundly clear. If soci-

ety cannot give a child a solid foundation in literacy, the child may easily grow into an adult who finds it more difficult than literate people to positively function in society whether creatively, socially, politically, or economically.

5 In addition to experiencing economic barriers, many of my adult literacy students found it difficult to take their full place in other parts of society. I once spent three weeks with one of my classes reviewing ballot initiatives before an election, only to find later that none of them actually voted because they were just too intimidated by the process or feared humiliation at the polling booths.

■ *intimidated:*
a. made afraid
b. excited

6 There are no measurements for the effects on individual people of the sense of narrow career options, or the poor self-esteem, or the feelings of failure and inadequacy that undereducated people cope with on a daily basis. (Rosenthal, pp. 121–22.)

Context Answers and Clues

embarked: a. set out (he came to the class)

hiatus: b. an interruption in time (returning to their education)

dire: b. alarming (the statistics are scary)

marginal: a. barely meeting a low standard (lumped together with the lowest group)

intimidated: a. made afraid (ended up not voting)

Discuss and answer the following in groups of 3–4.

1. "The differences between an adult learning to read and a child learning to read are significant." List the main differences that the author notes and add any others you can think of.

____

____

____

2. Explain the difference (¶3) between functional literacy and functional illiteracy.

____

____

____

3. According to the author, what active learning skills does a truly literate person have?

___

___

___

4. List three reasons (¶4) the author gives for supporting the funding of childhood education.

   a. ___

   b. ___

   c. ___

   Do you agree with the author's point of view? Why or why not?

5. "There are no measurements for the effects on individual people of the sense of narrow career options, or the poor self-esteem, or the feelings of failure and inadequacy that undereducated people cope with on a daily basis." Give any examples from your personal observation and/or experience of these effects of lack of education.

___

___

___

___

___

Reading Portfolio

WRITING CONTEXT SENTENCES

As a part of some of your Reading Portfolio assignments, you can increase your vocabulary by writing context sentences. When you select an article for a portfolio assignment, find one with words that challenge you, but not so many that you can't really understand what you are reading. If there are too many hard words, you won't be able to understand the article well enough to use the context. There should be around fifteen words in the article that you aren't sure of.

There are certain words for this exercise that are best not to use. Don't use the names of people, places, cities, countries, or organizations. These can only be identified or located, not defined. Also, avoid highly technical or scientific terms. It is very difficult, for example, to make a context sentence for chemical terms or for the names of illnesses. These usually require very technical definitions.

Select ten words, using the guidelines above. For each word, find the meaning in the dictionary that fits the context in which it is used. Then write your own context sentence, using a situation different from that of the article. Remember: you want to write a sentence that has enough specific clues that someone who doesn't know the word will be able to guess the meaning.

CHAPTER 7

Is There a Main Idea Here?

Stating Implied Main Ideas

After reading this chapter, you will know the answers to these questions:

- What is an implied main idea?
- How do the words *imply* and *infer* differ?
- How can implied main ideas be stated?
- What is a divided main idea?
- What are frames of reference?

Here is a paragraph that you read earlier on the topic of job satisfaction:

> Generally, older workers are more satisfied than younger ones. One reason is that older workers, being more advanced in their careers, have better jobs. Another reason is that younger workers are more likely to expect their jobs to be highly interesting and stimulating, hence are more likely to be disillusioned because of the difficulty in realizing their high aspirations. White-collar workers, especially professionals and business people, are also more likely than blue collars to feel genuinely satisfied with their jobs.

This paragraph gives us a number of ideas about job satisfaction:

- Older workers in general are more satisfied than younger ones.
- Because older workers are more advanced in their careers, they have better jobs.

- Because younger workers expect to be motivated and stimulated at work, they are more likely to be disappointed by their jobs.
- White-collar workers, especially professionals and business people, are more likely than blue collars to feel real job satisfaction.

The first two sentences tell about job satisfaction among older workers, the third about job satisfaction among younger workers, and the fourth about satisfaction among white-collar and blue-collar workers. None of these sentences is broad enough to be a main idea that will cover all the others. However, they are connected by something more than just a topic: the sentences in the paragraph all focus on job satisfaction as reported by different groups. We could form a question that all the details of the paragraph answer:

> Does job satisfaction vary between different groups?

The answer, though not directly stated in the paragraph, is a general idea suggested and supported by all the details:

> Job satisfaction varies from one group to another.

RECOGNIZING AND STATING IMPLIED MAIN IDEAS

Recognizing an unstated main idea like the above—what we call an "implied main idea"—is another important way we use inference to read for understanding. The words *imply* and *infer* are often confused. To imply is to suggest or hint: it is the writer or speaker who does the implying. To infer means to make a good guess or draw a conclusion from the evidence available: it is the reader or listener who does the inferring. As originally written, the preceding paragraph example did contain a stated main idea:

> *Studies have shown that job satisfaction varies from one group to another.* Generally, older workers are more satisfied than younger ones. One reason is that . . .

However, even without that sentence, an active reader would see the conclusion that the details lead to. Before you decide that ideas in a paragraph are organized around a topic only, read carefully to see if an implied idea brings them all together. There are a number of ways we can arrive at implied main ideas:

Drawing a Conclusion from Evidence We can sometimes draw a conclusion about a word's meaning from the details in the context. The same is true of implied main ideas; for example, in the paragraph example, the evidence about job satisfaction from a number of groups would point to an unstated main idea. Here is another example:

> On the one hand, the government estimates the number of homeless to be between 250,000 and 350,000, but advocates for the homeless, such as New York's Community Service Society, insist that there are well over 3 million homeless people. Sociologist Peter Rossi contends that most of the higher estimates are far off the mark because they are based on seriously flawed sampling methods. But [others] argue that Rossi's own lower estimate of 300,000 to 500,000 is questionable. It fails to include large numbers of the "hidden homeless." (Thio, p. 150.)

The evidence here consists of several estimates of the number of homeless. One question we could ask is "Approximately how many homeless are there in the United States?" Since there is no agreement among estimates, we would conclude that the paragraph has an implied main idea:

> No one is sure about the number of homeless in the United States.

A good test of an implied main idea that usually works is to put it at the beginning of the paragraph and see if it gives the paragraph unity. If we add the sentence to the paragraph above, we can see that it fits as a clear main idea that all the details support:

> No one is sure about the number of homeless in the United States. On the one hand, the government estimates the number of homeless to be between 250,000 and 350,000, but advocates for the homeless, such as . . .

Providing a Listing Phrase You learned earlier that one good clue to a main idea is finding a listing phrase such as "different types of," " a number of factors," or "for several reasons." If writers think the meaning is clear enough, they may leave out the listing phrase:

> Why do fashions occur in the first place? One reason is that some cultures, like ours, value change: what is new is good. Thus, in many modern societies clothing styles change yearly, while people in traditional societies may wear the same style of clothing for many generations. Many industries promote quick changes in fashions to increase their sales. Although a new style occasionally originates from lower-status groups, as blue jeans did, most fashions trickle down from the top. Upper-class people adopt some style or [symbol] as a badge of their status, but they cannot monopolize most status symbols for long. The style is adopted by the middle class, maybe copied by lower-status groups, pro-

viding people with the prestige of possessing a high-status symbol. By trickling down, however, the symbol eventually loses its prestige. The upper class adopts a new style until it, too, "trickles down" and must be replaced by another. (Thio, p. 372.)

The second sentence begins with "One reason . . ." This signal phrase begins a list and usually follows the main idea statement. A second reason for change in fashions is stated in the fourth sentence: to increase sales. The rest of the paragraph gives a final reason: the upper class, once the other classes start copying them, comes up with new fashions. Since we have been given a number of reasons, our implied main idea would include a listing phrase:

There are a number of reasons why changes in fashion occur.

Answering a Question The preceding paragraph also illustrates another process in stating implied main ideas. If a question occurs, especially near the beginning, the sentence that answers it is often the main idea sentence. If no one sentence in the paragraph answers the question, an implied main idea may be the answer to that question. In the example above, no single sentence answers the question "Why do fashions occur in the first place?" The implied main idea sentence answers the question by combining some words in the question (fashion/occur) with a listing phrase: "There are a number of reasons why changes in fashion occur."

Bringing Together a Divided Main Idea There are some main ideas that are somewhat in between stated and implied main ideas. That is, the main idea may be completely or partly stated in the paragraph, but it is not stated in a single sentence. It's left to the reader to put together a main idea from various parts. For example:

People with satisfying jobs have better mental health than those with less satisfying work. Thus, white-collar workers are less likely than blue collars to suffer from psychosomatic illnesses, low self-esteem, worry, anxiety, and impaired interpersonal relationships. People who are happy with their jobs also tend to have better physical health and to live longer. Although diet, exercise, medical care, and genetics are all related to the incidence of heart disease, job dissatisfaction is more closely linked to the cause of death. (Thio, p. 300.)

Finding a main idea here would begin with a question about the topic: "What about people with satisfying jobs?" Since the first sentence is a general statement that tells us about the topic—"People with satisfying jobs have better mental health"—we would guess that this might be the main idea of the paragraph. The example in the second sentence supports this main idea. However, the word *also* in sentence 3 widens the idea to include physical health and living longer. Now, to come up with a complete main idea sentence, we would need to combine information into a single main idea sentence: "People with more satisfying jobs have better mental *and physical* health *and tend to live longer* than those with less satisfying work."

The next three exercises will give you practice in working with implied main ideas in paragraphs and longer selections. In some of these exercises you will also practice using context clues to determine meanings.

EXERCISE 7.1

Recognizing Implied Main Ideas in Paragraphs

1. Flight demands high metabolic rates, which require a good deal of oxygen. A unique respiratory system greatly enhances oxygen uptake in birds. Flight also demands low weight and high power. The bird wing (a forelimb) consists of feathers, powerful muscles, and lightweight bones. Bird bones are strong and yet weigh very little because of air cavities in the bone tissue. The skeleton of a frigate bird, which has a seven-foot wingspan, weighs only four ounces. That's less than the feathers weigh. (Starr, p. 321.)

■ *enhances*: greatly increases

   a. Although birds may be very light, most are strong enough to fly.
   b. A number of physical features make birds well adapted to the demands of flight.
   c. Birds with long wingspans have better metabolic rates than those with short spans.
   d. Flight is a complicated and amazing process which no one really understands.

2. Each human starts out as a single fertilized egg. At birth a human body has about a trillion cells. Even in an adult, trillions of cells are still dividing. Cells in the stomach's lining divide every day. Liver cells usually don't divide—but if part of the liver becomes injured or diseased, they will divide repeatedly and produce new cells until the damaged part is replaced. (Starr, p. 321.)

   a. All human cells divide daily.
   b. Humans have many more cells than other animals.
   c. Humans of all ages have exactly the same number of cells.
   d. The cells of a human continue to divide throughout its lifetime.

■ *vigorous:* energetic, very active

■ *obesity:* condition of being very overweight

■ *incidence:* occurrence

3. Research evidence suggests that only one in five Americans exercises regularly and intensely enough to reduce his or her risk for disease and premature death. This is surprising, since it is now very well known that regular and vigorous exercise can significantly reduce coronary heart disease, even in the presence of other health risk factors, including smoking, obesity, high blood pressure, and high blood cholesterol. Moreover, some evidence suggests that even less vigorous forms of activity can be beneficial if done consistently. For example, people who walk regularly—at least four hours per week—have less than half the incidence of [high] cholesterol of those who do not. (Baron, p. 437–38.)

   a. Most Americans don't exercise vigorously enough to do any good.
   b. Regular exercise—even if not very vigorous—can reduce health problems.
   c. Easy exercises have higher health benefits for you than vigorous ones.
   d. Walkers actually receive more health benefits than those who run long distances.

■ *confrontations:* combative face-to-face meetings

■ *menace:* danger

■ *virtually:* practically, nearly

4. Conflict exists in all forms of social structure. It occurs between management and labor, whites and blacks, criminals and police, but also between friends, lovers, family members, and fellow workers. It can both harm and help a social structure. Wars between nations and violent confrontations between hostile groups clearly are harmful. Yet war may also unify members of a society. This is most likely to occur if various segments of society, such as leaders and the rank and file, agree that the enemy is a real menace to the entire country, that it warrants going to war and defending the nation, or that internal conflict, if any, can be resolved. Thus, the Vietnam War divided the American people because many did not agree with their government that South Vietnam was worth defending, but the Second World War was a unifying force because virtually all Americans looked upon the threat of Nazi Germany and Japan in the same light. (Thio, p. 64.)

   a. Conflict exists in all forms of social structure and can be both harmful and helpful.
   b. Conflicts that involve violence, such as riots and wars, are always wrong.
   c. America has had both popular and unpopular wars throughout its history.
   d. Conflict exists not only in business and politics, but in the family as well.

5. More than thirty years ago, most of the homeless were old men, only a handful were women, and virtually no families were homeless. Today, the homeless are younger, and they include a much higher proportion of women and families with young children. Today's homeless are also more visible to the general public because they are much more likely to sleep on the streets or in other public places in great numbers. They also suffer greater deprivation. Although in the past homeless men on Skid Row were undoubtedly poor, their average income from casual work was three to four times more than what the current homeless receive. (Thio, p. 150.)

- *proportion:* a part considered in relation to the whole
- *deprivation:* a state or condition in which something necessary is lacking or has been taken away
- *casual:* occasional

a. The number of homeless men has greatly decreased in the past 30 years.

b. Homelessness is only a problem when homeless people appear in public.

c. The homeless today show important differences from those in the past.

d. Homeless people today are much lazier than those of the past.

The rest of the paragraphs in this exercise deal with various aspects of health.

6. It is the high concentration of fats in the American diet, particularly saturated fats (largely animal fats), that appears to increase our risk for heart disease. Although too much sugar has been implicated in the development of many diseases, much of this information is inaccurate. Contrary to popular opinion, American consumption of sugar has not changed dramatically in recent years. In addition, the only disease associated with long-term excessive sugar intake is dental cavities. Most diet-related diseases are a result of increased consumption of fat. Over the years, several federal agencies have worked to modify the average American's diet through a series of dietary goals and guidelines. (Donatelle and Davis, p. 153.)

- *concentration:* large amount of
- *implicated:* thought to be connected to or caused by
- *modify:* change

a. Saturated fats increase our risk for heart disease and cause diet-related diseases.

b. The high concentration of fats, rather than sugars, seems to increase our risk for heart disease.

c. Too much sugar has been implicated in the development of many diseases, but consumption of sugar has not changed much in recent years.

d. Several federal agencies have worked to modify the average American's diet.

■ *speculated:* considered, guessed

■ *preliminary:* leading up to further action

7. Researchers have speculated that too much iron in the body may increase the risk for heart disease. They point to the low risk for heart disease in premenopausal women and the striking rise in risk in postmenopausal women as a possible indicator of such an association. Men who consume high-iron diets also appear to be at increased risk. But this research is preliminary; nutrition scientists are planning further studies of this possible connection. Blood donors and pregnant women may need to increase iron intake. (Donatelle and Davis, p. 166.)

a. Researchers think too much iron increases the risk for heart disease of both men and women.
b. The presence of too much iron, risks for men and women, with the need for further study.
c. Researchers have speculated that too much iron in the body may increase the risk for heart disease, but this research is preliminary.
d. Too much iron in the body may increase the risk for heart disease, but blood donors and pregnant women may need to increase iron intake.

■ *metabolic:* relating to vital bodily processes that maintain life

■ *unique:* special, one-of-a-kind

8. Men and women differ in body size, body composition, and overall metabolic rates. They therefore have differing needs for most nutrients throughout the life cycle and face unique difficulties in keeping on track with their dietary goals. Have you ever wondered why men can eat more than women and never seem to gain weight? Although there are many possible reasons for this apparent difference, one factor is that women have a lower ratio of lean body mass to adipose (fatty) tissue at all ages and stages of life. Also, after sexual maturation, metabolism is higher in men, meaning that they will burn more calories doing the same things as women. (Donatelle and Davis, p. 166.)

a. Because men and women differ physically and metabolically, they differ in nutritional needs and weight gain.
b. Men can eat more food than women and gain less weight because they have a higher ratio of lean body mass to adipose (fatty) tissue throughout life.
c. Differences in body shape, composition, metabolism, with big differences in nutritional needs and weight gain between men and women.
d. Men and women differ in body size and composition, and metabolism is higher in men.

9. Generally, people who follow a balanced vegetarian diet have lower weights, better cholesterol levels, fewer problems with irregular bowel movements (constipation and diarrhea), and a lower risk of heart disease than do nonvegetarians. Some preliminary evidence suggests that vegetarians may also have a reduced risk for colon and breast cancer. Whether these lower risks are due to the vegetarian diet per se or to some combination of lifestyle variables remains unclear. (Donatelle and Davis, p. 168.)

■ *per se:* in or by itself

a. People who are vegetarians, with fewer problems and risks, in combination with lifestyle variables.

b. A vegetarian diet causes a person to be in better physical condition and reduces the risk for some diseases.

c. People who follow a balanced vegetarian diet show a number of health benefits, although the reason for this is not clear.

d. People should follow a vegetarian diet along with a combination of other lifestyle variables.

10. Maintaining a nutritious diet within the confines of student life is difficult. However, if you take the time to plan healthy diets, you may find that you are eating better, enjoying eating more, and saving money. Understanding the terminology used by the food industry may also help you eat a healthier diet. In addition, these steps help ensure a quality diet:

- Buy fruits and vegetables in season for their lower cost and higher nutrient quality.
- Use coupons and specials to get price reductions.
- Shop at discount warehouse food chains.
- Plan ahead to get the most for your dollar and avoid extra trips to the store; extra trips usually mean extra purchases. Make a list and stick to it. (Donatelle and Davis, p. 172.)

a. There are several steps students can follow when shopping at discount warehouses.

b. There are some things students can do to have a nutritious diet on a limited budget.

c. Carefully planning a healthy diet, plus wise shopping to get the most for your money.

d. The most important thing students can do is shop wisely by using coupons and sticking to a planned-out list.

EXERCISE 7.2

Recognizing Implied Main Ideas in Passages

Parts A and B will give you practice in deciding on implied main ideas for paragraphs that are part of longer passages. Complete the vocabulary in context questions that follow some of the paragraphs. Be ready to explain your reasoning and the clues you used to arrive at your answers. Look up any other words that you are not sure of, using context as a guide to meaning.

■ PART A

Each paragraph in this passage develops an aspect of the topic of illness and disease. The implied main ideas for these are listed below. In the blank after each paragraph, write in the idea that fits the details.

- There are several reasons why women outlive men.
- Social class influences health.
- The incidence of sickness varies with age groups.
- Race and ethnicity are also correlated with health.

1 Old people are less likely than young people to suffer from *acute* and *infectious* illnesses such as measles and pneumonia. But they are more *susceptible* to *chronic* illnesses such as arthritis, heart disease, and cancer. Cancer deaths, in particular, have been climbing steadily among people aged 55 and older. Some illnesses have been attributed to exposure to workplace hazards some 30 or 40 years ago and a high-fat diet.

____

____

Using Context Clues

Which of these meanings best fit here?

acute

a. having a sharp point or tip
b. sensitive
c. fast moving and severe
d. very sharp or intense

infectious

a. able to be caught
b. relatively mild
c. incurable
d. unknown

susceptible

a. unaware
b. able to endure
c. likely to be affected by
d. immune

chronic

a. avoidable
b. curable
c. non-threatening
d. long-lasting, continuing

2 Women have higher rates of both chronic and acute illnesses than men of the same age, yet women live longer than men. Why? One reason is biological superiority. Women are more able to endure sickness and survive. A second reason is that women maintain stronger emotional ties with others than men do. By offering social support and *deterring* loneliness, intimate human relationships can reduce the *severity* and *duration* of illness. A third reason is the greater tendency of men to smoke, drink, and drive. Such behaviors increase the risk of serious chronic diseases and physical injuries. It is also possible that women are more *attuned* to their bodies and thus more likely to sense problems and seek medical help before an illness becomes serious.

____

____

Using Context Clues

deterring

a. increasing
b. ignoring
c. accepting
d. discouraging, preventing

attuned to

a. dissatisfied with
b. worried about
c. aware of, responsive to
d. shy about

Two important factors relating to a disease are how long it lasts and how serious it is. Which meanings do the words *severity* and *duration* have in this paragraph?

______________ length

______________ degree of seriousness

3 Blacks, Hispanics, and Native Americans all have shorter life expectancies than do Anglo Americans. Blacks are far more likely than whites to suffer from pneumonia, heart disease, kidney disease, AIDS, and high blood pressure. Blacks are more than twice as likely as whites in the same age bracket to die from most of those diseases. Hispanics, too, are much more likely than Anglo Americans to die from influenza, pneumonia, tuberculosis, and AIDS. Hispanics are also more likely to develop diabetes, kidney diseases, and stomach cancer. Native Americans suffer the most from acute diseases. They are 10 times more likely than other Americans to get tuberculosis and 30 times more likely to get strep throat. Both Hispanics and Native Americans, however, are less likely than Anglos to die from heart disease and cancer.

____

____

4 In particular, acute and infectious diseases, such as tuberculosis and influenza, are more *prevalent* among the lower social classes. Researchers have attributed the higher rates of disease among the lower classes to several related factors: *hazardous* and unclean environments; stress resulting from life changes, such as job loss and divorce; and inadequate medical care. More recent research has found another problem: unhealthy eating habits. Poor people are much more likely than others to eat high-sugar, high-salt, and high-fat food. (Thio, pp. 323–24.)

____

____

Using Context Clues

prevalent

a. unknown
b. widespread
c. understood
d. researched

hazardous

a. dangerous
b. foreign
c. attractive
d. urban

■ PART B

A section in a textbook begins with this introduction:

> If we try to pick the single item that has had the greatest impact on social life in this century, among the many candidates the automobile stands out. Let us look at some of the ways in which it changed U.S. society.

Which of the following is the most specific statement of the topic of the section?

a. social life in the United States
b. the automobile's effect on social life in the U.S.
c. some important influences on social life in the U.S.

Now state a main idea guess that is suggested in the introduction by adding a short listing phrase to the topic:

The automobile changed U.S. society ______________________

Each paragraph in the next selection deals with one of the ways in which the automobile has changed U.S. society. The implied main idea for each is listed. In the blanks after each paragraph, write in the idea that fits the details.

- Farm and village life was changed greatly by the automobile.
- A preference for private over public transportation changed the way Americans lived.
- The automobile also stimulated mass movements to the suburbs.
- The automobile helped to change the role of women in U.S. society.
- The automobile soon pushed aside the horse as a means of transportation.
- Changes in architecture of U.S. homes due to the car occurred in three steps.

1 When Henry Ford began to mass produce the Model T in 1908, people immediately found automobiles attractive. They considered them cleaner, safer, more reliable, and more economical than horses. Cars also [brought] lower taxes, for no longer would the public have to pay to clean up the tons of horse manure that accumulated on the city streets each day. Humorous as it sounds now, it was even thought that automobiles would eliminate the cities' parking problems, for an automobile took up only half as much space as a horse and buggy.

____

____

2 The United States had developed a vast system of *urban* transit, with electric streetcar lines *radiating* outward from the center of our cities. As the automobile became affordable and more dependable, instead of walking to a streetcar and then having to wait in the cold and rain, people were able to travel directly from home on their own schedule. The decline in the use of streetcars actually changed the shape of U.S. cities. Before the automobile, U.S. cities were web-shaped, for residences and businesses were located along the streetcar lines. When freed by automobiles from having to live so close to the tracks, people filled in the areas between the "webs."

____

____

Using Context Clues

urban

a. relating to a city
b. relating to a farm
c. relating to a nation
d. relating to the countryside

radiating

a. broadcasting
b. disappearing
c. extending in lines
d. being removed

3 Already in the 1920s, U.S. residents had begun to leave the city, for they found that they could commute to work in the city from outlying areas where they benefited from more room and fewer taxes. Their departure significantly reduced the cities' tax base, thus contributing to many of the problems that U.S. cities experience today.

____

____

4 Prior to the 1920s, most farmers were isolated from the city. Because using horses for a trip to town was slow and *cumbersome,* they made such trips infrequently. By the 1920s, however, the popularity and low price of the Model T made the "Saturday trip to town" a standard event. There, farmers would market products, shop, and visit with friends. As a consequence, mail order catalogues stopped being the primary source of shopping, and access to better medical care and education improved. Farmers were also able to travel to bigger towns, where they found a greater variety of goods. As farmers began to use the nearby villages only for immediate needs, these once *flourishing* centers of social and commercial life dried up.

____

____

Using Context Clues

cumbersome

a. steady
b. cheap
c. troublesome
d. exciting

flourishing

a. boring
b. doing well
c. deserted
d. dangerous

5 Before the car, each home had a stable in the back where the family kept its buggy and horses. The stable was the logical place to shelter the family's first car, and it required no change in architecture. First, new homes were built with a *detached* garage located like the stable, at the back of the home. Second, as the automobile became a more *essential* part of the U.S. family, the garage was *incorporated* into the home by moving it from the back yard to the side of the house, and connecting it by a breezeway. In the final step the breezeway was removed, and the garage *integrated* into the home so that Americans could enter their automobiles without even going outside.

____

____

Using Context Clues

detached
a. separated
b. uninterested, not curious
c. impersonal, without feeling
d. calm, cool-headed

essential
a. very expensive
b. vital, necessary
c. troublesome
d. unknown

incorporated
a. removed
b. rebuilt
c. joined; united
d. painted

integrated means about the same as
a. detached
b. sheltered
c. essential
d. incorporated

6 Because automobiles required skill rather than strength, women were able to drive as well as men. This new *mobility* freed women physically from the narrow *confines* of the home. As Flink observed, the automobile changed women "from producers of food and clothing into consumers of national-brand canned goods, prepared foods, and ready-made clothes. The automobile permitted shopping at self-serve supermarkets outside the neighborhood and in combination with the electric refrigerator made buying food a weekly rather than a daily activity." When women began to do the shopping, they gained greater control over the family budget, and as their horizons extended beyond the confines of the home, they also gained different views of life. (Henslin, pp. 620–623.)

____

____

Using Context Clues

mobility
a. wealth
b. ability to move easily
c. machine
d. regulation

confines
a. hallways
b. housework
c. highways
d. boundaries, limits

EXERCISE 7.3

Completing Implied Main Idea Sentences

In Parts A and B, you will need to supply key words and phrases to complete main idea sentences for paragraphs that are part of longer passages. Vocabulary in context questions follow some of the paragraphs. Look up other words that you are not sure of, using the context to decide on correct meanings.

■ PART A

Topic: Differences among the social classes

1 An infant born into a poor family is much more likely to die during its first year than an infant born into a nonpoor family. For adults, too, *mortality* rates—the number of deaths per 1,000 people—differ among the classes. Among whites between 25 and 64 years of age, lower-class men and women have a higher mortality rate than middle-class men and women. They are also more likely than higher-class people to obtain their medical care in emergency rooms or public clinics, rather than from a private doctor.

Implied Main Idea: There are differences among the classes in ______ __________________ and in choices about _________________________.

mortality

a. relating to death

b. relating to unemployment

c. relating to illness

d. relating to hospitals

2 Upper- and middle-class people are likely to be active outside their homes—in parent-teacher associations, charitable organizations, and various community activities. They are also likely to make friends with professional *colleagues* or business contacts, with their spouses helping to *cultivate* the friendship. In contrast, working-class people tend to restrict their social life to families and relatives. Rarely do they entertain or visit their friends from work. Many working-class men and women are also quite *reluctant* to form close ties with neighbors. Instead, they often visit their parents, siblings, and other relatives.

Implied Main Idea: Our life-styles tend to be shaped by ____________ ____.

colleagues

a. athletes

b. fellow workers

c. advisers

d. doctors

Which meaning of *cultivate* fits this context?

a. prepare land for crops, as by plowing

b. grow or tend a plant or crop

c. shape by education

d. encourage the development of

reluctant

a. not willing

b. not able

c. relieved

d. uncertain

3 Whereas the lower class is more likely to read the *National Enquirer* and watch soap operas or professional wrestling, the upper middle class is more likely to read *Time* and *Newsweek* and watch public television programs. The upper class does not go for TV viewing at all. More generally, when compared with those of higher classes, working-class people read less; attend fewer concerts, lectures, and theaters; participate less in adult education; and spend less on recreation—they are more likely to watch television, work on their cars, take car rides, play cards, and visit taverns.

Implied Main Idea: People ______________________________ tend to prefer different forms of media and recreation.

4 The middle class seldom uses the double negative ("I can't get no satisfaction"), whereas the working class often uses it. The middle class rarely drops the letter "g" in present participles ("doin" for "doing," "singin" for "singing"), perhaps because they are conscious of being "correct." The working class often drops the "g," probably to show that they are not *snobbish.* On the other hand, the middle class has a weakness for *euphemism.* To them, a toilet is a "bathroom," an undertaker is a "funeral director," or a prison is a "correctional facility." They also tend to go for "fake" elegance. They would say "vocalist" instead of "singer," "as of this time" rather than "now," or "subsequently" rather than "later." The upper class *distinguishes* itself by its tendency to use such words as "tiresome" or "tedious" instead of "boring." Upper-class women are inclined to describe something seen in a store as "divine," "darling," or "adorable." (Thio, pp. 151–52.)

Implied Main Idea: There are differences ______________________ ____.

snobbish

a. acting as if better than others
b. highly educated
c. without money
d. unemployed

distinguishes

a. brings honor to
b. makes fun of
c. undermines
d. sets itself apart from others

euphemism

a. owning things that are of material value only
b. saying things plainly and clearly
c. using fancy phrases for words thought to offend
d. bringing up subjects that are impolite

■ PART B

Topic: Differences between males and females

1 Boys are taught to behave, like men, to avoid being "sissies." They are told that boys don't cry, only girls do. If, even in play, they try on makeup and wear dresses, their parents are *horrified.* Boys tend to grow up with a fear of being feminine, which forces them to maintain a *macho* image as well as an *exploitative* attitude toward women. Boys are also encouraged to avoid being "mama's boys." They are more likely than girls to receive physical punishment, such as spanking, so that they develop a sort of independence. On the other hand, girls are taught to he "ladylike," to be polite, to be gentle, and to rely on others—especially males—for help. They are allowed to express their emotions freely. Seeing their mothers spend time and money on fashion and cosmetics, they learn the importance of being pretty—and feel that they must rely more on their beauty than on intelligence to attract men.

Implied Main Idea: Boys and girls are ______________________________

and so they ____.

horrified

a. wealth
b. shocked
c. amused
d. pleased

exploitative

a. taking advantage of
b. protective
c. very thoughtful
d. confused

macho

a. overly masculine, dominating
b. pretended, acted
c. friendly, eager
d. superior

2 When parents are asked, "In what ways do you think boys and girls are different?" many would say that boys are more active, stronger, more competitive, noisier, and messier and that girls are more gentle, neater, quieter, more helpful, and more courteous. If they consider boys stronger, for example, they are likely to handle them more roughly than girls and to protect girls more than boys.

Implied Main Idea: Seeing different traits in boy and girls has caused

parents to ____.

3 School textbooks have long conveyed the impression that males are smarter and more important than females. There are more stories about boys than girls and more biographies of men than of women. Clever boys are presented more often than clever girls. Moreover, girls are led to believe that they are not as *proficient* in mathematics as boys. Sometimes girls are directly discouraged from taking advanced math or pursuing math as a career. If a gifted female student has built a robot, her achievement may be *trivialized* with questions like "Did you build it to do housework?"

Implied Main Idea: Schools have ______________________________.

proficient

a needed
b. noticed
c. honored
d. capable

trivialized

a. emphasized
b. made unimportant
c. forgotten
d. increased

4 In virtually all the elementary and secondary schools, men hold positions of authority (as coordinators, principals, and superintendents), and women are in positions of *subservience* (as teachers and aides). In such a male-dominant atmosphere, children are led to believe that women are *subordinate* and need the leadership of men. As Laurel Richardson observes, "Children learn that although their teacher, usually a female, is in charge of the room, the school is run by a male without whose strength she could not cope; the principal's office is where the *incorrigibles* are sent."

Implied Main Idea: The structure of the school helps to create the idea that ____.

subservience

a. lower rank or function
b. great usefulness
c. high interest
d. danger

subordinate

a. not trustworthy
b. independent
c. of a lower rank
d. frightened

incorrigibles

a. those who are athletes
b. those who can't be controlled
c. those who are truants
d. those who excel in the classroom

5 In such traditional magazines as *Good Housekeeping* and *Family Circle,* there has, until recently, been the tendency to talk down to women as if they were children. Today, they are more *sophisticated,* but they still tend to define the female role in terms of homemaking and motherhood, and to offer numerous beauty tips to help attract men or please husbands. In less traditional magazines, such as *New Woman* and *Working Woman,* although women are portrayed working outside the home, they are nonetheless presented as responsible for housework and children—no protest being raised that women, much more often than men, are expected to perform two jobs *simultaneously.* If such magazines go all out to *demolish* the sexual stereotypes, they may lose many of their readers to the more traditional women's magazines. Today, the traditional "seven sisters"—*Better Homes and Gardens, Family Circle, Woman's Day, McCall's, Ladies' Home Journal, Good Housekeeping,* and *Redbook*— continue to *surpass* considerably in readership the new women's magazines, such as *Working Woman, Savvy,* and *Working Mother.*

Implied Main Idea: The most popular _______________ continue to portray women ______________________________.

sophisticated

a. experienced, worldly-wise
b. phony, unreal
c. angry, aggressive
d. thoughtful

demolish

a. present
b. increase
c. destroy completely
d. discuss

simultaneously

a. with great effort
b. without complaint
c. competently
d. at the same time

surpass

a. go down
b. go beyond
c. improve
d. lose

6 Television commercials present women as sex objects and dedicated housewives. Until recently, young sexy women were shown admiring an old cigar smoker who used an air freshener. Housewives were shown in *ecstasy* over their shiny waxed floors or the sparkling cleanliness of their dishes. Prime-time television programs also *reinforce* traditional gender roles and inequalities. Over the past 15 years before 1982, TV researcher George Gerbner analyzed 1,600 prime-time programs, including more than 15,000 characters. He concluded that women were generally typecast as either lovers or mothers. They were mostly portrayed as weak, passive sidekicks to powerful, effective men. (Thio, pp. 210–12.)

Implied Main Idea: Both ______________________________ and ______________________________ reinforce traditional gender roles and inequalities.

ecstasy

a. concern
b. great joy
c. extreme weariness
d. discussion

reinforce

a. counteract
b. reduce
c. add support to
d. confuse

RECOGNIZING IMPLIED MAIN IDEAS IN LITERATURE

In Chapter 5, you read "The Scholarship Jacket," followed by an exercise on inferences in reading literature. The story that follows will give you some more practice in learning to read between the lines by observing what characters say and do and what happens to them. The story deals with a situation that has a number of effects on children: the need for some families (mostly from minority groups) to keep moving to find work in fields across the country. Before you read, write down any information or experiences you may have had about the topic of migrant workers.

____

____

____

____

____

The Circuit

by Francisco Jimenez

1 It was that time of year again. Ito, the strawberry sharecropper, did not smile. It was natural. The peak of the strawberry season was over and the last few days the workers, most of them braceros, were not picking as many boxes as they had during the months of June and July.

2 As the last days of August disappeared, so did the number of braceros. Sunday, only one—the best picker—came to work. I liked him.

Sometimes we talked during our half-hour lunch break. That is how I found out he was from Jalisco, the same state in Mexico my family was from. That Sunday was the last time I saw him.

3 When the sun had tired and sunk behind the mountains, Ito signaled us that it was time to go home. "Ya esora," he yelled in his broken Spanish. Those were the words I waited for twelve hours a day, every day, seven days a week, week after week. And the thought of not hearing them again saddened me.

4 As we drove home Papa did not say a word. With both hands on the wheel, he stared at the dirt road. My older brother, Roberto, was also silent. He leaned his head back and closed his eyes. Once in a while he cleared from his throat the dust that blew in from outside.

5 Yes, it was that time of year. When I opened the front door to the shack, I stopped. Everything we owned was neatly packed in cardboard boxes. Suddenly I felt even more the weight of hours, days, weeks, and months of work. I sat down on a box. The thought of having to move to Fresno and knowing what was in store for me there brought tears to my eyes. That night I could not sleep. I lay in bed thinking about how much I hated this move. A little before five o'clock in the morning, Papa woke everyone up. A few minutes later, the yelling and screaming of my little brothers and sisters, for whom the move was a great adventure, broke the silence of dawn. Shortly, the barking of the dogs accompanied them.

6 While we packed the breakfast dishes, Papa went outside to start the "Carcanchita." That was the name Papa gave his old '38 black Plymouth. He bought it in a used-car lot in Santa Rosa in the winter of 1949. Papa was very proud of his little jalopy. He had a right to be proud of it. He spent a lot of time looking at other cars before buying this one. When he finally chose the "Carcanchita," he checked it thoroughly before driving it out of the car lot. He examined every inch of the car. He listened to the motor, tilting his head from side to side like a parrot, trying to detect any noises that spelled car trouble. After being satisfied with the looks and sounds of the car, Papa then insisted on knowing who the original owner was. He never did find out from the car salesman, but he bought the car anyway. Papa figured the original owner must have been an important man because behind the rear seat of the car he found a blue necktie.

7 Papa parked the car out in front and left the motor running. "Listo," he yelled. Without saying a word, Roberto and I began to carry the boxes out to the car. Roberto carried the two big boxes and I carried the two smaller ones. Papa then threw the mattress on top of the car roof and tied it with ropes to the front and rear bumpers.

8 Everything was packed except Mama's pot. It was an old large galvanized pot she had picked up at an army surplus store in Santa Maria

the year I was born. The pot had many dents and nicks, and the more dents and nicks it acquired the more Mama liked it. "Mi olla," she used to say proudly.

9 I held the front door open as Mama carefully carried out her pot by both handles, making sure not to spill the cooked beans. When she got to the car, Papa reached out to help her with it. Roberto opened the rear car door and Papa gently placed it on the floor behind the front seat. All of us then climbed in. Papa sighed, wiped the sweat off his forehead with his sleeve, and said wearily: "Es todo."

10 As we drove away, I felt a lump in my throat. I turned around and looked at our little shack for the last time.

11 At sunset we drove into a labor camp near Fresno. Since Papa did not speak English, Mama asked the camp foreman if he needed any more workers. "We don't need no more," said the foreman, scratching his head. "Check with Sullivan down the road. Can't miss him. He lives in a big white house with a fence around it."

12 When we got there, Mama walked up to the house. She went through a white gate, past a row of rose bushes, up the stairs to the front door. She rang the doorbell. The porch light went on and a tall husky man came out. They exchanged a few words. After the man went in, Mama clasped her hands and hurried back to the car. "We have work! Mr. Sullivan said we can stay there the whole season," she said, gasping and pointing to an old garage near the stables.

13 The garage was worn out by the years. It had no windows. The walls, eaten by termites, strained to support the roof full of holes. The dirt floor, populated by earth worms, looked like a gray road map.

14 That night, by the light of a kerosene lamp, we unpacked and cleaned our new home. Roberto swept away the loose dirt, leaving the hard ground. Papa plugged the holes in the walls with old newspapers and tin can tops. Mama fed my little brothers and sisters. Papa and Roberto then brought in the mattress and placed it in the far corner of the garage. "Mama, you and the little ones sleep on the mattress. Roberto, Panchito, and I will sleep outside under the trees," Papa said.

15 Early next morning Mr. Sullivan showed us where his crop was, and after breakfast, Papa, Roberto, and I headed for the vineyard to pick. Around nine o'clock the temperature had risen to almost one hundred degrees. I was completely soaked in sweat and my mouth felt as if I had been chewing on a handkerchief. I walked over to the end of the row, picked up the jug of water we had brought, and began drinking. "Don't drink too much; you'll get sick," Roberto shouted. No sooner had he said that than I felt sick to my stomach. I dropped to my knees and let the jug roll off my hands. I remained motionless with my eyes glued on the hot sandy ground. All I could hear was the drone of insects. Slowly I

began to recover. I poured water over my face and neck and watched the dirty water run down my arms to the ground.

16 I still felt a little dizzy when we took a break to eat lunch. It was past two o'clock and we sat underneath a large walnut tree that was on the side of the road. While we ate, Papa jotted down the number of boxes we had picked. Roberto drew designs on the ground with a stick. Suddenly I noticed Papa's face turn pale as he looked down the road. "Here comes the school bus," he whispered loudly in alarm. Instinctively, Roberto and I ran and hid in the vineyards. We did not want to get in trouble for not going to school. The neatly dressed boys about my age got off. They carried books under their arms. After they crossed the street, the bus drove away. Roberto and I came out from hiding and joined Papa. "Tienen que tener cuidado," he warned us.

17 After lunch we went back to work. The sun kept beating down. The buzzing insects, the wet sweat, and the hot dry dust made the afternoon seem to last forever. Finally the mountains around the valley reached out and swallowed the sun. Within an hour it was too dark to continue picking. The vines blanketed the grapes, making it difficult to see the bunches. "Vamonos," said Papa, signaling to us that it was time to quit work. Papa then took out a pencil and began to figure out how much we had earned our first day. He wrote down numbers, crossed some out, wrote down some more. "Quince," he murmured.

18 When we arrived home, we took a cold shower underneath a waterhose. We then sat down to eat dinner around some wooden crates that served as a table. Mama had cooked a special meal for us. We had rice and tortillas with "carne con chile," my favorite dish.

19 The next morning I could hardly move. My body ached all over. I felt little control over my arms and legs. This feeling went on every morning for days until my muscles finally got used to the work.

20 It was Monday, the first week of November. The grape season was over and I could now go to school. I woke up early that morning and lay in bed, looking at the stars and savoring the thought of not going to work and of starting sixth grade for the first time that year. Since I could not sleep, I decided to get up and join Papa and Roberto at breakfast. I sat at the table across from Roberto, but I kept my head down. I did not want to look up and face him. I knew he was sad. He was not going to school today. He was not going tomorrow, or next week, or next month. He would not go until the cotton season was over, and that was sometime in February. I rubbed my hands together and watched the dry, acid-stained skin fall to the floor in little rolls.

21 When Papa and Roberto left for work, I felt relief. I walked to the top of a small grade next to the shack and watched the "Carcanchita" disappear in the distance in a cloud of dust.

22 Two hours later, around eight o'clock, I stood by the side of the road waiting for school bus number twenty. When it arrived I climbed in. Everyone was busy either talking or yelling. I sat in an empty seat in the back.

23 When the bus stopped in front of the school, I felt very nervous. I looked out the bus window and saw boys and girls carrying books under their arms. I put my hands in my pant pockets and walked to the principal's office. When I entered I heard a woman's voice say: "May I help you?" I was startled. I had not heard English for months. For a few seconds I remained speechless. I looked at the lady who waited for an answer. My first instinct was to answer her in Spanish, but I held back. Finally, after struggling for English words, I managed to tell her that I wanted to enroll in the sixth grade. After answering many questions, I was led to the classroom.

24 Mr. Lema, the sixth grade teacher, greeted me and assigned me a desk. He then introduced me to the class. I was so nervous and scared at that moment when everyone's eyes were on me that I wished I were with Papa and Roberto picking cotton. After taking roll, Mr. Lema gave the class the assignment for the first hour. "The first thing we have to do this morning is finish reading the story we began yesterday," he said enthusiastically. He walked up to me, handed me an English book, and asked me to read. "We are on page 125," he said politely. When I heard this, I felt my blood rush to my head; I felt dizzy. "Would you like to read?" he asked hesitantly. I opened the book to page 125. My mouth was dry. My eyes began to water. I could not begin. "You can read later," Mr. Lema said understandingly.

25 For the rest of the period I kept getting angrier and angrier with myself. I should have read, I thought to myself.

26 During recess I went to the restroom and opened my English book to page 125. I began to read in a low voice, pretending I was in class. There were many words I did not know. I closed the book and headed back to the classroom.

27 Mr. Lema was sitting at his desk correcting papers. When I entered he looked up at me and smiled. I felt better. I walked up to him and asked if he could help me with the new words. "Gladly," he said.

28 The rest of the month I spent my lunch hours working on English with Mr. Lema, my best friend at school.

29 One Friday during lunch hour Mr. Lema asked me to take a walk with him to the music room. "Do you like music?" he asked me as we entered the building.

30 "Yes, I like corridos," I answered. He then picked up a trumpet, blew on it and handed it to me. The sound gave me goose bumps. I knew that sound. I had heard it in many corridos. "How would you like to

learn how to play it?" he asked. He must have read my face because before I could answer, he added, "I'll teach you how to play it during our lunch hours."

31 That day I could hardly wait to get home to tell Papa and Mama the great news. As I got off the bus, my little brothers and sisters ran up to meet me. They were yelling and screaming. I thought they were happy to see me, but when I opened the door to our shack, I saw that everything we owned was neatly packed in cardboard boxes.

EXERCISE 7.4

Recognizing Implied Ideas in *The Circuit*

None of the following ideas is directly stated. Some of them are strongly implied by the story, while others clearly are not. If an idea can be inferred from the story as probably true or very likely, write *Yes.* If an idea cannot be supported or the opposite is true, write *No.* Then explain your reasons and present any evidence (include paragraph numbers) that supports your position.

EXAMPLES

Yes The narrator's name is Panchito.

Evidence/Reasoning: Papa says "Mama, you and the little ones sleep on the mattress. Roberto, Panchito, and I will sleep outside." The next morning these three go to work. The narrator is the person between Roberto and "the little ones." (¶14–15)

No The family is very upset at having to stay in a rundown garage.

Evidence/Reasoning: Their reaction shows the opposite. (¶12–14) Mama is excited ("We have work! Mr. Sullivan said we can stay there the whole season," she said, gasping). Everyone pitches in to clean and repair it without complaint.

1. _____ In the strawberry fields, the workers normally did not get any days off.

Evidence/Reasoning: ______________________________

____

2. _____ Roberto is the oldest of the children in the family.

   Evidence/Reasoning: ____

   ____

3. _____ Papa doesn't know anything about car engines.

   Evidence/Reasoning: ____

   ____

4. _____ Papa is careful and uses good common sense in making purchases.

   Evidence/Reasoning: ____

   ____

5. _____ The sharecropper Ito is a fluent speaker of Spanish.

   Evidence/Reasoning: ____

   ____

6. _____ The family will eat at a restaurant on their way to the new job picking grapes.

   Evidence/Reasoning: ____

   ____

7. _____ Papa had a job promised to him before the family left to pick grapes.

   Evidence/Reasoning: ____

   ____

8. _____ The family's new home is much nicer than their old one.

   Evidence/Reasoning: ____

   ____

9. _____ Picking grapes is a much more pleasant job than picking strawberries.

   Evidence/Reasoning: ____

   ____

10. _____ Papa is able to do basic math.

Evidence/Reasoning: ____

____

11. _____ The family's home on the Sullivan property has an indoor shower.

Evidence/Reasoning: ____

____

12. _____ Roberto does not enjoy going to school.

Evidence/Reasoning: ____

____

13. _____ Panchito is eleven or twelve years old.

Evidence/Reasoning: ____

____

14. _____ When he enters Mr. Lema's class, he cannot speak or read any English.

Evidence/Reasoning: ____

____

15. _____ His classmates treated him badly.

Evidence/Reasoning: ____

____

16. _____ Mr. Lema is a thoughtful, giving teacher.

Evidence/Reasoning: ____

____

17. _____ Panchito spent more than one month in Mr. Lema's class.

Evidence/Reasoning: ____

____

18. _____ Mr. Lema knows how to play the trumpet.

    Evidence/Reasoning: ____

    ____

19. _____ The family has strong values and believes in hard work.

    Evidence/Reasoning: ____

    ____

20. _____ The narrator will not be going back to Mr. Lema's school this year.

    Evidence/Reasoning: ____

    ____

Often in stories, and sometimes in articles as well, the overall main idea is implied rather than stated. A main idea statement must always be a complete sentence. Which of the following is the best statement of the implied main idea of "The Circuit"?

a. Migrant farmworkers and their families were treated badly and paid unfairly low wages for their hard labor.
b. For a young person in a family of migrant farmworkers, moving often to find work makes getting an education difficult.
c. Having to work long hours in the fields, at last getting to go to school and get to learn to play the trumpet, and then having to move again.
d. Many young people are ignored or mistreated by society and by the system of education in this country.

EXERCISE 7.5

Guessing Foreign Vocabulary from Context

In a number of places in the story, Spanish words and phrases are used. Their meanings are not given, but for some there are enough context clues to come up with a meaning that might fit the situation. For the following, circle the letter of the meaning that best fits. If all the choices could fit the context, circle *d.* (If you already know the meaning of some or all of these, pretend that you do not.)

1. When the sun had tired and sunk behind the mountains, Ito signaled us that it was time to go home. *"Ya esora,"* he yelled in his broken Spanish. (¶3)

   a. "Let's take a short break."
   b. "You're all fired."
   c. "It's quitting time."
   d. All choices could fit.

2. Papa parked the car out in front and left the motor running. *"Listo,"* he yelled. Without saying a word, Roberto and I began to carry the boxes out to the car. (¶7)

   a. "Hurry up!"
   b. "Ready!"
   c. "Load it up!"
   d. All choices could fit.

3. The pot had many dents and nicks, and the more dents and nicks it acquired the more Mama liked it. *"Mi olla,"* she used to say proudly. (¶8)

   a. "My pot."
   b. "It's really a cheap one."
   c. "Buy me a new one."
   d. All choices could fit.

4. The bus drove away. Roberto and I came out from hiding and joined Papa. *"Tienen que tener cuidado,"* he warned us. (¶16)

   a. "Let's get back to work."
   b. "We must be careful."
   c. "Let's move to a new city."
   d. All choices could fit.

5. *"Vamonos,"* said Papa, signaling to us that it was time to quit work. (¶17)

   a. "Let's go!"
   b. "Watch out!"
   c. "Work harder!"
   d. All choices could fit.

6. Papa then took out a pencil and began to figure out how much we had earned our first day. He wrote down numbers, crossed some out, wrote down some more. *"Quince,"* he murmured. (¶17)

   a. 10
   b. 15
   c. 25
   d. All choices could fit.

7. Mama had cooked a special meal for us. We had rice and tortillas with *"carne con chile."* (¶18)

   a. chicken and vegetables
   b. soup and salad
   c. meat and chile
   d. All choices could fit.

8. Papa gently placed [the pot of beans] on the floor behind the front seat. All of us then climbed in. Papa sighed, wiped the sweat off his forehead with his sleeve, and said wearily: *"Es todo."* (¶7)

   a. "That's all of it."
   b. "It's time for school."
   c. "What time is it?"
   d. All choices could fit.

Active Learning

BUILDING FRAMES OF REFERENCE

If reading material has a lot of difficult vocabulary words and long sentences, the average reader will likely have problems understanding the ideas. But what happens when, even if most of the vocabulary and sentences are not very difficult, you still don't really have a clear idea what the author is taking about? When this happens to us, the reason is likely to be that we lack the background information and experience needed to make sense out of a topic. We can easily get lost and end up drawing a blank.

Learning about a field of knowledge is something like completing a large jigsaw puzzle. At the beginning it is very difficult to make much sense of all the pieces. We might begin to organize it by finding the straight pieces that make the framing edge. As various parts of the puzzle begin to take shape, we can fit new pieces at a quicker pace than before. Building knowledge is very similar. At the beginning, a subject seems like a confusing collection of separate facts. Gradually you begin to connect them into a bigger picture, with the main concepts of a field acting like a kind of skeleton that holds everything together. The more you know, the easier it is to add new information. After a while, you will have developed a "frame of reference" on a subject that will help you relate new knowledge to old.

You already have developed some of these from experiences in your life. What, for example, do you know about music, movies, television, or sports? It's likely that you are something of an expert in parts of one or more of these areas. For example, you might have a great deal of background on certain types of popular music. You may have an interest in a sport like football and know many facts about current players or you are able to recall all the Super Bowl winners.

Each field has a special body of knowledge and its own kind of frameworks. Learning about history, for example, is aided by a frame of reference we call a *time line.* This helps us see how events relate:

- Did the Greeks come before or after the Romans?
- When did the early civilizations of China, the Indus Valley, and Mesopotamia develop?
- What were the connections between the Olmec and Aztec civilizations of Mesoamerica?
- When did Rome fall?
- When did the Crusades occur?

In fields like geography and astronomy, *maps* are relied on to show connections in information. By studying these fields, you eventually build maps in your mind of how things relate together: maps of your city, your state, your country, your continent, the world, the solar system, and beyond. If you don't know, for example, where Honduras is, you will be able to place it mentally when you are told that it borders Guatemala, El Salvador, and Nicaragua—that is, if you already know where those places are. If you don't, the new information will stay disconnected because you have no frame of reference to add it to.

Learning is a lifelong process with much information coming through reading. As a lifelong learner, you need to build and add to your frames of reference. No one is expected to know everything, and some things are more important than others. Still, you should use every chance you get to store in memory what you learn about. The more information you are able to connect, the more you will be able to bring to the task of reading for real understanding.

EXERCISE 7.6

Using Frames of Reference

One passage in this chapter dealt with the important effect of the automobile on American life. What is your frame of reference for "automobiles"? Write down some things that you know about automobiles that make them important in American life:

____

____

____

____

____

____

Now here is some of the information you learned in the selection about automobiles. How many of these statements do you recall?

- The automobile replaced the horse as the main means of transportation.
- A preference for automobiles over streetcar travel changed the shape of cities.
- The automobile also stimulated mass movements to the suburbs.

- Farm and village life was changed greatly by the automobile.
- The automobile caused changes in the architecture of U.S homes.
- The automobile helped to change the role of women in U.S. society.

1. Was this new information for you when you first read it?

 ____

 ____

2. Did it connect to information you had before?

 ____

 ____

3. Did it change any ideas you had before about the automobile?

 ____

 ____

As this exercise shows, by adding information to what you already know, you will read with more understanding when you meet a topic again. In the chapters in Part Three of this text, you will do work with a variety of frames of reference. The following exercise will give you a better understanding of the process of building frames of reference.

Reading Portfolio

FRAMES OF REFERENCE

1. Decide on a topic from sports and entertainment. Pick one that you feel you know a lot about and are interested in. Here are some broad areas you can narrow down:

 movies (action, thriller, comedy)

 television (game shows, situation comedies, cop shows, soaps)

 television or movie actors

 singers, bands, types of music

 sports and star players

 Your topic: ______________________________

2. Write down some main points that you know about your topic.
3. Find an article on your topic, one that looks interesting and informative.

4. Read the article and write down the main points of information in it.
5. Compare what you learned with what you knew before. Write at least a full paragraph or more on each of the following:
   - What information did it give that you knew before?
   - What new information did it give that you could fit in with what you already knew?
   - What ideas that you previously had on the topic were changed by your reading?
   - Would someone with no background on the topic be able to understand the article fully?

CHAPTER 8

How Does This All Fit Together?

Using Outlines and Maps to Summarize

After reading this chapter, you will know the answers to these questions:

- In what way does reading material have a skeleton?
- What is plagiarism and how is it avoided?
- What skills are need to write a summary?
- What steps lead to writing a good summary?
- What are graphics and what information do they give?
- What previewing techniques will help for longer readings?
- What are mind maps?

Look at the two figures below for ten seconds. Then turn the page and, without looking back, redraw them.

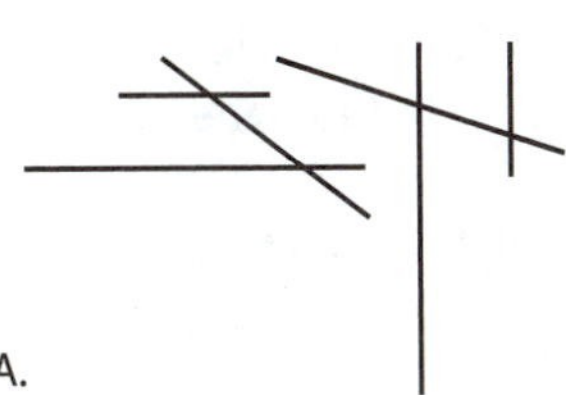

A.

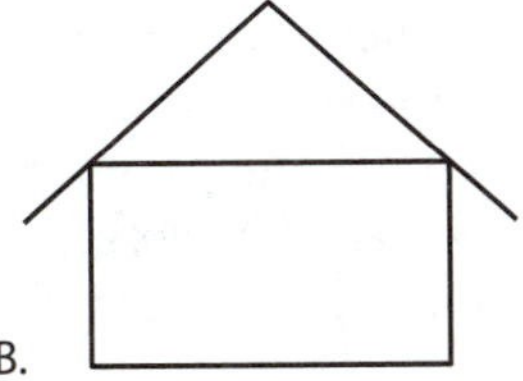

B.

A. B.

Both figures have the same number of lines with the same length, but most likely you came much closer to the original in B. Why do you think that is so? Reading the following will help you answer this question:

> Every book has a skeleton hidden between its boards. Your job is to find it. A book comes to you with flesh on its bare bones and clothes over its flesh. It is all dressed up. You must read the book with X-ray eyes . . . to grasp its structure. . . . You can penetrate beneath the moving surface of a book to its rigid skeleton. You can see the way the parts . . . hang together, and the thread that ties them into a whole.
>
> A book is like a single house. It is a mansion of many rooms, rooms on different levels, of different sizes and shapes, with different outlooks, rooms with different functions to perform. These rooms are independent, in part. Each has its own structure and interior decoration. But they are not absolutely independent and separate. They are connected by doors and arches, by corridors and stairways. Because they are connected, the partial function which each performs contributes its share to the usefulness of the whole house. Otherwise the house would not be genuinely livable.
>
> A good book, like a good house, is an orderly arrangement of parts. Each major part has a certain amount of independence. . . . But if they hang together at all . . . there must be a plan and you must find it. (Adler, pp. 160–64.)

In the exercise above, B was easier to remember and draw because all the lines (parts) came together into something you recognize: a house. In A, the lines stay separate; they are a jumble and don't connect as a skeleton. In the reading above, the author talks about skeletons in books, but it is the same for articles, chapters, sections, and paragraphs.

You have already worked with these skeletons in earlier chapters, in the form of outlines. These help us separate major and minor detail and thus show us what to remember or leave out. For example, the paragraph in a previous chapter was outlined in this way:

I. Overspecialization of work erodes responsibility/initiative of the worker.
   A. Bosses make workers feel controlled.
   B. Workers complain of "being spied on."
      1. plant foreman
      2. Ma Bell supervisor
      3. bus driver checker
II. Overspecialization dehumanizes workers.
   A. Worker tied to isolated task.
   B. Jobs lose meaning.
      1. spotwelder as a machine
      2. caged bank teller
      3. steelworker like mule
      4. receptionist like a monkey

Here items I A–B and II A–B give us the skeleton: the main idea and major details. The rest provide minor detail. If we wanted a really "bare bones" outline, we would leave these out.

SAYING THINGS IN YOUR OWN WORDS

All students need to be aware of the danger of *plagiarism.* This term refers to using and passing off the creations, ideas, or words of another as if they were one's own. It is serious business and has ruined careers. Charges of plagiarism have led to lawsuits over rights to songs, screenplays, and parts of novels. In education and medicine, professors and researchers have been fired and/or sued for taking the work of others without giving due credit.

Plagiarism also applies to student papers and research reports. Plagiarism is clear in cases where students turn in the work of others, copy from sources, or download reports from the Internet without giving any credit. But more often plagiarism is not deliberate. Sometimes students have left high school thinking that copying material is acceptable as long as the source is given. They do not understand that telling the source of material is not enough. Credit must also be given for any *phrasing* that is taken directly from a source, and this must be shown by using quotation marks. Anything else used must be put in the student's own words.

But "putting things in your own words" is not easy. Students sometimes have learned to switch parts of a sentence, change a word or two, and leave out a few words and phrases. But this patchwork quilt approach is not putting things into your own words. Explaining something in your own words means you have first read for understanding and thought long and hard about the ideas in the source. As an example of the thought needed to explain ideas, here is a common proverb (a wise saying that points to a general truth): "Don't cry over spilled milk."

Restating this as "Don't shed tears over milk that is spilled" won't get to the meaning here. This really isn't about milk or crying. The idea could be supported by many examples, of which spilled milk is one. Here is one way we might put the general meaning in different words: "Don't waste time over something that's happened but can't be fixed."

Working with information from texts presents similar problems. Below is part of a paragraph from an earlier exercise. Following it is one of the questions and a sample answer:

> *T. cacao* evolved in Central America. . . . Growers harvest its seeds, or "cacao beans." These are processed into cocoa butter and essences, which end up in chocolate products. Unknown interactions among the 1,000 or so compounds in chocolate exert compelling (some say addictive) effects on the human brain.
>
> ***Question:*** Why do Americans feel compelled to buy chocolate products?
>
> ***Answer:*** "Unknown interactions among the 1,000 or so compounds in chocolate exert compelling (some say addictive) effects on the human brain."

This answer is taken directly from the original. If you were, for example, making notes to prepare for a test, there would be nothing wrong with this. The danger is that such notes might accidentally end up in a later report. For safety and for the mental practice it gives you, it's best to follow this practice: WRITE ALL NOTES IN YOUR OWN WORDS.

Putting an answer to the question above in our own words requires us to think about and connect the things we learn about chocolate:

- it has compounds
- these react in certain ways
- no one really knows why we get hooked

By thinking about how these fit together, we could come up with a statement in our own words that shows we really understand the idea: "The ingredients in chocolate react in unexplained ways to hook us."

EXERCISE 8.1

"In Other Words . . ."

Work together in groups of 3–4 to complete this exercise.

■ PART A Expressing Ideas in Your Own Words

The proverbs below all give examples of a general idea. Discuss the meaning of that idea and then write it in your own words. Give any specific examples that the proverb might apply to.

1. "Let sleeping dogs lie."

   The point this makes, in my words, is: ______________________________

   ____

2. "When it rains, it pours."

   The point this makes, in my words, is: ______________________________

   ____

3. "If the shoe fits, wear it."

   The point this makes, in my words, is: ______________________________

   ____

■ PART B Stating Ideas from a Text in Your Own Words

Here is a paragraph you worked with in an earlier chapter.

> In 1945 psychologist Rene Spitz reported that children who received little attention in institutions suffered very noticeable effects. In one orphanage, Spitz found that infants who were about 18 months old were left lying on their backs in small cubicles most of the day without any human contact. Within a year, all had become physically, mentally, emotionally, and socially retarded. Two years later, more than a third of the children had died. Those who survived could not speak, walk, dress themselves, or use a spoon.

Do not look at the paragraph as you answer the following questions in your own words and sentence structure. Sometimes certain key words from the original can't be changed; these include names of organizations, places, professions, and people (*Spitz* and *psychologist* are examples above) or words that have no synonyms (e.g., *orphanage*).

1. What happened to neglected children in institutions? In my own words:

____

____

2. How were the children in one orphanage treated? In my own words:

____

____

3. How did they react in the first year? In my own words:

____

____

4. What happened to more than a third of the children? In my own words:

____

____

5. How did the rest act? In my own words:

____

____

MAKING A SUMMARY

"Get to the point!" we sometimes tell people. If you ask a friend about a movie, you don't want a dragged-out story: "and then . . . and then . . . and then . . ." What you want is a *summary:* a short form that still keeps the main ideas of the original. In college, you might have to summarize a chapter, an article, or even a book, sometimes in less than a page. Also, making summary notes is very important in studying for tests. Being able to summarize correctly, therefore, is one of the most important skills for success in college. You have already been learning the skills for writing a good summary: reading for understanding, finding the skeleton, creating an outline, and putting things in your own words. By following these steps you will be able to write good summaries.

1. You write a summary only after careful reading and thought. Ask questions to determine the topic and main idea. From this you can make an outline that shows you know what the main idea is, which detail is most important, and which is less important. Never begin writing until this preparation has been done.

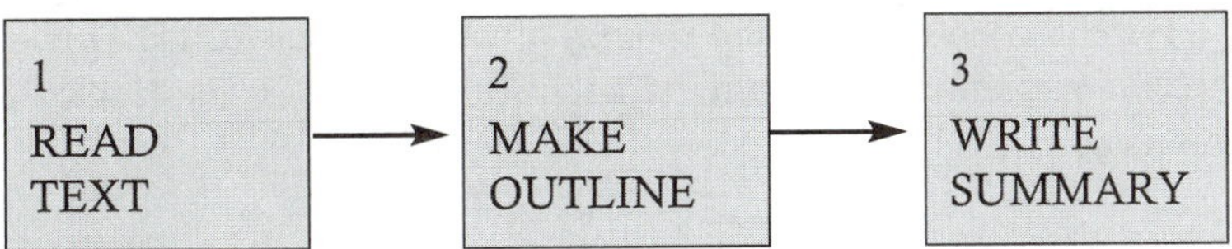

2. A summary is shorter than the original. If you try to do one line of summary for each line of text, you will not be able to shorten the original to the main points. To create a summary, think about the main point or conclusion of the entire paragraph. For example, review your answers to the paragraph about children in institutions. Then without looking back, in one or two sentences give an answer to the following question: What was Spitz's general conclusion about children in the care of institutions?

____

____

____

3. How much detail you leave in depends on your own purposes or what your instructor wants. For example, look again at the outline on specialization of work:

   I. Overspecialization of work erodes responsibility/initiative of the worker.
      A. Bosses make workers feel controlled, "spied on."
         1. plant foreman
         2. Ma Bell supervisor
         3. bus driver checker
      B. Tying the worker to small part of large task can dehumanize.
         1. spotwelder as a machine
         2. caged bank teller
         3. steelworker like mule
         4. receptionist like a monkey

   Your written summary could include all of these points. For a very short summary, points I, A, and B would be enough. For something in between, you might include one example of the minor detail under A and B.

4. The summary must be written in your own words. To do that, you must always be sure that the outline has been written in your own words. When you write the summary, you work only from the outline. If you start looking at the original, you will lose the big picture, and it will be very hard to say things in your own words.

Here is an example of the process of writing a summary. This is the outline you completed in an earlier chapter for the six-paragraph selection "The Conquistadores":

1. With fall of Granada (1492), Moors driven off by Spanish Christians
   A. Result: a class of intolerant men after honor/status
   B. After the Reconquista, great attraction to Spain's New World
2. Within fifty years, Aztec and Incan empires destroyed, territory taken by Spain
   A. Focus on mainland and wealth, not route to Asia through Caribbean
   B. 1519–1540, conquistadores in two groups spread through the Americas
3. Got victory with only about ten thousand men
   A. Cortes, Pizarro, others making contracts, raising money, signing up army
   B. Mainly soldiers/sailors, peasants, artisans—not nobles
4. Many different reasons for going on the venture
   A. Hoped conquering people and land for Spain would get them titles/favors
   B. Bring Christianity to those considered pagans
   C. Wanted excitement and adventure, get away from past mistakes
   D. All wanted gold, riches
5. Desires of most not achieved
   A. Very few got titles as nobles
   B. Ended up in debt forever to investors in Spain
   C. Did not get equal share of the booty
   D. Colonial administrators brought in, replaced them
6. Did receive "immortality" in a different way
   A. Spanish women scarce; married Indian women
   B. Offspring—mestizos—helped unify Latin America's races

The statements in the outline have been put into the writer's own words and sentence structure. As you learned earlier, some basic words in outlines may be those in the original, such as names of people, places, titles, occupations, and organizations. Here, for example, the outline includes words and phrases like *Moors, Spanish, Reconquista, colonial administrators, conquistadores, mestizos, Latin America,* etc. Figures and dates can sometimes be rounded off or stated differently. For example, the phrase in item 2—"Within fifty years"—replaces the text's phrase "Within half a century of Columbus's arrival . . ." Any long phrases from the source that you feel shouldn't be changed *must* have quotation marks both before and after, and they must be written exactly, word for word.

In writing the summary, always work from the outline. Go back to the text to check a point and make the change in your own words on the outline before beginning to write again. As you write, you should feel free to make more changes in your wording. Here is a sample of a summary of the outline:

> After the Spanish Christians took back Granada from the Moors in 1492, the winners began to look for honor and status in the New World. These conquistadores began to focus more on the mainland to find wealth rather than looking for a way to Asia through the Caribbean. From 1519–1540, in two groups they spread through the Americas. Within fifty years, they had destroyed the Aztec and Incan empires and taken their territory for Spain. They won their victory with only about ten thousand men. Cortes, Pizarro, and other leaders were busy making contracts, raising money, and signing up an army. These men were mainly soldiers, sailors, peasants, artisans, rather than nobles.
>
> They had many different reasons for going on the venture. Some hoped conquering people and land for Spain would get them benefits. Some wanted to bring Christianity to those they considered pagans. Some just wanted excitement and adventure, or to get away from past mistakes. All of them wanted gold and riches. But the desires of most were not achieved. Very few got titles. Many ended up in debt forever to investors in Spain. The men did not get equal share of the booty. Eventually, colonial administrators were brought in and replaced them.
>
> But they did receive "immortality" in a different way. Spanish women were scarce, so many of these men married Indian women. Their offspring (known as "mestizos") helped bring together the races of Latin America.

The original passage had over 600 words. This summary has kept the main points and important details, but shortened it to less than one half of the original. If needed, the summary can be even more to the point:

> After reconquering Granada, the winners looked for honor and status in the New World. In fifty years, the Conquistadores had destroyed the Aztec and Incan empires and taken their territory for Spain. They had many different reasons for going on the venture, but all wanted wealth. Though the desires of most were not achieved, they did receive "immortality" in that their offspring ("mestizos") from marriage with Indian women helped bring together the races of Latin America.

This version takes fewer than 80 words. It keeps the main points but leaves out minor details.

EXERCISE 8.2

Writing a Summary

Work together in groups to complete steps 1–4 that follow the passage. Look up any words that you don't know. Mark major detail, and be on the lookout for some key signal words—*one, another, third*—that will help you to make an outline.

Why Are They Homeless?

by Alex Thio

1 The causes of homelessness can be categorized into two types: larger social forces and personal characteristics. One social force is the shortage of inexpensive housing for poor families and poor unattached persons. This shortage began in the 1970s and accelerated in the 1980s, as the Reagan administration cut government funding for subsidized housing programs from $533 billion in 1981 to only $8 billion in 1988. Another social force is the decreasing demand for unskilled labor in the 1980s, which resulted in extremely high unemployment among young men in general and blacks in particular. A third social force is the erosion of public welfare benefits over the last two decades. Today, none of the states that have income support programs for poor unattached persons provides enough to reach $4,000 a year, and many states have no such programs at all. These three social forces do not directly cause homelessness. They merely enlarge the ranks of the extremely poor, thereby increasing the chances of these people becoming homeless.

2 Certain personal characteristics may explain who among the extremely poor are more likely to become homeless. These characteristics have been found to include chronic mental illness, alcoholism, serious criminal behavior, and physical health problems. Most of the extremely poor do not become homeless because they live with their relatives or friends. But those who suffer from any of the personal disabilities just mentioned are more likely to wear out their welcome as dependents of their parents or as recipients of aid and money from their friends. After all, their relatives and friends are themselves extremely poor and already living in crowded housing. We should be careful, however, not to exaggerate the impact of personal disabilities on homelessness. To some degree, personal disabilities may be the consequences rather than the causes of homelessness. (Thio, pp. 150–51.)

Step 1 Decide on the topic of the passage. The heading indicates that the topic is

____

Step 2 Decide if the article develops a main idea *about* the topic. Questions are often used to focus on main ideas. Does the first sentence answer the question in the title? If it does, it is likely to be the main idea. Write it here:

____

____

Step 3 Next, complete an outline showing the main idea and important details. Part of the outline has been completed for you. Make sure the wording in your outline is your own.

Main Idea: Homelessness results from ____________________

I. Three larger social forces don't directly make people homeless, but do make more poor people from whom the homeless come.

  A. First, there was a ____________________ which came about from ______________________________

  B. Second, in the 1980s ______________________________

  ____

  C. Finally, in the last twenty years ____________________

  ____

II. ______________________________ may determine who is homeless, though some disabilities may be an effect of homelessness.

  A. The homeless show mental and physical problems as well as _____

  ____

  B. ____________________ stop support because they can't afford it.

Step 4 When the map is completed, you are ready to write the summary. Work *individually* to complete a summary of around 100 words (one-third the length of the original) for the passage. After you write, look back only to check facts or to see if any important points have been left out. When you are finished, *exchange your summaries with others in your group;* check to see that they are complete and the right length. If any wording seems too close to the original, restate the idea in your own words.

PREVIEWING SKILLS

Would you walk down a stairway into a dark cellar where you had never been before, without first turning on the light? Would you dive into a swimming hole without first checking the water depth and looking for rocks, stumps, or garbage? There is an old saying, "Look before you leap." Yet many readers just plunge in and head straight on without really knowing where they're going. They ignore or aren't aware of the need for *previewing,* one of the most important active reading skills. One well-known study method that includes previewing techniques is called SQ3R:

> "*Survey*—look over the chapter
>
> Make up *Questions* about the material and write them in the margin
>
> *Read* the material looking for answers to the question
>
> *Recite* to yourself what you have learned
>
> *Review* the main points

You've already developed some preview skills in working with paragraphs, such as asking questions, looking at the title, finding topics, and making main idea guesses. For magazine and newspaper articles and longer sections from texts, you will need some more strategies. Before you begin each article in the rest of this text, you will first do a preview. It will include two sections:

Thinking About Reading This section will have directions and questions to help you do the following:

- focus on the topic
- think about what you know about the topic
- make predictions about the main idea
- consider what you might learn from the article

Reading with a Purpose This section prepares you to connect information by thinking about questions like these:

- What details are most important?
- How are the details organized?
- Does my main idea guess need to be changed?

Other questions and directions will sometimes occur in the text to help you be sure that you know what the author means. You may also be given some vocabulary from the article to look at before reading.

Previewing *The Customer Is Always Right: How to Return Practically Anything* by Laura Rich

Thinking About Reading Look at the title. What topic does it suggest?

____

Think about your experience with shopping and returning products. Have you done it often? Has it been easy or hard? How did you feel about it? Write down a few of your ideas here:

____

____

____

____

____

____

____

Look at the title again. It points to a main idea giving advice on how to return products, but you should always read the first and last paragraphs before making a guess. That's because the introduction often contains the main idea or a question that leads to it, and the last paragraph may repeat or make a complete statement of the main idea. In this case the introduction and conclusion tell us that the article is not only on **how** to take back products but on **what** policies companies are following and **why.** The sentence (¶1) that gives the best statement of the main idea would be our main idea guess:

> As more stores and manufacturers look for ways to improve customer relations, many are expanding their guidelines on returns and exchanges, which could save you time—and money.

The question at the end of the first paragraph—"So which companies are welcoming you and your damaged goods back, and why?"—suggests that the major details in the article will be examples of stores and their policies and some specific reasons for them.

Another important step in previewing is to look at the boldface headings that often show main points of an article. If we are on the right track, we would expect the article to include specific policies, reasons, and examples.

Write down the boldface headings in the article:

- ______________________________
- ______________________________
- ______________________________
- ______________________________
- ______________________________

Do some of these look like they would support the main idea?

Reading with a Purpose Look for and mark policies, reasons, and important examples. Make notes in the margin as indicated. These notes, along with the main idea, are the "skeleton" from which you can build your outline. Continue to check if the main idea guess is being supported or needs to be changed.

Some vocabulary words have enough context clues so you can guess their meaning. For these, choose from the meanings in the margin, the one that best fits. You can check the answers and clues to these at the end of the reading.

The Customer Is Always Right: How to Return Practically Anything

by Laura Rich

1 Sometimes it seems they just don't make things the way they used to. Seams tear, soles wear away, handbags fall apart—and why won't that watch ever keep time right? If you're tired of throwing things away and rushing all over town to find replacements, take heart. As more stores and manufacturers look for ways to improve customer relations, many are expanding their guidelines on returns and exchanges, which could save you time—and money. So which companies are welcoming you and your damaged goods back, and why?

Reason Why:

"The Customer Is Always Right" published in *Family Circle,* September 1, 1998. Reprinted by permission of the author.

Lifetime Guarantees

2 L. L. Bean, Eddie Bauer and Lands' End all advertise a "guaranteed for life" policy for customers' in-store and catalog purchases, and they seem to mean it. Lands' End, for one, insists it stands by this motto, accepting merchandise for any reason, at any time. Anna Schryver, a spokeswoman for Lands' End, explains that the company will accept merchandise for exchange or a return if you're unsatisfied with the product during its lifetime. (Of course, customers should be reasonable. "Even the best clothing ages," says Schryver. "We won't encourage someone to return a worn-out shirt after 20 years.")

Policy:

Example:

3 If you lose your receipt, you can write a note and stick it in the box, detailing when you bought it, for how much, and why you're returning it (even though an explanation isn't required). You pay for shipping to Lands' End; the company covers shipping costs on the way back. Schryver says the company now sees fewer returns, since it is working harder to get sizes just right. The No. 1 reason people return things, she says, is that they ordered the wrong size and need a different one. Wrong fit or not, though, Lands' End is ready to show returns respect. "We believe returns are a cost of doing business, and we'd much rather have happy customers," Schryver explains.

Reason Why:

4 Some might say the company has an obsessive interest in those happy customers. Not only is Lands' End ready to exchange merchandise from unsatisfied customers, it's also trying to please by returning any articles left behind in items that are shipped to its headquarters in Dodgeville, Wisconsin. Eight years ago a customer returned a bathrobe she'd worn once. Absentmindedly, she put a diamond ring in the pocket and forgot to take it out before sending the robe back. Shortly after shipping the package for an exchange, she realized her mistake and called Lands' End—which sent out a companywide alert to look for the ring. The customer, who was reunited with her ring, was so grateful to the company for having located and returned it, she sent a dozen longstemmed roses to the customer service department.

■ *obsessive:*
a. excessive
b. decreasing

Policy:

■ *absentmindedly:*
a. sneakily
b. without being aware

Example:

5 Though the flowers were lovely, Schryver says they weren't necessary. "We check all pockets. Anything belonging to the customer gets sent back as a matter of practice." In fact, there's an employee—the head of the company's "merchandise not ours" department—dedicated to tracking down and returning jewelry, car keys and other forgotten items.

An Understanding Merchant

6 Something that is broken should be accepted by the manufacturer—after all, it's their fault right? But what if you just don't want the product after you've bought it? Or worse, it's become damaged due to some unfortunate circumstances, having nothing to do with the manufacturer? "We'll still take it back," says a spokeswoman for J. Crew. That's exactly what the company did with a lamb's wool sweater that had been tossed in with the wash and shrunken during one of the spin cycles. Jenna Knudson, a student in Kansas, says she was at class one day when a relative washed her laundry and miniaturized her two-year-old sweater. What was once a size 8 became a size 2. "The company took it right back," says Jenna, who now owns a right size sweater.

Policy:

Example:

- *miniaturized*
  - a. shredded
  - b. made tiny

7 J. Crew's policy is similar to that of other quality mail-order companies: Return the product at any time, for any reason. For best results, the company recommends using the return label it includes in original packages. And since its clothes all bear its trademark label, J. Crew regularly accepts return merchandise without a receipt.

Long Term Relationships

8 Bring it back at any time, they say—and some customers actually do. Though merchants recommend returning purchases sooner rather than later, many still welcome your ripped, torn and broken goods years, even decades, later. Sears and J. C. Penney, for instance, whose similar policies request a receipt, have proven to be flexible on the matter. Sears says it will take a hammer, screwdriver or other hand tool back 50 years later if it comes from the store's Craftsman label line. And a J. C. Penney spokeswoman reports that the department store chain once accepted a box of T shirts unused by the deceased husband of a long-time widow. Ultimately, it's in these companies' best interest to take your appeal seriously, since it may mean the difference between a frequent shopper and one who never comes back again.

- *decades:*
  - a. months
  - b. periods of ten years

Examples:

- *flexible:*
  - a. unreasonable
  - b. adjustable
- *deceased:*
  - a. divorced
  - b. dead
- *ultimately:*
  - a. in the end
  - b. foolishly

Reason Why:

Thanks . . . or No Thanks

9 Rite Aid boosted its image among consumers last year when it launched a campaign unveiling a new return policy on makeup and fragrance, even if the products had been used. Calling it a "no-fault guarantee," the drugstore chain noted that customers sometimes accidentally choose the wrong shade of lipstick, for example. "Women can't try on most makeup in the store," says Jody Cook, a spokeswoman for Rite Aid, "but we

Policy:

Example:

don't want that to discourage them from trying new products." With a receipt in hand less than 60 days after the purchase, customers can get their money back on a cosmetics item that didn't work out, "for any reason."

It's All Up to You

10 Few stores actively spread the word about their lenient return policies, perhaps, in part, because additional returns can translate into lost sales. The computer electronics industry has revised its return policies in recent years in an attempt to curtail abuse. Circuit City, Best Buy and Sun TV are among the stores that have instituted 15 percent "open box fees" on computers and related products, such as printers and monitors, that are returned to stores without original packing intact. Morgan Stewart, spokesman for Circuit City, tells of students who buy computers to write term papers, then return them as "new"—with tell-tale files left on hard drives. "Once the box is opened, we can't sell the item as a new product," Stewart says. Opened products must be sold at considerable markdown, erasing "already extremely thin" profit margins. "This endangers our continued ability to offer the most competitive prices."

■ *lenient:*
a. easy
b. foolish

Policy:

■ *curtail:*
a. ignore
b. stop

Example:

■ *instituted:*
a. started
b. denied

11 Still, stores are prepared to take your requests seriously. So the next time something breaks down or doesn't meet your expectations, check with the store or manufacturer. You may come out with a better product—and in most cases, you won't spend a penny on the replacement.

Context Answers and Clues

obsessive: a. excessive (company seems very concerned—"not only . . . but also")

absentmindedly: b. without being aware (robe not a logical place to put a ring—later "forgot")

miniaturized: b. made tiny (washing can shrink things—went to size 2)

decades: b. periods of ten years ("even" suggests many years—Sears takes back "50 years")

flexible: b. adjustable (all examples show helpful attitudes)

deceased: b. dead (woman is his widow—T shirts not used)

ultimately: a. in the end (if it's in their interest, they'll do it sooner or later)

lenient: a. easy (all examples above show policies have become less strict)

curtail: b. stop (considered an "abuse"—therefore, would stop it)

instituted: a. started (it's something new they are doing)

EXERCISE 8.3

Questions on *The Customer Is Always Right*

■ Dictionary Skills

For the words below, decide on the part of speech that bests fits the context of the sentence and put your answer after each excerpt.

1. "It's in these companies' best interest to take your *appeal* seriously." (¶7)

   ____

   noun 1. An urgent request or plea. 2. A going to a higher authority, as for a decision. 3. The power of attracting or of arousing interest.

   verb 1. To make an urgent plea, as for help. 2. Law. To make or apply for an appeal. 3. To be attractive or interesting.

2. "Opened products must be sold at considerable markdown, erasing 'already extremely thin' profit *margins*." (¶10)

   ____

   noun 1. An edge or border. 2. The blank space next to the written area on a page. 3. An amount allowed beyond what is needed. 4. The minimum return a product or business earns and still pays for itself.

   verb 1. To give a margin to. 2. To border. 3. To write in the margin of a page.

3. "Rite Aid boosted its image among consumers last year when it *launched* a campaign unveiling a new return policy on makeup." (¶9)

   ____

   noun 1. A large ship's boat. 2. A large, open motorboat.

   verb 1. To throw with force 2. To put (a boat) into the water in readiness for use. 3. To introduce to the public or to a market. 4. To give someone a start in a career or job. 5. To plunge into something.

■ Reading for Information

1. The topic of ¶4 is
   a. the danger of obsessive companies
   b. how items get lost
   c. a policy on returning lost items
   d. grateful customers

2. The customer who got back her ring
   a. had to wait eight years for its return
   b. found it in a bathrobe she bought
   c. realized her mistake before she returned the robe
   d. gave her thanks with roses

Write the sentence with the main idea for each of the following paragraphs. Then circle the letter that shows the reason for your choice.

3. ¶2 Main Idea: ______________________________

   ____

   This is the main idea because it
   a. answers a question stated in the paragraph
   b. has a listing phrase
   c. is followed by an example
   d. has a change of direction signal
   e. both a and d

4. ¶6 Main Idea: ______________________________

   ____

   This is the main idea because it
   a. answers a question stated in the paragraph
   b. is followed by a "first item in a list" signal word or phrase
   c. is followed by an example
   d. has a summary/conclusion signal
   e. both a and c

5. In ¶10, there is one sentence that has background information on the topic:

   Background Sentence: ______________________________

   ____

   Main Idea: ______________________________

   ____

   This is the main idea because it
   a. answers a question stated in the paragraph
   b. is followed by an example
   c. has a change of direction signal
   d. has a summary/conclusion signal

6. Which is the best statement of the main idea of ¶8?
   a. Sears and J. C. Penney make every effort to keep customers happy, but you must have a receipt to exchange your purchases.
   b. Many merchants will accept returns even after many years because it's in their interests for customers to return.
   c. If a clerk at a store refuses to exchange your purchase, you should seriously consider taking your appeal to a supervisor.
   d. Even though customers may have been frequent shoppers, they may suddenly decide not to come back again.
7. Which is the best statement of the main idea of ¶9?
   a. Rite Aid helped its image by starting a "no-fault guarantee" campaign.
   b. Customers sometimes accidentally choose the wrong shade of lipstick.
   c. Despite the new policy, women can't try on makeup in the store.
   d. Rite Aid now allows women to try on lipstick in the store.
8. J. C. Penney accepted a box of unused T shirts because
   a. it has a special policy on T shirts only.
   b. a well-treated customer will return.
   c. it has a special policy for widows.
   d. government regulations force it to do so.

Circle T for True or F for False.

9. T F Despite less strict policies, no product can ever be returned without a receipt.
10. T F Stores widely advertise their return policies because it's good for customer relations.
11. T F Rite Aid customers don't need to give a reason for returning cosmetics.
12. T F Circuit City knew computers returned as new had been used because files were left on the hard drive.

■ Facts and Opinions

Label the following as *Fact* (can be proved or disproved) or *Opinion* (there is room for disagreement).

__________ 1. They just don't make things the way they used to.

__________ 2. L. L. Bean, Eddie Bauer, and Lands' End all advertise a "guaranteed for life" policy.

__________ 3. Of course, customers should be reasonable.

__________ 4. The No. 1 reason people return things is that they ordered the wrong size.

__________ 5. Eight years ago a customer returned a bathrobe she'd worn once.

__________ 6. The customer sent a dozen roses to the customer service department.

__________ 7. Something that is broken should be accepted by the manufacturer—after all, it's their fault.

__________ 8. J. Crew regularly accepts return merchandise without a receipt.

__________ 9. Ultimately, it's in these companies' best interest to take your appeal seriously.

__________ 10. Few stores actively spread the word about their lenient return policies.

■ Reading for Understanding

1. All of the following are examples of policies favoring the customer EXCEPT
   a. Lands' End's "guarantee for life" policy
   b. Rite Aid's "no-fault guarantee"
   c. Sear's policy on returned tools
   d. Circuit City's "open boxes" policy

2. "Sears says it will take a hammer, screwdriver or other hand tool back 50 years later if it comes from the store's Craftsman label line." What would this seem to indicate about the quality of Craftsman labeled tools?

   ____

   ____

3. What does "guaranteed for life" mean? What is the "lifetime" of a product?

   ____

   ____

4. Explain in your own words what these sentences mean. "Opened products must be sold at considerable markdown, erasing already extremely thin profit margins. This endangers our continued ability to offer the most competitive prices."

   ____

   ____

5. We could infer from the above statement about small profit margins that companies
   a. are going broke.
   b. charging way too much.
   c. will keep raising prices.
   d. must sell a lot of merchandise to show a profit.
6. What does the author's main purpose appear to be here?
   a. to promote certain stores and products
   b. to convince readers that return policies will benefit them
   c. to show how deceptive some store policies are
7. How would the author's tone (attitude) best be described?
   a. upbeat and informative
   b. purely scientific and neutral
   c. angry and resentful

USING WORD PARTS TO FIND MEANING

The following exercise has words with prefixes that appeared in the article you just completed. In some cases the words appeared in different forms (e.g., replace, replacement).

EXERCISE 8.4

Using Prefixes to Figure Out Meanings

■ PART A

The article has twelve words beginning with the letters *re.* These letters can be a prefix meaning "back, again." In three of the words in this article—*reason* (¶2), *realized* (¶4), *regularly* (¶7)—these letters do not form a prefix. They are part of a root. In the rest of the words, the meanings "back" or "again" are clear in some of the words, but not so clear in others. Give the meanings of as many of the words as you can, without going to the dictionary. Then check the columns *Useful* and *Not Useful* to indicate whether knowing that *re* means "back" or "again" helped you figure out the definition.

	Useful	*Not Useful*
1. replacements (¶1)	______________	______________
2. reunited (¶4)	______________	______________
3. receipt (¶3)	______________	______________

4. return (¶3) ____________ ____________
5. required (¶3) ____________ ____________
6. respect (¶3) ____________ ____________
7. recommends (¶7) ____________ ____________
8. request (¶7) ____________ ____________
9. revised (¶10) ____________ ____________

■ **PART B**

Explain how the prefix *un* changes the meaning of these words:

unsatisfied (¶4) ____________

unfortunate (¶6) ____________

unveiling (¶9) ____________

■ **PART C**

The article contains these sentences:

> "We won't *encourage* someone to return a worn-out shirt after 20 years." (¶2)
>
> "We don't want that to *discourage* them from trying new products." (¶9)
>
> "This *endangers* our continued ability to offer the most competitive prices." (¶10)

The root *cour* means "heart"; *en* means "in"; and *dis* means "away from." What do these words mean:

encourage: ____________

discourage: ____________

endanger: ____________

Active Learning

CREATING "MIND MAPS"

We build frames of reference so that we can get the big picture of a field of knowledge. This lets us connect new information to what we already know. In a similar way we also have "idea" frameworks. We share common ways of thinking about things in our world. The ways we can think about a thing—

our ideas about it—depend on our interests and purposes. The kind of questions that we ask determine the kind of ideas we create. For example, if you were curious about a friend's new house, you might ask **what it was like:** would it be described as cozy, spacious, or formal? You would ask about the floor plan: **how many** rooms were there and **how** did they connect? You might be curious about **what type of** house it was—Victorian, Colonial, or ranch? You might ask **how was it similar to or different from** other houses in the neighborhood? There are other questions that would be important also: **Where** is the house located? **Why** did the owner want to sell and **for what reasons** did your friend buy it? **What** problems did the house have and **how** would your friend solve them?

These questions lead to ideas that have different kinds of "skeletons." These can be shown by a traditional outline. These are very useful for material organized by a topic only. But the "one size fits all" outline form may not show the parts of an idea pattern as well as a map that shows a special skeleton. Many students find it more useful to use what are sometimes called "mind maps." In Part Three of this text, you will work with various idea patterns and learn how to make and use maps that work best with each.

An example of a pattern that we use daily is time order. Recall in the story "The Scholarship Jacket," a sequence of events happened before Marta finally got her jacket. Those events are the skeleton of the story. One way to see the structure clearly is to put these details in time order. A "mind map" showing sequence is easier to create and follow than an outline:

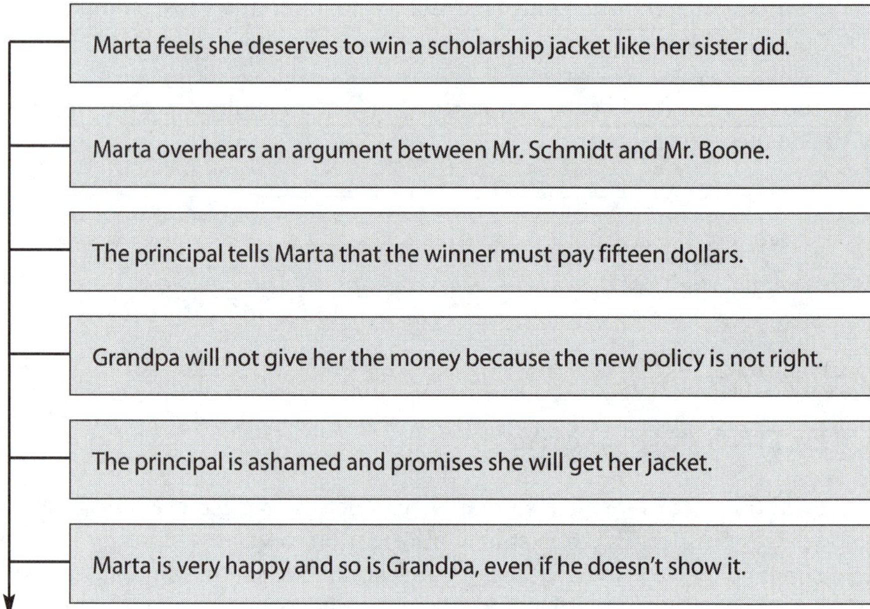

Marta feels she deserves to win a scholarship jacket like her sister did.
Marta overhears an argument between Mr. Schmidt and Mr. Boone.
The principal tells Marta that the winner must pay fifteen dollars.
Grandpa will not give her the money because the new policy is not right.
The principal is ashamed and promises she will get her jacket.
Marta is very happy and so is Grandpa, even if he doesn't show it.

For a longer example, compare an outline and a map of "The Customer Is Always Right." Here is an outline of the article.

I. Lifetime guarantees advertised for store purchases and from catalogs
  A. Examples: L. L. Bean, Eddie Bauer, and Lands' End
  B. Lands' End's view: returns a business expense, keeps buyers coming back
    1. No time limit, explanation not important
    2. But, buyer must be "reasonable"
    3. Just give information on purchase—no receipt needed
    4. Result: decrease in products returned
    5. Even has "merchandise not ours" return (example: woman's ring)

II. Return anything, anytime policy on quality goods ordered from companies
  A. J. Crew example: shrunken sweater exchanged
  B. Use return label, no receipt needed since label is on clothes

III. Long-range policies: receipts preferred, but will adjust policy
  A. Early return better but still accepted after many years
    1. Sears tradition of replacing all Craftsman-line tools
    2. Example: J. C. Penney taking back T shirts from widow
  B. Policy actually a benefit for company—more satisfied customers

IV. Rite Aid "no-fault guarantee" on return of used beauty products
  A. Example: woman chooses wrong shade of lipstick/can't try out in store
  B. Encourages trying out new products
  C. Have sixty days to decide

V. New computer policy to end abuses: "open box fees" (15%)
  A. Example: Circuit City
  B. Stop misuse of return policy—e.g., students writing term papers
  C. If box opened, can't sell product as new
  D. Weakens stores profits and ability to compete

Compare the chart on page 296 to a map of the article. The map and outline contain most of the same details, but the map is easier to take in. Putting information in a grid or chart gives us a better grasp of how parts connect. The four vertical columns have headings that identify these. We can focus quickly on the reasons, the policies, and the examples. In studying for a test, you would more easily remember the information.

Policies	Reasons	Examples	Details
lifetime guarantees advertised for store/ catalog purchases	a business cost; buyers return; fewer returns	Lands' End (also L Bean, Eddie Bauer)	no time limit, no receipt, no reason, but be reasonable; (also: returns lost items)
return anything, anytime policy on quality goods		J. Crew—shrunken sweater	use return label, no receipt needed (label on clothes)
long-range policies: receipts preferred, but adjust policy	benefits company in long run: more buyers return	Sears, J.C. Penney (widow's return of T shirts)	replacing line of Craftsman tools (even after 50 years)
"no-fault guarantee" on return of used beauty products		Rite Aid: woman choosing wrong lipstick	encourages trying out new products; have sixty days to decide
New computer policy to stop abuses: "open box fees"	protect store stop misuse of return policy	Circuit City—student's writing term papers	weakens stores profits/ ability to compete

This arrangement also gives more options in writing a summary. Depending on your purpose, you might follow the order of the original—that is, you would work horizontally across the columns and down. Your paper would be organized into five parts, each dealing with a policy. Or you could work down the vertical columns and across. This would lead to three major parts: why changes were being made (reasons), what the changes were (policies), and some key examples and details of those changes. The map also makes it easy to decide on length. For a shorter summary, the minor details column could be left out. For a summary of just the major points, both the details and the examples columns could be dropped.

EXERCISE 8.5

Writing a Summary from a Map

In Exercise 3.5 in Chapter 3, you matched subtopics to paragraphs and answered questions on the eight paragraphs of the article "Kicking Asphalt." Reread the article and the answers that you wrote. Then fill out the map with the answers to the questions for each paragraph. You will need to put the answers in your own words, since the phrasing of your original answers is probably too close to that of the article.

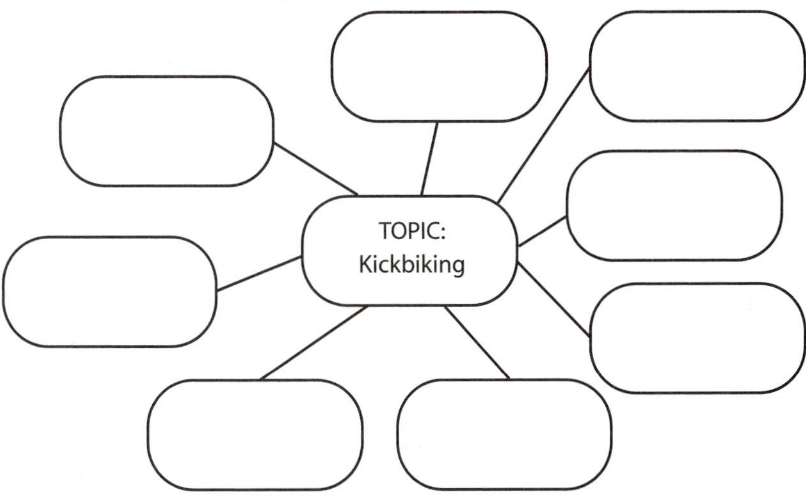

Now write a summary of the article. One key to good summaries is the ability of writers to establish their own voices. This results when writers really understand the organization of the original and are able to put ideas in their own words. You can gain control at the start by using the name of the article and the author at or near the beginning. When you write your summary, include this information in the first sentence. You can start with the name of the author or the title, or use one of many phrases to work the information in—e.g., "According to ______ in _______" or "In the article _______ by _______," etc.

Be sure to write only from the rephrased answers in the map. You do not need to follow the same order of the paragraphs if you see a better way to organize them. Your summary should be about 200–250 words long.

UNDERSTANDING GRAPHICS IN TEXTS

Most textbooks contain many *graphics* that go with the main text. Students sometimes think these are just extras that can be skipped over, but valuable information and ideas can be gained from them. Graphics like photographs and drawings are included to add interest and gain the reader's attention. Others, such as tables, maps, graphs, and charts, give in a short space a lot of information that wouldn't fit easily into the main text. The map above from which you wrote your summary is an example of a graphic.

Graphics require the reader to make inferences and draw conclusions from the data. Table 5.1 from a sociology text is an example of a graphic (Henslin, p. 124). It explains how tables work:

TABLE 5.1 How to Read a Table

Rapists' Account of Alcohol and Drug Use Prior to Their Crime

These are the results of interviews with men imprisoned for rape in seven maximum- or medium-security prisons in Virginia. *Admitters* are men who define their acts as rape, *deniers* those who do not define their acts as rape.

Use of Alcohol and Drugs	**Admitters** $n = 39$	**Deniers** $n = 25$
Neither the rapist nor the victim used alcohol or drugs.	23%	16%
The rapist used alcohol or drugs.	77%	72%
The rapist was affected by the alcohol or drugs.	69%	40%
The victim used alcohol or drugs.	26%	72%
The victim was affected by the alcohol or drugs.	15%	56%
Both the rapist and the victim used and were affected by the alcohol or drugs.	15%	16%

Source: Modification of Table 2 in Scully and Marolla 1984.

A table is concise way of presenting information. Because sociological findings are often presented in tabular form, it is important to understand how to read a table. Tables contain six elements: title, headnote, headings, columns, rows, and source. When you understand how these elements work together, you know how to read a table.

1. The *title* states the topic of a table. It is located at the top of the table. What is the title of this table? Please determine your answer before looking at the correct answer below.
2. The *headnote* is not always included in a table. When it is, it is located just below the title. Its purpose is to give more detailed information about how the data were collected or how the data are presented in the table. What are the first seven words of the headnote of this table?
3. The *headings* of a table tell what kind of information is contained in the table. There are three headings in this table. What are they? In the second heading, what does $n = 39$ mean?
4. The *columns* in a table present vertically arranged information. What is the fourth number in the second column and the second number in the third column?
5. The *rows* in a table present information horizontally. In the sixth row, who is listed as using and being affected by alcohol and drugs.
6. The *source* of a table, usually listed at the bottom, provides information on where the data shown in the table originated. Often, as in this instance, the information is specific enough for you to consult the original source. What is the source for this table?

Some tables are much more complicated than this one, but all follow the same basic pattern. To apply these concepts to a table with more information, see page 331.

Answers

1. Rapists' Account of Alcohol and Drug Use Prior to Their Crime.
2. These are the results of interviews with.
3. Use of Alcohol and Drugs, Admitters, Deniers. The *n* is an abbreviation for number, and $n = 39$ means that 39 men were admitters.
4. 26%, 72%.
5. Both the rapist and the victim.
6. A 1984 article by Scully and Marolla (listed in the References section of this text).

From Henslin, p. 124.

EXERCISE 8.6

Getting Information and Ideas from Graphics

The author tells the student, "To apply these concepts to a table with more information, see page —." One of the tables on that page appears below. Pay attention to any footnotes to the graphic. These may provide key information on identifying parts of the graphic or help to explain data. In the first column, for example, note how a raised letter *a* is used to refer the reader to a footnote. Study the table carefully, think about connections among the data, and answer the questions that follow.

TABLE 5.1 Education and Race or Ethnicity

	Less Than High School	High School Graduates	1–3 Years College	College Graduates	Number of Doctorates Awarded	Percentage of Doctorates Awarded
White Americans	18%	34%	25%	23%	23,996	83.8%
African Americans	27	36	24	13	1,288	4.5
Latinos	47[a]	44	NA	9	973	3.4
Asian Americans	15	25	19	41	2,004	7.0
Native American	35[a]	56	NA	9	114	0.4

Note: NA = Not Available. Totals except for doctorates refer to persons 25 years and over.

[a]Totals for Latinos and Native Americans are not listed in the same way in the source as they are for other groups.

Source: Statistical Abstract 1995: Tables 50, 52, 53, 997.

■ Reading for Information

1. What does NA stand for? ________________________________

2. Where did the author get the information to make the graph?

____

3. The group with the fewest *number* of doctorates degrees: ____________

4. The group with smallest *percentage* of doctorates: ________________

5. The two groups with the smallest percentage of college graduates:

____________________ ____________________

■ Reading for Understanding

1. Latinos and Native Americans with 2 years in college would be counted with which group?

 ____

2. In the second column, "High School Graduates," the figure 25% is listed for Asian Americans. Does that mean that only 25% of Asian Americans have a high school education? If not, what does it show?

 ____

 ____

 ____

3. For each of the five groups in the table, the percentages in the first four columns should add up to what? __________

 Do they? ________

4. A footnote states that "Totals except for doctorates refer to persons 25 years and over." Why would the data be recorded differently for doctorates?

 ____

 ____

 ____

5. High school dropout prevention programs should be aimed mainly at which two groups?

 ______________ ______________

Put *Yes, No,* or *Not Enough Data* for the following conclusions. Then explain your choices:

6. ______________ All minority groups are disadvantaged pretty much equally in education.

 Explanation: ______________________________

 ____

 ____

7. ______________ Whites have the highest percent of students who attend or graduate from college.

Explanation: ____

____

____

8. ____________ Female minority group members are more discriminated against than males.

Explanation: ____

____

____

9. ____________ Overall, Asian Americans show higher educational levels than whites.

Explanation: ____

____

____

10. ____________ A higher percentage of whites receive doctorates than do Asian Americans.

Explanation: ____

____

____

Reading Portfolio

SUMMARY AND RESPONSE

For your portfolio assignments in the chapters of Part Three, you will find, read, and write about articles organized in various patterns. Your report will have two parts.

Summary This gives the factual information of the article. It should be written from an outline or map that shows the skeleton of the article. Remember to write both the map and the summary in your own words. If you want to use part of the original, use quotation marks and be accurate. After you write your summary, reread it and make changes. A first draft can always be improved.

Response In this part you can bring in your own opinion. Here are some questions you can ask yourself:

- What did you know before you read? What did you learn?
- Do you agree or disagree with what the article says? Why or why not?
- Who would find the information in the article interesting and useful?
- Does the article connect to you in a personal way?
- Did you react emotionally to the article? Explain why.

Following these directions, write a response of 100–150 words to go along with your summary of "Kicking Asphalt." File both of these in your portfolio.

Part Three

Reading for *Patterns*

CHAPTER 9

What in the World Is This?

Describing People, Places, and Things

After reading this chapter, you will know the answers to these questions:

- For what purposes is description used?
- How do diagrams, maps, charts, and graphs convey descriptions?
- What is a spider map?
- What is an umbrella map?
- What is a profile?
- How are word parts used to create words?

It's natural for us to be curious about the traits of new people we meet. In school, on the job, or while socializing, we use positive labels such as "beautiful," "smart," "honest," or negative ones like "sneaky," "stuck up," "foolish." We want to know about their functions and achievements: "she runs a law firm," "he teaches school," "she led her team to the volleyball championship."

We are also curious about new things and activities: What is a new house like, or a new job? Like people, objects have traits and functions, but they also can be divided into parts. We therefore are interested in the components that make up the whole: what the parts of an engine are, how the floor plan of a house is laid out, what countries makeup a continent, how our solar system is arranged. Writing that gives us information on characteristics, functions, and the makeup of things we call *description.*

GRAPHICS OF DESCRIPTION

Textbooks use many visual aids to give a clearer picture of their topics. Graphics are usually listed under two labels: *tables* and *figures.* Figures include a number of different types of descriptive graphics that you will learn about in this section.

Drawings and Diagrams

Many textbooks in physical and life sciences use both text and graphics to give information on the structure of things. The text lists the specific names of parts of an object and may include a number of words that signal whole-to-part relationships or show how things are positioned in space:

component	body	top	bottom	middle
base	side	inside	outside	above
below	there	here	opposite	on
upon	over	under	by	near
adjacent to	next to	beside	between	in front of

Graphics are sometimes independent of the text, but usually diagrams and drawings relate directly to information in the text. They may also add more details.

EXERCISE 9.1

Understanding Structural Diagrams and Drawings

Here is a short selection from a biology text that includes text and a diagram. Look for and circle words that indicate parts and their relationships. Then answer the questions that follow.

Floral Structure
As a flower develops at a shoot tip, it differentiates into nonfertile components (sepals and petals) and fertile components (stamens and carpels). Directly or indirectly, all of these are attached to a receptacle, the modified base of the floral shoot (Figure 22.3). (Starr, p. 355)

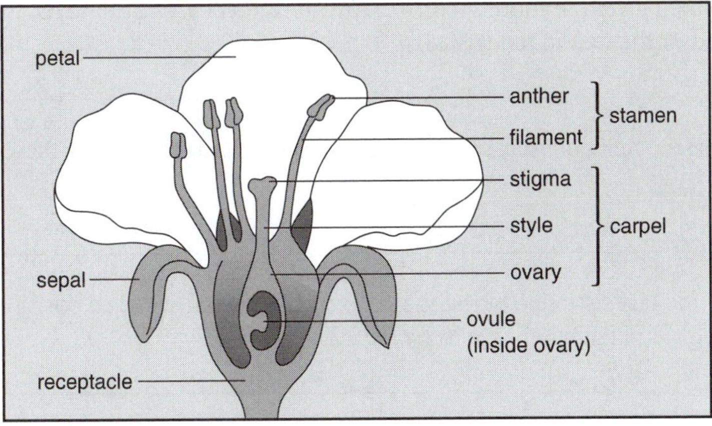

Figure 22.3 Structure of a cherry (*Prunus*) blossom. Like the flowers of many plants, it has a single carpel (a female reproductive part) and stamens (male reproductive parts). Flowers of other plants have two or more carpels, often united as a single srtucture. Single or fused carpels consist of an ovary and a stigma. Often the ovary extends upward as a slender column (style).

■ Reading for Information

1. What is the object (whole) that is being discussed in the main text?

   ____

2. What specific example of the object is shown in the diagram?

   ____

3. What parts are mentioned in the main text and the text in the graphic?

   ____

4. In the diagram, two things that are a part of the blossom can be viewed separately as wholes with parts of their own. One has two parts, the other three. List those here:

   A. ______________ B. ______________

   1. ______________ 1. ______________

   2. ______________ 2. ______________

   3. ______________

5. Which of the parts above has an even more specific subpart of its own?

   ____

   What is it called? ______________________________

6. Which gives the more specific definitions for *stamen* and *carpel,* the main text or the text in the figure?

 ____

7. Use the text and graphic to give a complete definition of the these terms:

 Stamen: ____

 Carpel: ____

8. In the last sentence of the main text, what signal word of position helps you visualize where the *receptacle* is?

 ____

Circle T for True or F for False.

9. T F Flowers of all plants have a style.
10. T F Some flowers have more than one carpel.

Question for Discussion

In doing a review for a test, which would you spend time looking at, the graphic or the text?

____

Why? ____

____

____

Maps

We all know how important maps are in our daily lives. We rely on road maps of our state or the country when we travel long distances, or city maps for activities nearer to home. It's natural that courses like geography and history would have many graphics with maps. These can give us, in a compact space, a picture of the parts and physical features of a very large area. Maps and text that deal with physical features use common words that show direction. These include fixed directions—north, south, east, west, northeast, northwest, etc.—as well as directions that show how things relate to a fixed point:

right	left	away	beyond	across
to	into	toward	up	down

Maps often give information other than the boundaries of countries and directions of travel. They can, for example, give statistics for specific regions on such things as population, divorce rates, education levels, employment rates, or the incidence of disease.

EXERCISE 9.2

Reading Geographic Maps

Study the map carefully to see how it works with the main text to give information. Then answer the questions that follow.

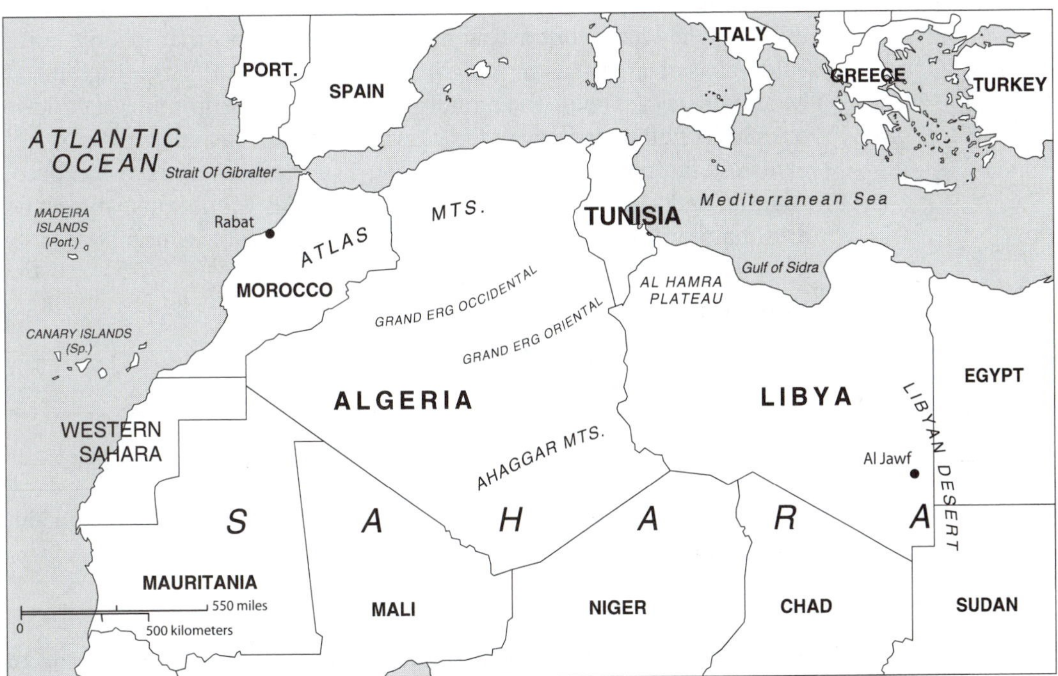

Figure 3.8 North Africa: countries, physical features, and main towns

North Africa

1 North Africa is the westernmost sector of the Arab world (Figure 3.8). It is closest to Europe and many of its past political ties and present economic links are northward. Algeria, Morocco, and Tunisia, in particular, retain close ties with France and there is a strong link to markets in Europe for selling products, buying goods, and emigrant labor. Libya reflects past links by selling much of its oil to Italy.

2 The North African countries, although a considerable distance from Southwest Asia, share an adherence to Islam as an almost exclusive religion and Arabic as the official language. In 1979, this link with other Muslim Arab countries was strengthened by the move of the Arab League headquarters from Cairo (Egypt) to Tunis.

3 Algeria, Libya, and, to a smaller extent, Tunisia are now oil producers and much of the income from this source has been invested in broadening the economic base into manufacturing. The oil income and more diversified economies place these countries higher in the world wealth list than other African countries.

4 The four countries of North Africa are Algeria, Libya, Morocco (with Western Sahara), and Tunisia. Algeria and Morocco had around 28 million people each in 1993, Libya had 4.9 million, and Tunisia, 8.6 million. They have contrasting natural environments that include cultivated coastal areas in the north, desert interiors, and the high Atlas Mountain ranges with their interior plateaus. Algeria and Libya have over 80% of their territory in the desert, but Morocco and Tunisia do not extend so far into the arid environment. The northern parts of Morocco, Algeria, and Tunisia are dominated by the Atlas Mountains, an upland area that is known collectively as the Maghreb. (Bradshaw, pp. 135–36.)

■ Reading for Information

1. List three words of direction that occur in ¶1:

   ____________________ ____________________ ____________________

2. Write in the word *Maghreb* in the area on the map where it belongs.

3. What two things do North African countries share with other Muslim Arab countries?

   ____

4. What two factors have made North African countries wealthier than other African countries?

   ____

5. Western Sahara is considered to be a part of what country?

   ____

6. Which North African country is not included as an oil producer?

   ____

■ Reading for Understanding

1. Why would it probably be easy and cheap to transport oil to Italy from Libya?

____

____

2. What would you need to figure out how far it is from Rabat, Morocco, to Al Jawf, Libya, with this map?

____

How far is it? _______________________________

3. Which two countries would be likely to have the most agricultural production?
   a. Algeria and Libya
   b. Morocco and Tunisia
   c. Libya and Morocco
   d. Tunisia and Algeria
4. From the figures in the text, what is the approximate population of North Africa?
   a. 28 million people
   b. 42 million people
   c. 70 million people
   d. 100,000 million people
5. The text states that North Africa's "link with other Muslim Arab countries was strengthened by the move of the Arab League headquarters from Cairo (Egypt) to Tunis." How does the map help to make this point clearer?

____

____

____

Pie Charts

An easy way to show what share of a whole each part has is by using a figure known as a *pie chart.* These are found in textbooks across many fields.

EXERCISE 9.3

Getting Information from Pie Charts

■ **PART A**

Read the text below before looking at the pie charts that make up the graphic. What information does it add?

____

____

____

A World of Striking Contrasts

Today, Asian Americans are the fastest-growing U.S. minority, increasing at fifteen times the rate of non-Hispanic whites, and doubling in just the past ten years (Chun and Zalokar, 1992). Most Asian Americans live in the West, as can be seen in Figure 12.9. The three largest groups of Asian Americans—of Chinese, Filipino, and Japanese descent—are concentrated in Los Angeles, San Francisco, Honolulu, and New York City. (Henslin, p. 336.)

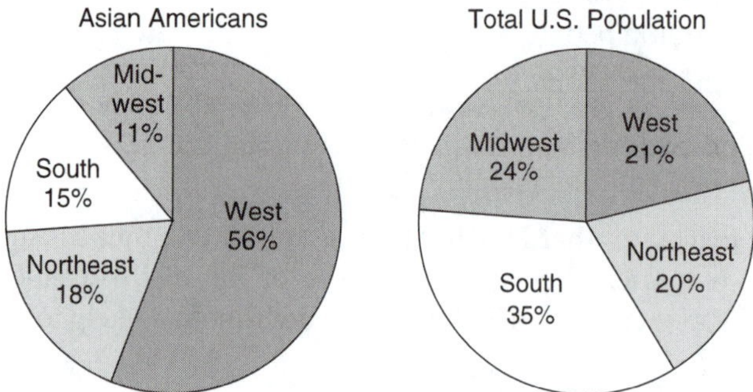

Figure 12.9 Residence of Asian Americans

■ Reading for Information

1. The term Asian Americans refers to people of
   a. Chinese descent
   b. Filipino descent
   c. Japanese descent
   d. all of the above

2. The fewest number of Asian American lives in what region? _________

3. In what year was the data for this figure published? _______________

Circle T for True or F for False.

4. T F As of 1992, Asian Americans made up 56% of the population of the West.

5. T F As of 1992, 15% of Americans lived in the South.

■ Reading for Understanding

1. The text says that the population of Asian Americans doubled in the past ten years. This ten-year period must have ended
   a. right after 1997
   b. in 1995
   c. before 1994
   d. before 1992

2. You would expect the percentages in these pie charts to add up to what number? _________

   Do they? _________

3. Asian Americans probably have their *highest* percentage of a region's population in which area?
   a. Midwest
   b. West
   c. Northeast
   d. South

4. Could you determine from the data in which area Asian Americans have their *lowest* percentage of a region's population? Why or why not?

5. Periods of heavy immigration by Asian Americans into the West occurred in the last half of the nineteenth century. That was also a time in the West of the discovery of gold and silver and the building of railroads. In what way are these events connected? Do some background reading on the history of immigration in this country to learn more about this topic.

■ PART B

As you read, underline the definition of *hydrosphere* in the first paragraph and circle terms that are used for different kinds of water.

The Hydrosphere

1 The hydrosphere includes water on the earth in all its forms. About 97.2 percent of the hydrosphere consists of ocean saltwater, as shown in Figure 4.2. The remaining 2.8 percent is fresh water. The largest reservoir of fresh water is stored as ice in the world's ice sheets and mountain glaciers. This water accounts for 2.15 percent of total global water.

2 Fresh liquid water is found both on top of and beneath the earth's land surfaces. Water occupying openings in soil and rock is called subsurface water. Most of it is held in deep storage as groundwater, at a level where plant roots cannot access it. Groundwater makes up 0.63 percent of the hydrosphere, leaving 0.02 percent of the water remaining.

3 The right hand portion of Figure 4.2 shows how the small remaining proportion of the earth's water is distributed. This proportion is important to us because it includes the water available for plants, animals, and human use. Soil water, which is held in the soil within reach of plant roots, comprises 0.005 percent of the global total. Water held in streams, lakes, marshes, and swamps is called surface water. Most of this surface water is about evenly divided between freshwater lakes and salty (saline) lakes. An extremely small proportion is held in streams and rivers as they flow toward the sea or inland lakes.

4 Note that the quantity of water held as vapor and cloud water droplets in the atmosphere is also very small—0.001 percent of the hydrosphere. Though small, this reservoir of water is of enormous importance. It provides the supply of precipitation that replenishes all freshwater stocks on land. . . . The flow of water vapor from warm tropical air oceans to cooler regions provides a global flow of heat, in latent form, from low to high latitudes. (Strahler and Strahler, p. 88.)

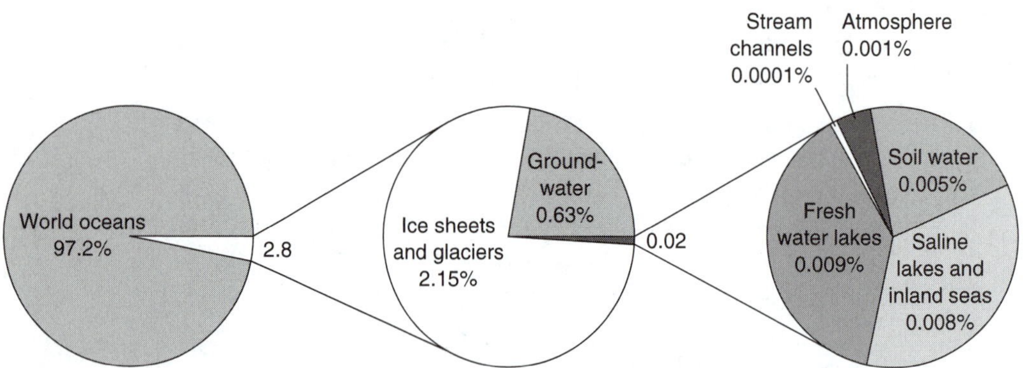

Figure 4.2 Volumes of global water in each reservoir of the hydrosphere. Nearly all the earth's water is contained in the world ocean. Fresh surface and soil water make up only a small fraction of the total volume of global water.

■ Reading for Information

1. What is groundwater? ______________________________

____

2. What is surface water? ______________________________

____

3. What does *saline* mean? ______________________________

____

4. Which of these statements is true of the three circles in the graphic?
   a. They each deal with the same percentages but in a different way.
   b. The second shows a part of the first and the third shows a part of the second.
   c. The percentage figures in each of them adds up to 100%.
   d. None of the above.

Circle T for True or F for False.

5. T F 0.001% of 2,000 would be 200.
6. T F Fresh liquid water is found both on top of and beneath the earth's land surfaces.
7. T F Soil water comprises 5 percent of the global total.
8. T F All surface water other than that in the ocean is fresh water.
9. T F Moisture in the atmosphere is not counted as part of the hydrosphere.
10. T F Fresh surface and soil water are only a small fraction of the earth's water.

■ Reading for Understanding

1. If the oceans warmed up, the percentage of water in ice sheets and glaciers would
   a. increase
   b. decrease
   c. stay the same
   d. double

2. If oceans warmed up, the percentage of water in groundwater, fresh surface water and soil water would
   a. increase
   b. decrease
   c. stay the same
   d. double
3. "Water occupying openings in soil and rock is called subsurface water. Most of it is held in deep storage as groundwater." From the context here, what do you think the prefix *sub* means in the word *subsurface?*

   ____
4. The numbers in both the second and third pie chart don't add up to 100, yet these circles do represent 100 percent of something. What is it?

   ____

Graphs

The main types of graphs are bar and line graphs. These can contain a lot of information or be fairly simple to read, as in the examples of a bar graph that follow.

EXERCISE 9.4

Understanding Descriptive Information in Bar Graphs

■ **PART A**

Before you read the following passage, find out what the term *median* means. How does it differ from the terms *mean* and *mode?*

Changes in the American Family

1 The traditional family, which consists of two parents living with children, is no longer the typical American family. As far back as 1970, the proportion of traditional families had already declined to 40.3 percent. In 1991 it was only 25.9 percent (see Figure 10.1). Increasingly, Americans are choosing either new patterns of family life or life outside the family; some are experiencing violence in the family.

Dual-Career Marriages

2 In the last 50 years, there has been a tremendous surge of married women into the labor force. The proportion of gainfully employed wives shot up from only 14 percent in 1940 to about 57 percent in 1990. Their employment has increased family income significantly. In 1987 the me-

dian income of dual-career families ($37,300) was more than 37 percent higher than the median for one-career families ($27,000). At the low end of the income scale, the wife's contribution is so great that relatively few dual-earner families fall below the poverty line. (Thio,p. 239.)

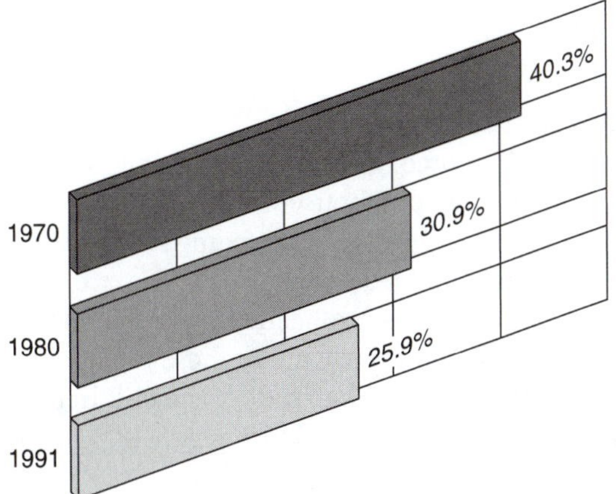

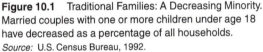

Figure 10.1 Traditional Families: A Decreasing Minority. Married couples with one or more children under age 18 have decreased as a percentage of all households.
Source: U.S. Census Bureau, 1992.

■ Reading for Information

1. What is the definition of the traditional family?

    ____

2. Before 1970, the proportion of traditional families was
    a. higher
    b. lower
    c. unchanged
3. The percentage of traditional families decreased most from
    a. 1970 to 1980
    b. 1980 to 1991
4. According to the text, in a fifty-year period (1940–90) the percentage of women working
    a. declined
    b. increased to twice as much
    c. increased to almost three times as much
    d. increased to more than four times as much

5. Having two wage earners in the family
   a. increases the family income
   b. keeps families above the poverty line
   c. both of the above
   d. none of the above

■ PART B

Single-Parent Families

With increased divorce, there has been a phenomenal rise in the number of children growing up in households with just one parent. From 1970 to 1991, the proportion of all families being single-parent families increased from 11 to 28 percent (see Figure 10.2). The overwhelming majority (90 percent) of such families are headed by women. About a quarter of the children today live for some time in these female-headed families. It has been estimated that more than half of the children born in 1980 will live with their mothers alone before they reach 18. (Thio, p. 240.)

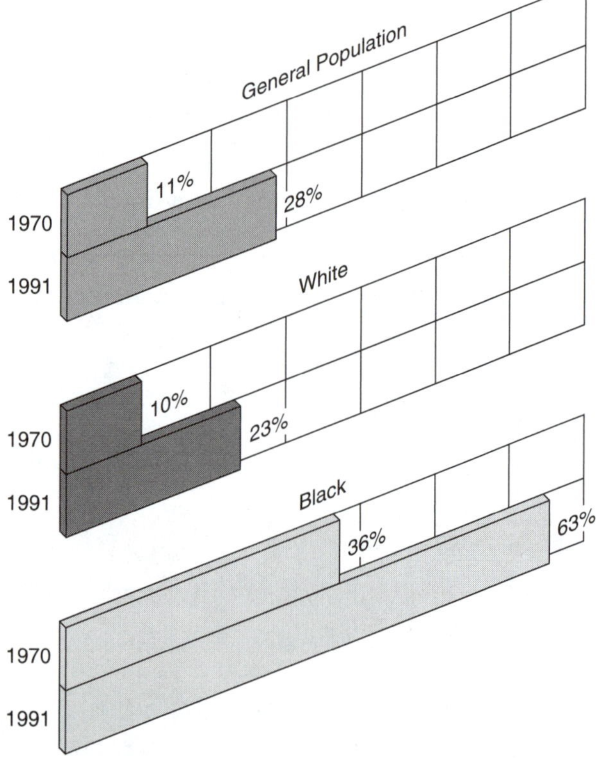

Figure 10.2
Single-Parent Families: A Fast-Growing Group.
Source: U.S. Census Bureau, 1992.

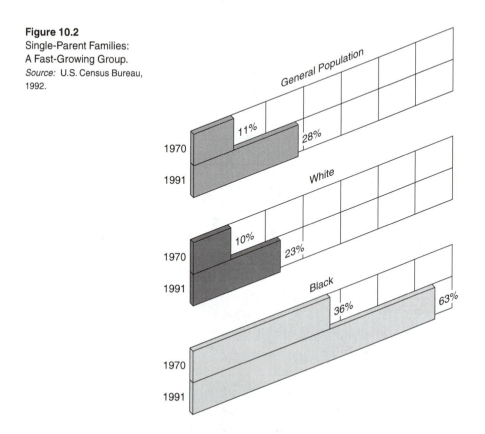

■ Reading for Information

1. What does the text suggest is responsible for the quick rise in single-parent families?

   ____

2. What percentage of single-parent families is headed by men? __________

3. Which group did *not* more than double in percentage of single-parent families?

   a. general population

   b. whites

   c. blacks

4. Which of the following conclusions is supported by the data in the graph?

   a. The percentage of black single-parent families in 1970 was higher than that of the general population in 1990.

   b. The percentage of white single-parent families has stayed much the same over the last twenty years.

   c. The percentage of white single-parent families will soon match that of black single-parent families.

5. The total *number* of black single-parent families

   a. is less than that of white single-parent families

   b. is more than that of white single-parent families

   c. can't be determined from the data in Figure 10.2

Reader Participation

Tables are sometimes used to involve the reader actively in a point the text is making. The next exercise is an example of a descriptive graphic that asks the reader to learn by doing.

EXERCISE 9.5

Graphics Requiring Reader Participation

Follow the instructions in the table on page 320 to learn something about self-consciousness and also how you would be described in relation to this trait. As you read, underline the definition of self-consciousness, and look up the meanings of any words you're not sure of.

TABLE 4.2
Private Self-Consciousness
Are you high in private self-consciousness? To find out, add the numbers you entered for items 1, 3, 4, 5, 6, and 8; then subtract the numbers you entered for items 2 and 7. The higher your score, the more you tend to be aware of your own inner feelings and reactions. (*Source:* Based on items from Britt, 1992.)

Indicate how characteristic or uncharacteristic of you each of these items is by placing a number in the blank space next to each.

0 = extremely uncharacteristic	3 = characteristic
1 = uncharacteristic	4 = extremely characteristic
2 = neither characteristic or uncharacteristic	

_____ 1. I'm always trying to figure myself out.
_____ 2. Usually, I'm not very aware of myself.
_____ 3. I think about myself a lot.
_____ 4. I'm often the subject of my own fantasies or daydreams.
_____ 5. I usually pay close attention to my inner feelings.
_____ 6. I'm aware of the way my mind works when I try to solve a problem or reason something out.
_____ 7. I never reflect on myself.
_____ 8. I frequently examine my own motives.

(Baron, p. 130.)

Mind Maps for Description

Mind maps let us show the special kind of skeletons that patterns have. Mind maps are more adaptable than outlines, are not so formal, and can show structure in a clearer and more easily remembered way. The most common map for descriptive writing is what is called a cluster or spider map. You completed this kind of map for a topic when you mapped the topical organization of "Kicking Asphalt."

Spider Map

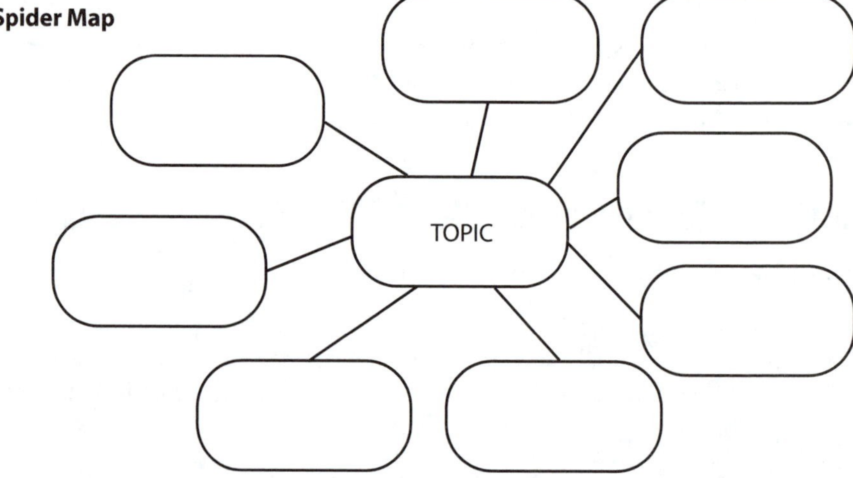

Descriptive spider maps put the subject or the whole at the center, with the details or parts extending out from it. This map is very useful for showing the functions and traits of things and people. For example, in Chapter 5 you completed an inference exercise on "The Scholarship Jacket." Some of these opinions about the main character, Marta, were supportable and some were not.

1. Marta dislikes physical activities.
2. Marta is smart.
3. Marta has very low self-esteem.
4. Marta will give in somewhat on her beliefs on what is right.
5. Marta wants to be recognized for her work.
6. Marta is snoopy.
7. Marta is usually lazy and inattentive.
8. Marta is not vain about her looks.
9. Marta is jealous of others.
10. Marta is respectful of her elders.

On these, most would agree that there is enough evidence to support the following traits, which are mostly positive ones:

2. Marta is smart.
4. Marta will give in somewhat on her beliefs on what is right.
5. Marta wants to be recognized for her work.
8. Marta is not vain about her looks.
10. Marta is respectful of her elders.

This information, along with some supporting detail, can easily be put into a spider map to serve as the basis for a summary or for review.

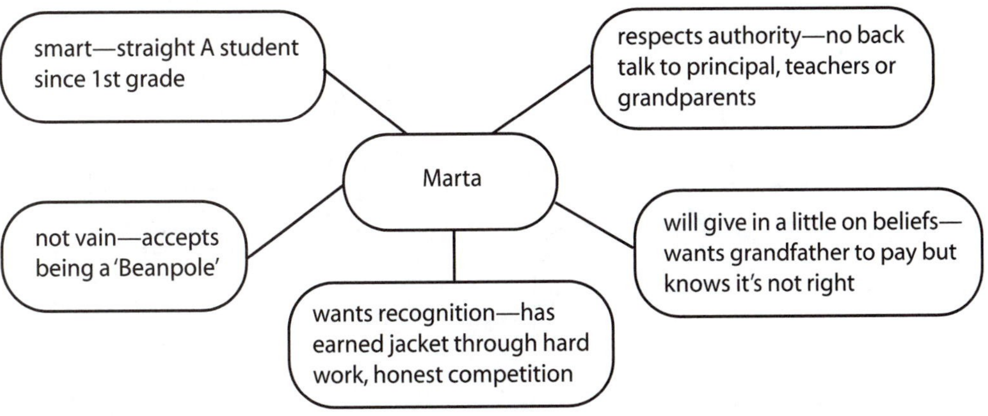

EXERCISE 9.6

Making a Spider Map

Work together in groups of 3–4 to complete this exercise. Review the story "The Circuit" in Chapter 7. Then discuss the inferences below about the main character, Panchito, and decide which *six* can be supported.

_____ 1. He shares the family value of doing hard, honest work.

_____ 2. He enjoys moving and traveling around.

_____ 3. He is around twelve years old.

_____ 4. He comes from a well-to-do family.

_____ 5. He is a serious student.

_____ 6. He is very shy.

_____ 7. He is unpopular with his fellow students.

_____ 8. He is eager to learn a musical instrument.

_____ 9. He is unable to read any English.

_____ 10. He likes his teacher, Mr. Lema.

Now use your six choices to complete a spider map showing the main characteristics of Panchito. Include a few details for each that support the inference.

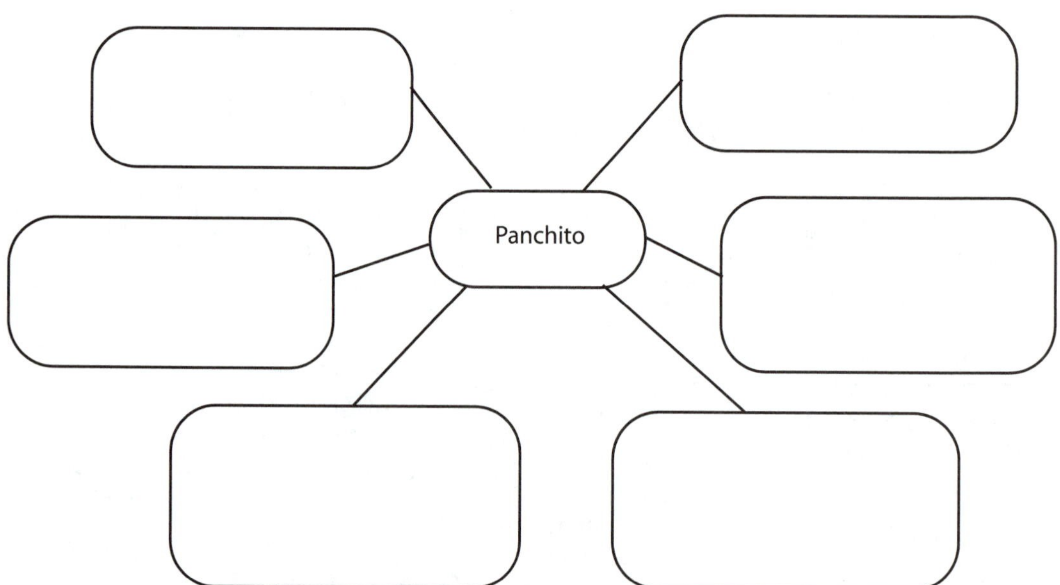

DESCRIPTION IN TEXTBOOK PASSAGES AND ARTICLES

A spider map is good way to show a topic with a lot of details and examples. It is also good, as you have seen, for showing the traits of a subject. A somewhat similar and very popular mind map is an "umbrella" map. This map is especially useful for main ideas supported by several key details and for main ideas with listing phrases such as "There are several reasons why . . ." "My uncle has several annoying habits. . . ." These maps are called umbrella maps because the top provides space for a main idea that is general enough to cover all the details beneath it.

Umbrella Map

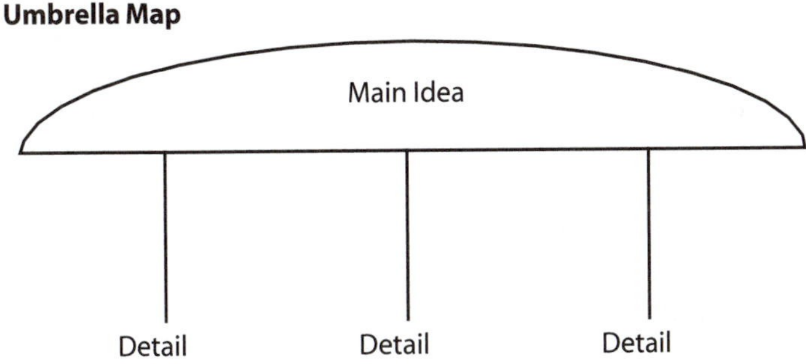

An umbrella map can be helpful for longer textbook passages and full-length articles like the two selections that follow. Your prereading activities will prepare you for completing an umbrella map for these.

Previewing *The Great African-American Migration* by Thomas A. Bailey, David M. Kennedy, and Lizabeth Cohen

Thinking About Reading The title tells you that the topic of this passage is

____

Write anything you know about African-American history in the last century.

____

____

____

____

Descriptions of events tell us not just an outcome but its significance as well. Preview the first and last paragraphs to answer this question: "Did African Americans gain or lose as a result of the Great Migration?" From your preview, which of the following main idea statements would most likely cover the major details of the reading?

a. The many black southerners on the roads during World War II crowded into boardinghouses, camped out in cars, and clustered in juke joints.
b. The trek to northern cities helped most African-Americans economically, but did not end racial discrimination and black poverty.
c. Southern farms gave work to all members of the family, whereas work is not easily found by African-American youth in today's decaying northern cities.

Reading with a Purpose If the text does not support your main idea guess, you will need to change it. If the main idea guess is on track, the passage will provide major details that connect to it. As you read, underline or highlight text and complete, in your own words, the headings in the margin. These will provide the major details of your map for this article.

Preview Vocabulary

The preview vocabulary defines words that do not have enough clues in the context for you to make a good guess.

sharecroppers: (¶2) tenant farmers who give back to landlords as rent a share of crops grown

ravaged: (¶2) destroyed, wasted

dispossessed: (¶2) had lands taken from

foundries: (¶3) places where metal is melted and then poured into molds

Mason-Dixon Line: (¶3) historical survey line separating North and South

creed: (¶4) system of principles, opinions, or religious beliefs

tactical: (¶4) skillful

intractable (¶6) unchanging, stubborn

scourge: (¶6) cause of severe problems

The Great African-American Migration

by Thomas A. Bailey, David A. Kennedy, and Lizabeth Cohen

1 So many black southerners took to the roads during World War II that local officials could not keep track of the migrants passing through their towns. Black workers on the move—a vast

population with no addresses or telephone numbers—crowded into boardinghouses, camped out in cars, and clustered in the juke joints of roadside America en route to a new, uncertain future in northern and western cities.

2 Southern cotton fields and tobacco plantations had yielded but slender sustenance to African-American farmers, few of whom owned their own land. Instead, most had struggled on as tenants and sharecroppers. The Great Depression had been yet another setback, for when the New Deal farm program paid growers to leave land fallow, many landlords pocketed the money, evicting the tenants from the now-fallow fields. Initially, the wartime defense boom only worsened matters, as new military bases and armories ate up farmland, uprooting still more tenants. With few other opportunities in the depression-ravaged country, dispossessed former sharecroppers toiled as seasonal farm laborers or found themselves without work, without shelter, and without hope for the future.

■ *sustenance:*
a. support of life
b. despair

■ *fallow*
a. irrigated
b. unseeded, without a crop

Situation in South in farming:

3 The shiny new war plants and busy shipyards of the South offered little solace to African-Americans. In 1940 and 1941, the labor-hungry war machine soaked up white unemployment but commonly denied jobs to southerners who had the "wrong" skin color. Government training programs in the South, designed to teach skills necessary for work in aircraft, shipbuilding, machine manufacture, electronics, and other war industries, enrolled few blacks. When the army constructed a camp near Petersburg, Virginia, it imported white carpenters from all parts of the United States, although hundreds of available black carpenters resided nearby. Nor was discrimination restricted to skilled positions. Federal investigators discovered that even unskilled jobs in defense industries were closed to black applicants. Fed up with such injustices, many African-Americans headed for shipyards, factories, foundries, and fields north of the Mason-Dixon line, where their willing hands found waiting work in abundance.

■ *solace:*
a. comfort
b. unhappiness

Situation in South in war industry:

Reaction of African-Americans:

4 Angered by the racism that drove their people from the South, black leaders pressured President Roosevelt into declaring that "there shall be no discrimination in the employment of workers in defense industries or government because of race, creed, color, or national origin." This executive order was but a rudimentary step; still, many blacks were heartened to see a presidential response to their protests. The war experience emboldened the civil rights movement, adding momentum and tactical knowledge to the cause.

Progress in civil rights:

■ *rudimentary:*
a. basic, first
b. useless

■ *heartened:*
a. afraid
b. encouraged

■ *momentum:*
a. increasing movement forward
b. money

5 By war's end many African-Americans made new homes in the North and Far West, shifting the heart of America's black

Conditions in the North in WW II:

community from southern plantations to northern cities. There they competed for scarce housing in overcrowded slums and paid outrageous rents to secure a foothold in the few neighborhoods of northern cities that would admit them.

Problems in America:

a.

b.

c.

■ *subsistence:*

a. support of life

b. discouragement

6 The entire nation was now grappling with the evil of racism, as bloody World War II–era riots in Detroit, New York, and other cities tragically revealed. And the trek to northern cities, while an economic boon for most African-Americans, did not end the intractable national problem of black poverty. African-Americans found themselves the first to be fired when the war plants closed down. And black teenage unemployment, a scourge to this day, dates from World War II. Southern farms, though providing the barest subsistence, had been all too generous in dispensing work to all members of the family—work not so readily found by African-American youth in today's decaying northern cities. (Bailey and Kennedy, pp. 856–57.)

Context Answers and Clues

sustenance: a. support of life (they were supporting themselves, but barely)

fallow: b. unseeded, without a crop (tenants evicted because there was nothing to grow)

solace: a. comfort (they were denied jobs)

rudimentary: a. basic, first (the words "but" and "still" indicate only a start toward a solution)

heartened: b. encouraged (they were "emboldened")

momentum: a. increasing movement forward (it was a step forward)

EXERCISE 9.7

Questions on *The Great African-American Migration*

■ Reading for Information

Completing an Umbrella Mind Map

Step 1 Your reading should have confirmed choice *b* as the best statement of the main idea:

> The trek to northern cities helped most African-Americans economically, but did not end racial discrimination and black poverty.

Begin to fill in the map on page 328 by writing the main idea at the top of the umbrella.

Step 2 Below are statements of the major details related to the migration. Compare these to the notes you made in the margins.

#1 The situation in the South at the time of WW II was bleak.

#2 Some progress was made in civil rights, but northern living conditions were very poor.

#3 There were major problems in America at the end of WW II.

Compare these to the major details you marked and noted in the margins as you read. Add these to the map by putting each major detail in its numbered box. Shorten each statement where possible. The first major detail has been done as an example.

Step 3 The answers to the following are the minor details. Shorten answers in your own words and put them in the minor detail boxes under the correct major detail. The answer to the first part of #1 is given as a sample.

Minor Details for #1 (¶s2–3)

What happened to African-Americans as a result of the New Deal and the defense boom?

They worked as farm laborers or were evicted and became homeless.

How were African-Americans treated regarding war industry jobs?

____

____

How did they react?

____

____

Minor Details for #2 (¶s4–5)

Why was Roosevelt pressured to ban discrimination in government employment?

____

____

What were housing conditions like for African-American workers?

____

____

Minor Details for #3 (¶6)

What occurred in Detroit, New York, and other cities?

____

____

____

What problem for African-Americans persisted despite the move to the North?

____

____

____

What new problem emerged that continues to exist today?

____

____

____

Main Idea (¶6):

(#1) bleak situation in South at WW II

- farmers became laborers or were evicted
-

(#2)

-
-

(#3)

-
-
-

Making a Paragraph Spider Map

The first paragraph and part of the second give the reader helpful background information on which African-Americans migrated and why. Fill in the spider map below with details that give important information about these items. Keep your answers as short as possible.

- number who migrated
- where they stayed
- what kind of work they had done
- effect of New Deal program paying farmers not to grow crops
- effect of creating new military bases and armories

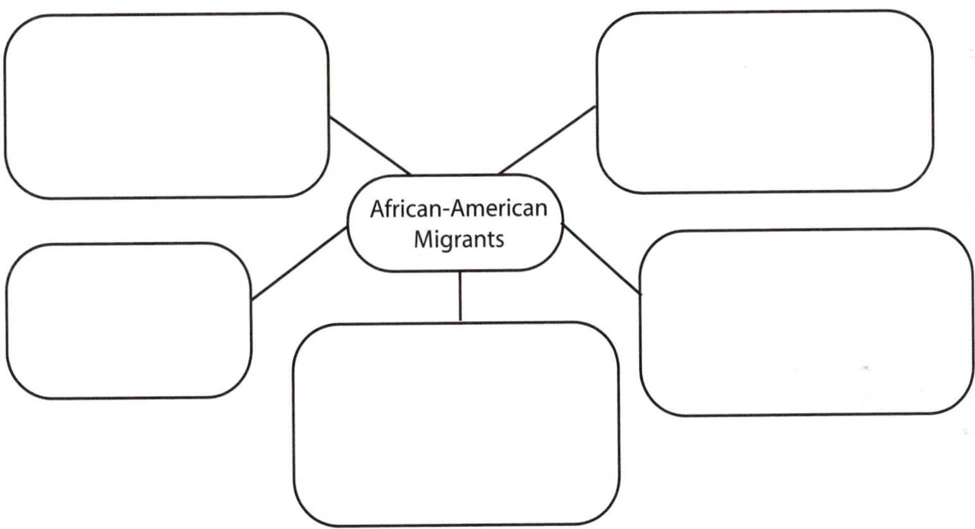

Circle T for True or F for False.

1. T F African-American farmers were not allowed to own land.
2. T F Paying farmers to leave land fallow was a big setback for landlords.
3. T F When lands went fallow, tenants were evicted.
4. T F The need for weapons of war created new job opportunities.
5. T F Only black carpenters were not discriminated against in hiring.
6. T F Black applicants were discriminated against only in skilled jobs.

7. T F African-Americans found work in the North in both factories and fields.

8. T F President Roosevelt's declaration ended all discrimination.

9. T F Most African-Americans returned to the South because of housing conditions.

10. T F When war plants closed, African-Americans were the first to lose their jobs.

■ Reading for Understanding

1. The author's purpose in this article is mainly to
   a. give facts about an important period in American history
   b. convince the reader to join the civil rights movement
   c. justify the actions by both North and South during this period
2. The author's tone (attitude toward the subject and the reader) is best described as
   a. scientific and objective
   b. humorous and sarcastic
   c. outraged and angry

The article mentions significant events that you need to know about and remember. Use reference materials to identify the following and the dates they are associated with.

- the Great Depression (¶2) ______________________________

  ____
- New Deal (¶2) ______________________________

  ____
- Mason-Dixon line (¶3) ______________________________

  ____
- World War II (¶1) ______________________________

  ____

Many magazines feature articles called *profiles.* This type of article focuses on the personalities and accomplishments of people. We draw conclusions about the subject of such articles by the words used to describe the subject, by the actions the subject has done, and by what others are reported to have said. Following is a typical example of this type of article.

Previewing *High School Hero* by Dr. JoAnn Jarolman

Thinking About Reading The title names a topic that most college students have had some experience with. What image comes to your mind when you think of a high school hero?

____

____

____

____

____

____

____

____

Now preview the first and last paragraphs. Does reading these change your views about what heroism means? State in your own words a main idea guess about the subject of the article; it should be based on the summary statements in the last paragraph.

Reading with a Purpose Underline text and make notes in the margin for key details that add to the profile of the subject. You can find this information best by asking questions about the things we base description on:

- What did the subject say?
- What did the subject do?
- What did others say about the subject?
- What judgments about the subject are made by the author?

The answers to these kinds of questions are the details that go into a mind map. Pay special attention in rereading the last paragraph, where some general summary opinions are stated.

Preview Vocabulary

dazzling: (¶1) bright, shiny

degenerative: (¶1) characterized by a gradual wearing down or destruction of cells and organs

muscular dystrophy: (¶5) disease where muscles slowly but steadily are destroyed

respiratory: (¶6) related to breathing

inhalation: (¶6) the act of drawing in air by breathing

adjunct: (¶9) member of a staff with part-time or extra status

self-actualization: (¶11) the fulfilling of one's highest possibilities

High School Hero

by Dr. JoAnn Jarolman

1 I looked through the throng of freshmen that dazzling September morning in 1992 and saw my new charge roaming about on the lawn with his peers. He was to be the first student I'd ever counseled who was suffering from a degenerative disease and in a wheelchair, and I wondered how well I would handle the challenge.

2 I took the plunge and went over to him, introducing myself. He responded like any other teenager: a little embarrassed, somewhat irritated that I had interrupted his conversation with his pals.

3 That's how Stephen Gold entered my life at Pascack Valley High School in northern New Jersey. I didn't know it then, but over the course of the next four years, he would turn the barrier of professionalism into a bond of friendship.

4 We soon became so familiar that he nicknamed me "JoJo," and I called him "The Kid." He was always attuned to how I was feeling. One morning I was very sad, having just learned that my dog, Chickie, had cancer and less than six months to live. Stephen's eyes caught mine, and he immediately came over and insisted I tell him what was wrong. When I told him about Chickie, he said, "JoJo, you can't believe those doctors; they're not God, they don't know." As he spoke, I realized he was talking about himself. His whole life was borrowed time.

■ *attuned to:*
a. understanding of
b. uninterested in

5 He suffered from muscular dystrophy, which had been diagnosed when he was a year old. By the time I met him, he had already exceeded his doctors' predictions in terms of life expectancy. His motto, "It's not over till it's over," was lifted from Yogi Berra. As he once explained in an essay, "It is an expression etched into the heart and soul of every underdog who ever was or will be."

■ *diagnosed:*
a. overlooked
b. found to exist through examination

■ *etched:*
a. imprinted clearly
b. rejected by

6 Stephen weighed only about 40 pounds and had little muscular power left in his limbs or even in his neck. He also suffered bouts of severe respiratory distress, which meant he often had to leave class for inhalation treatments. Yet he rejected any kind of assistance that he thought would give him an unfair advantage over other students. He once took a final algebra exam while hooked up to his breathing equipment. It took him six hours to complete the test, but he persevered.

■ *persevered:*
a. continued despite problems
b. complained

7 Stephen always knew that his time was short, and he accepted his fate. Why waste precious time railing against a situation over which you had no control? That was his philosophy of life. He had no room for dishonesty, no patience for anything but the truth.

■ *railing against:*
a. solving
b. complaining about

8 He did not ask for help from his teachers or his fellow students, nor did he try to elicit our sympathy. When his classmates elected him to the student council, they did so not because they felt sorry for him, but because he was known for getting the job done. And when, as a senior, he was asked to be the yearbook's business manager, it was because he had shown himself to be organized, effective and imaginative.

■ *elicit:*
a. bring out
b. avoid

9 On graduation day I felt bereft thinking of Stephen's departure. But he planned to go on to nearby Ramapo College, and that summer I was offered an adjunct professorship there. Our friendship could continue.

■ *bereft:*
a. cheated
b. lacking something greatly needed

10 But Stephen died on September 10, 1996, before he could start college. I was devastated. What would I do without this precious soul? My answer is to share him.

■ *devastated*
a. completely destroyed
b. surprised

11 Stephen was an inspiration to me and to all those who took the time to know him. We loved him for his ability to rise above bodily concerns and reach a level of self-actualization achieved by very few. He had a mission, and he was able to achieve it in his short life: to be a grand teacher. He taught all of us to persevere beyond our limitations and refuse to accept mediocrity. He also taught us not to make excuses for our shortcomings, but to embrace them and, in so doing, overcome them.

■ *mediocrity:*
a. authority
b. state of being only of average quality

Context Answers and Clues

attuned to: a. understanding of (he relates her situation to his own)

diagnosed: b. found to exist through examination (doctor has to discover it before predicting)

etched: a. imprinted clearly (it's his life motto)

persevered: a. continued despite problems (kept on going for six difficult hours)

railing against: b. complaining about (opposite of "accepted")

elicit: a. bring out (not trying to get sympathy fits with not trying to get help)

bereft: b. lacking something greatly needed (they have been close friends)

devastated: a. completely destroyed (would be expected response to loss of someone near you)

mediocrity: b. state of being only of average quality (if we exceed limits, we're above average)

EXERCISE 9.8

Questions on *High School Hero*

■ Reading for Information

Completing an Umbrella Mind Map

The statements below include one statement that is broad enough to cover the others (the main idea), and six statements that are major details. Compare these to the major details you marked and noted in the margins as you read. Then decide which of these statements is the main idea:

Stephen Gold

1. was very determined and self-reliant
2. suffered greatly and underwent treatments
3. had a philosophy of not complaining about fate
4. achieved a lot without appealing to pity
5. was able to relate to the feelings of others
6. had a mission to be a teacher
7. was an exceptional and inspirational person

Statement 7 is the main idea because the describing words *exceptional* and *inspirational* are developed and supported by the other details. Complete the umbrella map below by putting the main idea at the top of the umbrella. Then put the six major details in the numbered boxes. Shorten each statement where possible. The first detail has been done as an example.

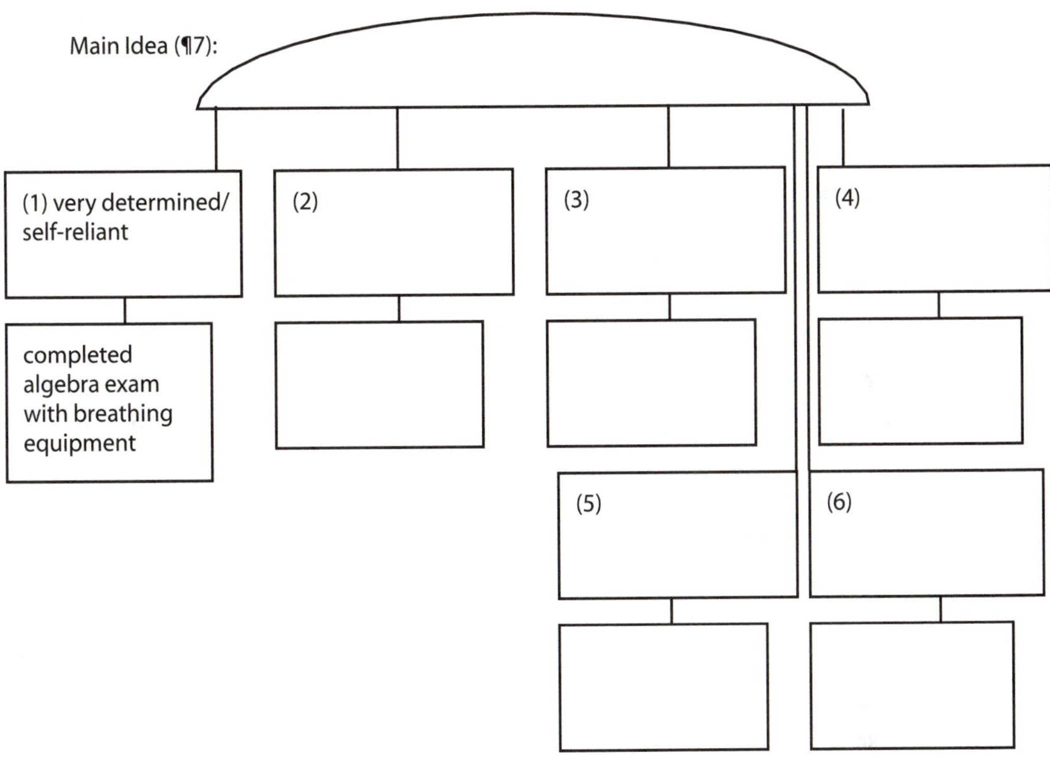

Finding Minor Details

Your answers to the following are the minor details. Put your answers, in as few words as possible, in the minor detail boxes under the same number. The answer to the first part of question 1 is given.

1. What example is given to show Stephen did not expect or want special help?

   He completed his algebra exam, even though it took six hours, using breathing equipment.

2. What discomforts and treatments did his illness create for him?

   ____

   ____

3. What was Stephen's attitude about using time?

____

____

4. What were Stephen's achievements in high school?

____

____

5. What incident showed Stephen's ability to understand the feelings of others?

____

____

6. What lessons did his way of living teach to others?

____

____

Finding Main Ideas

Write the sentence with the main idea for each of the paragraphs below. Then circle the letter that shows the reason for your choice.

1. ¶4 Main Idea: ____

   ____

   This is the main idea because it

   a. answers a question stated in the paragraph.
   b. has a listing phrase.
   c. is followed by an example.
   d. has a change of direction signal.

2. ¶7 Main Idea: ____

   ____

   This is the main idea because it

   a. answers a question stated in the paragraph.
   b. has a listing phrase.
   c. is followed by an example.
   d. has no signal but states a general conclusion that leads to all details.

3. ¶8 Main Idea: ______________________________

____

This is the main idea because it

a. answers a question stated in the paragraph.
b. has a listing phrase.
c. is followed by an example.
d. has a change of direction signal.

4. Which of these statements about Stephen Gold best gives the complete main idea of ¶6?

a. He had great physical problems, so he had to have special treatments.
b. He had to have special treatments, but he could still do algebra.
c. His physical problems, necessary treatments, but never giving up.
d. He had great physical problems, but he refused help he thought would be unfair.

■ Reading for Understanding

Circle T for True or F for False. Then give evidence for your choice.

1. T F The author had never counseled a disabled student before.

   Evidence: ______________________________

2. T F Stephen Gold was a freshman in high school when the author first met him.

   Evidence: ______________________________

3. T F JoJo had cancer and only six months to live.

   Evidence: ______________________________

4. T F Stephen saw himself as an underdog who had to battle to succeed.

   Evidence: ______________________________

5. T F Stephen got on student council because people felt sorry for him.

   Evidence: ______________________________

6. T F Stephen was never able officially to graduate from high school.

   Evidence: ______________________________

7. T F Stephen's doctor predicted he would live to be at least twenty-one years old.

   Evidence: ______________________________

8. T F Stephen weighed around 40 pounds and was not strong.

   Evidence: ______________________________

9. T F Stephen was ten years old when he became ill.

   Evidence: ______________________________

10. T F Stephen died in the middle of his freshman year at Ramapo College.

    Evidence: ______________________________

■ Purpose and Tone

1. The author's purpose in this article is mainly to
   a. give some information about disabilities.
   b. show how a person with handicaps can be a role model.
   c. tell about her experiences and achievements as a counselor.
2. The author's tone is best described as
   a. scientific and objective.
   b. humorous and lighthearted.
   c. sad but appreciative.

■ Questions for Discussion:

Work in small groups to discuss and answer these questions.

1. "We loved him for his ability to rise above bodily concerns and reach a level of self-actualization achieved by very few." Drawing from Stephen Gold as an example, list some characteristics of a self-actualized person and any examples you can think of.

   ____

   ____

   ____

   ____

   ____

2. "He taught all of us to persevere beyond our limitations and refuse to accept mediocrity." Explain in your own words what this sentence means. From your own experience and knowledge of history, give some examples of famous people who have taught a similar lesson.

____

____

____

____

____

3. "I didn't know it then, but over the course of the next four years, he would turn the barrier of professionalism into a bond of friendship." Explain what this statement means. What sorts of barriers would these be?

____

____

____

____

____

■ Summarizing

Write a summary of around 100 words on "High School Hero." Include only the main idea and the major details. Be sure to work in the name of the author and the article in the first sentence or two. Then write a response of about 50–75 words, which gives your reaction to the article.

WORD PARTS: MAKING DESCRIPTIVE WORDS

Words parts have been a handy source for making new words over the years. Certain word parts have been especially useful for naming new inventions in communications:

tele "far"	*vis/vid* "see"	*photo* "light"
phon "sound"	*graph* "write"	

From these have come the names of familiar inventions, such as *photograph, telephoto, phonograph, television, telegraph,* and *telephone.*

Word parts have also been a good source for science fiction stories, for movies (e.g., *Star Wars, Star Trek*) and for TV series like *Star Trek.* Writers give names to imaginative ideas and inventions, or simply have fun making up great-sounding phrases that probably don't refer to much at all. For example, a writer could take these word parts—*trans* (across), *tele* (far), *retro* (back), *port* (carry)—and make up a name for a device that will bring back space travelers who have been beamed elsewhere: "retroteletransporter."

EXERCISE 9.9

Making Descriptive Words from Word Parts

Here are some additional word parts that are good sources for making up descriptive names for ideas and inventions related to space travel and science. Pretend that you are a scriptwriter for a space travel movie or TV series, inventing words that sound like names for space terms and inventions. Using these and any other words or word parts that fit, make up as many words and phrases like "retroteletransporter" as you can think of.

spectro	scope	thermo	photon	gyro	tech
gamma	mega	giga	intra	stellar	hyper
galactic	tetra	quad	quadrant	poly	sphere
laser	tri	polar	neuro	force	reactor
bi	anti	nucleo	field	cyber	bio
warp	quark	phase	quasar	field	

Active Learning

GEOGRAPHIC MIND MAPS

One way of remembering information in a field of study is by building permanent "maps" in your mind. To do that, you need to begin by putting together information on paper. In studying geography, for example, you can create a descriptive map that shows the structure and parts of the world: countries, cities, physical features, etc. As you gain new information, you can add it to your map. As you do this, the world map on paper will eventually become a world map in your mind and you can apply this information to many more subjects than just geography.

EXERCISE 9.10

Building a Geographic Mind Map

Here is a list of some of the places you have read about so far in this textbook. Write the names of these in their proper location on a study map of the world (your college bookstore should have these inexpensive maps in stock). Write in the names of other cities, countries, continents, or physical features that you already know. As you continue to read this text and other reading materials, add any new information to this map as you run across it.

- Mexico
- Spain
- Europe
- areas where the conquistadores explored
- United States
- North America
- North Africa: Libya, Morocco, Tunisia, Algeria, Atlas Mountains, Maghreb
- areas of deserts: American Southwest, northern Chile, Australia, northern and southern Africa, Arabia, high deserts of eastern Oregon

Reading Portfolio

DESCRIPTIVE ARTICLES

Choose one of the following options for this assignment.

Option 1: A Profile. Look for an article in a magazine that runs features on people. Magazines like *People* and *Reader's Digest* and those featuring entertainment and sports figures are good sources. Newsmagazines like *Time* and *Newsweek* often feature world leaders but the vocabulary level of these magazines can make them hard to read. Profiles can also be done of places and things, but check first with your instructor if you want to do one of these.

Option 2: Part/Whole. Articles involving wholes and parts can be found in many different sources. Some examples are

- travel magazines (geography)
- home/garden (floor plans and layouts)

- crafts and building magazines (elements of a project)
- machines (cars and others)
- sports (leagues/components of a team)

1. Preview and read carefully for information and understanding. Make a map before you begin your summary. Use a spider or an umbrella map; for option 2, you may want to use a diagram if the article is very technical.
2. Write your summary from your map only. Clearly state the main idea or purpose at or very near the beginning. Say things in your own words. The summary should be about 150 words.
3. Be sure readers hear *your voice* leading them through the main points. Remember, one good way to establish control and voice is to begin by naming the author and title:

   Marian Lewis, in her article "You Can Get the Grade You Want," discusses some study strategies that students should use to . . .

4. Write a response of around equal length. In this section, you agree or disagree with points in the article or present any personal connection or application the topic might have for you.
5. From the article, select five words whose meaning you were not sure of. For each word, decide on the part of speech and its meaning as used in the article. Then write a context sentence of your own. Think of a situation different from that in the article. Be sure to include enough clues that someone could guess the meaning.

CHAPTER 10

What's the Difference to Me?

Comparing and Grouping

After reading this chapter, you will know the answers to these questions:

- What common signal words help us compare, contrast, and group?
- How do block and grid maps differ?
- How do graphics convey comparative information?
- What learning styles are most effective?
- Which prefixes make words into opposites?
- How have your learning behaviors improved?

Through description we identify and talk about the things we have an interest in. To understand things clearly, however, we must often think about how they are like or unlike other objects. This involves us in other very useful thinking processes: comparing, contrasting, and grouping (classifying).

You learned some signal words showing comparison and contrast when working with context clues. Below is a longer list of signal words and phrases of comparison and contrast, along with some that indicate grouping:

Signal Words of Comparison / Contrast

same	better than	although	but
like	worse than	however	yet
similarly	different from	in contrast	nevertheless
likewise	opposite	in spite of	while
resembles	on the contrary	rather than	despite

Signal Words of Classification

types (of)	kinds (of)	fall into	divide into
categories	groups	belong to	separate into

MIND MAPS FOR COMPARING, CONTRASTING, AND GROUPING

Comparing and contrasting always involves two or more things: cars, study methods, personality traits, solutions, etc. There are two common methods for mapping the skeleton (the most important ideas) in material organized by comparison and contrast.

Block: Items are discussed separately

SUBJECT 1	SUBJECT 2
Trait	Trait
Trait	Trait
Trait	Trait

Grid: Items are compared point by point

	SUBJECT 1	SUBJECT 2
Trait A		
Trait B		
Trait C		

In the following selection from a psychology textbook, note how questions lead to descriptions that create two different groups with contrasting characteristics. As you read, think about how the information might be arranged into a comparison/contrast map.

Type A Behavior

by Robert A. Baron

1 Think about the people you know. Can you name one person who always seems to be in a hurry, is extremely competitive, and is often hostile and irritable? Now, in contrast, can you

name one who shows the opposite pattern—someone who is relaxed, relatively uncompetitive, and easygoing in relations with others? If you succeeded, you now have in mind two people who could be described as showing Type A and Type B behavior patterns, respectively.

2 Interest in the Type A behavior pattern was first stimulated by medical research. Several physicians noticed that many patients who had suffered heart attacks seemed to share certain personality traits. Individuals who tend to be competitive, aggressive, hostile, and impatient are displaying a pattern of behaviors termed Type A. They are likely to be hard workers and tend to seek out the most challenging and stressful work conditions. Often, their efforts are rewarded with additional work from their superiors and coworkers. But some researchers now believe that only certain aspects of the Type A pattern may be related to increased risk of heart disease. Recent findings suggest it may be only those Type A individuals who fail to express their emotions—especially anger, cynicism, and hostility—and fail to ignore early symptoms of cardiovascular disease who are at risk. A particular type of hostility—*cynical hostility,* characterized by suspiciousness, resentment, anger, antagonism, and distrust of others—may be especially detrimental.

3 Yet there may also be some health benefits to being Type A. In a thirteen-year longitudinal study of Type A and Type B men, researchers found that although Type A had significantly more heart attacks than Type Bs, they were more likely to survive those heart attacks. It appears that the personality style that drove them to heart attacks may also include behaviors that increase adherence to post–heart attack treatment. In short, the very characteristics that threaten to kill Type As may, under certain circumstances, be the same ones that save their lives. (Baron, p. 432.)

- *cynicism:*
  a. suspicion, distrust of the motives of others
  b. rudeness
- *detrimental:*
  a. unusual
  b. harmful
- *longitudinal:*
  a. outdated
  b. over a number of years
- *adherence to:*
  a. refusing
  b. sticking with

Context Answers and Clues

cynicism: a. suspicion, distrust of the motives of others ("suspiciousness," "distrust")

detrimental: b. harmful (people with these characteristics are "at risk")

longitudinal: b. over a number of years (it took thirteen years)

adherence to: b. sticking with (survival depends on following the treatment)

EXERCISE 10.1

Comparing, Contrasting, and Grouping

■ Reading for Information

Fill in the grid using information from paragraph 1.

TYPE A	TYPE B
in a hurry	______________
______________	relatively uncompetitive
______________	______________

1. ¶1 Main Idea: ____

   ____

   This is the main idea because it
   a. answers a question stated in the paragraph
   b. has a listing phrase
   c. has a signal word or phrase of conclusion
   d. has a change of direction signal

2. ¶2 Main Idea: ____

   ____

   This is the main idea because it
   a. answers a question stated in the paragraph
   b. has a listing phrase
   c. has a signal word or phrase of conclusion
   d. has a change of direction signal

Circle T for True or F for False.

3. T F Interest in the Type B behavior pattern was stimulated by medical research.
4. T F Competitive, aggressive, hostile, and impatient individuals are termed Type A.
5. T F All Type A people are at equal risk of having a heart attack.

6. T F Type As who express their emotions have fewer heart attacks than Type Bs.
7. T F There are more health benefits to being a Type A than a Type B.
8. T F The Type As most at risk are likely those who show "cynical hostility."

■ Reading for Understanding

1. Reread the last paragraph. Now, imagine that a week from now you are discussing the subject of heart attacks and stress with a group of friends. Complete the following *in your own words,* without looking back at the original.

   I just finished reading a section in my psychology text on personality types and heart attack risks. It pointed out that an aggressive, at-risk type of person actually has a better chance of recovering from a heart attack because . . .

   ____

   ____

2. ¶2 goes into greater detail about the traits of Type A persons. Complete the grid below and rate yourself on whether or not these traits fit you.

	Describes me (check one)		
Type A Traits	**Closely**	**Somewhat**	**Not At All**
competitive			
aggressive			
hostile			
impatient			
hard worker			
seek challenging and stressful work conditions			
seek and get extra work			

GRAPHICS THAT COMPARE AND GROUP

Tables, graphs, and charts present a lot of material in condensed form. Sometimes graphics stand alone from the text; at other times, as in the next exercise, the text and the graphic work together to present the information.

EXERCISE 10.2

Comparing and Grouping in Graphics

Preview Vocabulary

adrenaline: (¶1) body substance that stimulates nerve action

cognitive: (¶2) relating to thinking and knowing

Of Larks and Owls

by Robert A. Baron

Before reading further, please answer the questions in Table 4.1.

TABLE 4.1 Are You a Lark or an Owl?

Respond to each of the following items by circling either "Day" or "Night"

1. I feel most alert during the	Day	Night
2. I have most energy during the	Day	Night
3. I prefer to take classes during the	Day	Night
4. I prefer to study during the	Day	Night
5. I get my best ideas during the	Day	Night
6. When I graduate, I prefer to find a job during the	Day	Night
7. I am most productive during the	Day	Night
8. I feel most intelligent during the	Day	Night
9. I enjoy leisure-time activities most during the	Day	Night
10. I prefer to work during the	Day	Night

1 How did you score? If you answered "Day" to eight or more questions, the chances are good that you are a morning person (a lark). If, instead, you answered "Night" to eight or more questions, you are probably a night person (an owl). Morning people feel most alert and active early in the day, while night people experience peaks in alertness and energy in the afternoon or evening. Such differences are more than purely subjective. Studies comparing larks and owls indicate that the two groups differ in several important ways. For example, morning people have a higher overall level of adrenaline than night people; thus, they seem to operate at a higher overall level of activation. Similarly, as you might expect, morning people experience peaks in body temperature earlier in the day than night people. While morning people have temperature peaks before noon, night people often experience their peaks in temperature in the evening, around 6:00 P.M. or even later.

■ *subjective:*
a. scientific
b. personal

2 In addition, some findings suggest that larks and owls also differ with respect to cognitive states. Not surprisingly, morning people report feeling more alert and do better on many cognitive tasks early in the day. In contrast, night people report feeling more alert and do better on such tasks later in the day. More surprising is the fact that these two groups also differ with respect to times at which they are most susceptible to hypnotism. Morning people seem to be most susceptible to hypnosis in the morning and early afternoon, while night people are most susceptible to hypnosis in the afternoon and evening. (Baron, p. 125.)

■ *susceptible:*
a. easily affected by
b. able to understand

Context Answers and Clues

subjective: b. personal (not based on studies)

susceptible: a. easily affected by (we know some people are more easily hypnotized)

■ Reading for Information

Mapping

Complete the grid on page 350 with the choices listed below.

- lower: less active
- before noon
- cognitive tasks
- morning/early afternoon
- temperature peaks
- do better later in the day
- active early in the day

	Morning People (Larks)	Night People (Owls)
feel alert/energetic		active in afternoon/ evening
level of adrenaline	higher: more active	
		6 P.M. or later
	do better early in the day	
susceptivity to hypnotism		afternoon/evening

1. The above paragraphs contain a number of words and phrases that indicated similarity or difference. Circle all the words or phrases in the paragraph that indicate these relationships.
2. Select the sentence that states the overall main idea for the two paragraphs:
   a. Morning people feel most alert and active early in the day, while night people experience peaks in alertness and energy in the afternoon or evening.
   b. Such differences are more than purely subjective.
   c. Studies comparing larks and owls indicate that the two groups differ in several important ways.
   d. Some findings suggest that larks and owls also differ with respect to cognitive states.

   This is the main idea because it
   a. answered a question in the paragraph
   b. contained a listing phrase
   c. was followed by an example with a signal word
   d. both a and c
   e. both b and c

Circle T for True or F for False.

3. T F A higher adrenaline level increases the level of activity.
4. T F Most studies of morning and night people are subjective, not scientific.
5. T F Morning people are more susceptible to hypnosis than night people.

■ Reading for Understanding

1. Why would the author select larks and owls to represent these two groups?

____

____

____

2. Why would morning and night people be easiest to hypnotize at the times listed?

____

____

____

3. What would you conclude about people who answered "day" or "night" to fewer than eight questions?

____

____

____

4. Based on your answers in the survey, what type do you lean toward being? What type would you like to be? Why?

____

____

____

Graphics often contain information on a variety of aspects involving two or more things. The text that accompanies the graphic will often call attention to some important conclusions from the graphic. By comparing and contrasting the data carefully, however, the reader can often draw other significant inferences.

EXERCISE 10.3

Drawing Conclusions by Comparing Data in Tables

The passage below mentions two important terms for political reference frameworks, *liberal* and *conservative.* After reading the passage, you should have a better understanding of these terms when you next run across them.

Political Parties and Elections

by James Henslin

1 After the founding of the United States, numerous political parties emerged, but by the time of the Civil War, two parties dominated U.S. politics: the Democrats, who in the public mind are associated with the working class, and the Republicans, who are associated with wealthier people. Each party nominates candidates, and in the pre-elections, called primaries, the voters decide which candidate will represent their party. Each candidate then campaigns, trying to appeal to the most voters. Table 15.1 shows how Americans align themselves with political

TABLE 15.1 How Americans Identify with Political Parties

	1960	1970	1980	1990	1994
Democrats					
Strong Democrat	20%	20%	18%	20%	15%
Weak Democrat	25	24	23	19	19
Independent Democrat	6	10	11	12	13
Total	51	54	52	51	47
Republicans					
Strong Republican	16	9	9	10	16
Weak Republican	14	15	14	15	15
Independent Republican	7	8	12	12	12
Total	37	32	35	37	43
Other					
Independent	10	13	13	11	10
Not political	3	1	2	2	1
Total	13	14	15	13	11

Note: Due to rounding, the totals do not always equal 100 percent.

Source: Statistical Abstract 1991:Table 452; 1995:Table 458.

parties. The realignment of party identification shown on this table reflects the more conservative stance Americans have recently taken.

2 Although the Democratic and Republican parties represent different philosophical principles, each appeals to such a broad membership that it is difficult to distinguish a conservative Democrat from a liberal Republican. The extremes, however, are easy to discern. Deeply committed Democrats support legislation that transfers income from one group to another or that controls wages, working conditions, and competition. Dyed-in-the-wool Republicans oppose such legislation. (Henslin, p. 411.)

Reading for Information

1. Between 1970 and 1994, the percentage of Democrats who switched to the Republican party
   a. increased.
   b. declined.
   c. stayed the same.
   d. can't be determined from the data.
2. The total percentage of voters identified as Independent in all three categories was greater than the total of Strong and Weak Democrats in
   a. 1970.
   b. 1980.
   c. 1990.
   d. 1994.
   e. can't be determined from the data.
3. Compared to 1960, for 1994 the percentage of Independents in the "Other" category
   a. increased.
   b. declined.
   c. stayed the same.
   d. can't be determined from the data.
4. Republicans had their biggest percentage gain between
   a. 1960 and 1970.
   b. 1970 and 1980.
   c. 1980 and 1990.
   d. 1990 and 1994.
   e. can't be determined from the data.

5. Democrats had their biggest percentage loss between
   a. 1960 and 1970.
   b. 1970 and 1980.
   c. 1980 and 1990.
   d. 1990 and 1994.
   e. can't be determined from the data
6. Democrats had their highest party identification and Republicans their lowest in
   a. 1960.
   b. 1970.
   c. 1980.
   d. 1990.
   e. 1994.
7. The total percentage adds up to 100% only in 1970. In other years it is 101 or 102. What reason is given for that?

   ____

   ____

   ____

■ Reading for Understanding

1. "The realignment of party identification shown on this table reflects the more conservative stance Americans have recently taken." Judging from the data in the table, we would conclude that the term *conservative* would be associated with
   a. Democrats.
   b. Republicans.
   c. Independents.
   d. those not political.
2. "Deeply committed Democrats support legislation that transfers income from one group to another or that controls wages, working conditions, and competition. Dyed-in-the-wool Republicans oppose such legislation." From the contrast clue in this sentence, we could guess that "dyed-in-the-wool" means about the same as what phrase in these two sentences?

   ____

3. From 1970 to 1990, over half the voters identified themselves as Democrats, yet there was only one Democrat elected president (Carter). In 1994, the Republicans had narrowed the percentage gap to its lowest point since 1960, but a Democrat (Clinton) was president and was reelected two years later. What can you infer from this about party identification and the way Americans vote?

____

____

____

COMPARING AND CONTRASTING: A LONGER TEXTBOOK PASSAGE

Textbook chapters often break up into sections that may be organized around different idea patterns. The following selection from a sociology textbook uses comparison and contrast to make some key points about differences in Japanese and American society.

Previewing *Japanese Society: Where Do You Fit?* by George J. Bryjak and Michael P. Soroka

Thinking About Reading The title asks a question that will likely point toward at least a part of the main idea. Read the first paragraph. From the title and your preview, you can see that two countries are being compared:

_______________________ and _______________________

Note from your preview that the authors know that the concepts they are presenting are difficult; therefore, they restate ideas and give definitions and examples. For a main idea guess, look for the sentence in ¶1 that begins with "In other words . . ." and complete it:

"In other words _______________________________________

____"

Reading with a Purpose As you read, mark main points and examples and make notes that will help you to understand, not just state, the key differences between Japanese and American views of social obedience.

Japanese Society: Where Do You Fit?

by George J. Bryjak and Michael P. Soroka

1 "So, what do you do?"

"I'm a sociology major at State."

During the course of a lifetime, we meet hundreds of people, and one of the first pieces of information we exchange concerns our present occupation or major activity. In Japan, however, neither the question nor the answer above would be appropriate or make much sense. Rather, the conversation would go like this:

"Dochira desuka?" "Where is it [that you work or belong]?"

"I am at the University of Tokyo studying sociology."

Do you see the difference between the two questions and answers? The first emphasizes attribute (personal trait or characteristic) while the second stresses what Nakane terms frame, one's place in an institution "or a particular relationship which binds a set of individuals into one group." In Western societies the emphasis is on attribute: "I am a sociology major. . . ." However, in Japan, frame is more important: "I am at the University of Tokyo. . . ." In other words, we emphasize who people are and what they do in life; for the Japanese what really matters is where an individual belongs.

2 Nakane noted that some frames can be even more significant than blood ties. For example, in Japan, relationships within the home are thought to be of utmost importance. Therefore, wives and daughters-in-law who come to the household from the outside are much more important than sisters and daughters who have married and now are members of other households. In this example, sister and daughter are characteristics of who an individual is, or attributes. Wives and daughters-in-law, on the other hand, are now part of the household frame. According to Nakane, the emphasis on frame has contributed to the weakening of kinship ties in Japan: "A married sibling who lives in another household is considered a kind of outsider."

3 This emphasis on frame or "belongingness" characterizes what many scholars believe is the most distinctive feature of Japanese social structure compared to Western societies. Not only do the Japanese place tremendous emphasis on group membership, but they also stress the individual's willingness to fulfill all of the obligations attached to his or her membership in the group.

4 The importance of group membership and the willingness to fulfill one's obligations within the organization are directly related to how the Japanese raise their children. Ian Buruma (1984) noted, "Being a Japanese child, especially a boy, and most of all the eldest son, is as close as one can get to being a God." Babies and small children are indulged and treated quite permissively. They are nursed for a relatively long time and are constantly held and fondled by their mothers. It is not uncommon for children to sleep with their parents until the children are quite large.

- *indulged:*
  - a. given what one wishes
  - b. disciplined

5 As a result of these child-rearing practices, Japanese children are accustomed to being the center of attention and having their needs promptly met. Children learn quickly that parents (especially mothers) are the source of all their physical and psychological support. They also learn to be compliant and to accept their mother as an authority figure. "In time this attitude becomes expanded into an acceptance of authority of the surrounding social milieu and a need for and dependence upon this broader social approval." (Reischauer, 1988) . . . These firmly held notions of duty and obligation, coupled with child-rearing practices that foster dependence and obedience, help explain the significance of group membership and a good deal of social behavior in Japan.

- *compliant:*
  - a. yielding to the wishes of others
  - b. critical
- *milieu:*
  - a. environment
  - b. approval
- *foster:*
  - a. ignore
  - b. encourage

6 From a Western perspective, the Japanese appear to be a nation of sheep, quietly and obediently doing what they are told when they are told to do it. More often than not, this conformity is interpreted as a sign of personal weakness. In our eyes, people who do not think for themselves lack the courage and inner strength to do what they want, regardless of the opinions of others. However, the Japanese view their behavior in a much different light. Rather than weakwilled conformists, they see themselves as possessed of tremendous self-control. It takes discipline to curb one's feelings, desires, and needs for the good of the group. Following the rules and doing one's duty is nothing to be ashamed of. On the contrary, conformity is the product of inner strength.

- *perspective:*
  - a. point of view
  - b. lack of information
- *conformity:*
  - a. cowardice
  - b. behavior in line with social customs, rules

Context Answers and Clues

indulged: a. given what one wishes ("treated quite permissively," examples given)

compliant: a. yielding to the wishes of others (accept authority)

milieu: a. environment ("surrounding")

foster: b. encourage ("dependence and obedience" are the result)

perspective: a. a point of view ("appear to be")

conformity: b. behavior in line with social customs, rules (do what they are told)

EXERCISE 10.4

Questions on *Japanese Society: Where Do You Fit?*

■ Reading for Information

1. Two terms are defined in the text in ¶1. Write the terms and the definitions here.

   A. ______________________________

   B. ______________________________

2. ¶2 Main Idea: ______________________________

   This is the main idea because it

   a. answers a question stated in the paragraph
   b. has a listing phrase
   c. is followed by an example
   d. has a change of direction symbol

3. List three signal words or phrases of contrast in ¶6 that present the Japanese viewpoint on social obedience.

Circle T for True or F for False.

4. T F The youngest Japanese daughter is most likely to get attention at home.

5. T F Accepting authority in the Japanese home leads to accepting it in society.

6. T F Group membership is more important in the United States than in Japan.

Reading for Understanding

1. Which of the following is the best statement of the main idea of ¶6?
   a. Doing what you are told shows a lack of courage and inner strength.
   b. Japanese and Americans have different views about social obedience.
   c. Differing views over obedience, the nature of courage and conformity.
   d. Everyone should follow their own opinion, no matter what society says.
2. Explain in your own words why a sister or brother living in a different household is considered to be an outsider in Japan.

   ____

   ____

3. Explain in your own words the difference between the way Japanese and Americans view following directions from others.

   ____

   ____

COMPARING, CONTRASTING, AND GROUPING: ARTICLES

Previewing *Study Styles* by Cintra Scott

Thinking About Reading What topic is clearly named by the title?

____

Preview by reading the first paragraph. Do you do better on learning tasks by hearing, reading, or doing something "hands on"?

____

____

____

____

Your main idea guess can be stated from the information in the first paragraph:

"There are a number of ______________________________."

Reading with a Purpose Survey the major headings. How many types of study styles will the article discuss? ________

Following discussion of each study style is a section of advice. What heading is given to each of these sections? ______________________.

From your preview, you can see that the article is organized by giving each style a name, describing it, and giving advice. As you read, mark key points and make notes in the margins where indicated. This information will be used to complete a grid that will show the skeleton of the article.

Preview Vocabulary

MOs: (¶1) methods of operation

elaborate: (¶2) fancy, very detailed

incriminate: (¶10) get involved in a crime or wrongful act

Study Styles

by Cintra Scott

1 You know whether you're a morning person or a night owl. You know whether you're a picky eater or a human garbage pail. But do you know if you learn better by reading or by hearing? . . . If you've survived school so far, you already have some sort of study routine—for better or for worse. We asked students all over the country for the lowdown on their MOs, and also collected some hard-won advice. See if you can recognize your own personal study method in the list below.

Type 1: The Dreamer

2 You may say you're studying. You may even *look* like you're studying. But your mind is in the clouds. Your test performance seldom reflects those long hours you spent at your desk, *almost* studying. Kim, from Montreal, says, "When I go to the library, I end up sitting there and people-watching. And then I go home realizing I haven't studied a thing." Cindy, from Lafayette, Pennsylvania, says: "Personally, I tend to write everything down on flash cards so I can quiz myself later. Every-

Style:

one else thinks that I'll ace the exam, but sometimes I find myself spending so much time writing down every little detail that I don't have time to actually study."

3 ***Warning:*** If you spend all day pretend studying, you'll pay all night cramming for real. (What a waste of socializing time!) This year's resolution: Stay on target by setting goals (like four chapters by Wednesday) and asking your friends to test you. Also, tune in to your interests: If you find yourself drawing elaborate doodles in the margins when you're supposed to be analyzing Shakespeare, take drawing classes and snap out of your reverie.

Advice:

■ *reverie:*
a. daydreaming
b. feeling of awe or devotion

Type II: The Grind

4 One look at your sock drawer, meticulously arranged in rainbow order, suggests control-freak tendencies. You never fail to do a fixed amount of studying each evening—and your good grades show it. You cautiously plot a course to conquer an unruly assignment, and you rarely break your routine. Gretchen, from Chicago, describes her hard-core method: "I completely organize all of my notes. Then, before I do anything else, I plan out exactly how many hours I'm going to study and how long I am going to take breaks. This way, I always stay on task. I read through my notes and then highlight the things I don't know well, to commit them to memory." But she's not done yet! "Then I read my assignments again and take notes and study these notes the same way I studied my class notes." *Whew.* Sarah, from Scarsdale, New York, also considers herself a worker bee. "I plan my work so that there's something I have to do every night of the week. But when there's a test, I'll do all my assignments before trying to do an overview. Studying comes last because I'll wait until the last minute to even try concentrating on something with so little structure."

■ *meticulously:*
a. hastily
b. very carefully

Style:

5 ***Warning:*** While your self-discipline will serve you well in college (or the military), you might want to add more inspiration to your perspiration. No amount of memorization, or color-coding your notebooks, will help you write an original, opinionated essay—and you'll be writing plenty. This year's resolution: Vary your routine and think about your own insights more. After reading an assignment, try closing your eyes and recalling what you found interesting before buckling down with your impeccable notes. And if you've got a half hour to spare in your study schedule, try something messy and creative, like writing a poem.

Advice:

■ *impeccable:*
a. perfect
b. useless

Type III: The Social Studier

6 You're the kind who learns out loud. You yak your way to enlightenment, so study buddies are a must. In school, you remember more from hearing the lectures than from doing the reading. Roberta, from Princeton, New Jersey, says: "I went to a study counselor to find out that I learn best by listening. It's true: Until I hear something out loud, it's not really real to me. When I'm studying and I don't understand something in our textbook, I'll call my friends to get the scoop." Amy, from East Lansing, Michigan, says: "Sometimes a bunch of us go to the library after school. It's a lot more fun in a group, and when . . . it's fun, it helps me stay on track. If I'm too bored, chances are I won't learn anything."

Style:

7 ***Warning:*** Set ground rules for your study party so you don't use your friends as excuses not to study. Limit your group to friends who know this is more than a chatfest. (Your slacker pals will be more fun to party with post-exam than to struggle with pre-test.)

Advice:

Type IV: The Crammer

8 You slack off for weeks, until the night before the exam. Then you *still* find reasons to dawdle: Gotta brew a pot of coffee, and—wait!—your favorite mug is missing! Finally the adrenaline starts pumping. Time to study triple-time. When you're startled awake at 4 A.M. with textbook creasemarks on your face, you resolve to do it differently next time. But next time rolls around, and you're in the same lame situation. Sara, from Hammonton, New Jersey, is a classic crammer: "My study habits are horrendous! I usually start studying about 11 P.M. and go until my eyes are sealed shut. Then I wake up panicked and whip out my notebook again on the bus." Christina, from Cambridge, Massachusetts, says: "I'll always wait until the last minute to study. It's like I need to get myself into panic mode to buckle down. Otherwise I stare into space with my book in my lap. But as soon as I start studying, I realize that I could have done really well, *if I only had more time. . . .*" Too late.

■ *horrendous:*
a. terrible
b. obvious

9 ***Warning:*** The hours after midnight aren't enough time to get all your work done or study a semester's worth of stuff. And get ready for "reserve" readings, where you and the whole class have to share one book on hold at the library. You won't have the option of doing it ALAP (as late as possible). This year's resolution: Improve your grades by adding casual study sessions before

Advice:

you hit high-stress mode. Bring your books outside or to your favorite cafe and skim the material. You may still get the most done when the pressure's on, but at least you'll know where to turn to make your cramming more efficient.

Type V: The Grade-Grubber

10 Have you no dignity? Don't you hear the snickers behind your back every time you ask, "But will it be on the test?" Maybe your fear of failing is stronger than your love of learning, and that's why you try to psych out the teacher or downright cheat. Katie, from Cold Spring Harbor, New York, says: "I knew plenty of kids who relied on old exams from people who'd taken the class before. Not to incriminate myself, but once I made photocopies of the teacher's answer book when he was absent. The test was take-home, so I shared the answer key with the whole class, and we each changed one or two answers to make it a little less suspicious. I don't know what I was thinking. Had I been caught, it could have been grounds for expulsion." Nora from Philadelphia says, "Sometimes I feel like my teacher doesn't care or he's not paying attention, so I do what I can to up my grade with minimal effort. One teacher, who'd been at my school forever, was notorious for alternating two final exams year after year. My friends and I were always looking for ways to cut corners or even cheat on his exams."

Style:

■ *expulsion:*
a. retesting
b. dismissal

■ *notorious:*
a. widely known
b. unfair

11 ***Warning:*** College classes are not the place to grade-grub. You'll waste your time . . . if you're focused on pleasing the prof, not learning the stuff. Besides, your college instructor will want to hear you brilliantly expound on the material, not parrot her words back. This year's resolution: Grow out of it. Here's a trick for you: Put your common sense to work and decide what's the most important material. That's probably what's on the test.

Advice:

■ *expound on:*
a. remember
b. explain in detail

Type VI: Too Cool for School

12 How much work can it take to get a C anyway? Face it: Your study technique is just to get by. Or to tell yourself that you're too busy for geometry. That laundry's been piling up for two weeks! No one calls you a nerd, but they don't call you Most Likely to Succeed either. You know you're capable of more, but you choose to keep your intellect under wraps. Alissa, from Syracuse, New York, admits: "I rarely study—even for finals. If it's convenient—say, I'm at a friend's house with people and

Style:

they're all studying—or if I don't even know the basic idea, then maybe. But usually I wing it."

Advice: 13 ***Warning:*** Consider taking some time off before college if you don't feel ready to seriously work. This year's resolution: Raise your standards! You may feel clever figuring out how to get away with hardly working, but . . . "winging it" won't fly for long. And out in the real world, where there are no grades, you'll find very little value in your most developed skill—doing as little as possible. That's for the retired-to-the-rocking-chair crowd.

Context Answers and Clues

reverie: a. daydreaming (doodling, not paying attention)

meticulously: b. very carefully (socks are in perfect "rainbow" order, called a control freak)

impeccable: a. perfect (notes are organized exactly)

horrendous: a. terrible (study methods clearly don't work)

expulsion: b. dismissal (cheating is a serious offense)

notorious: a. widely known (teacher had been there a long time)

expound on: b. explain in detail (explaining is the opposite of parroting back)

EXERCISE 10.5

Questions on *Study Styles*

■ Reading for Information

Mapping

- anything—including cheating—for a grade
- look ahead and plan/add casual study sessions
- learns from hearing/needs study buddies
- mind is elsewhere/wastes time/not really studying
- set ground rules for study/limit group to avoid chatfest
- think for yourself/be creative
- just gets by/does less than capable of
- The Grade-grubber
- The Crammer
- The Grind

TYPE	STYLE	WARNING
I. The Dreamer		have set goals/ have others test you
II.	too much planning/ not enough thinking	
III. The Social Studier		
IV.	always waits till last minute/ does worse than should do	
V.		grow up/look for what's important
VI. Too Cool for School		take time off or raise your standards

1. According to the author
   a. Most people learn better by hearing than by reading.
   b. More people learn better by reading than by hearing.
   c. Night owls and picky eaters learn best by hearing.
   d. Some people learn best by reading and others by hearing.
2. Grinds need to
   a. become more disciplined.
   b. become more organized.
   c. take more control.
   d. all of the above
   e. none of the above
3. Grinds are advised to
   a. vary routines.
   b. think more originally.
   c. be creative.
   d. all of the above
   e. none of the above

4. Which statement below is NOT true of grade-grubbers?
   a. They fear failing more than they love learning.
   b. They try to psych out the teacher.
   c. They explain ideas rather than repeat facts.
   d. They may resort to cheating.
5. Too Cool types
   a. are nerds.
   b. are Most Likely to Succeed.
   c. are antisocial.
   d. always study for finals.
   e. none of the above

Comparing and Contrasting: Choose the answer with the two types that best fit the description.

6. Most uncreative and unoriginal
   a. Dreamer and Social Studier
   b. Grade-grubber and Grind
   c. Social Studier and Grade-grubber
   d. Too Cool and Crammer
7. Do more socializing than studying
   a. Grind and Social Studier
   b. Social Studier and Grade-grubber
   c. Crammer and Too Cool
   d. Social Studier and Too Cool
8. Spend too much time working on notes
   a. Dreamer and Grind
   b. Crammer and Grind
   c. Social Studier and Grade-grubber
   d. Too Cool and Grade-grubber
9. Likely to try to study at the last minute
   a. Dreamer and Social Studier
   b. Social Studier and Grade-grubber
   c. Dreamer and Crammer
   d. Grade-grubber and Too Cool

10. Likely to worry most about grades
    a. Dreamer and Social Studier
    b. Crammer and Too Cool
    c. Social Studier and Too Cool
    d. Grind and Grade-grubber

Circle T for True or F for False.

1. T F The Dreamer type never spends long hours at a desk.
2. T F Dreamers often end up having to cram for exams.
3. T F Because they overorganize their notes, Grinds usually get poor grades.
4. T F Colorcoding notebooks can help a student to write an original essay.
5. T F The Too Cool types have less talent and intellect than the other types.
6. T F Social Studiers learn best by listening to their counselors.
7. T F Crammers know their study habits are bad but have difficulty changing them.
8. T F Crammers can improve their grades by drinking more coffee at a café.
9. T F Grade-grubbers may justify cheating by blaming teachers for being uncaring.
10. T F To do the best on a test, students should study the most important material.

■ Reading for Understanding

1. The main purpose of the author in this passage is
    a. to entertain the reader with lively stories
    b. to provide a way to group all students
    c. to suggest effective ways to study
2. The tone of the author in this article is best described as
    a. impersonal and matter-of-fact
    b. irritated and distrustful
    c. warm and chatty

The next article will give you a chance to practice techniques for reading comparison and contrast in a longer article. You will also be adding information to your frame of reference about American history.

Previewing *Our Two Greatest Presidents* by Charles B. Garrigus

Thinking About Reading What topic is clearly named by the title?

____

Preview by reading the first paragraph. The first sentence tells us that the discussion will be about two presidents:

____________________ and ____________________

Summarize anything you know about them:

____

____

____

____

Complete your preview by reading the first sentence in each of paragraphs 1–5. From this you can tell that the article will be about which of the following?

a. the main similarities between Lincoln and Washington
b. important differences between Lincoln and Washington
c. both of the above

Reading with a Purpose From your preview, you can see that the article will be organized by describing similarities and differences between Washington and Lincoln. As you read, circle all signal words and phrases that show similarity and contrast. Mark key points and make notes in the margins where indicated. You will use this information to complete a comparison/contrast grid.

Preview Vocabulary

consensus: (¶1) An opinion agreed upon by a group as a whole or by majority will

emancipating: (¶2) freeing

sinewy: (¶3) lean and muscular

burly: (¶3) strong and muscular; husky

ruddy: (¶4) having a healthy, reddish color

cadaverous: (¶4) of a pale color, like a corpse

vivacious: (¶7) lively, full of spirit

orthodox: (¶10) following closely the established faith or what is commonly accepted

Our Two Greatest Presidents

by Charles B. Garrigus

1 It is the consensus of historians, as well as most Americans, that George Washington and Abraham Lincoln are the greatest of American presidents, the most inspirational and influential. Each man had a character and quality of leadership Alike: adequate to the greatest challenges of his time: Washington for the achievement of American independence from England and the establishment of a democratic government, Lincoln for preserving the Union and emancipating the slaves. Both men led effectively because the majority of the people believed in their honesty and in their ability to lead.

2 Probably no two men could have been less similar in per- Different: sonal appearance. Washington, the plantation aristocrat, was 6'2", broad shouldered, deep chested, somewhat thick in the waist and hips and weighed over two hundred pounds. Yet he moved with astonishing grace and agility. No one looked better on a horse; and mounted, he was a commanding figure.

3 Lincoln was the taller, standing 6'4", but this height was often lessened by his tendency, when walking, to slouch or sag. Narrow across the shoulders, he was slender, sinewy, and rawboned. He was stronger than Washington, with muscles in his arms and back so developed that he could lift 500 lbs. In the prime of his youth he met only one man, a burly blacksmith from New York during the Blackhawk War, who could hold him to a draw in wrestling.

4 People who thought Washington handsome, with his wide Different: set, grey-blue eyes, ruddy complexion, and well-formed nose, would have quickly judged Lincoln as homely in comparison. Lincoln's face was long, sallow, and cadaverous; his cheeks leathery. His large ears stuck out nearly at right angles. His lower

Charles B. Garrigus, poet laureate of California, grew up in Lincoln country and has studied Lincoln's life for many years.

lip was too thick, and there was a dark mole at the right corner of his mouth. His high forehead was topped by nearly black random-tossed hair, and his Adam's apple protruded prominently. Yet, gaunt and awkward as he seemed in the company of friends in an informal situation, when he was on the public platform or in a formal social gathering, he projected a kind of majesty, his powerful figure dominated by a well-poised head, with eyes that demonstrated vigorous self-confidence.

Different:

■ *indifferent:*
a. unlike
b. uninterested

■ *slovenliness:*
a. untidiness
b. extreme poverty

5 From his early youth association with the aristocratic Fairfax family, clothing and personal appearance became increasingly important to Washington; but Lincoln, indifferent to how he looked in public, almost to the point of slovenliness, was frequently nagged by his wife Mary to maintain a dress standard barely equal to his public position as a successful lawyer.

■ *authentic:*
a. true, real
b. uneducated

Alike:

6 Both men were authentic frontier heroes. Washington was reared in the back country, virgin land of Virginia from 1740, while Lincoln, about eighty years later, was a young man in the wilderness areas of eastern Kentucky and southern Indiana and Illinois. Both were surveyors in their early twenties. Not only did they carry the chain, dividers, and scale, but they were also explorers and planners of the wilderness, and their characters were deeply marked by the natural beauty and vast resources of their country. Working two years as a surveyor for Lord Fairfax, young Washington saved enough money to buy 1400 acres near the Shenandoah Valley. Lincoln, doing the same kind of work, received about one tenth the daily wage of Washington and could save nothing.

Alike:

■ *lofty:*
a. high
b. fake

7 Both men idealized women, thought of them as more virtuous than men, and both had tragic love affairs in their youth. Lincoln's was with Ann Rutledge, who died shortly after their "understanding," a frontier term for engagement; Washington had the misfortune to fall deeply in love with Sally Fairfax, the vivacious, unattainable wife of his dull, good friend, George William Fairfax. Letters prove that Washington nourished this love for Sally throughout his life, but it is a most significant testimony to his self-control and lofty morality that in the small, tightly knit social circle in which he moved there was never the slightest hint of scandal regarding this relationship.

Different:

8 From his earliest manhood Lincoln's mind was political, and his chief ambition was to represent his fellow citizens in office. In sharp contrast Washington disliked politics intensely and left his experience in public office with a glad sense of relief to be rid of a burden he had assumed only as a patriotic duty performed on behalf of his countrymen.

9 Washington liked nothing better than to ride about his plantation, overseeing all the chores of management and productivity. Even his favorite amusement, fox hunting, was tied closely to the land. In pursuit of British soldiers fleeing from the battlefield at Princeton in 1777, he galloped beside his troops shouting, "It's a fine fox chase, boys!" In sharp contrast to such interests, Lincoln's chief pleasures were of the mind. Reading was what he most enjoyed, followed by conversation, argument, and story telling with congenial companions.

Different:

■ *congenial:*
a. bored
b. friendly and sociable

10 Both men were deeply religious. Both felt an overriding sense of duty to God, but their approach to this attitude was different. Washington's religion was straight-line faith, an acceptance of the orthodox rituals and theology of the Episcopalian church. But Lincoln was a mystic who slowly worked his way to discover his relationship with God. His honest, intellectual study of the religion of his day with its emotional fervor and hard line orthodoxy made it impossible for him to join any church, a condition that harmed him politically. Lincoln was grieved to see in a Springfield poll book that only three out of twenty-three of his home town ministers were going to vote for him for president. His eyes filled with tears as he told a friend, "I know there is a God and I see the storm coming. If He has a place and work for me, I believe I am ready."

Alike:

Different:

■ *fervor:*
a. one who preaches
b. intense feeling

11 Washington also felt that he was an instrument of God's choosing. This largely stemmed from an experience he had at the age of twenty-three. As the youngest aid-de-camp on the staff of the British General Braddock, he was the only officer to survive the massacre of the British by the French and Indians at the Battle of the Forks of the Ohio. During this disaster, four bullets tore through his coat and two horses were killed from under him. Soon afterwards, remembering the terrible carnage around him, he wrote: "I was suddenly aware of the miraculous care of Providence that protected me beyond all expectation."

Alike:

■ *carnage:*
a. noise
b. death, slaughter

12 Washington would have been irritated and embarrassed at the saintly image associated with his memory after his death. Like Lincoln, he took his complete honor and undisputed honesty for granted. He felt that such virtues were only what should be expected from all men of character. His writings and actions show consistently and clearly that he had a definite awareness of his faults and limitations, and it was likewise with Lincoln.

Alike:

13 At the present time American youth need heroic role models, probably more than at any previous time. But it is a sad fact that in the twentieth century there has been a steady loss of appreciation of the character and achievements of these two heroic

men who with selfless courage have contributed most to the American heritage. To really understand the lives of Lincoln and Washington is to understand that democracy is the best hope of mankind, that it works, and that it demands lives of honor to preserve it and keep it working.

Context Answers and Clues

indifferent: b. uninterested ("but" signals opposite—gave dress no importance)

slovenliness: a. untidiness (nagged by his wife to dress better)

authentic: a. true, real (details show they were the real thing)

lofty: a. high (great self-control; no hint of scandal)

congenial: b. friendly and sociable (he enjoyed their company; a social situation)

fervor: b. intense feeling (described as emotional)

carnage: b. death, slaughter (many men and horses had been killed)

EXERCISE 10.6

Questions on *Our Two Greatest Presidents*

■ Reading for Information

Mapping

Put the letter of the correct responses where they belong in the grid that follows. The notes you made in the margins of your text will help you in doing this. In *three* instances you will use the same letter for both men.

A. followed code of honor and total honesty
B. paid very little; unable to save any money
C. taller, stronger; raw-boned, homely; awkward; unconcerned with appearance
D. very religious; directed by a divine purpose
E. paid well, saved money, bought land
F. preferred mental activities: reading, storytelling
G. raised in back country of Virginia; surveyor
H. mystic/not a churchgoer
I. leader for American independence/democracy
J. idealized women/had tragic love affair

K. enjoyed politics
L broad-chested, thickset; handsome, graceful; clothes/appearance important
M. grew up in wilderness areas; surveyor
N. disliked politics
O. commanding presence; great horseman
P. straight-line faith
Q. liked physical activities: riding, fox hunting
R. preserved Union/emancipated slaves
S. majestic in public and social gatherings

	WASHINGTON	LINCOLN
ACCOMPLISHMENTS (¶1) Alike		
APPEARANCE (¶s2–5) Different		
Alike		
FRONTIER HEROES (¶6) Alike		
Different		
LOVE AND ROMANCE (¶7) Alike		
POLITICS (¶8) Different		
RECREATION (¶9) Different		
RELIGION (¶s10–11) Alike		
Different		
SENSE OF HONOR (¶12) Alike		

1. Which of the following is the best statement of the main idea of the entire reading?
   a. Lincoln was an important president, but Washington was this country's greatest.
   b. Washington and Lincoln, their achievements, appearance, and attitude toward women.
   c. Both Washington and Lincoln were strong, honest men who made great presidents.
   d. Although alike in many ways, Washington and Lincoln had some important differences.

2. Write the main idea sentence of ¶6: ______________________________

   ____

3. Write the main idea sentence of ¶7: ______________________________

   ____

4. Write the main idea sentence of ¶10: ______________________________

   ____

5. Write the main idea sentence of ¶11: ______________________________

   ____

6. Write the main idea sentence of ¶12: ______________________________

   ____

7. Which is the best statement of the main idea of ¶8?
   a. Lincoln's main ambition was to represent his fellow citizens as a patriotic duty.
   b. Lincoln's mind was political whereas Washington hated politics.
   c. Washington and Lincoln viewed political life as a heavy but necessary burden.
   d. Washington and Lincoln's different views of politics, being glad to leave office.

8. Which is the best statement of the main idea of ¶9?
   a. The very different habits of mind and pleasures of our two greatest presidents.
   b. Washington was too busy with fox hunting to read many books.
   c. Washington's personal pleasures were physical whereas Lincoln's were of the mind.
   d. Unlike Washington, Lincoln would neglect his duties sometimes to read and talk with friends.

9. What two words or phrases are used in ¶3 to show a contrast in physical characteristics?

_____________________ _____________________

10. What signal word in ¶4 marks the shift to a more favorable side of Lincoln's appearance?

____

Reading for Understanding

Inference

Based on your reading, decide which of the following statements is most true of Washington or Lincoln. Then give evidence from the reading to back up your choice.

1. __________ would enjoy wearing formal clothes for an affair of state.

   Evidence: _____________________

2. __________ would enjoy the long battle of today's typical political campaign.

   Evidence: _____________________

3. __________ had an image that would be easiest to sell in today's televised campaign ads.

   Evidence: _____________________

4. __________ would enjoy telling jokes and hearing them.

   Evidence: _____________________

5. __________ would appear regularly at church services.

   Evidence: _____________________

6. __________ would enjoy spending spare time alone in a library.

   Evidence: _____________________

7. __________ would be most at ease with people of high social standing.

   Evidence: _____________________

Purpose and Tone

1. The main purpose of the author in this passage is
   a. to give some facts about the lives of Lincoln and Washington.
   b. to highlight the traits of two great presidents.
   c. to destroy the traditional image of Lincoln and Washington.

2. The tone of the author in this article is best described as
   a. formal and serious.
   b. humorous and lighthearted.
   c. warm and chatty.

■ Questions for Discussion

1. How would you rate the qualities and honesty of recent presidents in comparison with Washington and Lincoln?

   ____

   ____

2. If Washington and Lincoln were running against each other in an election in this era, who do you think would win? Why?

   ____

   ____

3. If they were running against each other in this era, whom would you vote for? Why?

   ____

   ____

■ Reference Frameworks

Washington and Lincoln were leaders at very crucial moments in American history. You should have in mind some of the important events and dates of their times. Consult a history book or encyclopedia to learn more about the following. Match the events on the left with the dates on the right. One date is used twice.

_____ 1. American Constitution	a. 1861
_____ 2. American Revolution begins	b. 1732
_____ 3. American Revolution ends	c. 1809
_____ 4. Emancipation Proclamation	d. 1865
_____ 5. Civil War began	e. 1799
_____ 6. Civil War ended	f. 1787
_____ 7. Birth of Washington	g. 1775
_____ 8. Birth of Lincoln	h. 1863
_____ 9. Death of Washington	i. 1781
_____ 10. Death of Lincoln	

WORD PARTS: NEGATIVE PREFIXES

There are a number of common prefixes used to change meanings of words to the opposite.

non	nonviolent
dis	discontinue
a	apolitical
un	uncertain
in	indirect

There are variations of *in* that go with similar sounds at the beginning of a word.

im	impossible
il	illiterate
ir	irreplaceable

EXERCISE 10.7

Adding Negative Prefixes to Words

Do this exercise without going to the dictionary.

Step 1 To each word, add one of the prefixes above to make what sounds to you like a real word.

Step 2 Write what you think the meaning of your new word is.

Step 3 Use the word in a sentence whose context makes the meaning clear.

1. ___beaten:

   Sentence: ______________________________

   ____

2. ___typical:

   Sentence: ______________________________

   ____

3. ___voter:

   Sentence: ______________________________

   ____

4. ___responsible:

Sentence: ____

____

5. ___logical:

Sentence: ____

____

6. ___profit:

Sentence: ____

____

7. ___agree:

Sentence: ____

____

8. ___correct:

Sentence: ____

____

9. ___polite:

Sentence: ____

____

10. ___respectful:

Sentence: ____

____

11. ___active:

Sentence: ____

____

12. ___regular:

Sentence: ____

____

13. ___legal:

Sentence: ____________________

____

14. ___mature:

Sentence: ____________________

____

15. ___common:

Sentence: ____________________

____

Active Learning

SUCCESSFUL BEHAVIORS SURVEY, PART II

Earlier you rated yourself on a list of successful behaviors that active learners practice. Now is a good time to rate your progress toward making these behaviors your own. Rate yourself on the same scale. If you are not sure of the meaning of a question, look back in Chapter 1 at the explanation that followed each statement.

EXERCISE 10.8

Comparing the Results of Successful Behaviors Survey

4 Always
3 Most of the time
2 Sometimes
1 Seldom
0 Never

1. I make every possible effort to attend class.	4 3 2 1 0
2. I attend class on time.	4 3 2 1 0
3. I bring my materials to class.	4 3 2 1 0
4. I do my assigned homework.	4 3 2 1 0

5. I turn in all other assignments.	4	3	2	1	0
6. I turn homework and assignments in on time.	4	3	2	1	0
7. I read all handouts carefully and follow instructions.	4	3	2	1	0
8. If I have the choice, I choose to sit in a power seat.	4	3	2	1	0
9. I don't sit next to those I am tempted to talk to.	4	3	2	1	0
10. I am always ready to be called on for an answer.	4	3	2	1	0
11. I respond willingly if the teacher calls on me.	4	3	2	1	0
12. I volunteer to answer questions.	4	3	2	1	0
13. During lessons, I try to know exactly where we are.	4	3	2	1	0
14. I ask questions that show I am interested.	4	3	2	1	0
15. I do not talk to others, off task.	4	3	2	1	0
16. I show attention by keeping eye contact.	4	3	2	1	0
17. I want to know what the right answer is.	4	3	2	1	0
18. When I miss a question, I want to understand why.	4	3	2	1	0
19. I want to know more about subjects I read about.	4	3	2	1	0
20. I believe that wanting to learn is "cool."	4	3	2	1	0
21. I remember and use new learning strategies.	4	3	2	1	0
22. I give up old habits and strategies that don't work.	4	3	2	1	0
23. I accept responsibility for my actions; I don't give excuses.	4	3	2	1	0
24. I know the difference between public and private behavior.	4	3	2	1	0
25. I seek out the instructor when I have questions or problems.	4	3	2	1	0

Compare these results with your first rating.

1. Total your scores.

   1st Survey __________

   2nd Survey __________

   Is your total score higher or lower than your first rating? _____________

   By how many points? __________

2. On which items did your scores improve? ____________________

   Did your scores on any items go down? __________

   On which items did your scores stay the same? ____________________

3. On which items did your scores improve the most? ________________

4. List three behaviors you still need to target for improvement and tell what you intend to do to improve:

   a. ____

   b. ____

   c. ____

Reading Portfolio

ARTICLES THAT COMPARE AND GROUP

These articles are not as common as profile articles, but there are many examples in magazines and newspapers (look in the feature sections). Choose one of the following options for this assignment.

Option 1: Comparison/Contrast You can find these in many different interest areas. Be sure the article focuses on two or more subjects. Examples would include sports stars, politicians, entertainers, consumer products, etc. Use a grid or point-by-point map.

Option 2: Classification/Grouping The most common of these takes a large group of things and breaks it into subtypes. For example, an article might take a large group (salesmen) and break it into subgroups ("There are five basic types of salesmen."). In mapping types, note carefully the characteristics or traits that are used to separate the various types.

1. Preview and read carefully for information and understanding. Make a map before you begin your summary.
2. Write your summary only from the map. State the main idea at or very near the beginning. Put things in your own words. Make the summary about 150 words long.
3. Remember that a good way to let a reader hear your voice in control is to begin by including the name of the author and the title.

4. Your response should be of around equal length. Agree or disagree with the point of view in the article or give any personal application the topic has for you.

5. From the article, select five words whose meaning you were not sure of. For each word, decide on the part of speech and its meaning as used in the article. Then write a context sentence of your own. Think of a situation different from that in the article. Be sure to include enough clues that someone could guess the meaning.

CHAPTER 11

What in the World Is Going On?

Time Sequence and Process

After reading this chapter, you will know the answers to these questions:

- What signal words show time order and divisions in time?
- What is the difference between steps and stages?
- What is a process and how are processes organized?
- How do graphics help us to understand sequences and processes?
- How does a list differ from a sequence?
- What value is there to an historical time line?

Time sequence is the pattern we are most familiar with in our daily lives. Our home, school, and leisure activities are organized around schedules. We view our lives as a series of events, with some standing out as more important than others. Time sequence is the organizing pattern for three important types of reading:

1. *Stories (Narratives).* It's said that everybody loves a story, and from the time we are children, most of us are familiar with how stories relate an action from a beginning to an end.
2. *Histories.* These tell stories but are also concerned with explaining why events happened or how they came about.
3. *Processes.* These instruct us how to do something or explain how something is done or how it works.

You will become more familiar with these in brief passages, articles, and graphics. There are a number of common signal words that show sequences and divisions in time:

stage	first, etc.	before	since
phase	next	after	until
era	then	during	at last
step	now	earlier	finally
while	later	at the beginning, etc.	

TIME SEQUENCE IN NARRATIVES: MAPPING A STORY

In "The Scholarship Jacket" a sequence of events happened before Marta finally got her jacket. The best way to see how these provide the skeleton of the story is to create a time sequence mind map.

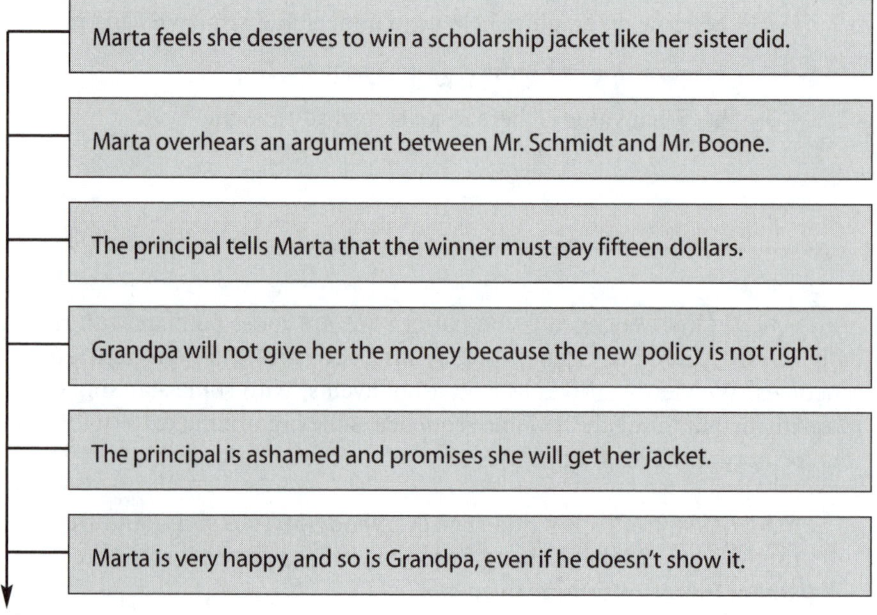

Marta feels she deserves to win a scholarship jacket like her sister did.
Marta overhears an argument between Mr. Schmidt and Mr. Boone.
The principal tells Marta that the winner must pay fifteen dollars.
Grandpa will not give her the money because the new policy is not right.
The principal is ashamed and promises she will get her jacket.
Marta is very happy and so is Grandpa, even if he doesn't show it.

Making sense of a time sequence, however, involves more than just relating one thing after another: "and then . . . and then . . . and then . . ." When we summarize stories, we think of the action as having a beginning, middle, and end. For example, the action in "The Scholarship Jacket" might be divided this way:

Beginning (problem or conflict introduced)

Marta feels she deserves to win a scholarship jacket like her sister did.

Marta overhears an argument between Mr. Schmidt and Mr. Boone.

Middle (development of action)

The principal tells Marta that the winner must pay fifteen dollars.

Grandpa will not give her the money because the new policy is not right.

End (the conflict is solved)

The principal is ashamed and promises she will get her jacket.

Marta is very happy and so is Grandpa, even if he doesn't show it.

Where we make divisions may vary depending on our point of view. For example, the division between the beginning and the middle might be made between the first and second events, or the division between the middle and end might be made between the last two events.

EXERCISE 11.1

Mapping Time Sequence in a Story: *The Circuit*

■ Reading for Information

Briefly reread "The Circuit" before completing the exercise. Below are a number of events from the story. Rearrange them in correct time sequence in the map on page 386. The order in which they occur in time is not necessarily the order in which the details appeared in the story.

- Panchito feels ill while working.
- Mr. Lema promises Panchito that he will teach him to play the trumpet.
- Papa buys the "Carcanchita" from a used-car lot in Santa Rosa.
- Roberto goes back to school.
- Panchito spends his lunch hours working on English with his teacher.
- Papa, Roberto, and Panchito begin their job picking grapes in a vineyard.
- The grape season ends and Panchito goes to school.
- The family gets work and a garage to stay in.
- Panchito meets Mr. Lema.
- The strawberry season ends.

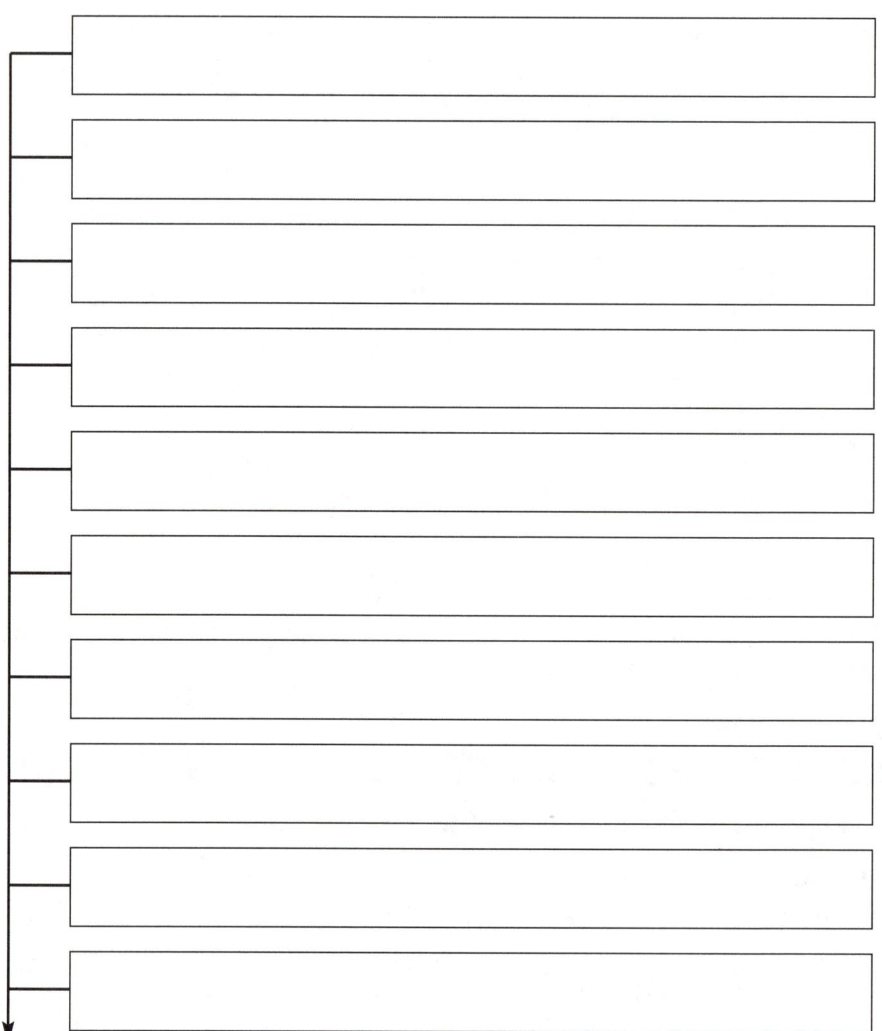

■ Reading for Understanding

Draw two lines to separate the events in the story into a beginning, middle, and end. Then compare your divisions with those of others in the class. If you differ, explain your reasons for making your divisions where you did.

MAPPING STAGES IN A SHORT HISTORY

The study of history explains and comments on events, but at its core history tells a story in time order, seeing the events as a series of small events making up larger stages. Historians divide events into eras and periods, based on political, social, economic, or scientific events. As with stories, where we make divisions into larger stages depends on our viewpoints and interests. For instance, if you compare a number of history textbooks, you will find big differences in their divisions within the same time period. The next passage gives a short history of a topic that is probably familiar to most of us. The author is editor-in-chief and publisher of *Indian Country Today,* a national weekly newspaper on American Indian issues.

Previewing *Gambling Addiction Taking Huge Tolls on Indian Families* by Tom Giago

Thinking About Reading From the title, you know that the article will be about what topic?

____

Write what is suggested to your mind by the words *gambling* and *addiction.*

____

____

____

____

Preview the article by reading the first and last paragraphs and by looking at the main headings. What three headings appear in the text?

______________ ______________ ______________

Reading with a Purpose As you read, notice the dates written in the margin. Write in the event or events associated with each date where indicated. You will use this information to construct a map in the exercise that follows.

Preview Vocabulary

preoccupation: (¶1) having one's attention directed on one thing

recoup: (¶1) get back, regain

injudicious: (¶1) not wise

pathological: (¶2) diseased

gulden: (¶6) (also called *guilder*) a unit of money in the Netherlands, similar to our dollar

havoc: (¶9) great confusion or destruction

inured: (¶11) made used to/no longer affected by something undesirable

plague: (¶12) a highly infectious, usually fatal disease

Gambling Addiction Taking Huge Tolls on Indian Families

by Tom Giago

1 There is a new addiction growing in Indian country. The addiction is gambling. The American Psychiatric Association, according to an article in the Harvard Magazine, lists the possible symptoms of gambling disorder as preoccupation with gambling; steadily increasing the size of bets; intolerance of losing and immediate efforts to recoup losses; gambling in response to disappointment in the other areas of life; neglect of family; losing one's job or marriage as a result of gambling, and engaging in illegal acts or injudicious borrowing or selling to finance betting.

■ *intolerance:*
a. unwillingness to put up with
b. a habit

2 According to the APA, any five or more of these symptoms qualifies one as a "pathological gambler." But that's still a somewhat murky definition.

Great proliferation

Before 1964:

In 1964:

Present time:

3 Gambling was limited to illegal dens or to Nevada before 1964. New Jersey didn't get into casino gambling until 1978. 1964 is the year New Hampshire started a state lottery. Since then, 36 other states have joined New Hampshire. Twenty other states now have some form of legal casino gambling. Hawaii and Utah are the only two states with no gambling allowed.

1974:

1980's:

4 Indian nations started with bingo halls in 1974 and in the mid-'80s started to build gaming casinos. Fearful this would get out of hand, the federal government passed the National Indian Gaming Act in 1987.

1998:

5 An article on Internet Gaming in the Jan. 26, 1998, edition of Sports Illustrated charged that the fastest growing segment of the gambling population are college students. They attribute this to the explosion of gambling over the past 30 years in America.

6 In his book "The Gambler," Fyodor Dostoevsky wrote, "At that point I ought to have gone away, but a strange sensation rose up in me, a sort of defiance of fate, a desire to challenge it, to put out my tongue at it. I laid down the largest stake al-

■ *defiance:*
a. fear of
b. bold resistance to

lowed—four thousand gulden—and lost it. Then getting hot, I pulled out all I had left, staked it on the same number, and lost again, after which I walked away from the table as though I were stunned. I could not even grasp what had happened to me."

Strong Dependence

7 These days I am hearing tales of Indian men and women reacting in a like fashion. One man, an employee of the Bureau of Indian Affairs, and his wife, who works for the tribal government, middle class Americans for all intent and purpose, find themselves over their heads in debt because of their frequent trips to their tribe's casino. They have reached the point where they are beginning to sell off some of their possessions in order to get back into the game.

8 Any Indian nation with a casino has among their customers those on welfare who have become addicted to gambling. They take what little they have and make a try for the pot of gold they hope to find at the slot machines or 21 tables.

9 We are just beginning to understand the havoc the gambling addicted people are bringing to their families. Just as many Indian tribes are beginning to win the battle against alcohol and drugs, this new addiction is pushing many families into deep poverty. Perhaps there is not the physical violence and the abuse associated with drinking, but the separation of mother and father from their children and the poverty brought about by the loss of money to the casino is creating many psychological problems, teen-age suicide for one.

Number of Addicts

10 The Harvard Magazine article estimates there are 2 million people, or 1.4 percent of the population, addicted to gambling. The magazine suggests that this report does not include the 2.2 million adolescents also addicted to gambling. In the scheme of things, 1.4 percent of the population seems pretty minute, but if this study had been restricted to American Indians only, how would this percentage shake out?

■ *minute:*
a. uneducated
b. small

11 John Lauerman, contributing editor of Harvard Magazine writes, "Although we're not exactly sure what defines problem gambling in individuals, its impact on the nervous system is undeniable. In many ways, problem gambling is like any other addiction. It appears to act as a stimulant, one to which frequent

risk takers can become inured. Research shows that problem gamblers exhibit patterns of brain activity familiar to experts on drug and alcohol addiction." Sound familiar?

12 Lauerman quotes Mohandas Gandhi who said, "No doubt war against gambling is not so simple as war against plague or earthquake distress. In the latter there is more or less cooperation for the sufferers. In the former the sufferers invite and hug their suffering."

13 This is an issue several tribal governments are just now beginning to address. Just as so many Indian nations declared war on alcohol and drug addiction among their own people, they must now declare war on this new addiction.

Context Answers and Clues

intolerance: a. unwillingness to put up with (tries to win losses back at once)

defiance: b. bold resistance to (wanted to challenge, put out tongue at fate)

minute: b. small (only 1.4 percent of the population)

EXERCISE 11.2

Questions on *Gambling Addiction*

■ Reading for Information

Mapping

Use the items below to fill in the time line that follows.

- college students fastest growing gambling population
- National Indian Gaming Act passed
- Indian nations building gaming casinos
- Hawaii and Utah only two states with no gambling allowed
- gambling limited to illegal dens or to Nevada
- New Jersey gets into casino gambling
- Indian nations started with bingo halls
- explosion of gambling begins in America
- New Hampshire starts state lottery
- twenty other states with forms of legal casino gambling

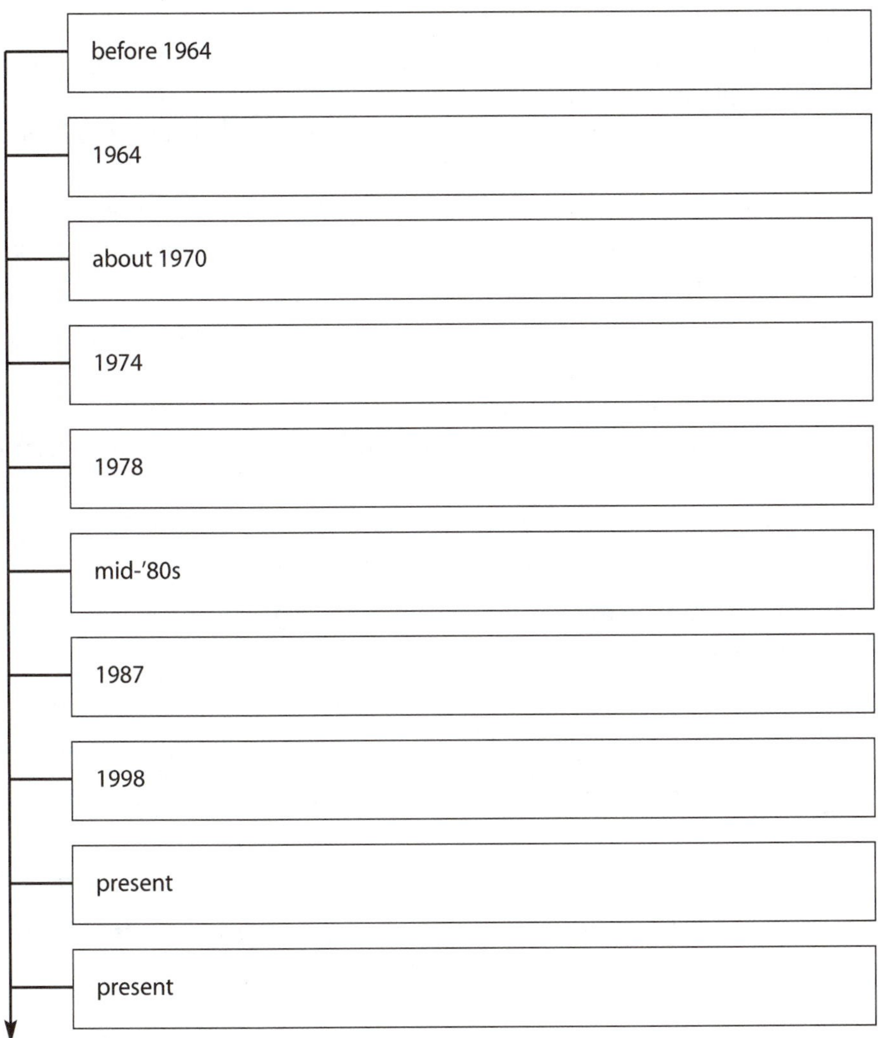

Main Ideas and Details

1. The best statement of the main idea of this article is
   a. Too many college students are involved in gambling.
   b. The costs of gambling and other addictions and the effect on families.
   c. The Indian nations must declare war on gambling.
   d. Indian men and women are finding themselves over their heads in debt.

2. The best statement of the main idea of ¶9 is
   a. We are just beginning to understand the havoc the gambling addicted people are bringing to their families.
   b. Many Indian tribes are beginning to win the battle against alcohol and drugs.
   c. This new addiction is pushing many families into deep poverty.
   d. Many psychological problems, including teenage suicide, have been created.
3. Which of the following is the best statement of the implied main idea of ¶3?
   a. Gambling is restricted mainly to states in the East and West.
   b. Over the years, most states have come to allow some form of gambling.
   c. Twenty states now have some form of legal casino gambling.
   d. Hawaii and Utah should relax their ban on gambling.
4. What reason is given for the rapid growth of gambling among college students?

   ____

   ____

5. The gambling compulsion of Dostoevsky's character in *The Gambler* is compared to that of which group?

   ____

6. A *Harvard Magazine* article estimates the total number of adults and adolescents addicted to gambling may be
   a. 2 million
   b. 3.4 million
   c. 2.2 million
   d. 4.2 million
7. How is problem gambling like any other addiction?
   a. It appears to act as a stimulant.
   b. Frequent risk takers can become used to it.
   c. Problem gamblers exhibit similar patterns of brain activity.
   d. all of the above

■ Reading for Understanding

Making Inferences

The author gives definition of "pathological gambling" that includes seven characteristics:

a. preoccupation with gambling
b. steadily increasing the size of bets
c. intolerance of losing and immediate efforts to recoup losses
d. gambling in response to disappointment in the other areas of life
e. neglect of family
f. losing one's job or marriage as a result of gambling
g. engaging in illegal acts or injudicious borrowing or selling to finance betting

The author cites two specific examples of compulsive gambling that show some of these behaviors. Reread the passages below and decide which behaviors the examples illustrate:

Passage A
"At that point I ought to have gone away, but a strange sensation rose up in me, a sort of defiance of fate, a desire to challenge it, to put out my tongue at it. I laid down the largest stake allowed—four thousand gulden—and lost it. Then getting hot, I pulled out all I had left, staked it on the same number, and lost again, after which I walked away from the table as though I were stunned. I could not even grasp what had happened to me."

1. Write the letters of three behaviors that are strongly suggested by this passage:

   ______ ______ ______

Passage B
One man, an employee of the Bureau of Indian Affairs, and his wife, who works for the tribal government, find themselves over their heads in debt because of their frequent trips to their tribe's casino. They have reached the point where they are beginning to sell off some of their possessions in order to get back into the game.

2. Which behavior does the couple in Passage B share with the person in Passage A?

____

3. Which behavior, not clearly suggested in Passage A, does the couple in B illustrate?

____

Purpose and Tone

1. The author's main purpose in the article is to
   a. convince the reader that action is needed now
   b. blame the government for its policies
   c. relate some facts about the history of gambling
2. The author's tone is best described as
   a. impersonal and objective
   b. urgent and concerned
   c. suspicious and irritated

Fact and Opinion

Label the following: *Fact* (can be verified and proved)
Opinion (differing viewpoints can be supported)
False (can be definitely proved to be untrue)

__________ 1. The APA definition of "pathological gambler" is a murky one.

__________ 2. Gambling was limited to illegal dens or to Nevada before 1978.

__________ 3. The federal government passed the National Indian Gaming Act in 1987.

__________ 4. More gambling in the past 30 years has caused more college students to gamble.

__________ 5. Some Indian families sell off possessions in order to get back into the game.

__________ 6. Some of those on welfare have become addicted to gambling.

__________ 7. Less physical violence and abuse is associated with gambling than with drinking.

_________ 8. Teenage suicide is a problem among Indian families.

_________ 9. Gambling has an impact on the nervous system.

_________ 10. Research shows that problem gamblers exhibit brain activity similar to that of drug and alcohol addiction.

MAPPING A PROCESS: HOW SOMETHING IS DONE

A process is a series of actions that will bring about a result or goal. A process can give specific directions on how to do something or describe how something is done. Most processes involving physical products are organized by time sequence. A set series of steps, if followed correctly, will lead to the desired end.

EXERCISE 11.3

Mapping a Process

A process is outlined in the first paragraph. As you read, place numbers in the text to indicate the major steps in the process.

Preview Vocabulary

Andean: (¶1) of the Andes mountain regions of South America

hamlets: (¶2) small villages

cuisine: (¶2) foods, cooking

Freeze Drying Food

by Jack Weatherford

1 The Andean farmers devised and perfected the first freeze-dried method of preserving the potato. At night, farmers put their potatoes out in the freezing air of the high mountains. During the day the sun thawed the potatoes, and the farm family

■ *devised:*
a. thought up
b. copied

■ *resembled:*
a. resulted in
b. looked like

■ *reconstituted:*
a. grown
b. returned to its original form

walked over them to press out the melting moisture. After several repetitions of this process, the potato dried into a white chunk which very much resembled modern plastic foam. In this very light form the Incas easily transported great numbers of potatoes to distant storehouses, where they could be preserved for five or six years without harm.

2 When needed, the potato could be reconstituted by soaking it in water, and then it could be cooked. Cooks also ground it into meal for making soups and other dishes. Today this entire procedure continues exactly as before in thousands of hamlets scattered throughout the Andes. The resulting *ch'uno,* as the dried potatoes are called in Quechua, still serves as a staple of Andean cuisine throughout the year.

3 The Incas also used drying techniques on a variety of other vegetable crops and even on meat. The dried meat, or *charqui* as it was called in Quechua, also found favor among the Europeans as a convenient and light way to preserve and transport meat. The name *charqui* was taken over and corrupted into "jerky," one of the few English words derived from Quechua.

Context Answers and Clues

devised: a. thought up (it was the first)

resembled: b. looked like (no real plastic until the modern era)

reconstituted: b. returned to its original form (can't be cooked until this happens)

■ Reading for Information

Mapping

The first paragraph and part of the second give a set time sequence that occurs in freeze-drying the potato. Put the steps into the correct time sequence in the map that follows.

- The potato could be reconstituted by soaking or ground into meal.
- The potato could be cooked.
- The farm family walked over the potatoes to remove moisture.
- Farmers put their potatoes out in the freezing night air.
- The potato dried into a white chunk like plastic foam.
- The sun thawed the potatoes.

The Process of Freeze-drying Potatoes

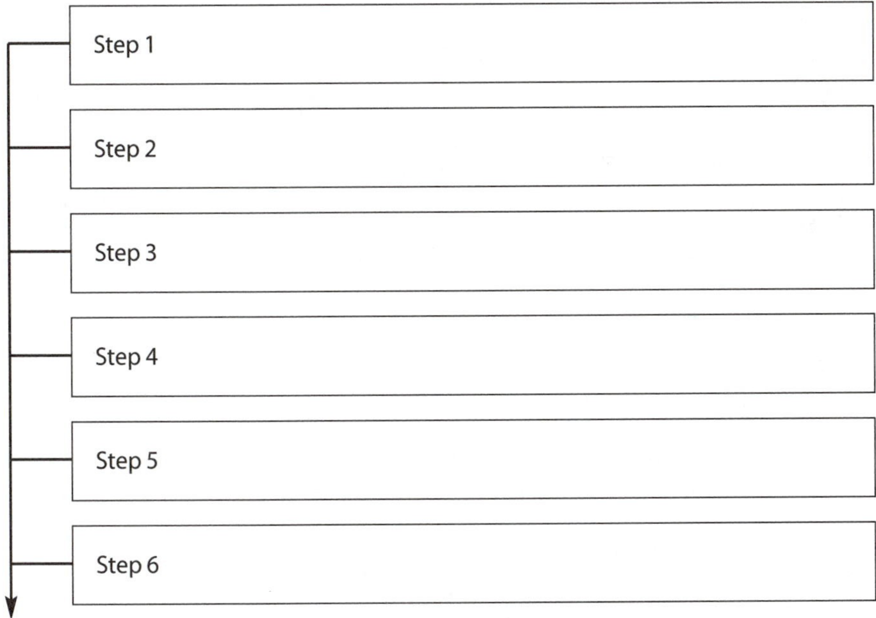

1. Write the sentence with the main idea of ¶1:

____

____

2. This is the main idea because it
   a. answers a question stated in the paragraph
   b. has a listing phrase
   c. is a general statement that all details develop
   d. has a change of direction signal

3. What word in ¶2 signals the change from talking about the past to talking about the future?

____

Circle T for True or F for False.

4. T F The family was involved in the process of freeze-drying.
5. T F Today everything continues exactly as before in small Andean villages.
6. T F Dried meat was called *Quechua* by the Incas.
7. T F Soups were part of the diet of the Incas.
8. T F The Incas were vegetarians.

9. T F For Europeans, meat in the form of jerky was easy to preserve and transport.

10. T F Unlike *charqui,* jerky tended to become corrupted and quickly rot.

■ Reading for Understanding

1. Select the best main idea for the three-paragraph passage from the following.
   a. Andean farmers developed the first freeze-drying method of preserving the potato.
   b. Today the process of freeze-drying in the Andes continues exactly as before.
   c. The process of freeze-drying the potato, making *charqui,* its use in Europe, and the continued use of the process today.
   d. The freeze-drying process developed by Andean farmers is still used even today.

2. List the answers given in ¶3 to the following questions:

   On what did the Incas use drying techniques? ____________________

   What was dried meat called in Quechua? ____________________

   Why did jerky find favor with Europeans? ____________________

   How did we get the word *jerky* into our language? ____________________

   ____

3. From the information above, what is the topic of ¶3?

   ____

4. Does ¶3 have a main idea organization—that is, do the rest of the questions help to answer a main question—or a topical organization? Map it below, using a cartwheel (main idea) or pinwheel (topical) map.

5. What advantages would being able to store food for many years give to the Incas?

____

____

____

GRAPHICS INVOLVING TIME SEQUENCE

Changes and developments over time are made much easier to picture and understand in texts through graphics. Health and science textbooks often deal with subjects that require tracing an ongoing or repeatable process. Graphics give a quick, visual summary of the time sequence in such processes.

EXERCISE 11.4

Following a Process in Graphics: *Ozone Layer Depletion*

Preview Vocabulary

membrane: (¶1) a thin layer of tissue separating or connecting regions/areas of an animal or a plant.

respiratory: (¶1) used in or relating to breathing

immune: (¶1) not subject to infection or disease

aerosol propellants: (¶3) compressed inert gas, such as a fluorocarbon, that acts as a vehicle for discharging the contents of an aerosol container

per capita: (¶4) per person

Ozone Layer Depletion

by R. Donatelle and L. Davis

1 We earlier defined ozone as a chemical that is produced when oxygen interacts with sunlight. Close to the earth, ozone poses health problems such as respiratory distress. Farther away from the earth, it forms a protective membrane-like layer in the earth's stratosphere—the highest level of the earth's atmosphere, located from 12 to 30 miles above the earth's surface. The ozone

layer in the stratosphere protects our planet and its inhabitants from ultraviolet B (UV-B) radiation, a primary cause of skin cancer. Ultraviolet B radiation may also damage DNA and may be linked to weakened immune systems in both humans and animals.

■ *depletion:*
a. explosion
b. using up

2 In the early 1970s, scientists began to warn of a depletion of the earth's ozone layer. Special instruments developed to test atmospheric contents indicated that specific chemicals used on earth were contributing to the rapid depletion of this vital protective layer. These chemicals are called chlorofluorocarbons (CFCs).

3 Chlorofluorocarbons were first believed to be miracle chemicals. They were used as refrigerants (Freon), as aerosol propellants in products such as hairsprays and deodorants, as cleaning solvents, and in medical sterilizers, rigid foam insulation, and Styrofoam. But CFCs were eventually found to be a major cause of depletion of the ozone layer. When released into the air through spraying or outgassing, CFCs migrate upward toward the ozone layer, where they decompose and release chlorine atoms. These atoms cause ozone molecules to break apart (see Figure 15.1).

■ *migrate:*
a. speed up
b. move from one place to another

■ *decompose:*
a. break up
b. enlarge

4 The U.S. government banned the use of aerosol sprays containing CFCs in an effort to reduce ozone depletion. In fact, the United States still has the highest per capita use of CFCs in the world, generating approximately 30 percent of all the emissions of ozone-depleting chemicals. Japan is close behind us.

■ *emissions:*
a. things left out
b. things released as by-products

5 Since 1987, many countries have worked to reduce CFC contamination. CFC-free refrigerators, air conditioners, and other products are becoming the norm in the United States. (Donatelle and Davis, p. 380.)

Context Answers and Clues

depletion: b. using up (concern is over a loss of protection)

migrate: b. move from one place to another (went upward to another place)

decompose: a. break up (they must break up before chlorine can be released)

emissions: b. things released as by-products (chemicals have gotten into the air)

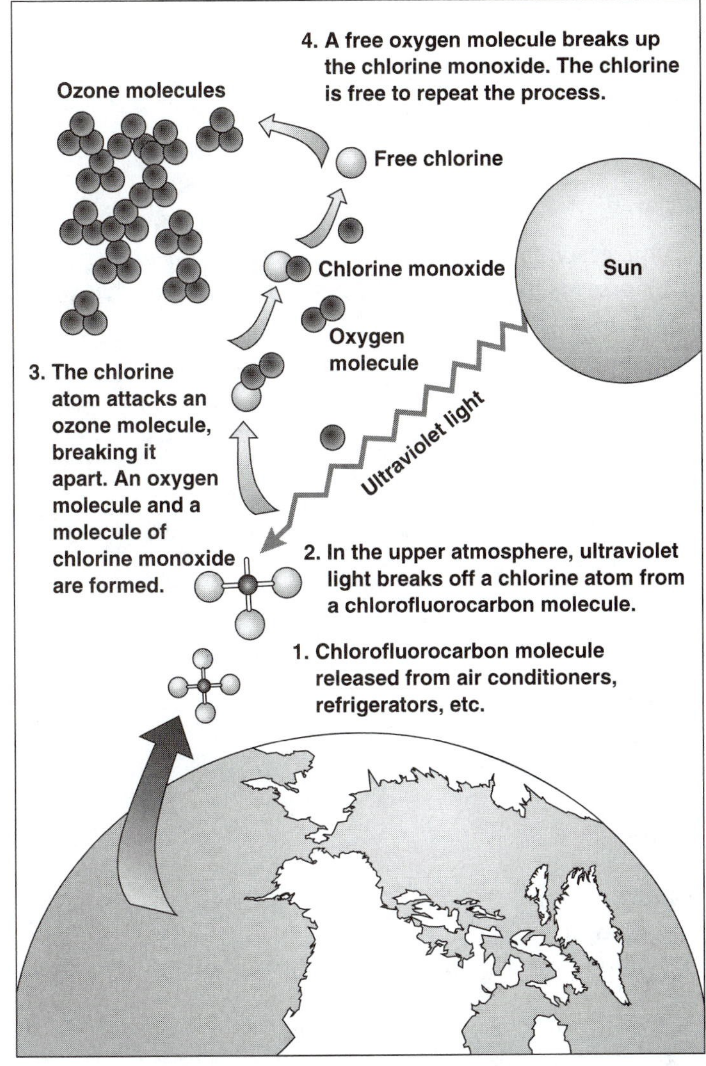
4. A free oxygen molecule breaks up the chlorine monoxide. The chlorine is free to repeat the process.
Ozone molecules
Free chlorine
Chlorine monoxide
Sun
Oxygen molecule
3. The chlorine atom attacks an ozone molecule, breaking it apart. An oxygen molecule and a molecule of chlorine monoxide are formed.
Ultraviolet light
2. In the upper atmosphere, ultraviolet light breaks off a chlorine atom from a chlorofluorocarbon molecule.
1. Chlorofluorocarbon molecule released from air conditioners, refrigerators, etc.

Figure 15.1 The diagram shows how the ozone layer is being depleted

Donatelle and Davis, p. 380. Adapted with permission.

■ Reading for Information

1. What definition is given in the text for these terms?

   ozone: ______________________________

   the stratosphere: ______________________________

   chlorofluorocarbons: ______________________________

2. The source of UV40 is
   a. chlorofluorocarbons.
   b. the sun.
   c. the ozone layer.
   d. the stratosphere.
   e. all of the above
3. According to the graphic, after the chlorine monoxide is broken up in Step 4, "The chlorine is free to repeat the process." If it did, what would be the next step?
   a. Step 1
   b. Step 2
   c. Step 3
   d. Step 4 (first part)
4. The real damage to the ozone layer occurs during what step?
   a. Step 1
   b. Step 2
   c. Step 3
   d. Step 4
5. CFCs can be released from use as
   a. refrigerants.
   b. hair spray.
   c. solid foam insulation.
   d. all of the above
   e. none of the above
6. Chlorofluorocarbons
   a. are a danger to the ozone layer.
   b. were invented in the 1970s.
   c. are considered to be miracle chemicals.
   d. all of the above
   e. none of the above
7. Ultraviolet B radiation (UV-B)
   a. is considered a primary cause of skin cancer.
   b. may cause damage to DNA.
   c. may weaken immune systems.
   d. all of the above
   e. none of the above

8. In the process of depleting the ozone layer, the function of ultraviolet light is to
   a. release aerosol propellants.
   b. break off a chlorine atom from a CFC molecule.
   c. weaken immune systems.
   d. all of the above
   e. none of the above
9. In its effort to solve problems with the ozone layer,
   a. the U.S. government encouraged the use of aerosol sprays.
   b. the United States now uses the fewest CFCs per person in the world.
   c. the government has banned all refrigerators and air conditioners that emit CFCs.
   d. all of the above
   e. none of the above
10. Which of the following is NOT true of ozone?
   a. It is formed from the interaction of oxygen with sunlight.
   b. It forms a protective layer against UV-B radiation.
   c. Scientists discovered in the 1970s that it was being depleted.
   d. It is always beneficial to human health.

Textbooks in the social sciences often use graphics to create time lines for periods and eras. Graphics are also helpful for understanding changes in an institution or policy over time.

EXERCISE 11.5

Tracking Changes in a Policy in Graphics

Social Insurance

by Karen O'Connor and Larry Sabato

1 Expenditures for Social Security have greatly increased during the last couple of decades because the number of beneficiaries is growing, they are living longer, and benefit levels are rising. More than 40 million people, including some 3 million workers with disabilities, currently receive benefits. Social Security is by far the national government's largest entitlement program (see Figure 17.2).

■ *expenditures:*
a. costs
b. arguments

■ *beneficiaries:*
a. those who get benefits
b. cheaters

■ *entitlement:*
a. unnecessary
b. having a right to something

Karen O'Connor and Larry Sabato, *American Government: Continuity and Change,* third edition, pp. 661–63. Reprinted by permission.

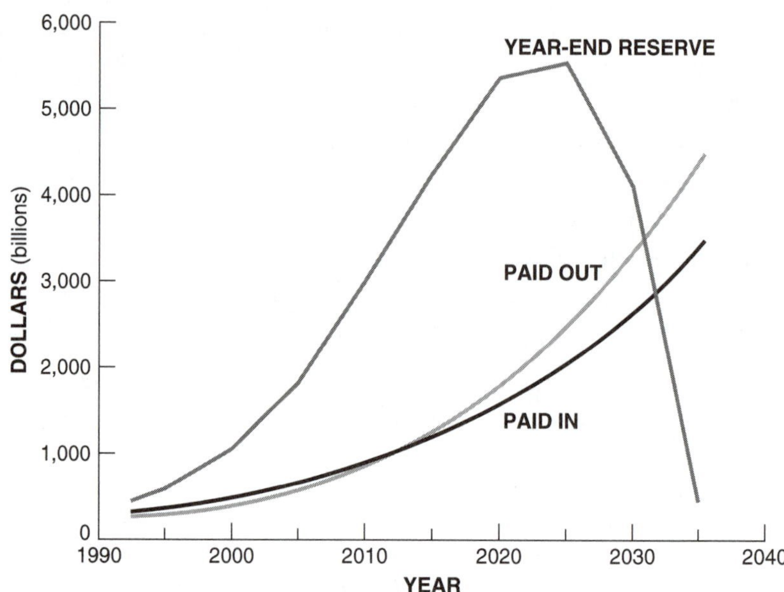

Figure 17.2 Social Security Receipts, Spending, and Reserve Estimates, 1992–2035. *Source:* U.S. Congress, House Committee on Ways and Means.

2 In the early 1980s, because of unstable economic conditions and a major increase in benefits, Social Security was in severe economic trouble. Benefits paid out were exceeding revenues, and the program's reserve fund was emptying, leading to fears that the programs would go broke. To solve this problem Democrats in Congress favored increasing Social Security taxes, while Republicans called for reduced benefits. Neither alternative drew much public support.

3 To lessen the political conflict surrounding the issue, President Ronald Reagan created the bipartisan National Commission on Social Security Reform. However, the commission was unable to reach agreement on a rescue plan. Consequently, in January 1983, a small group of White House officials, members of Congress, and private experts began negotiating a solution. After a few days of hard bargaining, they reached agreement on a bailout plan. Major components of the plan included higher Social Security taxes, reduced cost-of-living adjustments (COLAs) for retirement benefits, extension of Social Security coverage to all nonprofit organization employees and new federal workers, and taxation of the Social Security benefits of upper-income retirees. It was thought that this package would ensure the solvency of Social Security well into the twenty-first century.

- *bipartisan:*
  a. supported by members of both parties
  b. useless

- *components:*
  a. those who are against
  b. parts or pieces

- *solvency:*
  a. disappearance
  b. financial soundness

4 The proposal was enacted into law in 1983 with minimal changes by Congress. As it turned out, the Social Security solvency program has worked much better than expected in the short run. Annual revenues have greatly exceeded benefit payments, thus swelling the size of the Social Security Trust Fund. In 1993 the fund had a $46.8 billion surplus. Despite this success it is expected to be insolvent by 2030 because the ratio of workers to retirees will decline as baby boomers hit retirement age (see Figure 17.2). In anticipation of this problem, several members of Congress have called for a round of new reforms, including the removal of the Social Security Administration from the Department of Health and Human Services to make it an independent agency.

Context Answers and Clues

expenditures: a. costs (increases listed would lead to more expenses)

beneficiaries: a. those who get benefits ("currently receive benefits")

entitlement: b. having a right to something (qualifiers for Social Security are guaranteed benefits)

bipartisan: a. supported by members of both parties (intended "to lessen political conflict")

components: b. parts or pieces (various items in the plan are listed)

solvency: b. financial soundness (intention was to make the system strong)

■ Reading for Information

Mapping

Write the letters of the items below on the time line to show the correct sequence in which these events (¶s2–4) occurred.

A. Fund had a $46.8 billion surplus.
B. Agreement on a bailout plan.
C. Social Security getting into severe economic trouble.
D. Fund expected to be insolvent.
E. Bipartisan National Commission on Social Security Reform.
F. Bailout proposal enacted into law with minimal changes.

1. Figure 17.2 is mainly concerned with which time period?
   a. the past
   b. the present
   c. the future

2. In 2010, the year-end reserve is projected to be about
   a. $2,000.
   b. $3,000.
   c. $3,000,000.
   d. $3,000,000,000.

3. The year-end reserve will begin to drop drastically in approximately which year?
   a. 2020
   b. 2025
   c. 2030
   d. 2035

4. In which year is the amount paid out projected to begin to exceed the amount paid in?
   a. 2000
   b. 2005
   c. 2010
   d. 2015

5. The year-end reserve will become less than the amounts paid out and paid in between
   a. 2020 and 2025.
   b. 2025 and 2030.
   c. 2030 and 2035.
   d. 2035 and 2040.

6. The information in the graphic comes from
   a. the Social Security Administration.
   b. the Department of Health and Human Services.
   c. U.S. Congress, House Committee on Ways and Means.
   d. National Commission on Social Security Reform.

7. The text is mainly concerned with which time period?
   a. the past
   b. the present
   c. the future
8. Which of the following is NOT true of Social Security troubles in the early 1980s?
   a. Economic conditions were unstable.
   b. There had been a major increase in benefits.
   c. More money was coming out of the fund than going in.
   d. The reserve emptied and the program had gone broke.
9. Which of the following is NOT a reason why Social Security spending is increasing?
   a. The number of people getting benefits has increased.
   b. People are living longer.
   c. People are suffering from more disabilities.
   d. Benefit amounts have risen.
10. Which of the following was eventually adopted in the 1980s as a solution to the problem?
    a. Social Security taxes were increased.
    b. COLAs for retirement benefits were reduced.
    c. Social Security benefits of upper-income retirees were taxed.
    d. all of the above
    e. none of the above

STORY AND SEQUENCE IN LONGER ARTICLES

The study of history includes fascinating stories of individuals and particular events—for instance, the trial of Socrates or Amelia Earhart's attempt to fly around the world. We also learn about major events over periods of time. From these we can construct a time line—for example, for the events of an era (the Renaissance), a particular culture or civilization (Mayan), or an individual's life (Winston Churchill). The next story will give you an example, on a small scale, of both a specific story and a broader history of an event.

Previewing *Hero of Sugar Loaf Hill* by Malcolm McConnell

Thinking About Reading From the title, you can guess that the article is going to be about a

____

Preview by reading the first paragraph and first line of the second. Note that there is a big jump in time at the beginning of the second paragraph. When did the event take place?

____

What war is it a part of and during what years did it occur?

____

(Look back at "The Great African-American Migration" in Chapter 9 if you do not recall these dates.) Write anything you know about this period of time:

____

____

____

____

Two other wars are mentioned in the article. Look up their approximate dates:

Korean War: ________________ Vietnam War: ________________

Very often in material organized by time sequence, there is no single sentence that states the main idea. Read the last paragraph. You should be able to make a guess about the implied main idea by answering the question at the end of ¶1:

> But the report had never been acted upon—and a brave Marine had never received the honor due him. Was it too late?

Implied main idea guess: ____

Reading with a Purpose This article contains two time sequences. The first is a specific incident or story (¶s 2–9); circle all the signal words of time as you read these paragraphs. The second sequence covers a much longer period of time and gives many details of the subject's life and activities. In a number of places, the age of the subject and the year or date of certain actions is implied; write your inferences in the margins where indicated.

Preview Vocabulary

shrapnel: (¶3) shell fragments from a high-explosive shell

dengue fever: (¶4) a severe infectious tropical disease carried by mosquitoes causing high fever, headache, muscle and joint pain

melee: (¶5) wild, disorganized fighting

barrage: (¶6) a rapid and heavy discharge of artillery fire

phosphorous: (¶8) a poisonous, nonmetallic element; includes uses in matches, shells that cause fires

molten: (¶8) turned to liquid by heat

cloying: (¶9) supplying with too much of something

archives: (¶12) a place for collection of documents or other important historical materials

Semper Fidelis: (¶13) Latin for "always faithful"

Hero of Sugar Loaf Hill

by Malcolm McConnell

1 In Kentfield, California, Mark Stebbins was sorting through his deceased uncle's papers when he came upon a box marked "Jim Day." He recognized the name of a Marine who had served with his uncle. Stebbins glanced quickly through the box. It was full of old, smeared copies of what seemed to be a report. The papers were a recommendation for the Medal of Honor, including vivid witness accounts of savage combat in the Pacific. But the report had never been acted upon—and a brave Marine had never received the honor due him. Was it too late?

■ *deceased:*
a. rich
b. dead

2 By dawn of May 14, 1945, the Marines of Second Battalion, 22nd Regiment, had been pinned down on Okinawa for some 30 hours. The Japanese commanded a series of hills along a narrow section of the island, raining machine-gun and artillery fire down on the Americans. Cpl. Jim Day, 19, was ordered to try to hold the western slope of Sugar Loaf Hill, a steep hummock of gravelly mud that looked like a huge overturned bathtub. If the height could be secured, the enemy's cross fire would be disrupted, allowing the Americans to punch through.

■ *hummock:*
a. fence
b. a mound of earth

■ *disrupted:*
a. heard
b. interrupted

3 When the young man from Overland, Mo., quit high school to join the Marines two years earlier, he was 17, five-foot-six and 130 pounds. Now, five months from his 20th birthday,

Year:
Age:

he had grown to a full six feet—and was a survivor of bloody fighting on Eniwetak and Guam. Day and his men crunched up the hillside through heavy artillery fire. Finally they stumbled into a 30-foot crater almost five feet deep, dug by a bomb or a shell. They felt lucky to find cover, but almost instantly more than 20 Japanese soldiers attacked. As Day's squad rose to defend their position, they were hit by bullets and shrapnel. Day felt searing metal tear across his arms. Rolling and bobbing, he jammed fresh clips into his rifle, then threw grenades, aiming short so they'd bounce down among the enemy before exploding. After a furious firefight, the attack was beaten back.

4 His ears still ringing, Day heard moaning behind him. Of the eight men who'd made it with him to the crater, three were dead, three wounded. Another, Pfc. Dale Bertoli, was writhing in pain. "You hit, Bert?" Day asked. "It's the fever," Bertoli gasped. He had returned to the front lines only that morning after a debilitating bout of dengue fever. It had surged back, rendering the husky Marine almost powerless with spasms and a crippling headache.

■ *debilitating:*
a. restful
b. weakening greatly

■ *rendering:*
a. making
b. helping

5 Minutes later Sgt. Narolian West and two stretcher-bearers slid into the crater. Immediately the Japanese launched a second assault. Day spun around and shot three enemy soldiers who had dashed unseen to the hole. Their bodies tumbled onto West. During the melee two of the wounded Marines died. "Come on back with us," West now begged. Day refused. So did Bertoli and a badly wounded replacement named McDonald.

6 Night fell. Japanese soldiers slid under the chalky light of flares. Day waited until he could hear them coming up the hill. Then he threw grenades at the shadows. With daylight the slope around the crater was pounded with mortar fire. When the barrage lifted, enemy soldiers surged up the slope. Day rose to fire and cut down the attackers. This lonely outpost ahead of the main American lines put Day and his two comrades in a critical position. To reinforce their hill strongholds, enemy troops would have to cross open lowlands exposed to Day's fire. By holding off the Japanese, he gave the Americans time to find a way to push through. The Japanese knew it and were determined to drive them off Sugar Loaf Hill.

Date:

■ *barrage:*
a. a heavy discharge of artillery fire
b. a cloud

7 Late in the afternoon of May 15 another attack began. Day and McDonald were perched on the edge of the crater, firing long bursts down the slope, when a Japanese anti-tank gun cracked. McDonald was killed instantly. Shrapnel riddled Day's hands. Ignoring the pain, Day dragged a machine gun to the right lip of the crater and fired until the attackers retreated.

8 That night they faced a new peril: American phosphorous mortar shells exploded around the hole like a Fourth of July fireworks display gone bad. Day smothered flaming chunks on Bertoli's neck and arms with handfuls of mud. He felt stabbing heat in his right foot as a chunk of molten phosphorus burned through his shoe. Ripping it off, Day covered his foot with mud. The two men sprawled in the crater, floating on pain and exhaustion. At dawn, May 16, a cloying white mist rose from the valleys. Day heard the faint scrape of boots. By the time he could hoist his rifle, the enemy soldiers were only 40 feet away. He cut several down and drove the rest off. The day drifted by in bursts of noise and sudden, ringing silence. Flies swarmed in a hot stench of death. At nightfall Day fought to stay awake, firing at the enemy and taking out two machine-gun crews.

■ *hoist:*
a. lift
b. repair

9 Then it was morning, and a Marine lieutenant suddenly dropped into the crater, his feet crunching on hundreds of empty brass shell casings and tinkling steel grenade spoons. "Pull back, Corporal," he ordered, shouting so the deafened Day could understand. An American battalion was now sweeping their way. Day and Bertoli staggered down the slope through the advancing column. The Marines who finally relieved them counted dozens of enemy dead.

Date:

10 Day's defense of Sugar Loaf Hill for three days and nights would prove to be key to smashing the enemy's line across Okinawa. His battalion commander, Lt. Col. Horatio Woodhouse, immediately ordered witness statements to be taken from survivors in order to recommend the young man for the Medal of Honor. "Time is critical and events fleeting in our current situation," Woodhouse noted. Witnesses who were alive one day could be killed the next. Seven statements were collected, and a citation was drafted. Then the war brutally intervened. Woodhouse and Bertoli were killed in battle, and Day was badly wounded. His Medal of Honor recommendation never moved up the chain of command.

■ *drafted:*
a. lost
b. drawn up

■ *intervened:*
a. ended
b. came between events

11 After the war Day re-enlisted. Whenever new Marines would ask him about combat in the Pacific, Day would offer few details. In the Korean War Lieutenant Day led a platoon in hand-to-hand fighting, earning two Silver Star Medals and two Purple Hearts. In Vietnam, Maj. Jim Day earned another Silver Star and his sixth Purple Heart. In 1974 Colonel Day took command of the Fourth Marine Corps District in Philadelphia.

12 That year Owen Stebbins, who had been Day's company commander on Okinawa, heard about the lost Medal of Honor recommendation. Stebbins had been wounded and evacuated

Year:

■ *demurred:*
a. objected
b. remembered

■ *doggedly:*
a. unsuccessfully
b. with stubborn persistence

■ *posthumous:*
a. occurring after one's death
b. comical

from the battlefield just before Day's heroic action. He had never seen the citation. Now he called Day and told him he wanted to resubmit the report. Day demurred. "Okinawa was a long time ago," he said. Stebbins nevertheless worked doggedly over the years to secure medals for the forgotten Marines of Sugar Loaf Hill, including a posthumous Bronze Star Medal for Dale Bertoli and several other enlisted men. Finally, in September 1995, Stebbins wrote Day, who had retired from the Marines at the rank of major general and was running a home construction business in California. "I'm going ahead," Stebbins said. "You'll never do anything about it yourself."

Year:

■ *authenticity:*
a. age
b. truthfulness

■ *corroborating:*
a. typing
b. verifying, supporting

13 Stebbins forwarded the recommendation to Marine Corps headquarters in Washington, D.C. But like many of his comrades, Stebbins did not get to see Day receive his award. He died in 1996. Soon afterward his nephew, Mark Stebbins, found the box of Day's records among his uncle's effects. He did not realize the import of the papers, but he tracked down Day and sent him the box. Meanwhile Marine Corps officials debated whether to proceed with Day's medal. Most of the men who had signed the statements were dead, so there needed to be evidence of the documents' authenticity. Finally, an Awards Branch investigator found the service records of each witness in the military archives of the National Personnel Records Center in St. Louis. And there, in each yellowing folder, lay a carbon copy identical to those in Day's report, corroborating every word.

Age:

■ *unerringly:*
a. occasionally
b. consistently

14 On January 20, 1998, Maj. Gen. James Day (Ret.) stood in the East Room of the White House. Among the Marines who had gathered to see him receive the Medal of Honor were his son Lt. Col. James A. Day, and his grandson Lance Cpl. Joshua Eustice. "General," President Clinton said, "you are the embodiment of the motto 'Semper Fidelis.' You have been unerringly faithful to those who fought alongside you, to the Corps and to the United States. We are profoundly fortunate to count you among our heroes."

Context Answers and Clues

deceased: b. dead (not likely to be going through his uncle's papers unless he had died)

hummock: b. a mound of earth (it's a hill that "looked like a huge overturned bathtub")

disrupted: b. interrupted (can't "punch through" unless the enemy fire is stopped)

debilitating: b. weakening greatly

rendering: a. making (he was "almost powerless")

barrage: a. a heavy discharge of artillery fire (they were being "pounded with mortar fire")

hoist: a. lift (a soldier would be holding his rifle)

drafted: b. drawn up (the intention was to award a medal)

intervened: b. came between events (their plan to award a medal was interrupted)

demurred: a. objected (Day didn't want him to do it)

doggedly: b. with stubborn persistence (he kept at it over a period of time)

posthumous: a. occurring after one's death (Bertoli and the others were dead)

authenticity: b. truthfulness (they needed evidence to determine the truth about Day's heroism)

corroborating: b. verifying, supporting (the copies show the story is true)

unerringly: b. consistently ("Semper" means "always")

EXERCISE 11.6

Questions on *Hero of Sugar Loaf Hill*

■ Reading for Information

1. Select the best statement of the implied main idea of the article.
   a. Soldiers never get the recognition that they truly deserve.
   b. Jim Day's career, being wounded, with his heroism at last recognized officially.
   c. After many years and delays, Jim Day finally received the medal he deserved.
   d. Jim Day had a career in the military and in the construction business.

2. Find a signal words or phrases in the following paragraphs that helps keep the sequence of the Battle of Sugar Loaf Hill clear:

   ¶2: ______________________________

   ¶5: ______________________________

   ¶6: ______________________________

   ¶7: ______________________________

   ¶8: ______________________________

   ¶9: ______________________________

Tracking a Story Line

Below are the events that make up the story of the battle of Sugar Loaf Hill. Place them in the order in which they happened in the sequence map that follows.

- Day shoots three enemy soldiers in a second assault by the Japanese.
- An American Marine battalion relieves Day and Bertoli.
- Day's position is pounded by mortar fire.
- Day and Bertoli and McDonald refuse to withdraw.
- Day is wounded in the hands by shrapnel from anti-tank gun.
- Cpl. Jim Day is ordered to hold Sugar Loaf Hill.
- Day and Bertoli are burned by phosphorous mortar shells.
- Day is wounded in the arm by shrapnel.

Making a Time Line for Events

Put the letters for the major events in the story where they would approximately fall on the time line below:

A. Investigator finds carbon copies that support Day's report.
B. Day is running a home construction business in California.
C. Lieutenant Day earns two Silver Star Medals and two Purple Hearts.
D. Maj. Gen. Day receives Medal of Honor from President Clinton.
E. Jim Day quits high school and joins the Marines.
F. Woodhouse and Bertoli are killed and Day's citation is never acted on.
G. Mark Stebbins finds the box of Day's records.
H. Day heroically defends Sugar Loaf Hill.
I. Maj. Day earns third Silver Star and his sixth Purple Heart.

____

1943 1945 1950 1968 1975 1995 1998

■ Reading for Understanding

Making Inferences

Use the notes you made in the margins to help you determine the following:

1. Year that Day quit high school:
   a. 1925
   b. 1939
   c. 1942
   d. 1943
2. Year that Day joined the Marines:
   a. 1943
   b. 1944
   c. 1945
   d. 1972

3. Day's age at the time of battle of Sugar Loaf Hill:
   a. 18
   b. 19
   c. 20
   d. 21
4. Approximate month and year of Day's birth:
   a. October 1925
   b. December 1925
   c. October 1926
   d. November 1926
5. Day fighting on Eniwetak and Guam sometime in this period:
   a. 1941–1943
   b. 1942–1944
   c. 1943–1945
   d. 1949–1951
6. Date in 1945 that Day was relieved by battalion at Sugar Loaf Hill:
   a. May 15
   b. May 16
   c. May 17
   d. May 18
7. Year that Owen Stebbins called Day and told him he wanted to resubmit the report:
   a. 1945
   b. 1974
   c. 1995
   d. 1996
8. Year that Mark Stebbins found box of Day's records:
   a. 1993 or early 1994
   b. late 1994 or early 1995
   c. 1995 or early 1996
   d. 1996 or early 1997
9. Day's age when he received the Medal of Honor:
   a. 68
   b. 70
   c. 72
   d. 74

10. The correct time sequence of the wars Day fought in:
    a. Vietnam, Korea, World War II
    b. World War II, Korea, Vietnam
    c. Vietnam, World War II, Korea
    d. Word War II, Vietnam, Korea

Purpose and Tone

1. The author's main purpose in the story is to
    a. entertain the reader with exciting war stories.
    b. criticize the military for mishandling deserved awards.
    c. relate the facts about how a hero received his just reward.
2. The author's tone is best described as
    a. earnest and respectful.
    b. impersonal and scientific.
    c. suspicious and irritated.

TIME SEQUENCE AND LISTS IN "HOW TO" ARTICLES

"How to" articles are very common in popular magazines and in newspapers. They can follow two patterns of organization or a mixture of the two. One—strict time order—is usually more suited to mechanical operations where a series of steps are given in a strict time order: for example, building a deck or creating a quilt. A second type is more concerned with giving advice that will lead to a goal; how, for instance, to help your child do better in school. The advice is given in a list but not always in time order. When items are not in time order, they could be listed in a different order without confusing the reader.

Previewing *How to Manage Your Time, Part I* by Jan Farrington

Thinking About Reading "How to" articles give directions on reaching certain goals. Take note of the title and read the first two paragraphs. Then create a main idea guess for the article by completing this statement:

To reach the goals of ______________________________,

you need to ______________________________.

Think of your experiences with managing your time. Has it been a problem for you? For someone you know? Write down a few of your observations here:

____

____

____

____

____

Reading with a Purpose The article contains a mixture of advice organized by time and by lists. Number any series of pieces of advice that you think is organized by strict time sequence. In the last half of the article, write in information in the margins where indicated.

How to Manage Your Time: Part I

by Jan Farrington

The Busy-ness Syndrome

1 Do Americans glorify being busy? To many of us, being on the run and on the edge of exhaustion means: "I'm a really successful person." Maybe not. In a study released last summer, researchers found that people who worked hard at finding a good spouse and creating a solid family life actually made more money and had a higher rate of material success than people who classed themselves as "workaholics." Maybe the rat race isn't the competition you want to be in. Author Stephen Covey, in his best-selling book *The Seven Habits of Highly Effective People,* argues that the most successful and satisfied people aren't necessarily the busiest. They are the people who plan their lives so they have time to spend on activities that are important but not urgent—such as goalsetting, recognizing new opportunities, building relationships, and long-term papers and projects.

- *exhaustion:*
  - a. condition of feeling totally worn out
  - b. prosperity
- *"workaholics":*
  - a. rich people
  - b. people addicted to work

2 So how do you become less busy and more able to spend time on important stuff?

You PLAN.

You ORGANIZE.

You SET GOALS and PRIORITIES.

Learning to manage your time wisely is a way to make better grades, be more productive at work, and free up more leisure time. But it's also a technique you can use to think about and reach your goals in life. "If you're unorganized, you can't be as productive as you'd like to be," writes stress management expert J. Robin Powell in a recent book. "Being disorganized will leave you feeling overwhelmed and out of control." Being disorganized means you are living from hour to hour—and probably heading in no particular direction.

■ *overwhelmed:*
a. relaxed
b. overpowered completely

3 Once you start to think about priorities and goals, you may wind up doing a major rearrangement of the way you live your life every day. Take two blank sheets of paper. On the first:

- List the things that are most important in your life.
- Ask yourself what makes you feel good about yourself.
- Think about what you might do (now and in the future) if money were no object.

On the second sheet of paper, write short- or long-term goals for the following six areas:

- school
- work/career
- lifestyle
- personal growth
- relationships
- health

4 Now begin to think of how you can organize your time/life to make progress toward your goals. Here's a simple example. Let's say one of your "health" goals is to maintain an exercise routine to give yourself more mental and physical energy. You might look back at the weekly time log you kept, and try to identify times during the week that could be used for exercise. If you can't "see" times, you'll need to think about changes that will make time for exercise.

5 Of course, finding time to work toward a goal doesn't guarantee you'll make it. But time management skills can make a big difference. Once you know what you need to do, you can break the task of reaching the goal into smaller steps, set a time frame for reaching each goal, and then use organizational skills to be sure you make time for these important activities.

A Lifetime Skill

6 The need to manage time effectively will follow you through school, into the workplace, and into your personal life as an adult. Obviously, it isn't a skill you'll learn in a day or a week. But you can begin right now to make time your friend, not

your enemy. Think about the priorities and goals you wrote about on the sheets of paper—and get on the road to where you want to be next month, next year, or a decade from now. It's not just a matter of time. But if you can make the minutes and hours "do more," your time management skills can make the difference between having a life that just happens—and having the life you want.

Smart Study Tips to Try

7 Here are some smart study tips to help you learn more in the time you have.

Advice: 8 Become an "active" learner. Don't just sit there. Ask questions, make comments, actually think about what's being discussed. Read all assigned material. If possible, read ahead. Take good notes in class: key ideas, definitions, facts, questions you want answered, and so on. Read over your notes each night before you begin your homework in that subject.

Advice: 9 Write down assignments. You'll save time and worry if you keep a running list of homework assignments, long-term
Advice: projects (and when they're due), test dates, and so on. Keep one list, not slips of paper stuck in all your textbooks like confetti. Stationery stores have inexpensive notebooks for this purpose.

10 Learn to use little pieces of time. If you don't have big blocks of study time, learn to use the bits and pieces. If your teacher gives you time to study or start your homework in class, use it.

Advice: 11 Set up a good work space. If you have your own room, that's probably the best place to study. Don't sit on the bed, though. You're likely to wake up at 2 a.m. and wonder what happened. Use the desk and get a good desk lamp. If studying at
Advice: home doesn't work for you, take your books and find a quiet corner of the public library.

Advice: 12 Pay attention to your body's "rhythms." Are you a night
Def. of "biorhythms": owl or an early bird? The answer is in your biorhythms, the natural patterns your body follows from day to day. You can study more effectively if you choose the time of day when your body clock says "time to be awake and alert" instead of "time to crash."

Advice: 13 Plan study sessions. Do you study best alone or with one friend? Do you get more done if you tackle harder subjects first—or last? Set up study sessions that suit you. Concentrate on learning or doing one thing at a time, not on all the work you need to do. Keep yourself alert while you study: Make notes, ask somebody to quiz you, and give yourself a break every 45 minutes. Spend some time "overlearning" material you think you have "down cold." (Overlearning means knowing material so well that when questioned, you respond almost automatically.) Practice does make a difference in how much you remember and how easily you use what you know.

Def. of "overlearning":

14 Reward yourself for accomplishments. That can mean something as simple as checking items off your "to do" list as you finish them, or treating yourself to pizza after you've studied hard.

Advice:

EXERCISE 11.7

Questions on *How to Manage Your Time, Part I*

■ Reading for Information

1. Select the statement that best expresses the main idea of the article:
   a. People who are always busy and on the edge of exhaustion are the happiest and most successful materially.
   b. Managing time wisely pays off at school and work, in creating leisure time, and in reaching lifetime goals.
   c. The importance of time management, ways to accomplish it, and very important tips on how to study.
   d. You may not want to compete in the rat race, but the most successful and satisfied people do.
2. Smart time management can help you
   a. make better grades.
   b. produce more at work.
   c. create more leisure time.
   d. reach goals in life.
   e. all of the above
3. Being unorganized
   a. affects productivity very little.
   b. makes you feel more free.
   c. helps to relieve stress.
   d. all of the above
   e. none of the above

4. An "active" learner
   a. asks questions and makes comments.
   b. reads just the most important part of assignments.
   c. doesn't waste time in learning definitions.
   d. reads over notes only before tests.
   e. all of the above

5. To manage time effectively, you should
   a. put down goals on paper.
   b. break tasks for reaching goals into smaller steps.
   c. set a time frame for reaching each goal.
   d. use organizational skills to make time for important activities.
   e. all of the above

Recognizing Opinions

The author expresses opinions about a number of aspects related to time management. For each of the following statements, answer Agree if the author seems to support the statement and Disagree if the author does not.

_______ 1. Being busy all the time does not guarantee success.

_______ 2. If you can find time to work toward a goal, you won't fail to make it.

_______ 3. J. Robin Powell is an expert on how to manage stress.

_______ 4. Managing time is more important in school and on the job than in your personal life.

_______ 5. It is always best to study alone and tackle harder subjects first.

_______ 6. "Overstudying" anything is a waste of valuable time.

_______ 7. You are highly likely to have the life you want even if you don't manage time skillfully.

_______ 8. Keep assignments on slips of paper so you can rearrange them.

_______ 9. Your own room and the library can be good places to study.

_______ 10. Find a comfortable place to study, such as on your bed.

Time Sequence and Lists

Here are three groups of directions/advice on time management given in the article. Your task here is *not* to follow the directions, but rather to see if you can change the order of the items without creating confusion. If you can, the passage is a random list. If the items muststay in a set order, the passage is organized by time. For each group, check your conclusion as to whether the directions are a random list or in time order.

Group A
Directions as given in the text:

"Take two blank sheets of paper. On the first:

- List the things that are most important in your life.
- Ask yourself what makes you feel good about yourself.
- Think about what you might do (now and in the future) if money were no object."

Your rearrangement of the items:

- ______________________________
- ______________________________
- ______________________________

_____ Can change the order without confusion: A list

_____ Can not change the order without confusion: A time sequence

Group B
Directions as given in the text:

"■ Put down your goals on paper.
- Break tasks for reaching the goal into smaller steps.
- Set a time frame for reaching each goal.
- Use organizational skills to make time for these important activities."

Your rearrangement of the items:

- ______________________________
- ______________________________
- ______________________________
- ______________________________

_____ Can change the order without confusion: A list

_____ Can not change the order without confusion: A time sequence

Group C

Advice as given in the text:

"Here are some smart study tips to help you learn more in the time you have.

- Become an 'active' learner.
- Write down assignments.
- Keep a running list of assignments, and test dates.
- Learn to use little pieces of time.
- Set up a good work space.
- Pay attention to your body's 'rhythms.'
- Plan study sessions."

Your rearrangement of the items:

- ______________________________
- ______________________________
- ______________________________
- ______________________________
- ______________________________
- ______________________________
- ______________________________

_____ Can change the order without confusion: A list

_____ Can not change the order without confusion: A time sequence

■ Reading for Understanding

1. "You can begin right now to make time your friend, not your enemy." Explain in your own words what that sentence means.

   ____

   ____

2. In ¶12 the text asks "Are you a night owl or an early bird? You can study more effectively if you choose the time of day when your body clock says 'time to be awake and alert' instead of 'time to crash.'" Recall the results of the inventory you took in the previous chapter on being a lark or an owl. Which one were you? ______________ Based on that information, explain when the best study time would be for you.

   ____

   ____

3. The text states that you should "overlearn" material you think you know. Give an example from your own experience of overlearning—or failing to overlearn—material for a test.

____

____

____

4. Reread ¶8 on "active" reading, in the first part of Chapter 1. Recall what you learned about active learning in the first chapter in the text and elsewhere. What advice would you add about active reading?

____

____

____

5. The first boldface heading in the article is "The Busy-ness Syndrome." The dictionary defines a syndrome as a group of behaviors that show a characteristic pattern of behavior, often undesirable. Explain in your own words what this syndrome is and, if possible, give some examples from your own experience.

____

____

____

____

____

____

Active Learning

BUILDING TIME LINES

You will find in your college reading that articles and texts often make references to important people and events without citing specific dates or periods. That is one reason why building broad frames of reference for the histories of various countries and for the world are very important. These frameworks—called time lines—allow us to better understand an event by knowing what else was occurring during the same era. Time lines can cover very broad historical periods. They can, however, also be used for very specific histories in many different fields—for example, to track major events in the development of the automobile or in the discovery of a vaccine for polio.

EXERCISE 11.8

Building a Time Line for American History

In this text you have learned about some important people and events that can help you develop a frame of reference for American history. Use the skeleton time line on page 427 to construct a time line for American history. Below is a list of events that have been mentioned in this text. Use your index to find those whose dates you can't recall. The beginning and ending dates for the period covered are given. Put other dates on the line where needed and match the events on the list with the proper date or approximate period. Put in any other important dates in American history that you remember.

American Civil War
George Washington's birth and death
Vietnam War
Great African-American Migration
Spanish Reconquista of Granada
The New Deal
Korean War
American Revolutionary War
The Great Depression
First voyage of Columbus
Abraham Lincoln's birth and death
American Constitution
Emancipation Proclamation
World War II
Aztec and Incan empires destroyed
Model T mass-produced

1492

1973

Reading Portfolio

TIME AND PROCESS ARTICLES

1. For this assignment you will need to find a magazine or newspaper article that fits in one of the two categories below:

   True stories: "Hero of Sugar Loaf Hill" is a good example of this type of article. They can be about famous people and events or about ordinary people like Jim Day who have done something remarkable.

   "How to" articles: These are very common, making up the majority of articles in magazines focusing on such things as home, family, beauty, or fitness, and in specialty magazines on topics like woodworking, auto mechanics, crafts, etc.

2. Your summary should be 150–175 words. Try to come up with a pattern map like the samples in this chapter. For a story, use a time line and organize steps or stages into three sections: beginning, middle, and end. Use your own phrasing in your outline or map. That way you can write your summary directly from it. For a "how to" article, select the most important steps or pieces of advice; some articles will best be handled by lumping short steps into larger stages. Avoid articles that are very short or whose steps are already in outline form; trying to summarize very short steps in your own words can be hard to do.

3. Your response should be about the same length. For articles about origins and developments, do you have a new or better understanding? Has reading the article changed your attitude toward the topic, for better or worse? For "how to" articles, you might discuss how useful the information is. Will the process described work? Is the sequence correctly ordered? Or is there a better way? Your personal experience is very relevant here.

CHAPTER 12

Why Did It Happen and What Can We Do?

Explaining Events and Finding Solutions

After reading this chapter, you will know the answers to these questions:

- What is cause and effect?
- What is a fishbone map?
- What is a cycle map?
- What are the parts of the problem solution pattern?
- What are some important problems facing society?

Time order and process answer the questions **when** and **how.** But often we want to know not just when or how something happens, but **why.** This question leads us to examine *cause and effect.* One thing (the cause) leads to something that follows (the effect); without the cause, the effect would not have happened.

SIGNALS AND SEQUENCE IN CAUSE AND EFFECT

There are some common signal words that show cause and effect:

because	so	for	thus
therefore	so that	since	if . . .then
consequently	in order for	reason for	as a result

In addition, many verbs in the language suggest cause/effect relationships, but these are often harder to spot. Here are a few examples:

influence contribute to create determine lead to

In actual time, the cause always comes first and the effect follows. However, in reading, a cause/effect sequence can be difficult to determine at times because the effect often is placed in the sentence before the cause:

Because the carpenter had not been paid, he went home. (cause first)

The carpenter went home because he had not been paid. (effect first)

In order to get a rebate, customers must send in proof of purchase. (effect first)

The key is to be aware of whether a signal word points to a cause or effect:

Abel gets high grades because he studies hard. (Words like *because, for,* and *since* always point to the cause.)

Abel studies hard. Therefore, he gets high grades. (Words and phrases like *so, thus, therefore, consequently,* or *as a result lead* to the effect.)

EXERCISE 12.1

Determining Cause and Effect in Sentences

Pay careful attention to signal words and phrases of cause and effect and verbs indicating cause and effect relationships. Decide which part states the cause and which part gives the effect. Then identify the key signal word or phrase or verb that indicates cause and effect.

EXAMPLES

A. Melissa didn't eat breakfast, so she felt weak all morning.

Cause Melissa didn't eat breakfast

Effect she felt weak all morning

Verb/signal word or phrase so

B. Heredity determines most of your physical traits.

Cause Heredity

Effect your physical traits

Verb/signal word or phrase determine

1. Noe will not be considered for the job, since he did not complete the job application form.

   Cause ______________________________

   Effect ______________________________

   Verb/signal word or phrase ______________________________

2. The price of crude oil has increased; therefore, expect the price of gas to go up at the pump.

   Cause ______________________________

   Effect ______________________________

   Verb/signal word or phrase ______________________________

3. It did not rain all spring or summer; as a result, the wheat crop did not grow.

   Cause ______________________________

   Effect ______________________________

   Verb/signal word or phrase ______________________________

4. Smoking and the eating of fatty foods contribute to a high danger of heart disease.

   Cause ______________________________

   Effect ______________________________

   Verb/signal word or phrase ______________________________

5. Good study habits and strong motivation will lead to high grades.

   Cause ______________________________

   Effect ______________________________

   Verb/signal word or phrase ______________________________

6. The players were hungry after the football game, so they all went out for pizza.

   Cause ______________________________

   Effect ______________________________

   Verb/signal word or phrase ______________________________

7. Parental advice can strongly influence a child's success in life.

   Cause ______________________________

   Effect ______________________________

   Verb/signal word or phrase ______________________________

8. Karin stopped running so that Porfirio could catch up with her.

   Cause ______________________________

   Effect ______________________________

   Verb/signal word or phrase ______________________________

9. The voter turnout was somewhat low because the weather was very bad.

   Cause ______________________________

   Effect ______________________________

   Verb/signal word or phrase ______________________________

10. Both front tires of the racing car blew out; consequently, it spun into the wall.

    Cause ______________________________

    Effect ______________________________

    Verb/signal word or phrase ______________________________

11. The announcement of a postponement of a test creates a temporary joy in many students.

    Cause ______________________________

    Effect ______________________________

    Verb/signal word or phrase ______________________________

12. In order for us to be safe in our communities, we must have policemen and firemen.

    Cause ______________________________

    Effect ______________________________

    Verb/signal word or phrase ______________________________

13. The Dallas Cowboys won their last three games. Thus, they have reached the play-offs.

    Cause ______________________________

    Effect ______________________________

    Verb/signal word or phrase ______________________________

14. Drinking and driving only too often result in tragedy.

    Cause ______________________________

    Effect ______________________________

    Verb/signal word or phrase ______________________________

15. One reason for Kareem's success in business is his attention to detail.

    Cause ______________________________

    Effect ______________________________

    Verb/signal word or phrase ______________________________

MAPPING CAUSE AND EFFECT IN TEXTBOOK MATERIALS

Cause/effect does not always have a simple one-to-one relation. For example, if a football team begins losing (an effect), there might be a number of causes working together: injuries, attitude problems, ineligible players. A loss of a job (a cause) might lead to a number of bad effects: dropping out of school, getting behind on car payments, becoming depressed. Some causes and effects are linked in a chain where an effect becomes the cause of something else. For example, if a car won't start due to a bad battery, a student might get to school late and miss an important test. As a result, the student could fail the class and go on academic probation.

Because cause/effect can get complicated, mapping the many shapes it can take is very useful. For example, the various situations above could be mapped in these ways.

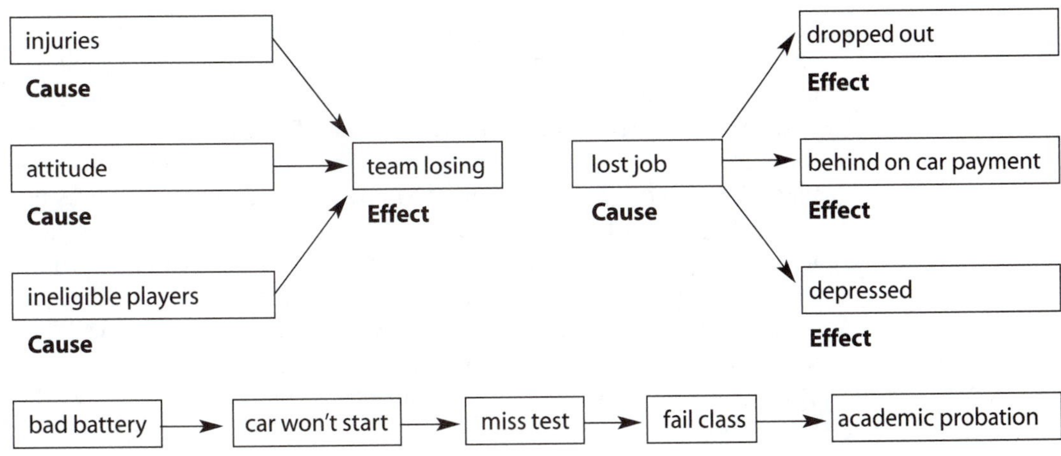

Maps often use arrows to show cause/effect without writing the words. As the last example shows, the connections are clear without the labels.

EXERCISE 12.2

Completing Cause-Effect Maps for Paragraphs

The following paragraphs are ones for which you found main ideas in Chapter 4. Look up any vocabulary words whose meaning you don't recall. Use the items following the paragraph to complete the map.

1. Studies have also shown that job satisfaction varies from one group to another. Generally, older workers are more satisfied than younger ones. One reason is that older workers, being more advanced in their careers, have better jobs. Another reason is that younger workers are more likely to expect their jobs to be highly interesting and stimulating, hence are more likely to be disillusioned because of the difficulty in realizing their high aspirations. White-collar workers, especially professionals and business people, are also more likely than blue collars to feel genuinely satisfied with their jobs.

   - older have better jobs
   - older workers more satisfied

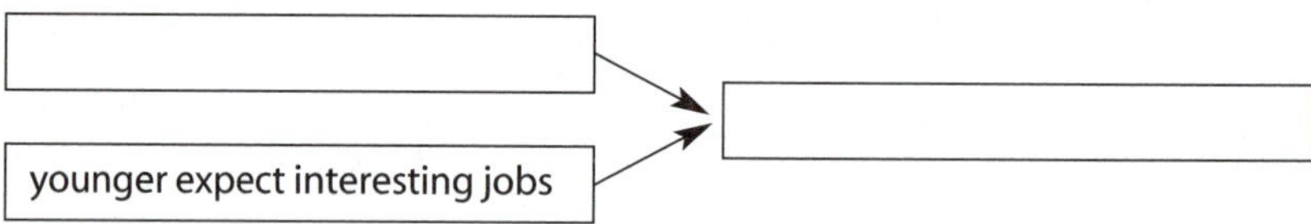

2. Specialization of work, if carried too far, leaves little room for responsibility or initiative by the worker. It can mean that some people are assigned the job of controlling those who actually produce goods or deliver services. When Studs Terkel interviewed workers, he found "the most profound complaint is 'being spied on.' There's the foreman at the plant, the supervisor listening in at Ma Bell's, the checker who gives the bus driver a hard time." Moreover, by tying the worker to an isolated task, to a small part of some large task, specialization can empty jobs of their meaning. The result can be dehumanizing for some workers, as Terkel found when he interviewed people across the country: "'I'm a machine,' says the spotwelder. 'I'm caged,' says the bank teller. 'I'm a mule,' says the steelworker. 'A monkey can do what I do,' says the receptionist."

- some control others
- feel less than human

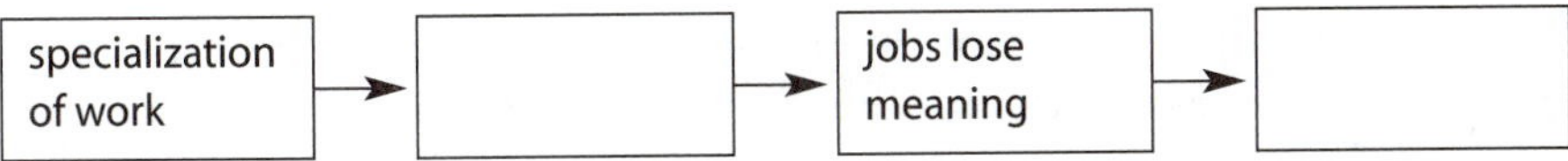

A more complicated map, called a "fishbone" map because it resembles the skeleton of a fish, shows how a number of causes and effects relate together.

3. Water plays several key roles on our planet. First, the oceans cover more than two-thirds of the planet's surface. They act as a huge heat storage reservoir and redistribute heat from low to high altitudes by ocean currents. Second, water falls on land in the form of rain or snow. As it runs off to the sea, water erodes rocks and soils and creates landscapes and landforms. This flow moves nutrients from one location to another, which also influences the distribution of plant and animal life. Third, water in the air moves huge quantities of heat from one place to another by absorbing surface heat in evaporation over warm oceans and releasing that latent heat in condensation over cooler regions.

- as runoff
- as reservoir
- moves nutrients, which affects placement of plant/animal life
- stores/redistributes heat through evaporation/condensation

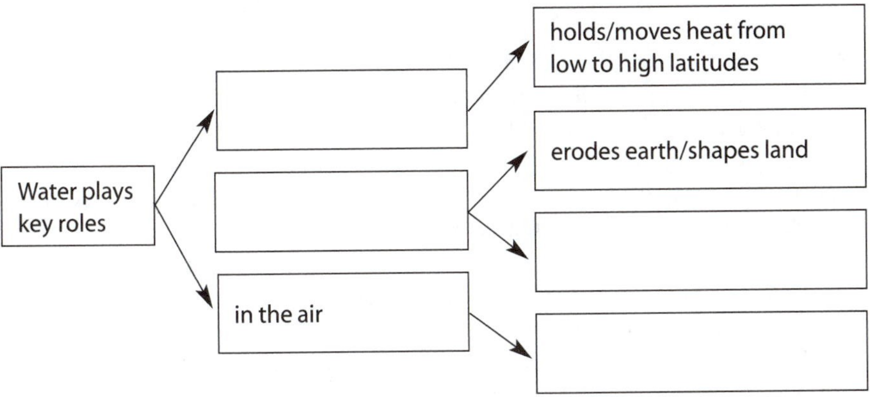

Longer passages, sections, and even chapters in textbooks may be organized by cause and effect. Identifying main ideas and making cause/effect maps is a good way to learn and remember information.

EXERCISE 12.3

Mapping Longer Textbook Passages

Try to use the context to figure out the meanings of words you're not sure of. If there aren't enough clues, use your dictionary.

Heredity and Weight Loss

by Cecie Starr

1 Why is it so difficult to lose weight permanently? The difficulty is partly a result of our evolutionary heritage. The fat-storing cells are an adaptation for survival. Collectively, they represent an energy reserve that may carry an animal through times when food just isn't available. Remember this when you start to put on unwanted fat. Once a fat-storing cell is added to your body, food intake may affect how empty or full it gets—but apparently that cell is in our body to stay. Dieting can decrease the fat stores. But research now suggests that the body interprets dieting as "starvation."

2 Dieting triggers changes in metabolism. With these changes, food is used more conservatively—so that fewer calories are burned. Meanwhile, the dieter's appetite surges, and "starved" fat cells quickly refill when a diet ends. In "yo-yo dieting," a person repeatedly gains and loses weight. This may alter cell metabolism in ways that make it more difficult to shed weight with each new round of dieting. Besides this, frequent changes in body weight may also increase the risk of heart disorders.

3 Some people opt to shed pounds by exercising, only to discover the going is slow indeed. Losing just a single pound of fat requires an energy expenditure of about 3,500 kilocalories. You can do this by, say, jogging for four hours or playing tennis for nearly eight hours straight. A more feasible way to keep off the fat is to combine a moderate reduction in caloric intake with increased physical activity. This approach might minimize the "starvation" response and increase the rate at which the body uses energy. Exercise also increases muscle mass. Even a resting muscle burns more calories than other types of tissues. Once you lose fat, the "starvation" response kicks in. To keep off unwanted weight, you have to continue to eat in moderation and maintain a program of regular exercise. (Starr, p. 411.)

■ Reading for Information

Mapping

Complete the top half of the map with the items below. Complete the bottom half of the map with the items that follow it.

- food used conservatively/fewer calories burned
- "starvation" dieting changes metabolism

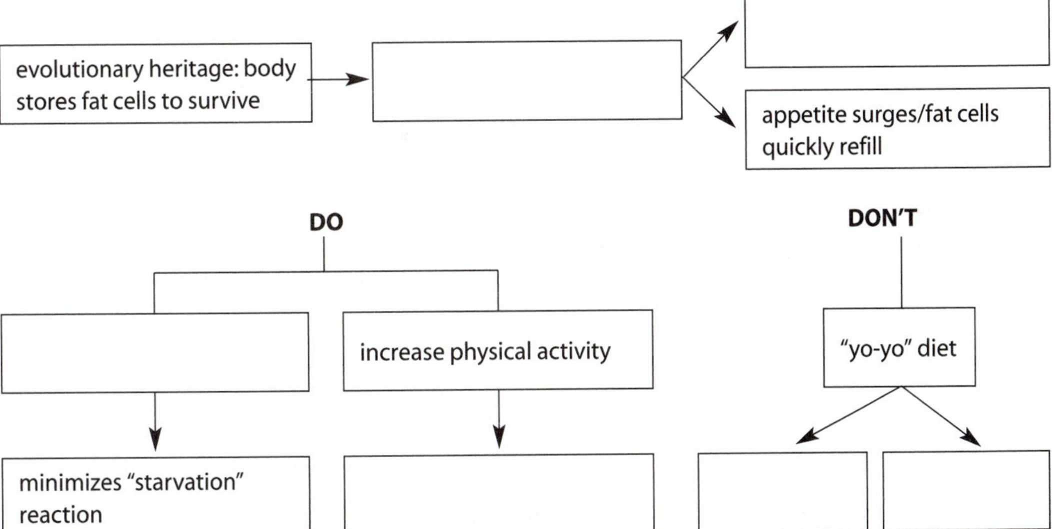

- reduce calories moderately
- more risk of heart problems
- makes losing weight difficult
- increases use of energy by body

Finding Main Ideas

Write the sentence with the main idea. Then circle the letter shows the reason for your choice.

1. ¶1 Main Idea Sentence: ____

   ____

   This is the main idea because it:

   a. answers a question stated in the paragraph
   b. is followed by a "first item in a list" signal word or phrase
   c. has a summary/conclusion signal
   d. has no signal but states a general conclusion that all details lead to

2. ¶3 Main Idea Sentence: ______________________________

____

This is the main idea because it:
a. answers a question stated in the paragraph
b. has a listing phrase
c. has a change of direction signal
d. has a summary/conclusion signal

3. Which of the following is the best implied main idea statement for ¶2? (Remember: a main idea must be a complete sentence.)
a. "Yo-yo" dieting is a major problem in America today.
b. Some bad results of "starvation" dieting, including the risk of heart disorders.
c. Any change in metabolism is dangerous to a person's health.
d. "Starvation" dieting can lead to some undesirable effects.

Circle T for True or F for False.

4. T F Dieting gets rid of fat cells.
5. T F If you run for 4 hours, you will lose about a pound of fat.

■ Reading for Understanding

1. What explanation is given in ¶1 for why the body wants to store fat?

____

____

2. Based on the information in ¶2, what would you say to a friend who is going to try a fad diet such as the "grapefruit only" diet?

____

____

3. Explain in your own words why "yo-yo" dieting is unwise.

____

____

4. "I work out all the time but I just can't seem to lose any weight." Based on the information in the passage, what would you tell someone who made this complaint?

____

____

5. People who exercise regularly will, when resting, continue to burn more calories than those who don't exercise. What information in ¶3 explains why this is so?

____

____

■ Writing Context Sentences

Here are some vocabulary words from the paragraphs above. Use the situation clues given or those of your own choosing (other than diet and exercise) to write your context sentences. Give enough specific detail so that someone could guess what the word means from the clues in your sentence.

1. **permanently:** in a lasting, unchanging way
   Situation clue: finding a residence or looking for a job
   Sentence: ____
   ____

2. **heritage:** things passed on from former generations
   Situation clue: things stored in grandparents' home or garage
   Sentence: ____
   ____

3. **reserve:** something kept back for use when needed; a stockpile
   Situation clue: losing a job
   Sentence: ____
   ____

4. **expenditure:** a cost, an expense
   Situation clue: supplies for school
   Sentence: ____
   ____

5. **minimize:** reduce to smallest amount or importance
   Situation clue: being part of a group involved in an action
   Sentence: ____
   ____

GRAPHICS OF CAUSE AND EFFECT

In the previous chapter, you worked with process maps that showed a series of events. A closely related map is the cycle map, which shows how events work together over and over in an endless cycle. This kind of map is often used to show weather patterns or the life cycles of plants and animals. It can take the form of a simple circle with arrows or it can be a more detailed illustration.

EXERCISE 12.4

Reading Graphics that Show Cycles

Here is a passage containing an illustration of a natural cycle.

The Hydrologic Cycle

by Allen Strahler and Arthur Strahler

1 The movement of water among the great global reservoirs constitutes the **hydrologic cycle.** In this cycle, water moves from land and ocean to the atmosphere as water vapor and returns as precipitation. Because precipitation over land exceeds evaporation, water also runs off the land to the oceans. We can summarize the main features of the hydrologic cycle, shown in figure 4.3. The cycle begins with evaporation from water or land surfaces, in which water changes state from liquid to vapor and enters the atmosphere. Total evaporation is about six times greater over oceans than land, however. This is because the oceans cover most of the planet and because land surfaces are not always wet enough to yield much evaporated water. Once in the atmosphere, water vapor can condense or deposit to form precipitation, which falls to earth as rain, snow, or hail. Precipitation over the oceans is nearly four times greater than precipitation over land.

2 Upon reaching the land surface, precipitation has three fates. First, it can evaporate and return to the atmosphere as water vapor. Second, it can sink into the soil and then into the surface rock layers below. This subsurface water emerges from below to feed rivers, lakes, and even ocean margins. Third, precipitation can run off the land, concentrating in streams and rivers that eventually carry it to the ocean or to a lake in a closed inland basin. This flow of water is known as *runoff.* (Strahler and Strahler, pp. 89, 91.)

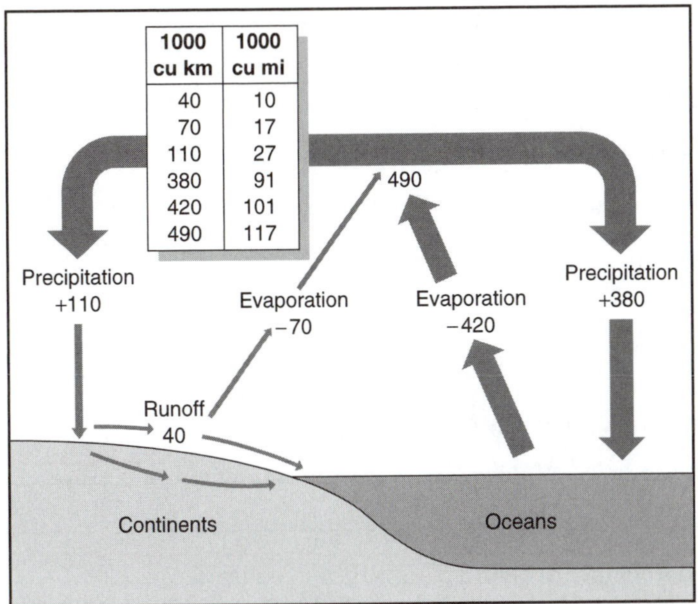

Figure 4.3 The global water balance. Figures give average annual water flows in and out of world land areas and world oceans. Values are given in thousands of cubic kilometers (cubic miles). Global precipitation equals global evaporation. (Based on data of John R. Mather.)

■ Reading for Information

1. What single sentence in ¶1 best summarizes the entire cycle?

____

____

2. Using the information in ¶1, fill in the cycle map of the hydrologic cycle:
   - precipitation evaporates, sinks, runs off
   - water vapor forms precipitation
   - rain, snow, or hail falls to earth

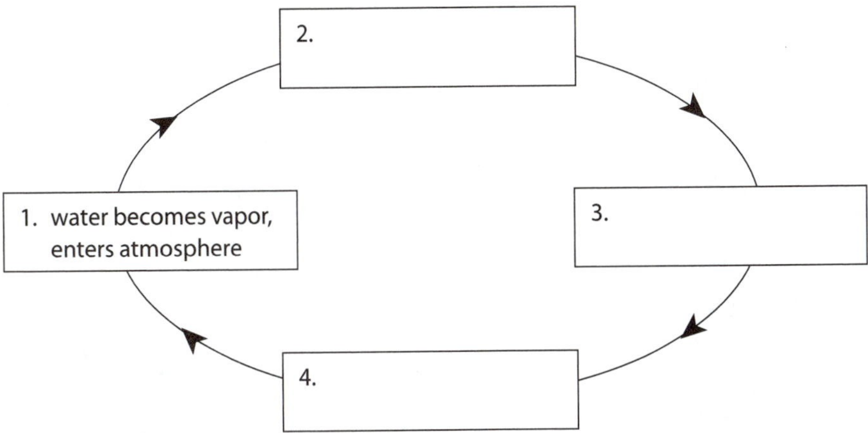

3. What two reasons explain why evaporation is much greater over oceans than land?

   a. ______________________________

   b. ______________________________

4. Which of the following is not a form of precipitation?
   a. rain
   b. water vapor
   c. snow
   d. hail

5. Write the main idea sentence of ¶2:

   ____

   ____

   Choose two from the list below. This is the main idea because it
   a. answers a question stated in the paragraph
   b. has a listing phrase
   c. is followed by a "first item in a list" signal word or phrase
   d. is followed by an example with or without a signal word or phrase
   e. has a change of direction signal
   f. has a summary/conclusion signal

■ Reading for Understanding

According to the passage, precipitation that falls to earth has three fates: (a) evaporates and becomes water vapor; (b) sinks into the soil and surface rock layers below; (c) becomes runoff.

1. _____ Write the letter of one of these that would be mainly caused by the sun.
2. _____ Write the letter of the two that are mainly the result of gravity.
3. _____
4. _____ Write the letter of the one that would probably be of *least* benefit to farmers.
5. _____ Which one would be of greatest benefit?

   Explain your answer.

   ____

   ____

6. *Hydro* is a word part that combines to make many words—for example, hydroelectric, hydrosphere, hydrophobia. From the context of this passage, what would you think its meaning in the word *hydrologic* and in these examples would be?

____

____

Figures and tables often give information that clearly shows cause-effect relationships from which these can be inferred. Below is a passage and figure that give information about the relationship between educational level and social class.

EXERCISE 12.5

Interpreting Cause-Effect Relationships in Graphics

Preview Vocabulary

conflict theorists: (¶1) those who believe there must be conflict between social classes

the bottom line: (¶1) the real truth; the important factor

elite: (¶1) social class with the highest status

perpetuates: (¶1) keeps going for a long time

affluent: (¶2) wealthy

Reproducing the Social Class Structure

by James Henslin

1 From unequal funding to IQ tests—what does it all mean? For conflict theorists, the bottom line is that education reproduces the social class structure; that is, education promotes the interests of a society's power elite and perpetuates a society's social class divisions. Regardless of their abilities, for example, children of the more-well-to-do are likely to be placed in college-bound tracks, children of the poor into vocational tracks, and each to inherit matching life opportunities laid down before they were born.

2 If this is true, then family background should be more important than test scores in predicting who attends college. Sociologist Samuel Bowles decided to find out. He compared the college attendance of the

brightest 25 percent of high school students with the intellectually weakest 25 percent. Figure 17.4 shows the results. Of the brightest 25 percent of high school students, 90 percent of those from affluent homes went to college, while only half of those from low-income homes did so. Of the weakest students, 26 percent from affluent homes went to college, while only 6 percent from poorer homes did so. And today? This same general relationship still holds. If you rank families from the poorest to the richest, at each income level the likelihood that the children will attend college increases.

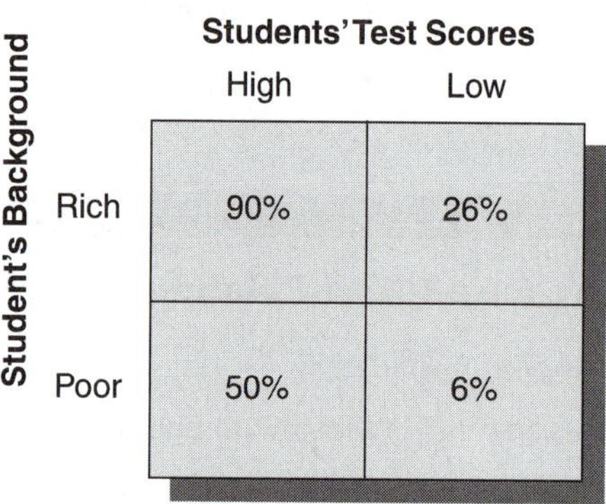

Figure 17.4 Who Goes to College? The Role of Social Class and Personal Ability in Determining College Attendance
Source: Bowles 1977.

■ Reading for Information

Based on the information in the figure, circle T for True or F for False for the following statements.

1. T F The percentage of Rich-Low who go to college is about 5 times that of the Poor-Low.
2. T F The grades of the Rich-High are 40% higher than those of the Poor-High.
3. T F Only 10% of the Rich-High don't attend college.
4. T F The percentage of Rich-Low who don't go beyond high school is larger than the percentage of Poor-Low who don't go to college.
5. T F The number of students who go to college is equal to the number who don't only in the Poor-High group.

■ Reading for Understanding

1. "Children of the more well-to-do are likely to be placed in college-bound tracks, children of the poor into vocational tracks." Explain in your own words what "tracking" is.

 ____

 ____

2. Which of three social classes—lower, middle, and upper—would conflict theorists likely believe will almost always come out on top?

 ____

 Why?

 ____

 ____

Explain why the following statements would NOT be accurate if made on the basis of this data.

3. "90% of the Rich-High students do well in college, whereas only 50% of the Poor-High students succeed."

 Explanation: ______________________________________

 ____

4. "56% of students who are poor attend college."

 Explanation: ______________________________________

 ____

5. "There are almost twice as many Rich-High students in college as there are Poor-High."

 Explanation: ______________________________________

 ____

THE PATTERN OF PROBLEM-SOLUTION

When we hear "problem-solution" we often think of a process. In solving a math problem, for example, we follow a series of set steps or a formula. If we do so correctly, the problem will be solved. But problem-solution is much broader when applied to everyday life. Radio and television talk shows, books, and many newspaper and magazine articles focus on personal and public problems—gangs, divorce, violence in the home, etc.—and how they should be handled. Problem-solution can be very complicated so it is helpful to look for four parts that occur in the pattern. You are already familiar with two of these because cause-effect is the core of the pattern:

> *The Problem:* This is a situation that needs to be changed. This section is often indicated at the beginning of a paragraph or article by the word "problem."
>
> *Causes:* This part gives one or more reasons why or how a problem has come about.
>
> *Effects:* These are undesirable results that have come about because of the problem. Often the three parts above are linked together in a chain of cause and effect.
>
> *Solution:* This section suggests ways to overcome the situation. Sometimes it warns us what will happen if we don't.

Problem-solution is very common in sections in textbooks and in popular magazine articles. Its pattern is also useful for organizing many reports and papers. A problem solution map is not difficult to construct. Here, for example, is the way a problem solution map would look for the reading "Tension Headaches" in Chapter 3. Notice how arrows are used to show cause-effect relationships:

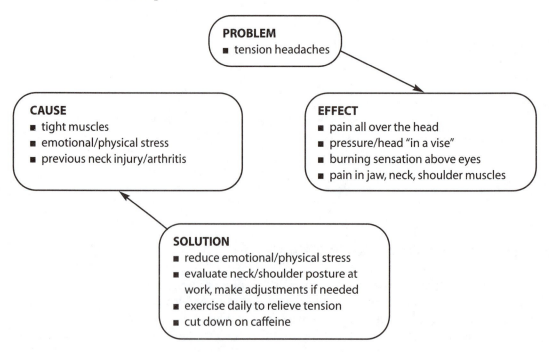

PROBLEM
- tension headaches

EFFECT
- pain all over the head
- pressure/head "in a vise"
- burning sensation above eyes
- pain in jaw, neck, shoulder muscles

CAUSE
- tight muscles
- emotional/physical stress
- previous neck injury/arthritis

SOLUTION
- reduce emotional/physical stress
- evaluate neck/shoulder posture at work, make adjustments if needed
- exercise daily to relieve tension
- cut down on caffeine

Recognizing the pattern in a reading will allow you to map its organization much more effectively. Because the parts of the problem solution pattern are not always in a set order, you must at times pull together information from different sections.

EXERCISE 12.6

Mapping a Problem-Solution Article

In the last chapter you created a time line for the article "Gambling Addiction Taking Huge Toll on Indian Families." The overall organization of the article, however, is not time sequence but problem-solution. Below are the most important items of information in the article. Use them to complete the problem-solution map that follows.

- those on welfare addicted
- explosion of gambling over past 30 years
- separates parents and children
- gambling addiction growing, especially among Indians
- creates psychological problems, including teenage suicide
- Indian nations must declare war on gambling

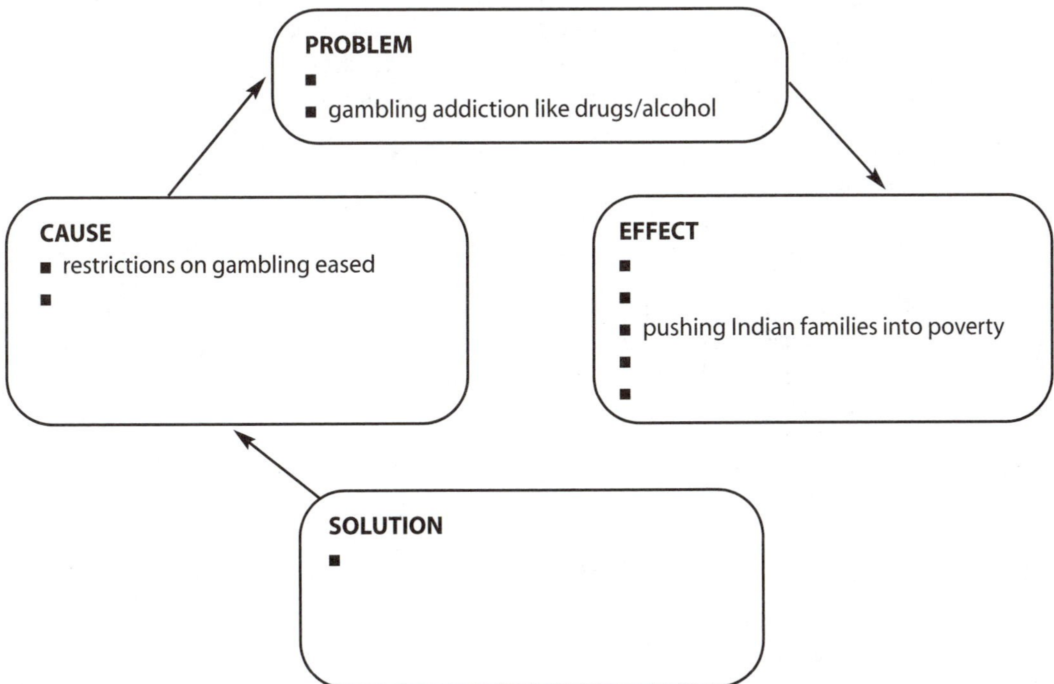
PROBLEM
■
■ gambling addiction like drugs/alcohol
CAUSE
■ restrictions on gambling eased
■
EFFECT
■
■
■ pushing Indian families into poverty
■
■
SOLUTION
■

Following are two articles that will give you practice in tracking problem-solution through longer readings. You read Part I of the first in Chapter 11. Review that before continuing.

Previewing *How to Manage Your Time, Part II* by Jan Farrington

Thinking About Reading Titles often alert us to the problem-solution pattern. Often words like *problem, cause,* or *solution* are in the title. The solution section can take different forms. Sometimes it gives reasons why a particular solution will work. It may also present a process—the "how to" pattern you worked with in the last chapter. Look at the title of this article. What part of the pattern does it point to?

a. problem
b. cause
c. effect
d. solution

From this title, what would you guess to be the problem?

____

The main idea of a problem solution article is usually a combination of the problem and solution. Because there may be no one sentence that combines these two, you must often put together the main idea from two or more sentences. In this article, the first two paragraphs work together as an introduction. Look for sentences in ¶2 that can be combined into this main idea statement:

"Because there will _______________________________,

you will always _______________________________.

Reading with a Purpose The parts of problem-solution do not always get the same emphasis. Usually it is the problem and solution that get the most space, but causes and effects are sometimes the main point of interest. Write down the boldface headings for the article:

_______________________ _______________________

_______________________ _______________________

From these, what part of the pattern is the article mainly concerned with?

____

To help you in bringing together information to make a pattern map, the parts of the pattern, as they occur, have been labeled in the margin. Underline or highlight key information and write it in the margin.

How to Manage Your Time, Part II

by Jan Farrington

1 It's always time to do something. You must have heard at
least one of the adults in your life say: "There just aren't enough Problem:
hours in the day!" Families juggling school and work schedules
(not to mention after-school sports practices, dance lessons, Effect:
part-time jobs, etc.) are doing well to find time to eat a meal together. Recent studies show that millions of American adults
and teens are actually "sleep deprived" from trying to keep up Effect:
with all the things they need or want to do. It's the song America
is singing in the 1990s: so much to do, so little time. Problem:

2 If you're like most American teens, having "enough time"
is already something you think about. So we'll let you in on a bit
of not-very-secret information: There will never be enough time
to do everything. That's how life is. You can't stop time, slow it
down, or speed it up. You will always have to make choices Solution:
about how you "spend" the time you have.

Work Smarter, Not Harder

3 When you're always rushed, always running, your only
thought may be: "If I can just work harder . . . If I can do it faster Problem:
. . . I'll make it." But what you really need to do is work smarter.
That means going with your strengths, talents, and habits in- Solution:
stead of against them. It means finding out how you learn, or
work, or study best—because doing it the best way (for you)
takes less time. "The challenge," writes Stephen Covey in *The
Seven Habits of Highly Effective People,* "is not to manage time, but
to manage ourselves."

4 Look at the people around you. How many of them seem Problem:
to think time is an enemy? How many of them spend every day
in a game of "beat the clock"? That may be OK for them—but
that's not the way your life has to be. Right now, you can learn
the skills you need to manage yourself—and make time work for
you, not against you. It's a set of skills you can use again and
again: in high school or college, on the job, and in your personal
life.

Making a List, Checking It Twice

5 The funny thing about "time planners" (weekly calendars, "to do" lists, etc.) is—they can give you more freedom, not less. How? If you write down and organize the work you need to do, you can stop worrying about remembering it all. You can concentrate on doing one thing at a time. And you can schedule some time for fun and relaxation, too.

Solution:

6 Before you start to make plans, find out how you are spending your time right now. For one week, keep a log of activities hour by hour. At the end of the week, take different color pens or highlighters and mark the time you spent on the following:

- school classes, homework, reading (non-school, too), long-term school projects
- sports and/or lessons (dance, music, etc.)
- work (part-time jobs, community service, etc.)
- at-home chores and obligations
- social life (activities with friends, family)
- watching TV, playing video games, etc.

7 Keeping the log will give you an idea of where your time goes, and how you might reorganize to get more done and have more fun. As you look over the log, ask yourself questions: Did I have trouble finding time for homework that week? Where was I just "hanging out" or wasting time—and not even enjoying it? What activities could I add to or subtract from my week to make my life less stressful, more fun, better organized?

8 Once you've evaluated how you spend your time, you can plan to use it more wisely. But how can you use lists and planners to manage your time? One good way is to set up a weekly calendar (like the time log you kept), and then sit down every night and make a "to do" list or "action plan" for the next day. On the calendar, fill in all the time you have to spend in school, lessons, work at home, or on a job. Then block out time to spend on: 1) homework, study, long-term projects; and 2) real social activity (more than just TV watching). If you don't seem to have time for these two categories, it's probably a signal that you need to reorganize: to watch less TV, work fewer hours at your part-time job, or talk to your parents about setting limits on your at-home duties.

Solution:

9 Every night, look at your weekly calendar and decide what you need to do the next day. Make a list and, as you accomplish the tasks, check things off. It's surprising how good it can feel to make those little marks—and know you're getting somewhere.

Why Put It Off?

10 "Yeah, I know it's Monday and my term paper is due in two days—and I haven't even hit the library yet. But ya know, I always do my best stuff at the last minute." Sound familiar? But is "at the last minute" really the way you want to live your life—rushing from one gotta-do-now to another? Writers Merrill and Donna Douglass in *Manage Your Time, Your Work, Yourself* say that: "More plans go astray, more dreams go unfulfilled, and Effect: more time is wasted by procrastination than by any other single Problem: factor." Why? Because we never put off unimportant things—only the important ones. You put off studying for a test because you suddenly realize you really need to phone a friend you haven't talked to in a while, or you really need to rearrange your book shelves. In the short term, you may feel good about your choice: You've substituted easier, more pleasant tasks for the hard one of studying. But (as you're cramming facts in the last minutes before the test), the choice is not one that will make your life better.

11 "Procrastination means doing low-priority activities rather than high-priority ones," write Merrill and Donna Douglass. But why does that seem like a good idea at the time? Think back on times when you've put something off. On the list below, check off any of the "reasons" that applied to the situations you remember.

_____ It seemed hard and I wasn't sure where to start.

_____ I don't enjoy doing this task; I find it unpleasant.

_____ My parents/friends were after me to do something else; I had to say yes.

_____ At the time, it suddenly seemed more important to do this other thing first.

_____ I like the excitement of the last-minute rush; I do good work under pressure.

_____ The deadline seemed so far away.

_____ I have to wait for the right mood.

_____ I couldn't decide what I wanted to do.

_____ I underestimated the difficulty of the work and overestimated the time I had to complete it.

12 We put things off because we're afraid of failure, because Causes: the task is difficult or unpleasant, because the job involves making a tough decision (and we aren't sure what to do). And many times, we put important things off by telling ourselves that we

have to handle some other "urgent" matter first. Having to baby-sit for your little brother or needing to take your car in for repair may seem like high-priority tasks. But the fact is, you could probably rearrange those things to give you time for something that's truly more important (studying for a test, researching a paper, practicing your music).

Get With It

13 Procrastination gets to be a habit with many of us—but habits can be changed. What can you do to get out of the procrastination trap? Here are a few ideas:

Solution:

- Check your weekly "action plan" every day. It will remind you of what you really need to be doing and give you a sense of what you can/can't put off.
- Cut down on "avoidance" behavior. Sometimes we don't realize we're putting things off, because we are very busy while we do it.
- Delegate, or make tradeoffs. OK, we know you can't "delegate" your schoolwork. But you can find creative ways to delegate or trade other tasks that aren't as important to your success. For instance, if baby-sitting for your brother is making you put off important schoolwork, you might ask an older relative to watch him—in exchange for your help with housework on the weekends.
- Do un-favorite tasks first. Bite the bullet, get it over with fast—and you can go on to work that is more appealing.
- Set a deadline, and stick to it. In school, your teacher will usually give you a deadline. But in work/life situations, that won't always be true. Learn to set deadlines for yourself.
- Start small—but start! Learn to break a task or project into smaller parts. Sometimes we procrastinate because we feel overwhelmed by a big project. Once you've made some kind of start, you're more likely to keep going.
- Don't wait for perfection. There usually isn't a "perfect" time to work, or a "perfect" decision, or even a "perfect" first line for your term paper. So don't procrastinate; take your best ideas, and go ahead. You can always go back and make changes as you go along. (*Career World,* 1995.)

EXERCISE 12.7

Questions on *How to Manage Your Time, Part II*

■ Reading for Information

Mapping

Complete the map with these items:

- check "action plan" daily
- plans ruined, dreams not fulfilled, time wasted
- get a start, no matter how small
- procrastination
- use "time planners"
- adults/teens: "sleep deprived"
- make and meet deadlines
- fear of failure
- trade jobs with others
- can't make tough decisions

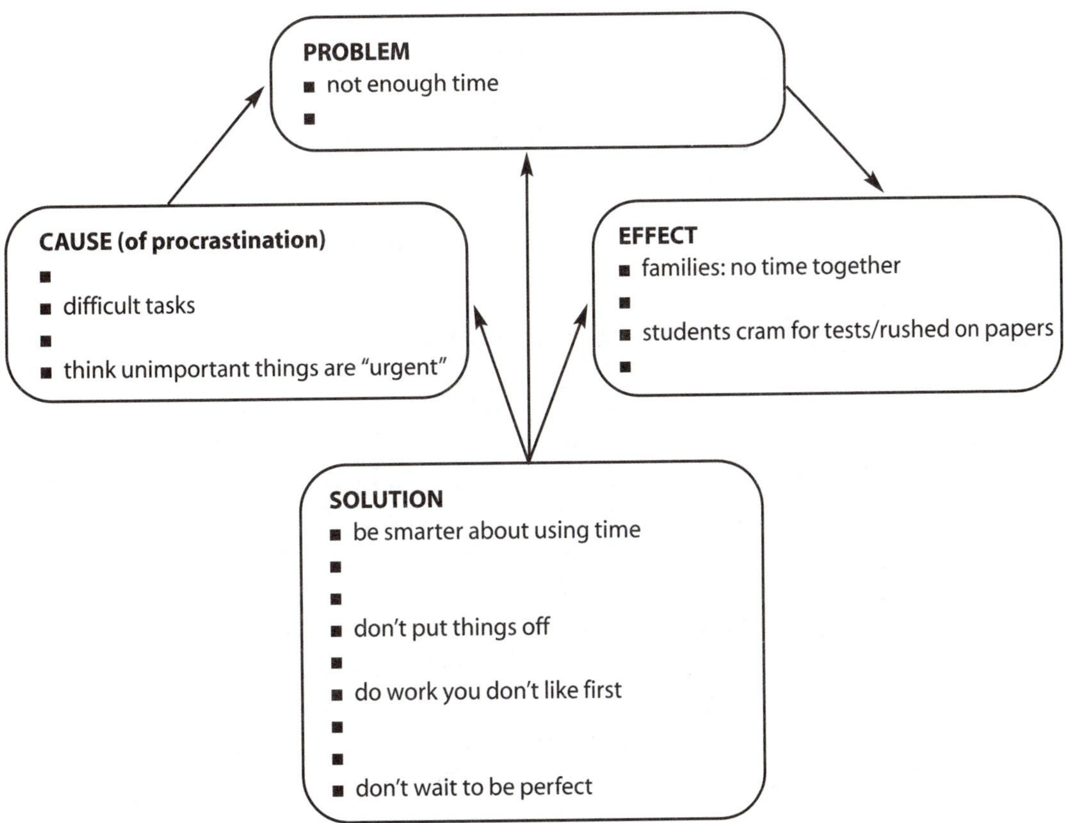
PROBLEM
■ not enough time
■
CAUSE (of procrastination)
■
■ difficult tasks
■
■ think unimportant things are "urgent"
EFFECT
■ families: no time together
■
■ students cram for tests/rushed on papers
■
SOLUTION
■ be smarter about using time
■
■
■ don't put things off
■
■ do work you don't like first
■
■
■ don't wait to be perfect

Finding Main Ideas

Choose the sentence with the main idea for these three paragraphs. Then indicate the signal that helped you make your choice.

1. ¶6 Main Idea Sentence: ______________________________

   ____

   This is the main idea because it:

   a. answers a question stated in the paragraph
   b. has a listing phrase
   c. has a change of direction signal
   d. none of the above

2. ¶8 Main Idea Sentence: ______________________________

   ____

   This is the main idea because it:

   a. answers a question stated in the paragraph
   b. has a change of direction signal
   c. has a signal word of conclusion
   d. all of the above

3. ¶13 Main Idea Sentence: ______________________________

   This is the main idea because it:

   a. answers a question stated in the paragraph
   b. follows a change of direction signal
   c. has a listing phrase
   d. all of the above

■ Reading for Understanding

1. Which of the following is the best implied main idea statement for ¶12? (Remember: a main idea must be a complete sentence.)

   a. There really are no unimportant things, so rearrange your scheduleto leave enough time for everything.
   b. We procrastinate for a number of very poor reasons.
   c. We must take care of urgent matter such as car repair before we can do anything else.
   d. Being afraid of failure, hard work, tough decisions, plus doing "urgent" things, all being very poor reasons.

2. *Rationalization* is a term used by psychologists for the way our minds sometimes come up with "good" reasons for our actions, but not the real reasons. Which paragraph gives reasons that are really rationalizations?

   ___

   Discuss any of the items you checked off in the list in this paragraph and give more details about the situations you were in.

   ___

   ___

   ___

3. "I like the excitement of the last-minute rush; I do good work under pressure." The author gives this as one example of rationalization. But, from your observation and experience, could "rush" and "pressure" work to the advantage of some students?

   ___

   ___

   ___

4. "We never put off unimportant things—only the important ones." Is that a statement of fact or opinion? Do you agree?

   ___

   Explain: ___

   ___

5. What is the difference between "delegating" and "trading off"? Explain why a student "can't delegate homework."

   ___

   ___

   ___

6. How do you manage your time? Do you have a planner? A weekly schedule? The figure on page 456 is a sample weekly schedule. Fill it in with what you plan to do this week or next, using any tips on time management that you got from the article above. Then compare your plan with that of others in the class. Discuss your plan with your instructor to see if it your management of time can be improved:

	MONDAY	TUESDAY	WEDNESDAY	THURSDAY	FRIDAY	SATURDAY	SUNDAY
6 a.m.							
7:00							
8:00							
9:00							
10:00							
11:00							
12 noon							
1:00							
2:00							
3:00							
4:00							
5:00							
6:00							
7:00							
8:00							
9:00							
10:00							
11:00							
12:00							
1 a.m.							

Writing a Summary

Use your map to write a 150-word summary of "How to Manage Your Time." You can be selective on how many details to include. For example, you may want to focus on the central problem of procrastination and the three or four main solutions to time management. Then write a 100-word response in which you may include any disagreement with the article or your own personal experience with this issue.

Previewing *When Good Kids Play Dangerous Games* by Dan Hurley

Thinking About Reading Look at the title of this article. What part of the pattern does it suggest?

a. problem c. effect
b. cause d. solution

What comes to mind when you think of "dangerous games"? Have you played—or do you continue to play—games that are dangerous? Do any of your family or friends play games you think can lead to tragic results? Write any thoughts that you have on this subject:

____

____

____

____

____

____

____

____

Writers often use two common strategies for introducing problem-solution articles. One is to give a clear statement of what the problem is. The other is to give a striking example before stating the problem directly. Which technique is used here?

____

How many paragraphs are used for the introduction? ________

Reading with a Purpose Boldface headings are used in articles to alert the reader to what parts of the pattern are being discussed. Below are the three major headings from the article. What part of the pattern—problem, cause, effect, solution—does each one suggest?

Why Kids Take Risks ________________________

Recklessness on the Rise ________________________

What Parents Can Do ________________________

To help you make a map, the parts of the pattern, as they occur, have been listed. Underline or highlight key information and write it in the margin. Also, note that the article contains a mixture of statements of fact and opinion. As you read, mark fact or opinion in the margin for key statements.

Preview Vocabulary

bizarre: (¶3) very weird, strange

spin: (¶3) version, variety

reflection: (¶3) a result of an influence

arrhythmia: (¶4) irregular heart rate

egocentrism: (¶5) a seeing of oneself as the center of everything

illicit: (¶9) illegal

stable: (¶9) not changing

When Good Kids Play Dangerous Games

by Dan Hurley

1 It was 11 P.M. on June 15, 1996, and a scene out of American Graffiti was heating up on the back roads of Cape Cod, Massachusetts. Patrick Swift, an 18-year-old high school junior whom friends called "Swifty," was riding with four girls in an old green car. They caravanned with friends from party to party, and most everyone had had a couple of beers—including Swifty and the 16-year-old girl behind the wheel. Maybe to impress one of them, maybe on a dare, or maybe just for a cheap thrill, Swifty decided to show off with a game he and his buddies had been playing the past few nights—car surfing.

■ *caravanned:*
a. argued, fought
b. traveled in a group of cars

2 With the car still moving, he climbed out the window and up onto the roof. Lying flat on his stomach, Swifty held on tight as the car took a sharp left turn. Then, although the car was traveling at about 33 miles an hour, he got to his knees and stood up. Suddenly, the girl driving swerved. Swifty pitched forward into the darkness, hitting the road headfirst. By the time his best friend, Chris DiGiacomo, arrived in another car minutes later, Swifty was lying facedown in a pool of blood. An ambulance pulled up as Chris, soaked in his friend's blood, tried desperately to administer CPR. But it was too late. Pam Swift would soon

Effect:

Reprinted by permission of the author. Originally published in *Family Circle,* September 1997.

receive the terrible news that her son was dead. "I never thought of him as wild," she says now. "He was a typical boy."

3 A growing number of "typical" boys and girls are being killed or maimed playing bizarre new dangerous games. Deaths or serious injuries due to car surfing have made headlines across the country in the past two years. Last summer, two teens in New York City put an urban spin on the "surfing" game and paid with their lives: One stood on the roof of a moving elevator, another rode atop a speeding subway train. These daredevil games are part of a national thrill-seeking trend that's also drawn millions of kids into "extreme sports"—downhill mountain biking, snowboarding, "aggressive" skateboarding and in-line skating. "I've never seen it to this extent," says Nancy Jane Vecchione, D.Ed., dean of Swifty's class at Barnstable High School. "There's a deep, underlying recklessness with kids today that's probably a reflection of society." "It's just been one after the other," says Swifty's sister, Maggie, of the teen deaths in their area in the past year. "It feels like an epidemic."

Problem:

■ *maimed:*
a. frightened
b. badly injured

Cause:

■ *epidemic:*
a. mystery
b. widespread event

Why Kids Take Risk

4 Teens have always taken risks that would make most adults cringe. The question parents ask is, *Why?* "I've been asked that a lot," says Elaine Scerbo of Central Islip, New York, whose 15-year-old son, Troy, died of an arrhythmia last October after playing a game called "Open Chest." The objective? To take as many punches to the chest as possible. "I can't seem to grasp it," admits Scerbo. "I suppose they get to that macho stage where they have to prove themselves." "The social pressure is definitely hard for teens to bear," agrees psychologist Baruch Fischhoff, Ph.D., of Carnegie Mellon University in Pittsburgh. "It's not that they're insensitive to the risks of dangerous games, but they're also very aware of the social risks of seeming afraid."

Cause:

■ *insensitive:*
a. lacking feeling for
b. opposed

5 Teens also take chances adults would avoid because of what Jeff Arnett, Ph.D., associate professor of human development at the University of Missouri, calls adolescent egocentrism—which tends to result in a teen's feeling of invulnerability. "It's a part of adolescent development," says Dr. Arnett. "They picture themselves doing all these dangerous things and always coming out on top."

Cause:

■ *invulnerability:*
a. self esteem
b. condition where one is not able to be hurt or killed

6 That's what Swifty believed. "He had a reputation for taking risks—people thought he was crazy," says his friend Joe Burgum, 18. Swifty was most likely a thrill seeker—a personality

■ *temperament:*
a. manner of thinking, reacting
b. bravery

trait that also plays a role in teen recklessness, says Frank Farley, Ph.D., of Temple University in Philadelphia. "Some kids are fearless from the first year of life," he explains. "Others back off. It's all about temperament."

Cause:

7 Experts say teens also take chances to discover boundaries. "They push the envelope to find out where the edge is," says Richard Schieber, M.D., a pediatrician at the Centers for Disease Control and Prevention. "When they find it, they usually withdraw." Tragically, many step back from the edge too late.

Problem:

Cause:

8 Teenagers aren't the only ones playing dangerous games, though; younger kids are doing it too. But their motivation is different: They simply want to have pure fun. Unfortunately, young children cannot fully comprehend the risks of their imaginative play, experts point out. Last December, for instance, 9-year-old Isaac Farr and his friends at a day-care center in Long Beach, New York, decided to play a game of "Execution." Isaac ended up hanging by his neck from a rope. Thankfully, he wasn't seriously injured. "They were kids playing a game that got horribly out of control," says Isaac's aunt, Sandra Farr. "That's why children need us—they don't know when too much is too much."

Recklessness on the Rise

Cause:

9 There is no single measure for youth risk taking, "but there are trends that tend to support the view that we're seeing an increase," says Dr. Farley. One of the most troubling is teens' use of drugs and alcohol—a reckless behavior in and of itself but also often a contributing factor in games like the one Swifty played. Between 1991 and 1996, the proportion of eighth graders using any illicit drug in the prior year more than doubled, from 11% to 24%, while the proportion of 12th graders doing so jumped by half, to a whopping 40%, according to the University of Michigan's Monitoring the Future Study. Teen alcohol use has been stable but remains alarmingly high: In 1996 the proportion of kids who'd had at least five drinks in a row in the prior two weeks was 16% for eighth graders, 25% for 10th graders and 30% for 12th graders.

Cause:

Effect:

10 Dr. Farley points to the rapid boom in extreme sports as another indicator of the increase in dangerous games. As the popularity of these so-called "thrill sports" grows, so too do the injury statistics: In-line skating—a sport which didn't even exist prior to 1980—caused an estimated 105,000 serious mishaps in 1995, up from 28,381 in 1992, according to the U.S. Consumer

Product Safety Commission. From January 1992 to mid-1995, a total of 25 deaths occurred during in-line skating, 15 of them among children under the age of 15. Skateboarding accidents requiring hospitalization also rose: from 25,486 in 1994 to 30,353 in 1995.

11 Of course, promoters of extreme sports insist that safety comes first and that people should wear protective gear. But just look around any suburb and try to find a child who actually does. Thirteen-year-old Matt Costello-Hurley of Belfast, Maine, doesn't always wear protective gear when he skateboards. Brian Farinas, 17, doesn't wear it either, although he practically lives on his skateboard in Boca Raton, Florida. One of his favorite sports videos shows kids skating down cement stairways, off the back of trucks and down busy streets. Whenever someone falls, Brian laughs. "Nobody really gets hurt," he says casually. "It's just fun." According to Dr. Schieber, "That's very characteristic of how teens think—and they are dead wrong."

Cause:

12 While older teenagers are almost always the ones playing the more outlandish games, such as car surfing, younger boys are increasingly likely to be injured in extreme sports and other innocent seeming games. Of the 25 in-line skating deaths previously cited, 11 of the victims were age 13 or under. It's not simply a matter of "boys will be boys," though. One-fifth of those killed while in-line skating are girls. And every case of car-surfing injury or death uncovered by *Family Circle* involved a girl—either behind the wheel or on the roof.

Effect:

What Parents Can Do

13 Many parents are so busy that they may not know what goes on when their youngsters play, according to a researcher at the National Center for Health Statistics. J. Thomas Kane, former principal of Holdrum Middle School in River Vale, New Jersey, agrees. Last summer he sent a letter to his students' parents warning them of a game the kids were playing called "California Knockout." A child stands against a tree or wall while several others press their hands against his chest until he grows faint or passes out.

Cause:

14 Many parents also believe that "as kids become adolescents, adults cannot exert influence over them," says Ruby Takanishi, Ph.D., president of the Foundation for Child Development in New York. "In reality, some of these high-risk behaviors can be lessened with more parental guidance." Here's how to help your child make smarter, safer choices:

Solution:

- **Start early.** "It's a lot harder to begin talking about safety when your child is 14 and already running around with a crowd you disapprove of," says Dr. Takanishi. "Start when kids are 8 or 9 and their peer groups are just beginning to become important."

■ *monitor:*
a. punish
b. watch and check on

- **Monitor behavior closely.** "When parents make it their business to know where their kids are going, who they're going to be with, and when they'll be home, adolescents tend to take fewer risks," says Dr. Arnett. But don't stop there. "Talk to your child's friends' parents," advises Dr. Takanishi. Make a pact not to allow one another's children to do certain things, such as going to the mall unsupervised, or attending parties where no adult is present.

■ *infractions:*
a. acts of rule breaking
b. curfews

■ *incentives:*
a. mistakes
b. rewards that motivate

■ *devastating:*
a. overwhelming, crushing
b. ignored

- **Be firm about infractions.** The time to come down hard is not when your child is 16 and has been in a near-fatal car accident, experts say, but when he's 10 and has failed to wear a helmet while skateboarding. "Develop a series of graded punishments for misbehavior and incentives for good behavior," says Dr. Schieber. "You cannot preach to kids, but you have got to set firm limits and guidelines," adds Swifty's dean, Dr. Vecchione. Otherwise, the consequences may be devastating. "I never thought anything horrible would ever happen to my child," Pam Swift says softly. "Until it did."

Context Answers and Clues

caravanned: b. traveled in a group of cars (they are in one car, the friends in another)

maimed: b. badly injured (not killed, but hurt)

epidemic: b. widespread event ("one after another")

insensitive: a. lacking feeling for ("they're also very aware . . .")

invulnerability: b. condition where one is not able to be hurt or killed (do dangerous things while "always coming out on top")

temperament: a. manner of thinking, reacting (quotation says kids are born different)

monitor: b. watch and check on (parents know what kids are doing)

infractions: a. acts of rule breaking (examples show misbehavior)

incentives: b. rewards that motivate (opposite of punishment, lead to good behavior)

devastating: a. overwhelming, crushing (mother's natural reaction to "horrible" accident)

EXERCISE 12.8

Questions on *When Good Kids Play Dangerous Games*

■ Reading for Information

Mapping

Complete the problem-solution map with the items below.

- boom in extreme sports
- failure to use helmets
- be tough on rule breaking
- teen use of drugs and alcohol
- check behavior closely
- kids playing new, reckless games
- feel need to prove selves
- teens like Swifty get killed or injured

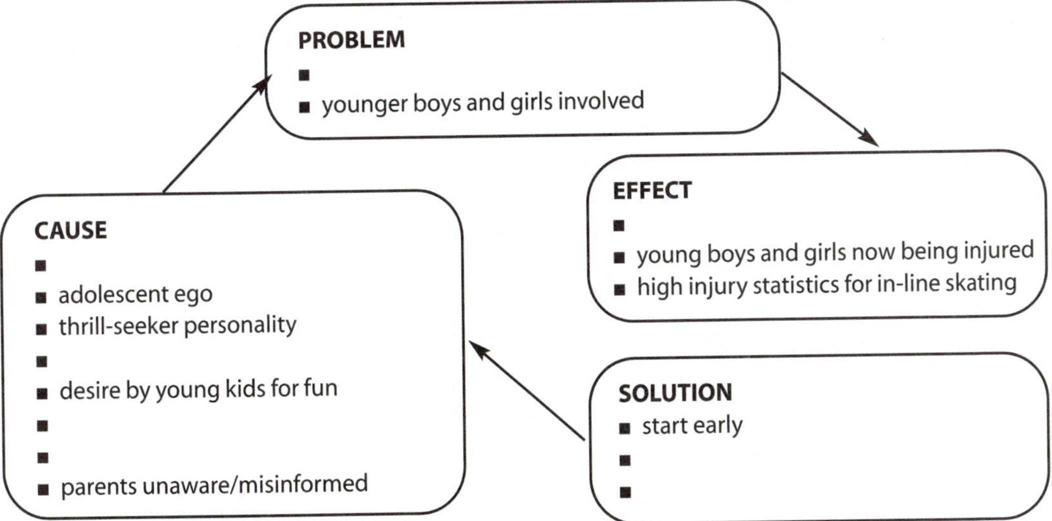
PROBLEM
■
■ younger boys and girls involved
EFFECT
■
■ young boys and girls now being injured
■ high injury statistics for in-line skating
CAUSE
■
■ adolescent ego
■ thrill-seeker personality
■
■ desire by young kids for fun
■
■
■ parents unaware/misinformed
SOLUTION
■ start early
■
■

■ Reading for Information

Finding Main Ideas

Choose the sentence with the main idea for the three paragraphs below. Then indicate the signal that helped you make your choice.

1. Which sentence best expresses the main idea of ¶3?
   a. A growing number of "typical" boys and girls are being killed or maimed playing bizarre new dangerous games.
   b. Deaths or serious injuries due to car surfing have made headlines across the country in the past two years.
   c. Last summer, two teens in New York City put an urban spin on the "surfing" game and paid with their lives.
   d. "I've never seen it to this extent." says Nancy Jane Vecchione, D.Ed., dean of Swifty's class at Barnstable High School.

2. This is the main idea sentence because it
   a. answers a question stated in the paragraph
   b. has a listing phrase
   c. is followed by a "first item in a list" signal word or phrase
   d. is followed by an example with or without a signal word or phrase
3. Which sentence best expresses the main idea of ¶14?
   a. Many parents also believe that adults can't exert influence over adolescents.
   b. In reality, some of these high-risk behaviors can be lessened with more parental guidance.
   c. Parents must start early with children and monitor their behavior closely.
   d. "I never thought anything horrible would ever happen to my child," Pam Swift says softly.
4. This is the main idea sentence because it
   a. answers a question stated in the paragraph
   b. is followed by a "first item in a list" signal word or phrase
   c. is followed by an example with or without a signal word or phrase
   d. follows a sentence with a change of direction signal

■ Reading for Understanding

1. ¶s 1–2 work together to give an introductory example. Choose the best implied main idea statement for this unit. (Remember: a main idea must be a complete sentence.)
   a. Swifty was out to impress his friends through car surfing.
   b. Patrick Swift made the fatal mistake of standing up.
   c. A dangerous game—car surfing—ended tragically for Patrick Swift.
   d. Thrill riding and partying with friends, then a fatal decision with a tragic result.
2. ¶s 4–7 work together to focus on the causes of the problem. Choose the best implied main idea statement for this unit. (Remember: a main idea must be a complete sentence.)
   a. Teens have always taken risks and sought for thrills due to social pressure.
   b. There are a number of reasons why adolescents take dangerous risks.
   c. Tragic risks due to acting macho, due to social pressure and being egotistical.
   d. We will always have thrill-seeking teenagers willing to push the envelope.

3. Choose the best divided main idea statement for ¶8.
   a. Older teenagers play outlandish games, while younger ones just want to have pure fun.
   b. Younger kids playing for fun, with many risks and getting out of control often.
   c. Isaac Farr was playing a game that got out of control but he wasn't seriously injured.
   d. Younger kids play dangerous games for pure fun but don't fully understand the risks.

Fact and Opinion

Some of the following statements are opinions. Some are facts for which evidence is included or could be found. Other statements are false—they are contradicted by information in the article. After making your choice, give your reason for it. An example is given here.

Fact "One-fifth of those killed while in-line skating are girls."

Reason: This is a statistic whose source could be found.

Opinion "You cannot preach to kids, but you have got to set firm limits and guidelines."

Reason: Many people might agree with this as common sense, but it can't be proved by factual evidence and some people would definitely not agree.

False Skateboarding accidents requiring hospitalization declined from 1994 to 1995.

Reason: The article cites statistics that show these rose from 25,486 in 1994 to 30,353 in 1995.

______ 1. A growing number of "typical" boys and girls are being killed or maimed playing bizarre new dangerous games.

Reason: ______

______ 2. "There's a deep, underlying recklessness with kids today that's probably a reflection of society."

Reason: ______

_______ 3. 9-year-old Isaac Farr's death by hanging resulted from a game called "Execution."

Reason: ____

____

_______ 4. Fewer eighth graders were using drugs in 1996 than in 1991.

Reason: ____

____

_______ 5. In 1996 the proportion of 10th graders who'd had at least five drinks in a row was higher than that for 8th graders but lower than that for 12th graders.

Reason: ____

____

_______ 6. In-line skating caused approximately a little over 100,000 mishaps in 1995.

Reason: ____

____

_______ 7. Although statistics for in-line skating before 1980 were not included in the article, these could be obtained.

Reason: ____

____

_______ 8. Almost all teens involved in extreme sports wear helmets.

Reason: ____

____

_______ 9. Injuries and deaths from dangerous sports is not a serious problem for girls.

Reason: ____

____

_______ 10. "As kids become adolescents, adults cannot exert influence over them."

Reason: ____

____

Writing a Summary

Use your map to write a 150-word summary of "When Good Kids Play Dangerous Games." The examples of the terrible effects of the problem get most of the space in the article, but as your map shows, the most important section is really the causes of this problem. Make this section and the solution the focus of your summary—don't go into detail about the examples. In your response (about 100 words), include your own personal experience with this issue. If you disagree with some things the article says, discuss other possible causes or a different solution.

Active Learning

PROBLEM ISSUES

Radio, television, articles, books—all of these sources constantly give information about problems we face as individuals and as a society. Some of these are fairly new—for example, AIDS or pornography on the Internet—but some of them have been with us a long time and continue to cause friction: racial prejudice, poverty, divorce, child abuse, famine, etc. Courses you take in general education will help you to develop frames of reference for important problem areas. The more background information you can bring, the better you will be able to understand readings that deal with problems. For example, in the exercises in this text you have already touched on some historical and current problem issues:

television viewing
prejudices and stereotypes
specialization of work
work-related mental and physical health
children in orphanages
mistreatment of the Indians of the New World
homelessness
migrant workers
muscular dystrophy
time management
diet and heart disease
anorexia and bulimia
dangerous games that kids play

EXERCISE 12.9

Building a Reference Framework for Issues

In groups of 4–5, look through a newspaper that deals with international, national, state, and local news. Work together to identify some current problem issues in each of these areas. Then, individually, track these issues in newspapers and magazines for a week. Find as many titles as you can for the areas you identified earlier and for any new ones you discover. Then get back together and compare findings. Share your list with other groups; from this, your class will be able to compile a selective list of articles on the problems of greatest interest and concern.

Reading Portfolio

PROBLEM-SOLUTION ARTICLES

Look over the list of articles that your class has compiled. Select an article in a problem area that interests you.

1. *Summary:* As you read, mark and label parts in the margin. Then compile a problem-solution map that shows the four parts of the pattern. When you write your summary, you will probably find that your organization of the information in the article is different from that of the original. For example, if the article begins with an illustration, your summary should begin with a problem statement. Keep minor details from examples to a minimum. Your summary should be about 200 words.
2. *Response:* This should be about 100 words long. There are a number of directions you can go in responding to problem-solution. You can respond by answering any of the following: Is there really a problem? Are the causes indicated for the problem the real ones? Are there others? Is there a better solution? You can also relate the problem to your own personal experiences or to those of someone you know.

Index